Frederick William Faber:
A Great Servant of God

Frederick William Faber (*c*.1860)
Engraving by Joseph Brown.

Frederick William Faber:
A Great Servant of God

Melissa J. Wilkinson

GRACEWING

First published in 2007

Gracewing
2 Southern Avenue, Leominster
Herefordshire HR6 0QF

© Melissa J. Wilkinson 2007

ISBN 0 85244 135 5
978 0 85244 135 0

Typeset by
Action Publishing Technology Ltd, Gloucester, GL1 5SR
Printed in England by
Biddles Ltd, King's Lynn, PE30 4LS

Contents

Illustrations

Cover
Portrait of Frederick William Faber, Elton, *c*.1840.

Frontispiece
Frederick William Faber (*c*.1860). Engraving by Joseph Brown.

Plates
Vicarage of St Wilfrid's Church, Calverley, Yorkshire. Birthplace of Frederick William Faber.

Watercolour portrait of Frederick William Faber. Probably painted to commemorate either his ordination to the diaconate (1836) or priesthood (1839) in the Church of England.

Frederick William Faber in the Lake District (1839–40). Colour miniature on ivory by Simon Rochard. Reproduced by permission of Sir Richard Faber.

St Nicholas Church, Elton. Photograph by the author (2003).

St Wilfrid's, Cotton, Staffordshire (*c*.1900).
Cotton Hall is to the left of the picture. The extension to Cotton Hall and St Wilfrid's Church were both built for F. W. Faber by A. W. N. Pugin. The foundation stone of the church was laid on 12 October 1846 and the opening ceremony performed on 25 April 1848.

The first London Oratory Church at King William Street, Strand (*c*.1850).

The London Oratory House and original church, Brompton Road, designed by J. J. Scoles (1778–1863).

Frederick William Faber (1863).

With the exception of those noted, all illustrations are reproduced with permission of the Fathers of the London Oratory.

Foreword

F. W. Faber has not lacked biographers and editors of his volu-
minous correspondence, from his fellow Oratorian John
Bowden's *Life and Letters of Frederick William Faber* (1869)
through those of Wilfrid Meynell's *The Spirit of Father Faber*
(1914), Ronald Chapman's *Father Faber* (1961) and Raleigh
Addington's *Faber, Poet and Priest* (1974). Sheridan Gilley's
magisterial *New DNB* entry on Faber (2004) is also an invalu-
able source of information and interpretation. Without these
works, Melissa Wilkinson's task would have been more difficult, but she skilfully builds on and develops the picture of
Faber which emerged from those earlier studies. In her careful
analysis of what she identifies as seven chronological stages in
Faber's spiritual development, she has not been content with
analysing Faber's corpus of printed works but has utilised the
vast corpus of Faber's correspondence with his friend John
Brande Morris at the London Oratory to a greater extent than
any previous author.

F. W. Faber is largely known as an exponent of 'extreme'
Mariolatry and as the author of triumphalist and sometimes
sugary Catholic hymns, some of which (in edited or expur-
gated form) became and remain popular among other
denominations and have been the subject of recent study by a
Methodist scholar, Andrew Pratt (1997). Within the historiog-
raphy of the nineteenth-century Catholic Church in England,
however, Faber's reputation has suffered through his unfortunate personality clashes with his fellow-Oratorian John Henry
Newman, a rift opening up between the founders of the
Birmingham and London Oratories. As Dr Wilkinson puts it in
her introduction to this carefully researched and nuanced
reassessment of Faber, the accepted historical picture of him is
as that of 'a fat, ebullient, over-emotional, occasionally bad-
tempered individual'. Wilkinson does not deny that such traits
existed (indeed she admits that these included a volatile

personality, and a certain immaturity, or 'silliness' that clung to him throughout his life). However, in so far as such character flaws manifested themselves, they can be partly, if not largely, explained by the nature of Faber's illness (Bright's disease) and exacerbated by his medication (laudanum and 'blue pills') which induced mercury poisoning, on the subject of which historians have hitherto remained largely silent. Whereas Faber's illnesses were not always taken seriously by Newman and by some of his hagiographers such as Meriol Trevor, Dr Wilkinson persuasively shows that chronic illness occurred earlier than previously recognised in Faber's life and not only took a heavy physical toll, destroying his early good looks and bloating him, but also distorted his mature and later intellectual and spiritual development. She even suggests that the attempted 'cure' may have been worse than the apparent disease itself and raises the intriguing possibility that mercury poisoning rather than Bright's disease largely explains Faber's deteriorating medical condition. Dr Wilkinson is highly original in the way in which she skilfully weaves discussion of Faber's troubled medical history into her analysis of Faber's complex (and sometimes contradictory) spiritual and theological development, showing how it also warped his personality, fostering indecisiveness, but also feelings of solitariness (and yet fear of solitude and craving for companionship), melancholia, making him hysterical and bad-tempered at times. Faber was well aware how he had made enemies at Oxford, conceding that 'my temper would almost create them in the Sahara Desert' (Faber, *Unkind Judging*, Sonnet LXXXVI, *Poems*, p. 248). His medical condition might also partly explain certain attitudes and actions in his career which must have seemed irrational to contemporary friends and followers. It could have been a factor in his nostalgia for Elton and unhappiness in the early months following his conversion to Rome. It almost certainly underlay his sudden decision in February 1847 to close the Brothers of the Will of God or 'Wilfridian' community (which he had set up after his submission to Rome in November 1845) and join Newman's Oratory, a decision made at the last minute and at the most insensitive time for those who were about to take the community's vows. Moreover, it perhaps also encouraged his trend towards disenchantment with the 'unreality' and superficiality of the present world and recurring strictures on the 'spirit of the age' and sharpened his almost mystical sense of the reality of the afterlife for which he yearned.

Dr Wilkinson marshals the albeit limited biographical evidence on Faber's upbringing and early life, dwelling on the evangelical family influences of his uncle George Stanley Faber, and the Romantic influences of Wordsworth and the 'Lake Poets'. She sensitively navigates her way through an elucidation of his intellectual spiritual development as an undergraduate at Balliol and at University College, Oxford, in the turbulent period of the 1830s when the Tractarian movement under Newman's influence was beginning to hold sway. She shows, through careful analysis of Faber's many letters to his Oxford friend John Brande Morris, how he, like others of his religious background, came gradually to abandon Calvinistic Evangelicalism precisely because it 'had not allowed him to develop spiritually' (p. 25). She explains that Faber's dissatisfaction with Evangelicalism was because he felt it 'made religion a series of frames of feeling', and because it 'feeds the heart at the expense of the head'. She notes the significance of these admissions, given the fact that Faber 'remained an individual for whom emotion and feeling were two important facets of religious expression'. Dr Wilkinson's analysis of Faber's shift from evangelical to High Churchman fits in with and complements recent (e.g. by David Newsome and Sheridan Gilley) and not so recent wider studies of the complex and problematic relationship between Evangelicalism and the Oxford Movement.

Dr Wilkinson stresses the formative years of Faber's time as curate at Ambleside in his beloved Lakes from 1837–42 and his being caught up in the Romantic 'Young England' movement associated with Lord John Manners (1818–1906) and George Smythe (1818–1857), escaping the influence of the latter when he scented moral danger. Faber had a considerable influence on Manners and was portrayed by Disraeli as the Revd Aubrey St Lys in his novel *Sybil*. Faber's own poetic gifts, which Dr Wilkinson subjects to critical examination in the later part of her study, found an early outlet in his *The Cherwell Water-Lily* (1840), earning him the ambiguous *soubriquet* of 'Water-Lily

Faber' on account of his good looks and charm of manner. Faber's poetic style and instincts found a more influential and substantial outlet in his *Sights and Thoughts in Foreign Churches and among Foreign Peoples* (1842), a sort of travelogue which asked the reader to look on Europe in the spirit of the Middle Ages. However, as Dr Wilkinson observes (p. 54), 'unlike a number of his contemporaries, Faber did not idealise the Middle Ages or view it in isolation as an ecclesiastical utopia'. Nonetheless, the chief point of the work was to show that during the Middle Ages, 'there was one church in which the pilgrim felt at home because of its sacramental and doctrinal unity and continuity'.

Dr Wilkinson is particularly revealing in her depiction of Faber's almost cult of childhood, an attitude exacerbated from his own feelings of parental loss and nostalgia for his early past. Such feelings of loss encouraged a spirit of introspection and solitariness, as well as a sense of ridicule and cynicism, and a reaction against what he called 'the idolatry of domestic affections'. She also draws out Faber's unusual form of spiritual humility, a conscious aim to achieve an intellectual and literary second best rather than excellence or originality; an attitude again attributed originally to a parental source – Faber divulged in his *Spiritual Conferences* (1859) that as a child he had been taught that it was wrong to be original, as originality was tantamount to showing off, and that this notion had remained with him throughout his life. Interestingly, given Faber's fabled reputation for emotional exuberance and outspokenness, it was an attitude that also accorded with the Tractarian *ethos* or moral temper of reserve which John Keble (who also disapproved of originality) especially exemplified. However, in Faber's case, Wilkinson suggests (p. 156) that while 'the notion of forgetfulness of self shows the influence of scholasticism on his thought, the Medievalist would have used his best work to glorify God, not his second best, making this a perversion of such a tradition'.

Dr Wilkinson also rightly stresses the fact that while Faber often had difficult relations with fellow clergymen and those with whom he was in community, he was always very popular with his parishioners, both in the Anglican parish at Elton, and in the parishes served by the Wilfridian community and by the

London Oratory. A vivid illustration of this often overlooked side of Faber comes in a letter from Arthur Stanley to his sister Mary Stanley, dated 7 December 1845, cited in R. E. Prothero's *Letters and Verses of Arthur Penrhyn Stanley* (London, 1885), which is not reproduced by Dr Wilkinson. It deserves to be quoted in full as highlighting Faber's remarkable personal gifts, and deserves to be set alongside the aspect which he too often conveyed to his mature contemporaries of an awkward and highly wrought persona. After relating to his sister that another Fellow of University College, Piers Claughton, had just taken Faber's Elton living, after Faber's abandonment of the Church of England for Rome in November 1845, Stanley stated:

'It seems that Faber had devoted himself wholly to the parish, and, with the great energy of his character and the fascination of his manners, had produced an effect on the people which I should think was really very extraordinary, whilst the faults which his friends knew did not strike them. He had lived on terms of great familiarity with them, having the young men etc. constantly to dine with him, and read with him in his own drawing room, and having pulled down all the divisions in the Rectory grounds, so as to turn it into a kind of park, and throw it open to the whole parish to walk in, so that on Sunday evening there used to be promenades of one hundred or three hundred people, the poorer classes, and he walking about from group to group and talking to them. And thus, while the old people liked him for his kindness, there had grown up a "young Elton" which quite adored him, and most of them (about sixteen) have gone over with him, and when Claughton came he found these young farmer boys talking of "The Church of St Peter, out of which there is no salvation". The churchwarden described the last Sunday, and the departure on the Monday evening, as the most piteous sight he ever saw; all the people weeping and lamenting, and following him along the road as he went, and wandering about disconsolate all the next day.'

This attractively charismatic side of Faber is easy to miss when the focus is only on his undoubted inability to get on well with his equals (the 'Wilfridians' were even mischievously called the 'Brothers of the Will of Faber' by Dominic Barberi) and the more negative aspects of his personal history such as his unfortunate (but by no means one-sided) misunderstandings with Newman. The latter was related to a dispute between the two Oratories in the mid-1850s ostensibly based on the London Oratory's wish to hear nuns' confessions but it was undoubtedly exacerbated by personal tensions between the two men.

The great strength of Dr Wilkinson's study is in her cogent and revealing analysis of Faber's spiritual writings, lectures and sermons as well as hymns and poems. She is balanced in her appraisal and not afraid to offer candid and searching literary and stylistic criticism where she feels it is due. As Sheridan Gilley has commented: Faber's 'emotive combination of romanticism and evangelicalism is a little strong for modern sensibilities'. Although many of his works were an unsatisfactory hybrid – too devotional to be a theological work and too theological to be devotional work – Dr Wilkinson is able to show that at its best, Faber's literary style was imbued with impressive poetic sensitivity and an Ignatian use of the imagination. On the other hand, several of his published works were overwrought and hagiographical, especially his *Life of Rose of Lima* (1847), edited for the *Lives of the Saints* series, which earned measured criticism from Bishop Ullathorne. Faber's *All for Jesus* (1853), in which Dr Wilkinson argues that he brought the emotional side of the religiosity of the saints to the fore, was also subject to strident criticism along with praise from some quarters. Criticism among Catholics of his work, however, became muted after he had been awarded a doctorate of divinity by Pope Pius IX in 1854. Moreover, his devotional works, especially those on the Virgin Mary, sold very well: his *Sorrows of Mary* (1858), for example, went through ten editions by 1886.

The Faber who emerges from these pages is a complex and problematic figure, not easy to pigeon-hole and certainly far more than the emotional and unstable practitioner of saccharine verse. Although in his later Anglican years Faber has often been bracketed with 'Romanising extremists' among the Tractarians such as W. G. 'Ideal' Ward and Frederick Oakeley, Dr Wilkinson rightly concludes that he was never a typical Tractarian, certainly never a 'true disciple' of Newman, and that he remained very much an individualist in his spiritual journey. She draws attention to his 'Ultramontane stress' as a

Catholic 'on the unity of Catholic countries', an emphasis which led him to take up a highly unpopular negative view of the British 'Protestant empire' which he contrasted unfavourably with Ireland. Faber was utterly uncompromising in his view of Protestantism, urging Catholics to shun 'daily intercourse with unbelievers and heretics'. He even believed (p. 238), quite impracticably, that Roman Catholics should not live in countries which were not Catholic.

Dr Wilkinson charts a previously absent contemplative strand in Faber's spirituality during the last five years of his life, though notes that this remained undeveloped in his sermons and lectures. While strongly emotional and inclined to excess in expressions of Marian devotion, Faber's spirituality was also practical, severe and austere with a profound emphasis on the Passion of Christ (in 1858 he stated that he possessed one hundred books on the subject). While a great exponent of spiritual friendship, playfulness and 'sweetness' alongside an openness to the poor, Faber had a deep-rooted cynicism, sarcasm, pessimism, and mistrust of intellectualism, and often seemed to set an almost unattainable spiritual ideal: he was frequently discouraging of an individual's ability to achieve higher perfection in this world. As Wilkinson argues (p. 244), Faber manifestly lacked 'one of the fundamental instincts of the spiritual genius, the ability to encourage individuals to a higher level of attainment'. On the contrary, Faber 'consistently highlighted the propensity of the individual to avoid effort in the spiritual life, and frequently returned to the idea that individuals cannot be sufficiently religious, holy, or serious about God'. In this as in other aspects of his spiritual make-up, Faber seemed to retain and combine elements of his early Evangelicalism, tinged with Calvinism, alongside his later Ultramontane Roman Catholicism. As he informed his friend J. B. Morris in August 1846, 'ye more Roman I get, ye more I seem to recover ... old boyish evangelical feelings'. The wheel had turned full circle.

Dr Wilkinson shows that Faber had as much of a hand in the foundation of the English Oratory as did Newman. Although in his oft-quoted reply to Faber's letter in December 1847 offering himself and his Wilfridians for the Oratory, Newman doubted whether Faber had 'fully mastered what Oratorianism is', Dr Wilkinson suggests that he actually may have been better acquainted than Newman with the *cultus* and spirit of St Philip Neri (Faber had embraced it while still an Anglican), emphasising the need for his community to be always cheerful, cultivating 'playful ways and sweet manners' and shunning aloofness. Moreover, Faber only undertook the hearing of nuns' confessions, the point on which Newman opposed him, at the request of Cardinal Wiseman. In the last resort, while Faber undoubtedly, in the words of Sheridan Gilley, 'defined the tone and temper of mid-Victorian Ultramontane Catholicism', Dr Wilkinson is surely right in her assessment that 'Faber was essentially an apologist for his own individual reading of Roman Catholicism'.

Peter Nockles
University of Manchester
November 2006.

Preface

This book is the result of four years' research and writing which produced the thesis for my Ph.D., the first academic study of Frederick William Faber (1814–1863).

Faber's contribution to the ecclesiastical history of the mid-nineteenth century has not been developed, and twentieth-century historians who mention him do so *en passant*. The purpose of this study is to present as complete a picture of Faber as possible, based on all available manuscript and printed material, in order to explore the minutiae of the complex series of intellectual, moral, spiritual and emotional factors that marked the progression in Faber's spirituality from evangelical Anglicanism to Roman Catholicism. This progression has been divided into seven stages, which mark the spiritual phases through which Faber progressed during his life. Each stage has continuity with its preceding and succeeding stage, and a definable character of its own.

As well as presenting a comprehensive picture of Faber's life and spiritual development, we shall examine his sermons and major writings, in order to illustrate the development of Faber's thought and the influences, both historical and contemporary, upon him. Faber was a controversial figure during his lifetime, and his responses to doctrine, spirituality, theology and the personalities of those around him were frequently contradictory. We shall, therefore, identify external religious and theological influences on Faber, as well as looking at what he indicates of the deeper recesses of his spirituality. In doing so, we shall demonstrate that Faber inhabited a more sophisticated, complex and multi-faceted spiritual world than has previously been assumed.

Biographers of Faber have not discussed his medical history in detail, whilst historians who mention it in the context of other works fail to present a complete picture. However, knowledge of Faber's illness is vital to our understanding of his life and spirituality; therefore, we shall present a comprehensive survey of Faber's medical history during this study. This is because illness and medication affected Faber's character to such an extent that it seems certain that the accepted historical picture of him, as a fat, ebullient, over-emotional, occasionally bad-tempered individual were caused, or exacerbated, by them.

Acknowledgements

I should like to express my gratitude to the following people:

Fr Ignatius Harrison and the Fathers of the London Oratory, particularly Fr Ronald Creighton Jobe, for the use of their archive. Professor Nigel Yates of the University of Wales, Lampeter, the supervisor of my Ph.D., for his wisdom and counsel. Dr Peter Nockles, for his guidance and advice, and for writing the Foreword. Sir Richard Faber, for an enjoyable day spent discussing the Faber family.

This book is dedicated to my parents, Christopher and Dee Wilkinson, in recognition and appreciation of their continuous encouragement and support.

Chapter 1

Early Life: 1814–1832

Post mortem

On Tuesday, 29 September 1863, the priests of the Roman Catholic Church of the London Oratory recited vespers of the dead for their founder and provost, Frederick William Faber, who had died early in the morning of Saturday, 26 September, aged 49 years. Faber's body had been displayed in the Little Oratory, in alb and purple chasuble, 'on a plain mattress on the floor'[1] from the morning of his death until 28 September, when it was placed in a closed lead-lined coffin. Parishioners and admirers visited the Little Oratory, and, before the coffin was closed, many individuals presented 'rosaries [and] medals'[2] to be blessed by contact with his hands.[3] Faber's Requiem Mass was celebrated in the old Oratory Church, Brompton Road,[4] at 9.30 in the morning of the 30th,[5] 'a fine autumnal day'.[6] The obituarist in the *Dublin Review* observed: 'F[ather] Faber's bier ... was surrounded by more than a hundred priests, representing the reverence and affection of the diocese, and a great multitude of mourners, representing the love of his spiritual children.'[7]

After the service, Faber's body was interred alongside other deceased members of his community at Sydenham,[8] in the cemetery within the grounds of St Mary's, the country house of the London Oratorians.[9]

H. E. Manning (1808–1892) described Faber as 'a great servant of God',[10] noting 'for beauty of mind, and eloquence of speech, he stands almost unequalled';[11] whilst in a sermon preached in the London Oratory Church the Oratorian J. E. Bowden (1829–1874) described 'the bright example of his life, the noble presence ... the singleness of heart ... the chivalrous fervour ... and many other things on which we cannot bring ourselves to speak but on which our love can dwell'.[12]

In a letter to the London Oratorians, W. B. Ullathorne (1806–1889), the Roman Catholic Bishop of Birmingham, wrote: 'Your departed superior ... not only raised the London Oratory, and moulded it in his own fervid and laborious character; he has also left an impress of the supernatural life upon the Catholic heart in this country',[13] whilst Cardinal Wiseman (1802–1865), in a letter to Faber, whose tone is of one who is meditating an obituary, wrote of 'the great work which you have founded, and which will remain, not long, but for ever, to perpetuate the good you have done while living'.[14]

The, anonymous, obituarist in the *Morning Post* opined: 'Of all the converts to Roman Catholicism from the Anglican Faith, none have been more zealous, more successful, more earnest, than Dr Faber.'[15]

A number of obituaries are primarily concerned with Faber's early life and contribution to the Church of England. The *Athenaeum* refers to Faber as a poet of 'moderate merit'[16] and at least one author has a high view of Faber's early intellectual capacity.[17] *Blackwood's Magazine*[18] cites Faber's Anglican period as being more important, and his sphere of influence therein greater, than his Roman Catholic period. The former is seen as showing a promise which was subsequently unfulfilled, and although this article describes Faber as being 'far more successful than Newman, or than any of his companions'[19] as a Roman Catholic, he notes that the Roman Church 'dimmed the fine gold of his genius, and trailed through his devotional writings ... [a] thread of coarse exaggeration and materialistic devotion'.[20] This is connected to the idea, present in a number of obituaries, that Faber and other Oxford converts, such as 'Manning ... Newman [and] ... Oakeley',[21] distanced themselves from the broader social life of the country, as well as from the Establishment and from the Church of England, by converting to Rome. One author writes of Faber's funeral: 'We should have preferred to see the first of the more remarkable great converts ... laid in his grave with as much silence as was possible.'[22] In the obituary in *Blackwood's Magazine*, Faber's Anglican period is postulated as being of more interest to the reader, as: 'interest attaching to the spread and development of the Anglican revival is greater, and ... more enduring than that which can be aroused by the struggles which preceded ... the formation of a new Roman Catholic order in England'.[23]

A significant number of writers indicate an antipathy towards Rome which is expressed either by remarks that express openly anti-Catholic sentiments, or as a sense of unease or by innuendo. We cannot automatically conclude that these were anti-Catholic in origin, although we can hypothesise that this was at the root of some, due to the climate of suspicion of Catholicism that existed during the nineteenth century. A number of articles point to past or ongoing controversies associated with Faber's conduct as a Catholic, which seem to be calculated to prey on the fears and superstitions of the reader. The *Athenaeum* refers to 'the way in which the captain of Westminster School was rapidly converted into a Roman Catholic, at the Oratory, and was recommended to conceal the fact from his masters'.[24] The writer concludes, 'Dr Faber has passed away soon after the late revelations in that unhappy matter.'[25]

Only one obituary, in *The Saturday Review*,[26] is completely unfavourable towards Faber; and, though anonymous, it is usually attributed to Mark Pattison (1813–1884),[27] a contemporary of Faber's at Oxford. This article demonstrates Pattison's dislike of Faber, an attitude that may have had its roots in Pattison's failure to obtain the Fellowship which was subsequently awarded to Faber.[28] He describes Faber whilst an Oxford undergraduate as 'a diligent tuft hunter'[29] and exhibits lack of sympathy for Faber's religious standpoint as an Anglican, whilst regarding him as being too Roman for the Anglican Church.[30] The article is laden with innuendo, which was clearly intended to arouse the suspicions of the reader regarding both Roman Catholicism and Faber's conduct whilst a Roman Catholic. Pattison describes converts to Rome as inhabiting 'a desert of unfulfilled promise, blighted powers, and wasted life'[31] and characterises Faber as being insincere 'silly ... unreal ... [and] effeminate'.[32] He concludes: 'If we have seemed to unveil the littlenesses of Frederick Faber ... we can only say that the semi-canonization which his friends have inflicted on him made it necessary to show that they were the littlenesses of an average, not of a great man.'[33] Another Oxford contemporary, Roundell Palmer, wrote of Faber: 'His nature was tender and emotional; he thought and felt in superlatives, and though his feelings were real and true they were surrounded by a *nimbus* of artificial light.'[34]

Early life

Frederick William Faber was born on Friday, 28 June 1814, in the vicarage of the Church of St Wilfrid at Calverley, Yorkshire. The house, which is no longer in existence, was described in a late nineteenth-century guidebook as 'a low irregular building, but with its strip of ever verdant lawn, shaded by tall beeches and its old grey front almost covered with trailing plants ... a very cosy dwelling'.[35] Faber was baptised into the Church of England on 12 August by his grandfather, the Revd Thomas Faber (1729–1821),[36] at the font of the small eleventh-century church,[37] the inside of which was plain, with monuments, fifteenth-century stained glass and box pews.[38]

Thomas Faber had three sons, the first of whom was George Stanley Faber, (1773–1854),[39] a clergyman, theologian and Fellow of Lincoln College, Oxford, whose works 'advocated the evangelical doctrines of the necessity of conversion, justification by faith, and the sole authority of scripture as the rule of faith'.[40] They are concerned with providing an apology for Christianity as distinct from other religions, for Evangelicalism as distinct from Roman Catholicism, and for groups within Anglicanism. They include dissertations relating to prophecy and scripture, and others dealing with controversy, such as the Tractarian Movement and Catholic emancipation. G. S. Faber's importance to F. W. Faber's life is that his evangelicalism supplemented the religious milieu of the Faber family, which was fundamentally Low Church and tinctured with Calvinism, but devoid of any form of excess in piety and worship.[41]

Thomas Faber's second son was Charles David Faber, JP (1777–1857), and his third son was Thomas Henry Faber (1779–1833), F. W. Faber's father. He had lived in Bradford prior to his sojourn in Calverley, and is described on his son's certificate of baptism as a merchant[42] and in later documents as a solicitor. The date of his marriage to Betty Atkinson (1784–1829), the daughter of a Bradford textile mill owner,[43] is unknown; however, they produced five male and three female children between 1802 and 1816.[44] F. W. Faber was the seventh of these, and one of five who survived into adulthood.

In December 1814, Thomas Henry Faber moved to Bishop Auckland with his family to take up the appointment of secretary to Shute Barrington (1734–1826), the Bishop of Durham;[45] a position which continued during the episcopate of his successor, William van Mildert (1765–1836), the last Bishop Palatine.[46] Although historical evidence relating to F. W. Faber's childhood is scarce, his older brother, Francis Atkinson Faber, notes that he showed 'precocity at a very early age',[47] and that 'his whole nature ... was a joyous one'.[48] It is also documented that he was influenced by his early impressions of the ceremonies of Durham Cathedral, the pageantry surrounding the Bishop of Durham, and the scenery and history of the city of Durham and its surrounding countryside.[49] Several early character traits continued throughout Faber's life, particularly his 'great reliance on himself and his own powers'[50] and 'the use of exaggerated forms of expression ... in talking or writing'.[51]

Faber received his early education from two clergymen. The first of these was Robert Thompson at the Grammar School at Bishop Auckland,[52] which he attended for an unspecified amount of time.[53] The second was John Gibson,[54] at Kirkby Stephen, Westmorland, where he stayed from 1824[55] until 1825. Faber's first biographer, the Oratorian John Bowden (1829–1874), notes that Faber's interest in, and affection for, the Lake District began during this year,[56] whilst Francis Atkinson Faber opined that his experiences at Kirkby Stephen shaped his interests and subsequent character.[57]

In 1826, at the age of 12, Faber went to Shrewsbury School, and transferred to Harrow School during the following year, for reasons that he does not specify. Among the important influences on Faber's spiritual and intellectual development whilst at Harrow was C. T. Longley, who became headmaster in 1829.[58] Longley was an old High Churchman, a fact that highlights a third religious influence on Faber, along with the Low Church

Anglicanism of his family and G. S. Faber's evangelicalism. In an article which provides one of few references to his early life,[59] Faber described the importance given to the study of Divinity at Harrow. This article also provides an insight into the books that he read whilst at school; a list that centred upon the study of scripture,[60] Classics, English Literature, 'to the detriment of his classical studies',[61] and poetry. Faber's temperament at this time can be ascertained by his comment, 'When I was at Harrow I felt always quite wild – wild with power of intellect.'[62] In the same letter he wrote, 'I had *volumes* of poetry written then, and an immense quantity of melancholy Byronical journal.'[63] The latter he destroyed, and it is notable that for the remainder of his life Faber did not keep any form of diary or journal, and actively discouraged others from doing so. In writing of his childhood, Faber noted that he had, 'been brought up ... self-indulgently',[64] probably because of early ill-health, and Addington describes him as an individual whose 'nature was ... deeply flawed by the circumstances of his early life'.[65] It is worth noting that Faber attended the Eucharist at the Roman Catholic Church at Warwick Street, London, some time during 1827 or 1828; however, he does not record his thoughts about this experience.[66]

Faber's mother died in 1829[67] after three years' illness,[68] and this event, together with memories of childhood, continued to resonate with Faber for the remainder of his life. He retained his initial feelings of grief, which were never resolved, and eleven years after his mother's death he described himself as one who had been 'deprived of home and all home thoughts ... in early boyhood'.[69] He wrote, 'my early loss of home and people to love, joined to my exuberant temperament ... have considerable influence on me'.[70] These sentiments are particularly noticeable in poems, such as 'The Easter Guest', in which he wrote:

> Dear Mother! Through the long, long year
> I never think without a tear
> Of thee so soon departed:
> And, weariest penance! All the things
> Which memory from her storehouse brings
> Are seeds of bitter thought, and stings
> Which keep me broken-hearted.[71]

During the same year, Faber underwent a period of scepticism about Christianity, the first of two such occasions during his life,[72] and because of this he 'stood on a tomb in Harrow Churchyard, and lifted up his hand to heaven, defying God if a God there was, to strike him dead!'[73] The experience of evangelical conversion which followed this episode[74] was caused, at least partially, by the influence of the vicar of Harrow, J. W. Cunningham,[75] a prominent evangelical. From this point onwards, evangelicalism was in the ascendant in Faber's adolescent spiritual life and, in retrospect, he wrote of this time, 'my characteristics at Harrow were wildness, impetuosity, imperiousness [and] pride'.[76] At one level, it seems possible that it was part of the experience of conversion to create in Faber a sense of his pre-conversion wickedness. However, there is an equally strong sense that it was caused by his flamboyant and ostentatious temperament, early attributes which were never erased from his character.

Several of Faber's Harrow contemporaries[77] recurred later in his life, notably Henry Edward Manning, who was six years older than Faber, and A. Beresford Hope. However, his foremost, and most enduring, friend[78] was John Brande Morris,[79] whose home was Egglesfield House, New Brentford, Middlesex, and whose father, the Revd John Morris DD, was vicar of St Nicholas Church, Elstree, near Harrow. Morris's parents, brothers and sister became a surrogate family for Faber, and he frequently stayed with them at both of these addresses during the school holidays. Illness provides one explanation of why Faber did not return home more often, and it seems possible that he stayed with Morris's family in order to avoid the long journey by steam packet along the Thames, around the coast to Newcastle[80] and by coach to his family home in Bishop Auckland. This is corroborated by Faber's note, written during the summer of 1833, that he had been exhausted, both physically and mentally, by the return sea voyage from his family home to London.[81] Faber mentioned ill-health in a number of letters written during the early 1830s,[82] and from these references we can gather that he had been in poor health for much of his childhood and adolescence. Thus, he wrote to Morris, 'I had no idea ... how extremely weak my constitution was, and how completely the struggles I had for life in early boyhood had shattered me.'[83] Faber does not provide details of definite illnesses, but only general references; indicating, for example, that he took laudanum for seasickness and experienced recurrent headaches.[84] As we shall see in the course of this study, both of these influenced Faber for the remainder of his life.

Notes

1   J. E. Bowden (1869), *The Life and Letters of Frederick William Faber, DD: Priest of the Oratory of St Philip Neri*, 5th edn, London, Burns & Oates, p. 444. [Hereafter referred to as Bowden, *Life*.]
2   Ibid.
3   Ibid.
4   The old church was used from 1854. It 'was enlarged in 1856, and various additions were made between 1856 and 1880'. E. Kilburn (1987), *A Walk Round the Church of the London Oratory*, London, Caldra House, p. 10. The old church was demolished in 1880, and the new church was completed in 1884.
5   Bowden, *Life*, p. 444.
6   Ibid. p. 445.
7   Anon (1864), 'Father Faber', *Dublin Review*, NS, Vol. 2, January, p. 163.
8   Bowden, *Life*, p. 445.
9   Faber's remains were reburied in St Wilfrid's Chapel of the new Oratory Church, on 16 February 1952, after the closure and demolition of St Mary's, Sydenham. The guide to the new church contains the following: 'Father Faber's body was ... laid in a vault prepared in front of St Wilfrid's Altar. The grey marble slab which covers it bears an inscription of which the following is a translation: This stone covers the remains of the first Provost of the London Congregation of the Oratory, Frederick William Faber. He died on 26 September 1863, when he was 49 years of age and had worn the habit of St Philip Neri for 15 years. R. I. P.' E. Kilburn (1987), *A Walk Round the Church of the London Oratory*, London, Caldra House, p. 21.
10 Bowden, *Life*, p. 445.
11 Ibid. p. 446.
12 *Notes of Fr John Bowden's sermon at the High Mass, Sept[ember] 27 1863, the day after Fr Faber's death* in London Oratory Archives [hereafter referred to as LO], Vol. 23, Doc. 99.
13 W. B. Ullathorne to J. B. D. Dalgairns, LO, Vol. 24, No. 230, 3 October 1863.
14 N. Wiseman to F. W. Faber, 14 July 1863, in Bowden, *Life*, p. 438.
15 Anon (1863), 'Obituary of F. W. Faber', in *Morning Post*, 28

September, p. 5, in LO, Vol. 22, p. 248.

16   Anon (1863), 'F. W. Faber' [Obituary], in *Athenaeum*, Vol. 2, 3 October, p. 436.

17   Anon (1869), 'F. W. Faber's Life and Letters', in *Blackwood's Magazine*, Vol. CVI, December, p. 694.

18   Ibid. pp. 693–700.

19   Ibid. p. 693.

20   Ibid.

21   Anon [M. Pattison?] (1863), 'Frederick William Faber', in *The Saturday Review*, 10 October, p. 488.

22   Ibid.

23   Anon (1869), 'F. W. Faber's Life and Letters', in *Blackwood's Magazine*, CVI, December, pp. 693–700.

24   Anon (1863), 'F. W. Faber' [Obituary], in *Athenaeum*, Vol. 2, 3 October, p. 436.

25   Ibid.

26   Anon [M. Pattison?] (1863), 'Frederick William Faber', in *The Saturday Review*, 10 October, pp. 488–9.

27   R. Faber (1987), *Young England*, London, Faber, pp. 51–2. [Hereafter referred to as Faber, *Young England*.]

28   Ibid. p. 29.

29   Anon [M. Pattison?] (1863), 'Frederick William Faber', in *The Saturday Review*, 10 October, p. 488.

30   Ibid.

31   Ibid. p. 488.

32   Ibid.

33   Ibid. p. 489.

34   Roundell Palmer, quoted in Faber, *Young England*, p. 32.

35   W. Cudworth (1876), *Round About Bradford*, n.p., p. 454. This building was demolished in the 1880s. Letter to the author from E. W. Garnett, Calverley Archivist, 30 March 2001.

36   Thomas Faber (1729–1821) was the longest serving incumbent, from 1770–1821. (Letter to the author from E. W. Garnett, Calverley Archivist, 30 March 2001.) Thomas Faber attended St John's College, Cambridge, a college patronised by men from the north of England.

37   Author's interview with Sir Richard Faber (great-grandson of F. A. Faber and great-nephew of F. W. Faber) 8 August 2005. [Hereafter referred to as R. F.]

38   The church was restored during 1869–70. Letter to the author from E. W. Garnett, Calverley Archivist, 31 March 2001.

39   *G. S. Faber (1773–1854)*, in *Dictionary of National Biography* [hereafter referred to as DNB], London, Smith Elder & Co, 1889, Vol. XVIII, pp. 111–12.

40   Ibid. p. 111.

41   R. F.

42   Certificate of Baptism F. W. Faber. Letter to the author from E. W. Garnett, Calverley Archivist, 30 March 2001.

43 R. F.
44 Thomas Henry (1802–1850), Francis Atkinson, BD, MA (1804–1876), Charles Edward (1807–1868), Frederick (n.d.–1813), Frederick William (1814–1863), Caroline (1809–n.d.), Eliza Sophia (n.d.–1813), Ellen (1816–1898).
45 Barrington was Bishop of Durham from 1791–1826. See *The Oxford History of the Christian Church* (London, OUP, 1957) p. 134. [Hereafter referred to as OHCC]
46 Van Mildert was Bishop of Durham from 1826–36. He was also involved in the foundation of the University of Durham during 1832. See OHCC, p. 1407. It is interesting to note the, unverified, Faber family anecdote that T. H. Faber was involved with the foundation of the University of Durham. See R. F.
47 F. A. Faber (1879), *A Brief Sketch of the Early Life of the Late F. W. Faber DD*, London, Thomas Richardson and Son, p. 7. [Hereafter referred to as F. A. Faber, *Brief Sketch*.]
48 F. A. Faber, *Brief Sketch*, p. 10.
49 Ibid. pp. 5–7. See also Bowden, *Life*, pp. 2–3.
50 F. A. Faber, *Brief Sketch*, p. 8. It is evident that Bowden had used F. A. Faber's book, as he employs similar language to describe this trait of Faber's early life. See Bowden, *Life*, p. 2.
51 F. A. Faber, *Brief Sketch*, p. 8. See also Bowden, *Life*, p. 2.
52 Bowden, *Life*, p. 3.
53 R. Chapman (1961), *Father Faber*, London, Burns & Oates, p. 6. [Hereafter referred to as Chapman, *Father Faber*.]
54 Bowden, *Life*, p. 3.
55 This date is given in R. H. L. Addington (ed.) (1974), *Faber: Poet and Priest: Selected Letters of Frederick William Faber from 1833–1863*, Cowbridge, D. Brown & Sons, p. 27. [Hereafter referred to as Addington, *Faber: Poet and Priest*.]
56 Bowden, *Life*, p. 3. See also F. A. Faber, *Brief Sketch*, p. 14.
57 F. A. Faber, *Brief Sketch*, p. 14.
58 C. T. Longley (1794–1868). Christ Church College, Oxford (1812), BA (1815), MA (1818), DD (1829). Tutor Christ Church College, Oxford (1825–1828), Curate, then Vicar of Cowley (1823), Vicar of West Tytherley, Hampshire (1823), Headmaster of Harrow (1829–1836), Bishop of Ripon (1836), Bishop of Durham (1856), Archbishop of York (1860), Archbishop of Canterbury (1862). See J. R. Garrard, *C. T. Longley (1794–1868)*, in DNB (Oxford, OUP, 2004) Vol. 34, pp. 399–402.
59 *The Oxford University Magazine*, Vol. 1: 1834, pp. 200–7.
60 Ibid. p. 205.
61 Bowden, *Life*, p. 6.
62 F. W. Faber to J. Manners, 16 May 1839, in Addington, *Faber: Poet and Priest*, p. 74.
63 Ibid.
64 F. W. Faber to J. B. Morris, LO, Vol. 17, No. 41, 22 October 1840.

65   Addington, *Faber: Poet and Priest*, p. 24.
66   F. W. Faber to J. H. Newman, LO, Vol. 2, No. 231, 19 February 1850.
67   F. W. Faber to J. Manners, 16 May 1839, in Addington, *Faber: Poet and Priest*, p. 74.
68   F. A. Faber, *Brief Sketch*, p. 16.
69   F. W. Faber to J. B. Morris, LO, Vol. 17, No. 41, 22 October 1840.
70   Ibid.
71   F. W. Faber (1857), 'The Easter Guest', in *Poems*, 3rd edn, London, Richardson & Sons, No. CXXV, p. 328. [Hereafter referred to as *Poems*.]
72   The second, brief, episode was during 1846 after his conversion to Roman Catholicism, which took place in November 1845.
73   H. Wilberforce to J. E. Bowden, 17 July 1869, in Addington, *Faber: Poet and Priest*, p. 17.
74   Ibid.
75   J. W. Cunningham (1780–1861). St John's College, Cambridge, BA (1802), MA (1805). Fellow St John's College, Cambridge. Ordained Deacon (May 1803), Priest (December 1803). Vicar of Harrow from 1811 onwards, and Governor of Harrow School from 1818. Students from Harrow School attended the parish church until 1839, when a chapel was built. See A. F. Munden, *J. W. Cunningham (1780–1861)*, in DNB (Oxford, OUP, 2004) Vol. 14, pp. 693–4.
76   F. W. Faber to J. Manners, 16 May 1839, in Addington, *Faber: Poet and Priest*, p. 74.
77   For a list of Faber's contemporaries at Harrow, see Andrew Jukes to Hon. Revd G. T. O. Bridgeman, in '125 Years Ago', in *The Harrovian*, May 17 1956, pp. 88–9.
78   Faber destroyed Morris's letters to him; however, Morris kept Faber's letters and returned them to the London Oratory after Faber's death. The letters, which span the period from 1833 until 1863, present a valuable record of Faber's personal and spiritual thoughts.
79   J. B. Morris (1812–1880). Balliol College, Oxford (1830), BA (1834), MA, Fellow Exeter College, Oxford (1837), Lecturer in Hebrew, Priest (1836), Roman Catholic (1846), Priest (1849), Lecturer at Prior Park School, Canon of Plymouth Cathedral (1851), various chaplaincies. See W. A. G. [*sic*] *J. B. Morris (1812–1880)*, in DNB (Oxford, OUP, 1921) Vol. 13, pp. 996–7. (Morris is also in the latest DNB – see G. Martin Murphy, *J. B. Morris (1812–1880)*, in DNB (Oxford, OUP, 2004) Vol. 39, pp. 282–3.)
80   F. W. Faber to J. B. Morris, LO, Vol. 17, No. 1, 8 June 1833.
81   Ibid.
82   F. W. Faber to J. B. Morris, LO, Vol. 17, No. 15, 5 January 1836; LO, Vol. 17, No. 16, 22 May 1836; LO, Vol. 17, No. 23, 30

November 1836; LO, Vol. 17, No. 25, 10 January 1837.

83   F. W. Faber to Roundell Palmer, 20 December 1835, in Bowden, *Life,* Letter VI, pp. 25–6.

84   F. W. Faber to J. B. Morris, LO, Vol. 17, No. 15, 5 January 1836; F. W. Faber to J. B. Morris, LO, Vol. 17, No. 16, 22 May 1836; F. W. Faber to J. B. Morris, LO, Vol. 17, No. 23, 30 November 1836; F. W. Faber to J. B. Morris, LO, Vol. 17, No. 25, 10 January 1837; F. W. Faber to J. B. Morris, LO, Vol. 17, No. 39, 28 September 1840.

Chapter 2

Pre-conversion: 1833–1843

Stage One of Faber's spiritual development: evangelical, January 1833–December 1834

Faber matriculated at Balliol College, Oxford, on 26 July 1832, and commenced his Classical studies in January 1833. His father, Thomas Henry Faber, who had 'always regarded him with a love equal to that of his mother',[1] died on 3 April,[2] and Faber's grief affected the whole of his first year at Oxford. In retrospect he observed, 'I was so stunned that ... my intellect was struck dead. It was kept in ice.'[3]

Faber's initial response to the religious climate of the university was critical, and, because of this, he remained on the periphery of the religious scene in Oxford throughout his undergraduate career. The fundamental cause of Faber's dissatisfaction was the conflict between his own Low Church evangelical[4] Anglicanism and the High Church Anglicanism of the Oxford Movement, which was founded in June 1833, during Faber's second term at Oxford. Faber believed that the style of church advocated by the Tractarians was fundamentally wrong for Anglicanism as a whole; and, although he did not articulate his dissatisfaction fully during 1833–4, he continually underlined the doctrinal differences between the two parties. Faber particularly deplored the Tractarian emphasis on apostolic succession,[5] writing: 'I love the Church of England most fervently and affectionately ... But ... I suspect and mistrust that sort of religion in which <u>Apostolicity</u> – <u>Establishment</u> – <u>Episcopacy</u> ... are terms in more frequent usage than <u>depravity</u>, <u>atonement</u>, [and] <u>justification</u>.'[6] Faber also distrusted the cult of personality, particularly that which surrounded John Henry Newman, and what he saw as undue stress on the necessity of affiliation to a religious party. He noted: 'The greatest evil which I seemed to perceive at Oxford was the substitution of ... zeal for the exterior of religion, for the inward spirit of faith and love. How easy it is to mistake love of our party for the love of our God.'[7]

In correspondence written during 1833–4, Faber exhibits boundless confidence in his theological position. He demonstrates an evangelical emphasis on scripture, particularly the Epistles of St Paul,[8] and opined to J. B. Morris: 'I think that we best serve our venerable church, not by always <u>lauding</u> her <u>ordinances</u> but by practising in their primitive purity, her truly scriptural doctrines.'[9] In August 1834 he informed Morris, 'on leaving Oxford ... I did not bring down one single volume relating directly or indirectly to religion'.[10] He also indicated that he had not attended the College chapel for eight months,[11] which he described as 'a very sufficient sign of a very <u>unsafe</u> state as to religion'[12] and ascribed it to the pressure of work.[13] He did not record whether he had substituted another place of worship more suited to his evangelicalism, or whether his doubts were connected with the rightness, or otherwise, of remaining an evangelical. There is a constant tension inherent in Faber's spirituality at this time, and perhaps work became an excuse for his antipathy to the organised religion available to him. There is also a sense of dissatisfaction and depression, which may be attributable to the death of his father during the previous year.

During September 1834, Faber exhibited a preoccupation with the way in which faith is acquired, and with the experience of conversion, the primary indicator of an evangelical. Unlike the flamboyant nature of his descriptions of other events in Oxford,[14] Faber's comments on his own conversion are restrained. They are expectant of spiritual experience as proof of their authenticity, a trend which continued throughout Faber's life, although he indicated that his own 'hours of extatic [*sic*] enthusiastic devotion'[15] were fragmentary and of short duration.[16] He repeatedly compared and contrasted his own religious experience with that of others: 'It somewhat disheartens me to see the maturity of faith, and the spiritual perfection, to which many good men arrive so early. They seem to be made Christians all at once. Their conversion appears to have been almost miraculous.'[17]

During August and September 1834, discussion of theology assumed the central position in Faber's correspondence. In a letter to Morris, he articulated his intention to start reading theology, particularly the New Testament, in preparation for examinations prior to his ordination.[18] He wrote: 'Religious biography, which has ever been my favourite study, has ... occupied almost all my extra classical hours; and it would be no difficult matter ... to compile a ... code of Christian experience from my reading.'[19]

Faber's spiritual reading mirrored the type of Anglicanism which he espoused,[20] and its evangelical content is represented by G. S. Faber's *Treatise on the Holy Spirit,* which he indicated had been particularly useful.[21] He had also read Pearson's work on *The Creed,* and Abbot's *The Cornerstone* and *The Young Christian.* He wrote of the latter in disparaging terms, but commented that it 'contains many fanciful speculations, but is nevertheless calculated on the whole to do an infinity of good'.[22] It is interesting to note that Faber did not think that fanciful speculations were a problem; and this is perhaps an early indication of the strand within Faber's thought that espoused the evangelical idea that the emotional effect on the individual is more important than the depth of theology represented. It is noticeable that Faber's reading was frequently influenced by taking part in discussion of the interests of his friends. The *Life of Adam Clarke*[23] was concerned with the study of biblical criticism, and was clearly influenced by Morris's interest in biblical scholarship and his study of Greek and Hebrew. Faber wrote, 'it contains ... a fund of the most valuable ... information for one whose ambition it is to become a sound Biblical critic'.[24] Faber was also influenced by Morris's father, a Doctor of Divinity and lecturer at Oxford; and in a number of letters Faber asked for his 'valuable opinion'[25] and views on literary and theological matters. Faber was also, at this time, reading books which may have been outside his religious world, such as the works of Cyprian,[26] Newman's *Prophetical Office,* and *Sermons,*[27] although he does not comment on these.

Faber indicated a number of books which were of particular

significance. One of these was Walton's *Lives of the Saints*,[28] of which he wrote to Morris: 'If you have not read Walton's Lives, I beseech you to read them ... There are a thousand interesting ... questions involved in them.'[29] Faber also possessed an enduring enthusiasm for the works of Hooker, and indicated that 'the lives of Hooker and Herbert are my favourite ones in Isaak Walton's volume'.[30] This interest was primarily intellectual, but it also seems to have fulfilled a religio-emotional function, which is indicated by the phrase 'I feel so painfully ... the controversiality of my own disposition; that a perusal of it always produces considerable self abasement'.[31]

Towards the end of 1834, Faber's style of writing became more sophisticated and mature, both in his use of the language and in its content. Both were closer to his mature style, and it is noticeable that this has similarities to Walton's florid and elaborate style of seventeenth-century English. This is particularly apparent in the sympathetic empathy and emotionalism of both individuals, and in their somewhat rambling mode of expression. Faber's correspondence was not solely filled with discussion of theological matters. He discussed poetry, particularly that of Burns and Wordsworth, and letters, lectures and sermons which he had attended; also, his own composition, such as poetry and essays, and references drawn from the Philosophy and Classics which he was reading in preparation for his degree.[32] A magazine article which is probably by Faber, entitled 'Life in Oxford',[33] indicated that he was studying Greek, Latin, Modern History, Poetry, Philology, Philosophy, Religion and Logic.[34] He wrote, 'I have read so far two books of the *Aeneid* ... Thucydides ... Aeschylus ... Potter... Shakespeare ... and Livy.'[35]

In *Father Faber*, Chapman notes that, during this time, the defining attribute of Faber's theological vocabulary[36] was a 'Calvinistic bias';[37] however, Addington contradicts Chapman and casts doubt over the depth of Calvinistic influence on Faber's spirituality.[38] This tendency towards Calvinism was part of the process of spiritual re-organisation taking place within Faber's spirituality, one which shows that Faber was, even at this early stage, capable of drifting towards theological extremes. Faber worked through his feelings towards Calvinism in debates with his contemporaries, and with Morris, who indicated an antipathy towards Calvinists.[39] He informed the latter that his Calvinism had been underlined and strengthened by his reading of the New Testament, particularly the epistles.[40] Faber's attitude to Calvinism was contradictory and a matter of degree, which he described as 'a bias towards some of their opinions'.[41] The tendency towards Calvinism was clearly an ingrained part of Faber's religious and intellectual makeup. He justified himself by concluding that the traits he held were not his own, but inherited from his family, and that he did not have the knowledge of history needed to distinguish doctrinal niceties, or to 'decide where the best and wisest of men have doubted'.[42] The influence of Calvinism was both positive and negative. It seems possible that overtones from it affected Faber's spirituality for the remainder of his life, remaining in the background of his thought at a sub-conscious level after he had formally rejected it.

Faber indicated Calvinistic doctrines which he did not hold, such as the predestination and salvation of the elect, the rejection of which is a central part of the theology of Arminianism, and underlined this by saying that 'the Calvinism of Calvin is not connected in the most remote degree with fatalism'.[43] 'I, like my uncle, [G. S. Faber] disavow all Arminianism and all Calvinism: but I have lost ... all prejudice which I had against the latter opinions.'[44] Faber wrote that his reading of Hooker's 'sermons on justification by faith, and on the certainty and perpetuity of faith in the elect'[45] had influenced him, and he mentioned his reading of the *Laws of Ecclesiastical Polity* and *Sermons* in several letters.

Calvinism affected Faber's opinions on a significant number of concerns, such as the Bible as the most important repository of faith, denial of human free will, and justification by faith alone. The idea that the State should be subjugated to the power of the Church was an important doctrine in a number of readings of Protestantism, such as Calvinism, and was also the central concern of the early Tractarians. The Oxford Movement is not mentioned in extant correspondence of this period. However, this does not preclude its being in the background, possibly causing some of Faber's stronger assertions of evangelicalism, and veiled comments about worries over religious matters.[46] Faber was aware of Tractarian ideas, and these highlighted concerns that were already present in his thought; and, because of this, Faber founded and edited the *Oxford University Magazine*, to promote 'Conservative principles in church and state, without refusing to acknowledge the necessity and advantage of practical improvement'.[47] Three issues were printed during 1834, containing articles, poetry and essays, the majority of which are unsigned, although Faber indicated in letters those which were of his authorship and indicated that contributors to the magazine had been few.[48] In one of these articles, Faber considered that the main problem for the Church was its relationship to the State,[49] in particular the balance of power between the two. He presented the view that the State was 'the gift of God ... God's moral government on earth, for the present and eternal welfare of mankind'.[50] He was critical that the Church had not given moral leadership and authority,[51] leading people to dissent or to Roman Catholicism, which he considered the two enemies of the Church of England.[52] Faber considered that the 'appointment of bishops by the Crown'[53] was problematic, particularly if Roman Catholics and dissenters in Parliament were allowed to influence the decision. Another article in the same publication further underlined Faber's view of the inadvisability of giving autonomy to other religious groups. His reasons are revealing, as for Faber the problem with admitting dissenters and Roman Catholics into Oxford lay in the number and diversity of religious opinions generated. His argument was that it is easier if everyone believes the same, because there is less room for heresy.[54] Although this article is anonymous, it has the crispness, logic and enjoyment of argument which is increasingly a feature of Faber's style.

It is important to recognise that in letters where Faber discusses theological points, such as ideas relating to the existence of God, the argument from design,[55] and the necessity of an intelligent creator, he does not go into detail. Faber indicated that he held the Reformed Church's view of justification by, and salvation through, faith, advocated by Paul in the Epistle to the Romans;[56] writing that 'no human beings have attained unto righteousness by works'.[57] He also discussed transubstantiation, writing: 'Transubstantiation has been bothering me: not that I lean to it: but I have seen no refutation of it!'[58] He viewed transubstantiation as being both improbable and contradictory, but his primary reason for rejecting it was because it was unscriptural.[59] However, he also rejected the arguments against transubstantiation given by the Anglican Divines because they were also contradictory, writing: 'I have had some trouble in finding out the cause of what I much deem their error.'[60] The tone of these two letters is that of an individual who, although he is enjoying discussing theology and controversy as an intellectual exercise, is still relatively shallow.

Faber emphasised that the way in which the Christian life was lived was of fundamental importance, an idea which was also expressed in sermons after his ordination as an Anglican, and as a Roman Catholic. This forms part of a sense of austerity, which was a life-long component of Faber's spirituality, and which was related to his Calvinistic awareness of the fallen nature of humanity. Faber exhibited a pessimistic view of the human state, in which the depravity and moral hopelessness of human nature meant that it is difficult to avoid damnation, which is counterbalanced by an emphasis on the need for atonement, and the centrality of the Cross to Christian life. A major contradiction in Faber's spirituality is that he often comes near to presenting a pessimistic view of Christ's atonement. In Faber's view, few of the rich would ultimately be saved, a judgement that hints at predestination, as it had no bearing on whether or not they had been philanthropic and charitable.[61] This is incongruous, because, throughout his later career, Faber relied on the rich members of his congregation to provide money for building and decoration of his churches.

Although Thomas Henry Faber had left provision in his Will for Faber to stay at Oxford until he had completed his degree,[62] Faber experienced monetary difficulties throughout his first year.[63] Because of this, he transferred to University College, Oxford, on 6 December 1834.[64] University College awarded him a Freestone exhibition,[65] and was less expensive than Balliol. It was also popular with students who were, like himself, from the north of England.

Faber's responses to Newman and Tractarianism during 1835

During 1835, the primary concern of Faber's spiritual development was his response to Tractarianism, and between January
and June he openly indicated his aversion to it. However,
Tractarianism represented the third major influence on
Faber's spirituality, and despite his distaste he began increasingly to fluctuate between Low and High Church theories of
churchmanship. This aspect of Faber's intellect was also
present in his mature theology, in which he was capable of
working himself round between several potentially conflicting
positions.[66] It is not always clear from his writings whether
Faber's espousal of one theory represented the complete abandonment of the other and, in a number of letters, Faber seems
to play the role of devil's advocate with his correspondent. He
does not usually give the impression of being indecisive, rather
as though he is progressing through an intellectual process of
distinguishing between different sectarian and doctrinal standpoints. This highlights the imprecise nature of the use of
epithets such as 'High' and 'Low' Church and 'evangelical' for
anything other than concrete doctrinal statements, particularly
when applied to the complex process of religious change in the
individual.

Faber's primary concern was that the Tractarians were in
danger of becoming a heretical sect within Anglicanism. He
wrote, 'his [Newman's] followers are likely to become a sort of
Christian Essenes',[67] and described the progress of their ideas
as 'more like the blind march of error than the steady unifor-
mity of truth'.[68] This strand was particularly apparent in
Faber's criticism of the cult of personality, which we noted at
the beginning of this chapter as being associated partly with
the adulation given to Newman.[69] Faber was not one of the
undergraduates who queued up to sit at Newman's feet, at
least not all of the time. This distinction is important, because
Faber's indecision, whether or not to support Newman, was a
trait that continued throughout their mature relationship,
which began in 1838 after Faber had become a Fellow. During
1835, Faber singled out the teaching and influence of Newman
from that of other Tractarians, in order to represent aspects of

the Tractarian Movement with which he disagreed most strongly. Faber was undoubtedly aware of the power of Newman's oratorical style, writing, 'I can answer from personal experience for the manner in which it captivates a mind which is in the least imaginative.'[70] Although Faber was both an academic and a biological generation younger, circumspection did not prevent him from criticising Newman,[71] and, in correspondence written in January 1835, Faber's language was scathing. He indicated that he had distanced himself from Newman's influence[72] and spirituality because he 'had become ... convinced of its falsehood'.[73] Faber wrote, 'Newman's mind has become deeply tinctured by that mystical allegorising spirit of Origen and the school of Alexandria.'[74] He characterised Newman as an individual who had been deluded by his own theological intellectualism, which was leading him via a false logic towards a heretical mysticism.[75] There seems to be both irony and evangelical rebelliousness in Faber's comment to Roundell Palmer that 'after having been an unprejudiced acolyth of Newman's ... I found the impressive simplicities of the Bible irksome to me ... and vague, bodiless Platonic reveries were the food my soul craved for'.[76] This somewhat cynical portrait contains within it the underlying criticism that Newman was putting forward a theological stance that was in a sense unreal, an idea that was always anathema to Faber.

Faber also characterised Newman as one who presented a Christianity that was excessively esoteric; a system which made religion suitable only for those who possessed the intellectual capacity to understand and interpret it.[77] This aspect of Newman's Christianity was emphasised for Faber by the idea that there were, for him, 'thoughts which it is scarcely right to enlarge upon in a mixed congregation'.[78] On the surface, Faber's comments are surprising, because Newman's role at Oxford was pastoral in the context of education. However, the root cause of this criticism was Faber's consciousness that a generation of clergy were being formed by such ideas, an idea which was unacceptable. He wrote, 'a very serious blow may be given to the Church by bodies of young men going out to be parish priests believing that there are inner doctrines which it is as well not to reveal to the vulgar'.[79] This represents one of the fundamental distinctions between the two individuals, as

Faber distrusted distinctions made between religion for the educated and religion for the general population. One of Faber's most enduring traits is an interest in the poor and uneducated, particularly those who were outside his academic and social circle, an idea which is particularly apparent during his Roman Catholic period.

Faber's correspondence during 1835 included increasing use of disparaging and negative comments about his studies, referring to them as 'heathen classics'.[80] It is also noticeable that references to classical literature become less frequent in Faber's extant correspondence of this period, and that the only authors mentioned are Aristotle,[81] Pliny,[82] Homer, Euripides and Seneca. Faber increasingly contrasted Classics with the writings of Christianity, and it becomes apparent that he was not making a straightforward distinction between two words and worldviews: 'Christian' and 'pagan'. Firstly, he was reinforcing the idea that studying Classics was diverting him from the study of Theology, which perhaps contains an element of guilt that theology was not the first of his intellectual priorities. Secondly, Faber increasingly believed that the literature he was reading for his degree was morally suspect in its subject matter, and he wrote of 'the deadening effect of so much heathen reading upon the soul's health'.[83] This is important in the context of Faber's concern for individuals, as he viewed Classical Studies as leading to temptations for those who studied it, particularly those who were not sufficiently morally developed to cope with them.[84] It may also represent an oblique sense of unease, or dissatisfaction, with aspects of the education which he had received that was, at one level, evangelical in origin.

Faber discussed a number of his literary interests in correspondence written at this time. He continued to return to the subject of Hooker's theology and poetry,[85] and indicated that he was writing articles for the Oxford University Magazine on the poetry of Burns and Byron.[86] Faber's response to reading the poetry of Herbert, one who 'takes a first rank among the poets of our land',[87] was significant in that it contrasted with his reaction to Newman. He wrote, 'I feel that under the blessing of God the study of Herbert ... is ... effecting the restoration of my mind's equilibrium, destroyed by my recoil from Newman's theology and Platonism.'[88] His remark that, 'to read him and appreciate him you must be a ... dutiful Church of England religious quiet thinking mind',[89] echoes Hooker's phrase 'a peaceable and quiet mind'[90] in Book V of the *Ecclesiastical Polity*. Such phrases provide an indication of the spirit of his reading of Anglicanism, and his desire to avoid controversy.

Faber was also reading Butler's *Analogy*,[91] a book which he indicated his antipathy towards in several letters.[92] In reviewing 'Pearson on the Creed'[93] Faber remarked that 'it is a kind of Divinity much more interesting than the department to which the Analogy belongs'.[94] Faber described the reserved philosophical intricacies of the *Analogy* as 'the greatest book of pagan wisdom I ever pursued'.[95] It is apparent that Faber's criticism refers not only to the style but also to the content of Butler's writing, and he wrote, 'I should be better employed if I substituted in its place some more Christian book.'[96] Morris and Faber had been discussing Butler's 'low view of the atonement',[97] and it is revealing of Faber's ideas that he did not view Butler's low view of the atonement as a problem, whilst Morris did. Despite this, it is clear that Faber felt that there was a discrepancy between his view of Christianity and Butler's,[98] and that here, as elsewhere, the word Christian can be translated as evangelical. Faber's criticism of Butler is essentially an emotional as well as an academic and theological criticism, and he was concerned that Butler's view of Christianity was too dry, philosophical and unemotional, an idea that echoes his criticism of Newman. Faber wrote, 'if <u>that</u> is Christianity, I <u>am</u> not, and God grant I never <u>may</u> be a Christian'.[99]

Despite his distrust of the power of individual personalities, such as that of Newman, Faber was clearly aware that he possessed a certain amount of influence among his undergraduate acquaintances. During 1835, Faber began a series of prayer meetings, to carry out 'a ... series of aggressive efforts in favour of religion'.[100] As in our discussion on Butler, we can infer that by 'religion' Faber was referring to Evangelicalism. It is noticeable that he was promulgating a reading of Christianity in which holiness of life, mortification of the flesh, prayer and judgement, were important and constantly recurring ideas.[101] These ideas were enduring ones for Faber; however, they are not specifically evangelical ideas, but ones that could be applied to the general religious climate in England during the early nineteenth century. Faber also highlights ideas that were important to the reformers, such as the inspired character of scripture, particularly the Gospels, and the inspiration of the Holy Spirit.[102] His thought was influenced by the Pauline Epistles, and on several occasions he made use of the Pauline contrast, in the Letter to the Corinthians, between human philosophy and that of the Holy Spirit.[103] The underlining of the gulf between human and divine philosophy was part of Faber's pessimistic view of the sinfulness of human nature, and the depravity of humanity.[104] On a number of occasions during 1835, Faber highlighted the impossibility of discovering a personal God, and the helplessness of humanity, which leads to discussion of humanity's need for God, more specifically Christ.[105]

Faber had not been attending services in the College chapel; however, during October he wrote that he had 'resumed my attendance at St Peter's,[106] which I hope will be now uninterrupted till [*sic*] the month of June 1836'.[107] The tone of Faber's letters at this time is interesting because it indicates an inherent tension in his personality, between an individual who at once distrusted and courted showiness. He seems to have circumvented potential difficulties associated with a Faber personality cult by stressing that his primary concern was for the cause of evangelical religion. This shows itself in his interest in the spiritual state of others, particularly those who had given up the practice of Evangelicalism.[108] Conversely, a number of his letters exhibit a mercurial, enthusiastic fervour. There is an element of showing off, of arrogance and blustering,[109] which we would associate with an individual who is determined to project his personality onto others; and on one occasion he describes himself as one who has 'been blessed with an assurance not often found in one so young'.[110] In a further example of the complexity of Faber's religious personality, this attitude contrasted with an element of insecurity, in which he was concerned that he was not as able intellectually as other individuals with whom he associated. This was because he was concentrating upon defending the cause of Evangelicalism and writing poetry[111] to the detriment of his studies.[112]

Stage Two of Faber's spiritual development: disavowal of Evangelicalism, 1836

The year 1836 marked a watershed in Faber's spiritual development, during which he moved away from Low Church Anglicanism towards a number, but not all, of the ideals of the Oxford Movement. In a letter to Roundell Palmer, he described the processes which his religious beliefs had undergone since his arrival in Oxford. He indicated that, during his first year, he had been briefly influenced by Newman towards a form of religion that was primarily intellectual; and that he had rejected Newman's intellectualism in favour of the emotional Evangelicalism which he had held prior to Newman's influence, and thereafter until 1836.[113] Faber's movement, in 1836, away from Evangelicalism, was also caused by his moving towards a more intellectual form of religion,[114] although not on Newman's terms, rather on the terms of Faber's interpretation of ideas associated with Tractarians other than Newman, such as Keble and Pusey. It is interesting that Faber was in the second term of his third year at Oxford before he began to question any of his religious motives. The significance of this fact is that historians generally present the influence of the Oxford Movement as being impossible to avoid, and it is indicative of the strength of Faber's religious opinions, and perhaps a lack of openness to disputation, that he was able to do so successfully until 1836.

There were several reasons for his rejection of Evangelicalism. The most serious of these was that the religious climate of his upbringing had not allowed him to develop spiritually.[115] He wrote, 'I feel even now the trammels of that human system, of which all my religious friends were advocates. It impedes my progress wherever I turn.'[116] Faber was also concerned that Evangelicalism had a tendency to 'make religion a series of frames of feeling';[117] it had no structure, or coherent system of doctrine,[118] which made the doctrines which it did hold over-simplistic, and that there was in consequence no depth to his religion.[119] Faber reflected that as an evangelical he had 'lived upon the religious excitements of the passing day',[120] and that his religion '[fed] the heart at the expense of the head'.[121] These comments are particularly revealing, as Faber remained an individual for whom emotion and feeling were two important facets of religious expression. However, his concern was that religious feelings should have a concrete doctrinal base in order to be valid, and to avoid 'the tremendous delusion of excited feelings'.[122] These sentiments indicate a major change in the position of the intellect and the emotions in Faber's spirituality, and form the basis of his religious change. It is significant that he came to the above conclusions immediately after a period of intense evangelical enthusiasm, which may have served to highlight what he was lacking spiritually.

Between his arrival at Oxford in 1833, and December 1835, Faber's spiritual maturity had not kept pace with his intellectual maturity, and the two came more into line during the first six months of 1836. Correspondence written at this time shows an ever-increasing sophistication and confidence, both in the style and content of Faber's thought. His manner of writing points towards his mature style, and one of its consequences was variety and depth of questioning, both of his own thoughts and those of others. Faber's writing exhibited a poetic sense of place, and he consistently used ideas and scenes drawn from nature, particularly those associated with his home environment in various places in the north of England. These provide a counterpoint to other thoughts, whether religious, theological, philosophical, or academic, which he was discussing. One of the ways in which Faber differed from Newman was that Newman possessed a more profound and intellectually precise scholarship. However, Faber had an immense sympathy for nuances of feeling and, as we have said, emotions were a central part of his temperament, which was Romantic in all senses of the word. The following, from an essay, is worth quoting in full as an example:

> I was sitting alone in my rooms the other evening, and the College clock had just struck ten with a melancholy pathos. It was a fine starry night, and the mild flowing of the Autumn wind through my open window bore with it but little 'of the fading year's inclemency'.[123]

One of the problems of Faber's impressionistic style is that it can be imprecise, and because of this the reader is frequently led to ask: Where is he going? What is he saying? What does he mean? Why is he telling us this? One of Faber's enduring traits was a certain immaturity, or 'silliness', which was present in varying degrees throughout his life. This provided one of a series of tensions in Faber's intellect, in that he could be, almost at the same time, absurd and profound, untheological and theological, fanciful and down to earth. It is highly probable that, in later life, this was the part of Faber's temperament that Newman distrusted.

The process of religious and intellectual change heightened Faber's sense of dissatisfaction with Oxford and with Anglicanism. During 1836, he further distanced himself from the religious parties at Oxford[124] and moved away from public argument, disputation, and controversy about religion, towards an attitude which we can interpret as being quietist. Faber indicated that he intended to build up a religious personality and spirituality based on an intellectually valid system of doctrine.[125] He wrote, 'There is no possibility of measuring the harm done to a man's religious habits by the admission and temporary entertainment of an error.'[126] It is possible that this was connected with his wish to be ordained, and a desire to appear to follow a middle path of Anglican orthodoxy, rather than being seen as an individual on the fringe, susceptible to passing fads. Church doctrine was also important to Faber for more intellectual reasons, and by his statement 'I find ye doctrine of ye church such an inestimable privilege'[127] he implied that the judgement of the Church relieved the responsibility of the individual for conclusions relating to doctrine, in contrast to Evangelicalism. He wrote of the Church: 'there I cease to be an individual . . . and the noiseless path of childlike obedience . . . offers a calm and peaceful prospect of spiritual growth'.[128]

The idea of childhood appeared first in Faber's writing during 1836, and retained its importance throughout his life. Faber's treatment of this theme exists on two interrelated levels, the first of which is a personal response to his own circumstances and history. This was conditioned by the fact that, by 1836, both of his parents were dead; and, although he did not provide details, we cannot underestimate the effect that this had on Faber, spiritually, intellectually or emotionally. In letters from Oxford Faber made several references to his boyhood, adolescence, and family life as an idyllic world which was now irrevocably lost to him. His letters indicate, not always overtly, that he was an individual who was profoundly lonely because of this, despite good friendships, and he contrasted his own family with Morris's complete family.[129] It is possible, in this context, that Faber looked upon Newman as a father-figure, a role which Newman could not, or would not, fulfil. The second was an academic response to a scheme of study, and Faber referred to childhood several times in the relatively, but not totally, impersonal context of essays. One of these discusses friendship, and in doing so he gives as an example the importance of friendships formed during childhood and continued into adolescence and adulthood.[130] In the essay *The Idea of Man,* Faber wrote about the moral development of the individual. He represented childhood as a time of innocence. This contrasted with adulthood, a backward step which corresponded to the moral fall of humanity from its original state.[131] He wrote, 'the shock which our Moral Being received at the fall has thrown our passions into a state of insurrection against our higher and nobler powers'.[132] The essay contrasted Christian pessimism regarding human sin with a more positive view inherent in Plato and Greek philosophy. Faber wrote of childhood in this context as an ideal world, in which the child 'has lately come from the Presence-chamber of God: he is possessed of a nature which he must <u>unlearn</u> before he is fit for the world he is born into'.[133]

Faber was not dissatisfied enough at this time to consider leaving the Church of England, despite his altered conception of churchmanship. He was still firmly rooted in Anglicanism, and retained a distrust both of the Church of Rome and of Romanising tendencies within Anglicanism. The latter may indicate that the roots of Faber's dislike of Tractarianism were still present; although if they were, and it seems probable that this was so, they were slowly being eroded.[134] Correspondence written during 1836 indicates the beginnings of a subliminal ingestion of Tractarian ideas, mainly through the thought and influence of John Keble, E. B. Pusey, Richard Hurrell Froude, William Palmer and Isaac Williams. In contrast to his views on

Newman, Faber was more positive in his comments and responses towards these five individuals, and each influenced his thought to varying degrees. It is noticeable that he did not hero-worship any one individual to the extent that he ceased to work through an intellectual process in order to decide which facets of their influence to keep, and which to reject. Pusey was Faber's undergraduate role model, and the theme of Pusey as a holy individual recurs during his letters of 1836. Pusey represented the ideal attributes of a Christian and an Anglican: 'ye beauty of holiness ... tranquil piety ... unruffled quietness ... [and] Christlike meekness'.[135] It seems probable that Faber intended this rather reserved evangelical group of epithets to contrast with the more showy expression of religion that he associated with Newman; however, he did not meet either Newman or Pusey until the following year.[136]

Our picture of Faber's political stance is somewhat fragmentary, as he seems to have written about political matters only in the context of discussions concerning religion.[137] During 1836, Faber's views on the Church–State relationship were similar to what they had been between 1833 and 1834. He continued to stress that the Church should give moral leadership to the State,[138] and exhibited a personal dissatisfaction with the increasing amount of political influence given to dissenters and those who were not Christians. The latter convinced Faber that the State was no longer a Christian State.[139] Indeed, he was concerned that the State had passed legislation which was disadvantageous to the Church, and wrote, 'scarcely a vote has passed the House of Commons which has not been an insult to God, and ... a death blow to his religion'.[140] A new idea, expressed in Faber's thought during 1836 and important during his later life, was a sympathy for the Irish people. Faber was particularly concerned with situations where he felt that they had been placed at a disadvantage by the British government, such as withdrawal of funds for education.[141] During 1836, all of the preceding views were expressed as an awareness that the priorities of the Church and those of the State and the secular world were, and were likely to remain, fundamentally different from each other. It is possible that Faber had acquired these views partly from Keble's statements about the relationship between the Church and the political establishment, such as those in his Assize sermon, and that they had been deepened by Faber's closer ties with Tractarianism during 1836.

Faber discussed the phrase 'spirit of the age'[142] in both essays and correspondence during the first part of 1836, and it becomes apparent that he thought in terms of two levels of definition for this term. He first wrote of its popular definition, used to describe the superficiality of popular culture, which was 'like the breeze ruffled surface of a mountain lake'.[143] He countered this idea with the notion that there are profound depths in the thought of each age which are the real basis of its thought; these cannot be adequately defined, although they define the age itself.[144] Likewise, he did not feel that he could adequately or completely analyse the prevailing religious temper of the 1830s. He wrote: 'its subtlety seemed to baffle analysis'.[145] Faber was aware that the problems caused by the State's involvement with the Church were mirrored by a corresponding threat to church unity from within the Church itself. He described the inspiration for dissent as the spirit of Antichrist,[146] 'disturbing ... the peace of the Church'[147] and it is possible that he was, at least partially, referring to the tension between High and Low Church parties within Anglicanism. In May 1836, Faber wrote of the 'spirit of the age' as the process by which the Church is affected by 'the spirit of wickedness and sin',[148] and, although he does not explicitly say so, it is apparent that he believed that its inspiration came, like dissent, from inside and outside the Church. Faber wrote, 'he [Antichrist] manages to insinuate a religious modification of ye spirit of ye age into some portion of ye church. So that that portion is unconsciously doing ye work of ye devil.'[149] He put his reasoning behind this statement thus, 'I first look for ye spirit of ye age, and when I have found it I look for some school in ye church whose teaching is ye spirit of ye age Christianised.'[150]

Faber wrote, 'the spirit of the age is mercantile, in fact utility',[151] and he contrasted this with the thought that there has to be a higher mysticism within the Church, which is beyond a purely utilitarian standpoint. Faber seems to have used this concept in a practical as well as in a philosophical sense. He implied that the higher mysticism of the Church is at odds with a society that is disparaging of the rites, ceremonial and fabric associated with its religious practice. Faber wrote disparagingly of those who 'think magnificence misplaced in churches, and imagine church-room within four walls of brick to be as good as in a temple fit ... for the House of the Most High'.[152]

In essence, this was an idea that was held by a number of the Tractarians, and is almost identical to that expressed in the late 1830s by Isaac Williams in Tract 80,[153] and by Keble in Tract 89. Keble's Tract is concerned with mysticism in the Early Church. He wrote, 'Mysticism conveys the notion of something essentially ... remote from common sense and practical utility: but common sense and practical utility are the very idols of this age.'[154] For Faber, the significance of this idea was that it was part of his intellectual, moral and emotional process of realising that the Church was more multi-faceted than he had previously held.

During this period, Faber's reading of theology began to show greater variety in its subject matter, which both influenced and was a result of the process of religious and doctrinal change, and there is greater depth and profundity in Faber's language with regard to religious matters. Faber read a number of the books that were listed as recommended further reading in the volumes of Tracts, such as the *Sermon on Repentance* in Volume 1 of Taylor's *Life of Christ*, and Pearson's writing on the Creed.[155] His study was broader than theology written since the Reformation, although this was a matter of degree, as it had not been solely confined to post-Reformation theology prior to 1836. A result of this was that Faber was becoming increasingly influenced by patristic theology and the doctrines of the Early Church. This interest was fuelled and developed by his discussions with J. B. Morris, who became lecturer in Hebrew, Oriental and Patristic Theology at Oxford in 1838.[156] Morris and Faber discussed the translation of the Fathers by Newman and Pusey;[157] and, as he was unacquainted with Newman, Faber indicated to Morris his wish that they could be introduced, so that he might have some part in the translation process. He wrote: 'I should be truly rejoiced to find myself ... employed in such a work ... especially where the object is a wider dissemination of the majestic ... teaching of the Old Catholic theology.'[158]

During the latter part of 1836, Faber's conviction that he had been wrong in the sacramental ideas that he had grown up with became absolute,[159] and he seceded from Evangelicalism, Protestantism and Low Church Anglicanism. From this point onwards, Faber believed that the only credible Church was one with a highly developed sacramentality; and that, in order to be valid, Anglicanism had to eschew Protestantism and exhibit continuity with the rites and sacraments of the primitive Church. He wrote of evangelicals: 'I hold them to be fundamentally wrong ... in their doctrine of faith ... because wrong in their doctrine of the Sacraments.'[160] Faber put forward the idea that the primary reason for the adoption of the Low Church doctrine of the Sacraments was to provide refutation of the doctrines of the Church of Rome, rather than put forward a reformed interpretation of Sacramental Theology.[161] He therefore concluded that sacramentality was indelibly related to the idea of the Church, and that this tie had been broken by evangelicals.[162] He wrote,

> There can be no such thing as a consistent Low Churchman. There is no stopping short of Calvinism, if you have once left the primitive doctrine of the Sacraments; because your faith must depend on election, and election you must have separated from the Sacraments beforehand.[163]

Faber exhibited a high view of the role of the priest in conferring the Sacraments; and, although it is possible that this was due to the influence of the Tractarians, it seems more likely that it was an integral part of Faber's own spiritual development, and stemmed from his evangelical desire to convert those with whom he came into contact. One example of Faber's change of thought was that reading Book VII of the *Ecclesiastical Polity* led him to question his own belief in Hooker's theology of absolution, 'as merely declaratory'.[164] He wrote, 'I believe absolution to be sacramental ... as ye helping of ye church to the individual's repentance, and ... conferring ... what it declares.'[165]

In September 1836, ten months before his ordination, Faber characterised the sacramental role of the priest as being also a teaching role;[166] and from this point onwards studied theology in order to enable himself to be a moral teacher to his parishioners, rather than for purely academic reasons. After Morris's ordination,[167] in early October, their letters were concerned almost exclusively with discussions of how they would use their knowledge of theology in their respective parishes. Both individuals shared similar ideas and, at this early stage in his development, Faber was aware of the importance of the presentation of religion to those who were uneducated. Faber was concerned for those who were outside the academic and social environment with which he had always been familiar, and commented: 'Intellectually speaking, I am inclined to think we underrate the poor.'[168] Faber had distinctive ideas about the relationship between religion and the intellect, writing: 'Religious mysteries seem exempted from that ordinary operation of ye mind which causes indifference ... they give ye mind a dignity and exaltedness of tone ... and thus they keep us from sin.'[169]

We can hypothesise that the combination of these social and intellectual factors forms the root of his later development of a narrative, storytelling approach to religion, which is concerned not with straightforward exegesis but as being an aid to understanding for his parishioners. It becomes apparent that Faber wrote in a popular style in order to be read by, and be accessible to, as many people as possible; although he clearly expected a reasonable level of intellectual understanding and empathy from his readers. The significance of this for later sections of this study of Faber, is that it enables us to take away any suspicion that he was a quaint eccentric who was incapable of writing good theology. His writing style has a definite purpose, which is not the same as academic theology. However, as we shall see later, Faber's style of writing formed the root of the controversial nature of his theology, leading to accusations of heresy and bad taste.

In November, Faber graduated with a second class degree in Classics,[170] a consequence of his having been ill during the previous summer and being unable to study.[171] He viewed this result as failure, and was concerned that it had adversely affected his prospects of acquiring a Fellowship, pupils, and a good position within the Church.[172] This career was clearly anticipated by his family, probably because of his uncertain financial situation, and a primary concern of Faber's was his brother's 'miserable dejection and wretchedness'[173] at his degree result. Despite this, Faber wrote: 'How long, and oh! how painfully, I have been kept from my favourite studies.'[174] We have already noted[175] that Faber was critical of aspects of his Classical studies, and it seems possible that his private reading of Theology rather than Classics may have been the root of his failure to obtain a first class degree. During the same month, Faber was unsuccessful in his first attempt at gaining a Fellowship.[176] In December, he travelled to Mannheim with Francis Atkinson Faber, the first of eight journeys outside Britain, and stayed until early January 1837. In contrast to later travels, Faber discussed few details of the religious climate which he observed whilst in Germany. In a letter to Morris he wrote as though he was still in Oxford, leaving only the briefest of notes to indicate that he had attended church and had seen artisans and peasants praying there, and that there were a large number of crucifixes visible in the surrounding towns.[177]

Stage Three of Faber's spiritual development: espousal of Tractarianism, January 1837–April 1843

During the period from 1837 to 1839, the changes in Faber's religiosity were more subtle than the fundamental changes of opinion that had occurred during the previous four years. From January 1837 onwards, Faber consolidated the position which he had reached by the end of the previous year, and the effect of this was an increasing affinity with the ideals of Tractarianism. Faber ceased to be an outspoken critic of the religious climate in Oxford, and his language with regard to religion in general became more discriminating. This point may be illustrated by comparing his thoughts in 1834, regarding party spirit in Anglicanism – 'How easy it is to mistake love of our party for the love of our God',[178] – with those in January 1837 – 'party spirit is not the worst vice of a religious man. Like other moral evils, it is mixed with much of good.'[179] Faber implied that the difference between these two points of view is agreement or disagreement with the aims of the group.[180] He did not connect the aforementioned extracts himself; however, he must have been aware that the latter represented a change of opinion that would allow him to empathise with Tractarianism.

During 1837, Faber was studying in preparation for his ordination examination, and because of this his reading became more eclectic. In a letter to Morris, Faber commented on an interview with the Bishop of Ripon,[181] C. T. Longley, who was to ordain him during August. As we have already observed, Longley had been headmaster during Faber's sojourn at Harrow, and it seems possible that he ordained Faber because of their previous acquaintance. Faber exhibited concern about the severity of the examination: 'eighteen out of forty were rejected at his last ordination'.[182] However, his unease was mitigated by his conclusion that a severe test of knowledge of 'Church history and ... the Anglican formularies'[183] ensured that the clergy were better qualified to be apologists for their beliefs, particularly against dissenters within the Church of England.[184] It is interesting that he was more concerned that the clergy should be aware of dissent within the Church rather than from outside, such as from Roman Catholicism. In this way he differed from G. S. Faber, who was, as we have seen, concerned with refuting any theology that conflicted with evangelical doctrines.

For Faber, biblical criticism was the central and most important facet of theology, and he indicated that it would provide the basis of his studies.[185] We have seen that Faber's reading of scripture had been extensive throughout his undergraduate life, and in January 1837, he wrote that he intended to study the Pentateuch, Ecclesiastes, and the historical books of the Old Testament. In order to give greater depth to his study of the latter, Faber began to study Hebrew,[186] an event which may have been prompted by Morris, a Hebrew scholar; and it is notable that throughout his life Faber was a competent linguist, studying French, Italian and Spanish, as well as Greek, Hebrew and Latin. During 1837, he was also reading the Epistles of the New Testament,[187] and discussed with Morris the idea of giving lectures on scripture to poor people. He wrote of the

Acts of the Apostles, 'I think a few plain lectures might be delivered from them to the poorer people, eliciting in a very clear and popular way the doctrines of the Church from the practices of ... St Paul and St Barnabas.'[188]

It is significant that, as on earlier occasions, Faber's attitude to the poor was not patronising or limiting in what he was prepared to put before them. His theological interest in tradition extended to traditions found in scripture; he wrote of 'the traces of tradition, visible all through ... Acts'.[189] He and Morris discussed whether many of the traditions of the Apostles were retained in the post-scriptural Church: 'If Wordsworth talked an hour with us how much would be remembered ... and how much more an Apostle, and one who always excited so much deep personal interest as St Paul.'[190]

Faber began to read Christian History and Theology in a pre- as well as post-Reformation context during 1837. His choice of reading reflected both his own interests, and preoccupations of his older contemporaries; and he indicated that it would provide background material, so that he had 'a more extended and accurate acquaintance with modern controversies'.[191] He read Pusey's *Life of Vincent of Lerins*,[192] and the *Lectures on Noah*,[193] and attended the reading of a paper by Keble entitled *Mysticism imputed to the Early Christian Writers*, which he described as a 'masterly historical sketch'.[194] In the same letter he wrote of, but did not comment on, the agenda for the Theology Society, which included papers by Isaac Williams 'on the reserve of the ... early church; [and] in hearing sacred subjects before persons unprepared to receive them; [and] one by Newman on the Epistles of St. Ignatius considered as a witness of Catholic doctrine'.[195]

Other reading included Bishop Kaye writing on Justin and Origen, Clement and St Ignatius.[196] It is unclear whether Faber's reading of patristic literature, and the comments of his contemporaries upon it, was inspired by the wish to understand the Tractarian position or to defend his own position against the Tractarians. However, it is certain that, whether or not this was so initially, he progressed beyond a purely apologetic stance towards the adoption of the Early Church as a doctrinal and spiritual role model for the Anglican Church of which he was a part.

Faber's interest in the Anglican Church, an important facet of thought since his arrival in Oxford, was transformed into a preoccupation with the nature and character of Anglicanism during 1837. His ecclesiology became less sectarian and less inward-looking, and there are an increasing number of references to the Catholic Church within discussions of the role of Anglicanism within the wider Church.[197] Faber's definition of the Church–State relationship provides an indication of his change of ecclesiology from the previous year, in that he now characterised the Church as being morally aloof from the State. In discussing the appointment of bishops in March 1837, he indicated that, despite the responsibility of parliament for choosing bishops, the sacramental aspect of the Church ensured that it remained apart from worldly matters.[198] Faber, using a favourite Tractarian concept, identified the Anglican Church as being part of the universal, catholic, Christian Church rather than being a Protestant sect. He wrote, 'the church catholic has a substantive existence, independent, and gifted with indefectibility, her sacraments being to her as bundles of myrrh to keep her from corruption'.[199]

On 1 February 1837,[200] Faber was successful in obtaining a Fellowship of University College[201] and was awarded the Johnson Divinity Scholarship.[202] The beginning of the process of empathising with Newman's churchmanship began some time during the period from February to June 1837. The roots of this empathy were that Newman's ideas, as well as those which were central to the Tractarian worldview such as the *Via Media*, were now, or were becoming, a central part of Faber's intellectual and spiritual vocabulary. In March, Faber read Newman's *Prophetical Office,* which he described as 'a deep and difficult book which … will give rise to abundant cavil among the ill instructed'.[203] The major premise of the *Prophetical Office* is that the religion of the day did not comprehend the concept of the Anglican Church as the *Via Media*[204] between Roman Catholicism and Protestantism. Faber, who had referred to the dislocated factions within the Anglican Church as being like the valley of the bones,[205] indicated to Morris that he was in agreement with the 'old and wholesome truths'[206] expressed by Newman. Faber repeated a criticism that he had made during 1836,[207] that it was theologically incorrect to define Anglican

theology as being expressible only in terms of being the opposite of those which were put forward by the Church of
Rome.[208] He wrote, 'Newman's lectures ... supplied me with
what I had long wanted – clear and positive statements of
Anglican Principles.'[209] His description of Newman's work as
'one of the noblest, apostle-like consolations ... stamped with
the utmost majesty of thought',[210] is typical of Faber's descriptive style. It also has overtones of the zeal of a new convert to
Newmanism, although how long this honeymoon period lasted
is a matter for conjecture. He was, however, interested enough
to read other Newman works at this time, such as the *Lectures
on Justification*. The distance put by Faber between his new allegiance to Tractarianism and his old Low Church
Evangelicalism was expressed forcefully in a reply to a letter
from Roundell Palmer, in which Faber defended himself from
Palmer's charge that he (Palmer) had been referred to in
derogatory fashion as 'a thorough Protestant'.[211] In the same
letter, Faber also objected to Palmer's reference to his admiration for Pusey, in which Palmer had written that Faber had
been interested only in Pusey[212] to the detriment of other
points of view. It seems probable that this letter indicated to
Faber the distance that had been placed between his new allegiance to the Tractarians and his former beliefs.

During June 1837, Faber's attitude towards the Reformation
underwent a change of emphasis. He began to identify himself
less and less with the Reformers, writing to Morris, 'I am quite
sick of all Reformers. I have been studying that mournful history
for ordination exam and it has ruffled my spirit more than it
ought.'[213] His studies had convinced Faber that there were no
good histories of the Reformation, and he expressed the opinion
that the task of researching and writing one would be 'far beyond
the compass of any individual mind'.[214] The depth of Faber's
involvement with the ideals and ideas of Tractarianism is indicated by the desire to subscribe to Newman's publication of the
Library of the Fathers, and his concern that they would not be well
received on publication.[215] Faber had been involved with the
aforementioned work since April, and was translating the seven
books of St Optatus against the Donatists[216] for the series. He
wrote to J. B. Morris that he was inspired by his translation, and
by his reading of the Fathers,[217] to such a degree that he contem-

plated writing a history of the fourth-century African Church.[218] This may indicate that he wanted to write something that was original, and to contribute something that was significant and new. He indicated that he was interested in this period because he thought that he saw parallels between the Church of 'Tertullian, Cyprian, Austin, [and] Optatus'[219] and the Anglican Church of the late 1830s; firstly, in a common distrust of Rome, and secondly, in that he viewed the position of the African Church after the Donatist schism as being similar to the situation regarding Anglican bishops in Ireland.[220] It is interesting that Faber was still not convinced that the Anglican Church was Apostolical, as following this parallel he wrote of the African Church, of the 'peculiarity of its history in its not being an apostolic church: a fact which I suspect to have been our own call'.[221] Faber's personal distrust of Rome was highlighted in the context of a discussion of the difference in number between Sacraments of the Anglican and Roman Catholic Churches, in which he wrote, 'how frightened one is when one gets near Rome'.[222] This indicates that we have to view this stage of Faber's spiritual development as being one within Anglicanism, and that it would be too simplistic to be tempted to look upon it solely as being a step nearer to Rome.

Faber took a reading party of three of his undergraduate students from Oxford to Ambleside from June until the end of August 1837.[223] During this time, he began to link nature and God, two ideas which had in their separate forms been a consistent part of his thought. This identification was particularly apparent in his poetry,[224] and may have been inspired both by the scenery around him and by his meeting with Wordsworth, which took place at this time. However, although Faber's relationship with Wordsworth was an important influence on his early life, it is outside the limits of this study of Faber's spiritual development. Several other themes recur in Faber's thought and poetry, such as retrospective thoughts of Oxford,[225] the transience of childhood and the irrevocability of past youth:

> The springs of silent thought and purpose high
> Rise at our manhood's threshold. Let us drink
> Deep ere we quiet them, and life's sultry sky
> Hath stol'n their freshness.[226]

Faber celebrated his twenty-third birthday on 28 June 1837, and on 6 August, Bishop C. T. Longley ordained him deacon in Ripon Cathedral.[227] Although it seems probable that his choice of vocation was one that was expected by his clerical family, the role of clergyman was clearly the only one which appealed to Faber, as three years earlier he had written, 'I could never be happy or content in any other profession.'[228] The majority of Faber's references to his new status are restrained, such as, 'I believe God has been much with me since my Ordination.'[229] In a line that echoes Newman, he wrote, 'I have now no masters but God and my bishop to whom may I always be obedient.'[230]

After ordination, Faber became curate at St Anne's Chapel, Ambleside,[231] and lived at Rothay Cottage.[232] His letters to Morris indicate the social strata present within his congregation. He noted that there were 'Twenty one Cantabs ... three Oxonians, [and] many candidates for Holy Orders',[233] and it seems probable that the large number of University men in the congregation was the result of individuals spending their vacation in Ambleside, possibly undergraduates reading with a tutor. Faber also noted that there were 'about thirty or so educated gentry, ignorant but well inclined to the Church'[234] and a 'few poor people'.[235] By 1838 this had not changed significantly, in that the majority were educated, 'serious people'.[236]

Faber was formally admitted to his Fellowship on Friday, 27 October 1837.

The now familiar theme of concern for the worldly status of the Anglican Church was uppermost in Faber's correspondence during 1838. He reiterated the idea that the Church has to be above the influence of secular institutions, a thought which was inspired by parliament making decisions such as the appointment of bishops. Faber believed that the Church should not be manipulated in this way, and that it was important that society realised that the Church was part of a superior divine order.[237] The reasoning behind these comments was that Faber's ecclesiology had completely changed. He was now critical of the uncatholicity[238] of factions within Anglicanism, and thought of it not as a Reformed Church, or Protestant sect, but as part of the Catholic Church.[239]

It is possible that some of Faber's ideas were influenced by R. H. Froude, who had died in 1836 whilst Faber was an undergraduate. It seems probable that Faber had heard Froude discuss his ideas, or that he had heard them expressed by another individual who espoused Tractarian ideals. Certainly, a number of Faber's ideas about the Reformation mirrored those expressed by Froude in his *Remains,* and were supported by Newman and Keble, who edited the work. Faber does not appear to have hero-worshipped Froude to the extent of copying actions such as recording his moral and spiritual oversights in a journal. It is certain, however, that although Faber wrote that he was 'unfeignedly glad at the subsiding of the Froude mania'[240] because it was 'apt to run off into the typhus of popery',[241] he identified with portions of Froude's thinking. In a poem, *Sent to a friend with a copy of Froude's Remains,* he characterised Froude as an individual whose reverence for chivalry and the ecclesiastical past was contrary to the spirit of the nineteenth century. He wrote,

> It was his lot to live in times uncouth
> that shrank from ought so hard and stern as truth.[242]

By highlighting this, Faber was identifying Froude with concepts that he associated in his own mind with the 'spirit of the age'. The idealisation of the Early Church, and disparaging comments about the 'spirit of the age', come together in the preface to the *Remains,* in which Newman described the Early Church's 'reverential reserve with regard to holy things; of all its characteristics the most unaccountable to the spirit of this present age'.[243] During May, Faber edited Laud's *Private Devotions*, which he described as 'a delightful book . . . so different from the long, weary, wordy prayers of modern manuals'.[244]

The idea that the Church of his contemporaries contrasted with the Early Church continued to influence Faber's thought, and was developed in sermons, as we shall see in Chapter 6. His reading reflected these interests, and he discussed with Morris the Chaldean and Monophysite Church of the seventh and eighth centuries, and wrote that he found the ninth-century Church particularly interesting because it was a missionary Church.[245] In July he wrote, 'I am slowly progressing with the Donatist Controversy.'[246] Newman was concerned to translate and publish a selection of anti-Donatist writings by Optatus and Augustine, and wrote to Faber requesting his advice.[247] However, although Faber had completed a considerable portion of his translation of the three books, he had not, by September 1838, sent them to Newman, who wrote: 'it will be welcome when it comes'.[248] An editorial note at the end of this letter reads, 'Faber did not complete anything for the Library of the Fathers',[249] and the manuscript evidence concurs with this note. Faber did not provide an explanation as to why he did not finish the work, which ends with a line of indecipherable scribble.[250] It seems pointless to try to draw any conclusions as to the reason for this, which could have been due to pressure of work, illness – which was a common complaint of Faber's throughout this period – boredom, or impatience. It may be significant that Faber was having problems at Ambleside because he was preaching Tractarian doctrines, and perhaps he became temporarily disillusioned. Newman wrote an encouraging letter to Faber which contained the line, 'I am not surprised at the misconceptions which have attended to you in the North. It must be so for a time.'[251] From our historical perspective it is disappointing that Faber did not contribute any writings to the Tractarian cause. Firstly, because he had already indicated his eagerness to write something for a movement which he admired, and secondly, because it would undoubtedly have been advantageous to Faber's wider reputation to have completed this task for Newman. An important contrast between Faber and individuals such as Froude, Keble and Newman, was that they had the capacity to produce abundant writings in support of their cause, an attribute which Faber does not seem to have had, at least not at this time.

During July 1838, a group of Oxford undergraduates joined Faber in Ambleside for a reading party. The Cambridge undergraduates Lord John Manners (1818–1906) and G. S. S. Smythe (1818–1857) were also staying in Ambleside, and they are significant as they were 'both future MPs and founders with Disraeli of the "Young England" Party',[252] a movement within the Tory Party, during 1842.[253] Their intense friendship with Faber dates from the summer of 1838, and the subsequent cross-fertilisation of poetical and political ideas which stemmed from it, led to Faber also becoming a member of the Young England Party. In *Young England*, Richard Faber explores the friendship between Faber and the other founders, noting that Faber's contribution to the movement was to provide its spiritual foundation.[254] Addington concurs with this assessment, opining, 'His influence ... was more moral and literary than directly political.'[255] This intensity of their friendship during 1838 is apparent in Faber's letters to Manners, and the latter wrote of him, 'The magic of his voice and the charm of his society and conversation were irresistible.'[256] The clergyman Aubrey St Lys, in Disraeli's novel *Sibyl*, is a portrayal of Faber at this stage in his life. His character possesses a high view of the Church of England, views himself as a pastor of both rich and poor,[257] and, like Faber, exhibits equal concern for the temporal and spiritual welfare of both groups.[258] Manners provides the only extant description of Faber's demeanour in the pulpit during the summer of 1838; writing, '[I] did not quite like his style of reading prayers; too inanimate; the high church idea of not presuming to invest things sacred with any human ornaments.'[259] He was, however, impressed with Faber's sermons, which he described as 'eloquent, earnest and gorgeous beyond what I had anticipated'.[260]

Faber's unhappiness at Oxford has been a recurring theme throughout this chapter, and during July[261] he decided to move away, although he did not formally resign his Fellowship until 1843. Addington attributes Faber's unhappiness[262] to his friendship with G. S. S. Smythe;[263] however, he was discontented with life in Oxford before he met Smythe, and so there is no conclusive link between the two. Faber's complicated personality was the cause of his problems, although it is impossible to say precisely why. He wrote: 'I am ... well aware that my character and temperament are peculiarly liable to misapprehension and consequently Oxford is not the place for me. It is one mass of cruel misunderstandings from top to bottom.'[264]

Faber did not provide any further details as to why this should be so, or ascribe his comments to a particular incident or individual(s). The fact that both his contemporaries and those older than himself mistook his motives is significant, as throughout Faber's later life his manner and character were frequently misunderstood by those around him; indeed later on, he seems almost to have expected misunderstanding. Faber's antipathy towards Oxford was directed at both the people and the institution: 'Human nature, in spite of the abundantly profuse gifts and graces of the place, is of more dwindled stature there than elsewhere. Good men are less good there than in any other place.'[265] This comment echoes Faber's disparaging comments regarding the cult of personality at Oxford, made during 1834.[266] Here, as elsewhere in Faber's writing about his own experiences of life, there is an element of unhappiness and regret: 'I loathe the ethos of a great part of it – I hate it for its own foulness sake, and also because it has not left myself unhaunted.'[267]

Faber remained an individual despite the diversity of influences around him. The idea that a significant number of undergraduates became willing clones of Newman has become commonplace, and we have become used to reading the reminiscences of Newman by individuals who were influenced and inspired by him whilst at Oxford.[268] Faber does not fit into this norm, if that is what it is. Despite taking up significant Tractarian ideas, which had by 1838 affected his whole view of the Church of England, Faber did not surrender his intellectual integrity in order to conform to the views of another individual. Faber's confidence in his own ideas is part of the same character trait as that which made him resist the influence of Tractarianism for nearly the whole of his undergraduate years. It seems possible that Faber's outspokenness caused an unrecorded disagreement with Newman whilst he was at Oxford, or that Newman disliked what he had heard about Faber. We can suggest that one of the reasons why the relationship between Newman and Faber did not represent a meeting of minds, was that Faber was unwilling, or temperamentally unable, either to subscribe to adulation of Newman, or to relate to him in the way in which others did.

On Trinity Sunday, 26 May 1839,[269] Faber was ordained priest in Christ Church Cathedral, Oxford,[270] by Bishop R. Bagot,[271] an old High Churchman who empathised with Tractarian aims for reforms within the Church of England.[272] Faber 'read ye absolution for ye 1st [*sic*] time with a trembling voice in college chapel at 4 [*sic*] o'clock that afternoon',[273] and celebrated his first

Eucharist at St Andrew's Church, Sandford,[274] near Oxford, sometime during the following week. During August Faber travelled to Belgium,[275] which he described as 'the most purely Catholic country in Europe, excepting England'.[276] His emphasis on the catholicity of the Church is consistent with his thoughts throughout this period, and he notes as a contrast, 'the multitude of Protestants and unbelievers'[277] and the 'falsehood [of] the Roman Church'.[278] Faber contrasted the Church abroad unfavourably with the Anglicanism of his contemporaries in England.[279] He was particularly disapproving of ecclesiastical practices which he had observed, the over-elaborate decoration of the churches, and the number of 'tin offerings hung on the limbs of images'.[280] He compared these excesses with the linguistic purity of the prayer book services, cathedral worship and the church decoration with which he was familiar. Although these are undoubtedly spiritual concerns, we can interpret Faber's antagonism as being also the complaint of an individual who is nostalgic for home.

At the beginning of 1840, Faber had been living in Ambleside for almost two and a half years. However, although he had left Oxford bodily, he was unable to do so mentally; and the criticisms of Oxford that we have noted as a constant aspect of Faber's life during the 1830s, resurfaced and continued into the 1840s. On one level, his criticisms were directed towards the general climate within the university, both religious and secular.[281] These criticisms were related to the 'spirit of the age' idea, and expressed in the form of cryptic asides to Morris, which deplore notions such as 'eighteenth centuryism'[282] and 'high mindedness'.[283] Education was a recurring subject in Faber's sermons, and he stated a number of his views in the *Sermon on Education*, a work that was both praised and criticised by Christopher Wordsworth.[284] A number of parochial sermons also discuss this subject, and he frequently referred to the necessity of educating individuals so that they could understand Christian faith and practice.[285] The second level was personal; Faber dwelt on the idea that the primary reason for his rejection by Oxford in 1836 had been 'academic harshness',[286] and expressed the view that the authorities had not been sufficiently sympathetic towards him. Faber was particularly concerned that his reputation among his contemporaries had been irrevocably damaged by his failure to gain a first class degree, an observation that shows how much he was concerned to have the approval of his peer group. Faber's feelings amounted to an overwhelming sense of betrayal, which was often expressed in the form of satire and irony:

> I confess that while I have an affectionate reverting to ye cold night air that is circulating in High Street, Broad Street, and ye other arteries of Oxford, still the blustering howl of wind upon these mountains ... feels more soothing to me.[287]

This was combined with hints that Faber had made enemies whilst at Oxford,[288] and he wrote 'my temper would almost create them in the Sahara Desert'.[289] If this is so it is unsurprising, as throughout his life individuals either liked or disliked him, with equal intensity; however, Faber seems to have overlooked the fact that he had subsequently been awarded a Fellowship by his college, an appointment which presumably indicated that they were not unimpressed by his abilities. This is a good example of Faber's emotional response to a situation and of the extremeness of his judgement, which was frequently much harsher than that of other individuals who had assessed the same group of facts.[290]

Harshness, failure and disappointment are the central ideas in the octave of Faber's sonnet *Unkind Judging*.[291] The sestet develops the idea that the results of such treatment are either positive, in which the subject grows in humility, or negative, a type of martyrdom, 'a gloomy screen, fencing our altered lives from praise and glare'.[292] The notion of wilfulness, an idea which recurs constantly in letters of this period, is also present in the background of this sonnet; particularly in the forced Christianised stoicism with which Faber accepts the 'unmeet sternness'[293] of those around him. Faber's sonnet *Admonition*[294] is also autobiographical. It expresses his anger at his exile from Oxford, which no longer either belongs to, or recognises, him because it has passed to another generation. The sonnet is a warning to succeeding generations of Oxford undergraduates that their sojourn in the university is transient, and that it will eventually reject them.[295]

There is no place for thee; be warned in time.
Thou must go haunt some free and breezy knoll,
Ere this grey city come with spell sublime;
Freezing her heartless state into thy soul.[296]

In another, undated, sonnet written whilst abroad, Faber presented Oxford as an ideal place, the reminiscence of which surpassed all of the European cities which he had visited on his travels.[297] In this sonnet, Faber stressed the moral neutrality of the city of Oxford, an aspect that contrasted with his criticism of the moral culpability of certain, unnamed, individuals within the university.

Another significant recurring idea of Faber's, that of childhood as an ideal which is lost upon growing up, is present in the background of this sonnet, although it is not explicitly stated; as is the sense that moving into adulthood is a type of exile, rather than a necessary stage in the development of the individual.[298] Both of these notions are reflections of Faber's complicated responses to his own childhood and adolescence as, even at this stage, the grief caused by his parents' death was unresolved. This led to contradictions, such as the occasional hints that family life was unimportant, and distrust, rather than dislike, of any form of excessive emotional and bodily comfort. This is further highlighted by his expression that he had been a 'most spoiled child'[299] and had been brought up 'indulgently'.[300] There is a significant covert element of defensiveness and mental flagellation in these responses, as though Faber was frightened to think otherwise or to dwell on what he no longer possessed. In phrases such as 'my early loss of home and people to love … have considerable influence on me',[301] Faber's feelings are ongoing, rather than in the past. He connected the aforementioned ideas with the need to become more disciplined;[302] indeed, throughout his life Faber exhibited a lack of sympathy for signs of weakness, self-love and excuses, both in himself and others. His rebukes are particularly astringent when applied to his own spiritual life, and he wrote, 'my occupation in religion hitherto has been exclusively the putting off of soft habits'.[303]

In contrast to this rather defensive stance, Faber also wrote of his need for companionship, and the phrase 'you see what a craving I have after sympathy. It is my weakness – almost a disease'[304] occurs in a letter to Manners. This idea, which recurred throughout the early 1840s,[305] was expressed principally in the context of whether or not he would eventually marry.[306] Faber's primary reason for indecision was that he had not found the celibate all-male environment within Oxford congenial.[307] However, it is significant that one of the reasons which Faber gave for remaining unmarried, and being celibate, was as penitential reparation for his 'idolatry of comfort and sympathy'.[308] This was related to the ongoing idea of the necessity of mortification of the flesh. The idea of celibacy was also moral,[309] linked to a priestly ideal which was held by the Tractarians, and by Faber before he joined the Movement. Faber's espousal of the celibate state was also influenced by his high regard for Newman;[310] although Faber's difficulty in mentally accepting it highlights one of the essential temperamental differences between the two men.

In a letter of November 1840, Faber replied to Morris's[311] criticisms of Anglicanism by stating positive and negative points of his own. 'I have,' he wrote, 'meditated long and gloomily on your letter against Anglicanism; and I think it a little hasty.'[312] Faber's reply indicates that he was aware both of the validity of the points made by Morris and of his agreement with them, although as Morris's letter is not extant it is impossible to tell whether he instigated Faber's doubts. However, it is interesting to note that Morris has been described thus: 'Though an Anglican priest, he was always fond of ridiculing and finding fault with the English church.'[313] It would be possible to view what follows as the first stage of Faber's move towards Roman Catholicism. However, this seems over simplistic, and it is more likely that it was a continuation of the process of spiritual discernment which had been ongoing since the 1830s. Faber's writing in this letter exhibits the contradictions which were part of his character, although during this period they are the result of his ability to empathise with positions other than his own.

Faber wrote that the importance of Anglicanism is that it admits contrasting theological views, a standpoint which ensures that individuals can formulate a legitimate religious ethos which is suitable for their individual temperament.[314]

This is, for Faber, true Anglicanism; however, he continues that 'the essence and soul of such a system will ... be <u>caution</u>',[315] because of the necessity of admitting diversity. Faber states that this caution can be misunderstood, but that in its negative sense it does not represent the ideal of true Anglicanism. Faber contrasts the ideal Anglican ethos with a group of ideas which both he and Morris found uncongenial in Anglican writings: 'Coldness, unclear statement, gadarene humility, fearfulness of mysticism ... the ... unintelligent dislike of Rome, and a general absence of ye marked characteristics of Catholic childhood.'[316] Several of these ideas are related to those which we have already discussed, and their development from 1840 onwards is a symptom of Faber's move away from a certain dryness or lack of religio-emotional depth. We have already seen that Faber moved away from the excess emotionalism of Evangelicalism towards formality, and this is now counterbalanced by a progression away from formality towards the doctrinally orthodox emotionalism which we associate with mature Faber.

Faber indicated that he was influenced by the ecclesiology and theology of Newman's Anglicanism, particularly in the context of its position as an historical church. In the same letter, Faber is critical of much of the history of Anglicanism. He wrote that post-Reformation Anglicanism was not a direct result of the Reformation, but the articulation of a tendency towards religious 'idiosyncrasy' (*sic*),[317] the 'peculiar character [of] the English Church'[318] that was present in Britain before the Reformation. This was caused by geographical distance from Europe, particularly from Rome, with the result that the Church in England was, even whilst Roman, a unique, island church, retaining the ethos of the primitive church. During this period, Faber's writings from abroad present the English Church as being a part of the wider Christian Church, but free from the later corruption of the post-Reformation Western Church. His criticism of Anglicanism extended to the tendency towards Gallicanism, which he viewed as a significant trend in the contemporary church.[319] He wrote, 'were I a French priest [I] should belong to ye school of de Maistre',[320] a comment which exhibits sympathy with the importance of authority, particularly Ultramontane authority in the Church, and the authority of the State.[321] This comment is significant because of Faber's stress on Ultramontanism after he became a Roman Catholic, and it seems probable that his move away from Anglicanism was caused, wholly or in part, by the question of Church authority. He writes scathingly of contemporary Anglicanism as being tainted with Erastianism, a further example of the problematic nature of the influence of the State over the Church. The State prohibits the Church from acting as an autonomous body because of its control over it, particularly over the bishops, which is why Faber writes that true Anglicanism is found only among certain members of the clergy.[322] It seems probable that he is referring to those clergy who are practising the principles of the Oxford Movement.

For Faber, 'Anglicanism is a ... tendency, in aspiration, incomplete – a real view yet never hitherto realised.'[323] This is because it lacks catholicity, in the sense of being universal, and is therefore not fully representative. He wrote that Anglicanism:

> Has realised to a great extent primitive teaching – it has not realised primitive ethos, because it has not realised catholicity. Catholicity cannot be realised without considerable approach to Catholic communion; and ye nearest approach we have made is to communion with Catholic antiquity.[324]

Faber puts forward the view that the Anglican reliance on the primitive church does not prevent it from being schismatic.[325] However, he does not see Rome as a valid alternative to Anglicanism, and writes of the Roman Church: 'We make neither head nor tail of ye present church.'[326] Faber rarely referred to works of theology in the extant correspondence written during 1840. However, he did mention that he owned a copy of the French translation of Möhler's *Symbolik*,[327] a work which had been published in 1832 and not translated into English until 1843.[328] Faber was enthusiastic about Möhler's theology, and expressed the wish that he could travel to Germany in order to study theology.[329] The *Symbolik* is concerned with presenting the differences within the doctrines relating to the Church and Sacraments which are held by the

Roman Catholic Church and all forms of Protestantism. Faber seems to have been interested primarily in the way in which the idea that Protestantism was heretical was expressed in the *Symbolik*, as he mentioned the 'resemblance between ultra Protestantism and Nestorianism'.[330] Elsewhere, his language underlines a deeply rooted pessimism, which portrays the impossibility of recognising any branch of Christianity as being completely orthodox. This, coupled with 'If we cannot make any use of western Christendom, we cannot',[331] provides one reason why Faber remained an Anglican, despite being outwardly critical.

Pastoral responsibility was one of the central concerns of the letters written by Faber to Morris. Faber was a conscientious and successful curate who had 'more than doubled ye congregations and disseminated many good books among them'.[332] Because of this, Faber's discussions of theology are always pastoral in emphasis; and controversy, such as that between Anglicans and dissenters,[333] is always related to practical, rather than intellectual, concerns. However, despite his success at Ambleside Faber was unsettled and depressed. Between November 1840 and January 1841, the three main sources for this malaise were overwork, spiritual crisis and illness, each of which fed upon the other two, and were therefore inseparable from each other. It is impossible to say conclusively whether this crisis was related to the Bright's disease from which Faber suffered from 1840 until his death, aged 49, in 1863. Chapman wrote that Bright's disease began to affect him during 1846, although he does not deny the possibility that its symptoms began to occur at an earlier, unspecified, date.[334] We can postulate that the first stages of the disease did begin earlier, as his health deteriorated significantly from November 1840 onwards. Our theory is corroborated by the following statement, written by Faber in January 1841, which describes an ongoing process, namely: 'I cannot help suspecting that my constitution is undergoing some change; and that I shall not be quite well until the resolution has taken place.'[335]

Bright's disease, which was not classified until 1854, is 'chronic nephritis, or chronic renal failure'.[336] Its symptoms include 'raised blood pressure and, because of this, cardiac problems including heart failure causing, among other things,

severe breathlessness'.[337] Faber 'would have been anaemic ...
short of protein ... and because of this and the heart failure
would have had swollen legs and feet'.[338] It seems possible that
some of the traits of Faber's character were caused or exacerbated by illness; particularly as Bright's disease also caused
'what the Oxford Textbook of Medicine calls a "decline in
higher mental function" with confusion, memory loss, apathy
and irritability and, very probably, depression'.[339] All of these
symptoms were present, to a greater or lesser extent, from
November 1840.

In a letter to Morris, Faber described the amount of work
involved in managing a 'parish, wh[ich] is in an awfully desti-
tute condition'[340] on his own. The reason for the lack of help
was the advanced age and illness of the incumbent,[341] and
Faber's letter provides an interesting snapshot of the problems
inherent in being a curate in an isolated country parish. In the
sonnet *Brathay Bridge*,[342] Faber contrasted his own feelings of
depression and fatigue with the scenery around him, which is
beautiful but ultimately isolating:

> Month after month more languid do I grow,
> Struggling and striving in life's sterile round,
> And in each strife and struggle losing ground ...[343]

The spiritual dimension of this situation was that Faber
contemplated giving up both his curacy and the clerical life,[344]
but was held back from doing so by re-reading the ordination
service.[345] Faber's youthful inexperience had caused him to try
to do too much on his own, and his response shows that he was
discharging his spiritual charge seriously and conscientiously
but, characteristically, without moderation. We can hypothesise
that this was also the beginning of a period of inward spiritual
change, which continued during the next four years and
reached a watershed during his visit to Rome in 1843.

By November 1840, Faber was using several different
medications, such as quinine,[346] which caused him to have
headaches. Headaches were not only symptoms of Bright's
disease,[347] as Faber had suffered with them throughout his life;
however, they seem to have been exacerbated by periods of
stress and tension, such as the overwork of his first years of

Anglican ministry. This led to a breakdown during the Christmas Day Eucharist, on Saturday 25 December,[348] after which Faber wrote to Morris, 'I lost all control of my mind during [the] service; but somehow or other I found the prayers over and myself in the vestry with the medical men.'[349] He described the moments immediately before the breakdown thus: 'While administering the H[oly] elements to 96 people without help at a small altar, I got quite confused between the paten and the cup and made mistakes.'[350]

We have already noted that confusion was a symptom of Bright's disease. However, confusion does not seem surprising in the light of his comment that, 'On Xmas day I took 12 drops of Laudanum before church, and three doses of brandy in the vestry.'[351] It is impossible to say conclusively whether Faber did this because of overwork or stress, because of his disease, or because of an addiction to opium, which affected his mental state. It is also not possible to prove the extent to which Faber was mentally and physically affected by laudanum, as its effects are dependent on the size of the dose which he was taking and of the amount of opium in each dose, and we do not have this information.[352] However, it seems probable that Faber's attempts to relieve his symptoms, which also included indigestion for which he was taking gentian,[353] sleeplessness[354] and problems with his liver,[355] made a significant contribution to his problems. Faber had recovered sufficiently by the end of January to describe the events of Christmas Day to Morris in a lucid manner, a fact which seems to indicate that his lapse had been of short duration. Faber was also taking blue pill, a mixture of 'mercury ... confection of red roses ... [and] liquorice root'[356] and he wrote, 'a course of blue pill has done wonders for me'.[357] Mercury, or blue, pills were used as a diuretic,[358] and it seems probable that Faber was taking these to combat swelling caused by fluid retention, another symptom of Bright's disease.

Newman published Tract XC on 25 January 1841, although, despite its importance to this period of the nineteenth century, it is not mentioned by Faber in extant correspondence. On 24 February 1841, Faber left Ambleside in order to accompany his pupil, Matthew Harrison, on the first part of a tour[359] which included France, Italy, Greece, Constantinople, Hungary,

Austria and Germany.[360] During this time Faber kept a
journal[361] in which he recorded his impressions of the scenery
through which he travelled, the buildings and churches which
he visited, and the religious ceremonies attended. He also
wrote about the history of the places through which he travelled. He rarely mentioned the people he encountered, or his
travelling companion, although he did indicate to Morris that
he was writing letters to the father of his pupil.[362] The journal
presents an interesting and descriptive travelogue, although it
is noteworthy that the printed edition is more polished than
the manuscript, with the result that the former is didactic
whilst the latter is outspoken and spontaneous.

The journal contains a number of notions that are important
to this study. Many of these are part of the Tractarian worldview, although despite this Faber retained, at one level, the
vestiges of Evangelicalism; whilst others are typical of Faber's
poetic and individual temperament. Faber's empathy with
Church history bridges these three influences.[363] As a
Tractarian he emphasised Church history from the early
Christian Church to that immediately preceding the
Reformation, a period which he presented as being one of
Church unity. This notion appears in the opening pages of the
narrative, in which he put his own travels into context by
writing of the popularity of visiting holy places during the
Middle Ages. It is notable that, unlike a number of his contemporaries, Faber did not idealise the Middle Ages or view it in
isolation as an ecclesiastical utopia. However, the distinction
drawn by Faber was that, during the Middle Ages, there was
one church in which the pilgrim felt at home because of its
sacramental and doctrinal unity and continuity.[364]

Faber's awareness of history also affected his interpretation
of his surroundings; indeed, the past often seems more acutely
and sensitively observed than the present. This is particularly
apparent with regard to Faber's travels through the Greek
islands, which enabled him to visit, for the first time, sites associated with the history and literature which had been part of
his education both at Harrow and Oxford. Faber's retrospective rehabilitation of his Classical Studies may have erased the
evangelical scruples as to their moral validity, which he had
espoused whilst at Oxford. If this is so, it underlined the

continuing influence of the mental world that he had inhabited during his childhood and adolescence.[365]

As we would expect, Faber responded particularly to the position occupied by religion in the countries through which he passed. He was particularly concerned with aspects of morality, and put forward the opinion that cities are immoral and/or amoral places.[366] This idea was essentially the same as the condemnation of the 'spirit of the age' by Faber and Keble; and, in this context, Faber wrote that the spirit of the age is characterised by 'prosperity, wealth ... commerce, luxurious domestic living ... and boastful self-praise'.[367] For Faber, the nation which epitomised these characteristics was America.[368] He also commented on the irreligious behaviour of the population of Dresden, particularly the profanation of Sunday with street entertainment.[369] Whilst in France he wrote of the irreverent treatment of religious subjects in the theatres of Paris,[370] and commented that 'there is little religion at all among the bulk of the people, especially in the northern departments'.[371] He was also interested in theological developments in the countries which he visited, such as the decline of Gallicanism and the prevalence of Ultramontanism in France.

The Reformation was anathema to Faber, not only for reasons of doctrine, but also because of the Reformers' desecration of images and churches.[372] The latter is a constantly recurring idea in the journal. Faber did not distinguish between beauty, both in church architecture and religious art, and the worship of God; consequently, the destruction of one was synonymous in Faber's mind with disrespect to the other.[373] Faber was wary of, rather than openly hostile to, Roman Catholicism. His descriptions fluctuate between intellectual interest, such as the detailed account of the ceremonies of Holy Thursday, in which he contrasts Anglican and Roman Catholic rites,[374] and suspicion, such as at Genoa, where he made the impersonal observation: 'I saw mass performed in the Cathedral.'[375] Faber demonstrated scepticism of a number of the claims of the Roman Church, particularly those which related to the uncertain authenticity of relics of saints; and was concerned that he could not appreciate such relics because of this uncertainty.[376] Faber was also critical of excessive Roman devotion to Mary,[377] which he contrasted with the observation that Protestants and Anglicans do not honour Mary.[378] Faber's Marian sympathies were somewhere between the two, and this is indicated in his descriptions of the festivities in Genoa for the Feast of the Annunciation.[379] He also wrote at length about the position of Mary in the piety of the Middle Ages, and in the writings of St Bonaventure.[380]

Travel through Italy created in Faber the sense that being an Anglican made him an outsider in religious matters,[381] and he described his presence in Milan Cathedral as being that of a tourist rather than a worshipper.[382] As in previous travels, Faber frequently referred nostalgically to his home in England, and to the English Church. His whole outlook whilst abroad was defined by his ecclesiological position: the belief that the Anglican Church was the *via media*. Thus, England was necessary for Faber's spiritual equilibrium, and he wrote of the 'speedy prospect of returning once more into the bosom of my own branch of the Church Catholic'.[383] However, Faber frequently contrasted Tractarian Anglicanism with a sense of dissatisfaction with the manner in which religion was presented in 'Protestant' England.

Faber's health did not improve on his travels, despite his hopes that it would.[384] His letters and journal describe headaches and other symptoms as well as providing, in graphic detail, information about the vermin and fleas which he encountered, and his efforts to avoid them.[385] Faber's references to illness[386] frequently ascribe it to lack of discipline, rather than to any physical or medically recognisable source.[387] He disliked all signs of weakness and self-love and, because of this, he dismissed his affliction in a flippant manner, saying, 'to a man of my soft habits it is a hard thing to read and write in the face of a refractory digestion'.[388] It seems probable that this mechanism enabled Faber to cope with symptoms that his doctors could not relieve; and we can assume that he was unsure whether his illness was real, or the result of inherent hypochondria. Faber returned to Ambleside at the beginning of September 1841.

In January 1842, Faber informed Morris that he had been ill for several weeks. He was 'suffering from an ulcerated sore throat'[389] and was experiencing problems with his heart, which had been diagnosed as indigestion.[390] Both of these were symptoms of Bright's disease. However, they may also be attributable to mercury poisoning, which causes 'irregular action of the heart'[391] disease of the mouth,[392] particularly 'ulceration',[393] 'a state of excessive irritability and ... heightened and intense emotional reactivity',[394] all of which are symptoms from which Faber suffered. Writing of chronic mercury poisoning, Bidstrup[395] states that 'The kidney plays an important part in the elimination of mercury from the body, and is also the organ in which the highest concentrations of mercury are localised following absorption.'[396] He also notes that, 'some cases of chronic nephritis have been attributed to the effects of mercury in the kidney'.[397] We can, therefore, postulate that Faber was not only suffering from Bright's disease but also from mercury poisoning, caused by taking an excessive number of blue pills over a long period of time, although we cannot be sure in what order these occurred. Faber's health deteriorated significantly from his first written indication that he had begun to take blue pills. However, we do not know whether he had been taking them before this, and only if he had not can we state categorically that he was already unwell, with Bright's disease or some other illness, before he began to take them. It is, therefore, impossible to say conclusively whether, and to what extent, Bright's disease harmed him and to what extent he was harmed by mercury; however, it seems probable that mercury caused the most damage to Faber. It is interesting to note that Newman was also aware of the unwelcome effects of taking blue pills, as he wrote to J. W. Bowden, 'do not take too much blue pill, it is a most shattering medicine'.[398]

During December 1842, Faber was offered the College living of Elton, a parish that offered a stipend of £450 per annum;[399] however, he declined the appointment several times.[400] After accepting the parish, on the advice of the College authorities,[401] Faber wrote to Morris quoting Pusey in resigned tones, 'events not of our own seeking are mostly God's ordering'.[402] In the same letter, the revealing phrase, 'ye whole <u>pastoral</u> office ... is very unacceptable to me',[403] indicates that Faber was now questioning his suitability for the clerical life. It is not easy to say for how long this sense of unhappiness or depression had been part of Faber's life. However, it is probable that it was not only spiritual, but originated with Faber's chronic ill-health at Ambleside during 1840–41, which had made the amount of work he had to do overwhelming. References to ill-health fill the letters written to Morris[404] during this period; they provide Faber with an emotional safety valve through which he confides his worst fears. Faber does not say that he regretted taking orders, or that he did so only because it was expected of him; however, he had clearly thought seriously about returning to Oxford to pursue an academic career. About this time, Faber sold much of his library in order to pay debts accumulated since he had been a Fellow, and was depressed to receive only £130, a fraction of its value, in return.[405]

During 1842, the influence of Newman gradually supplanted the influence of Pusey; and Faber's Tractarian circle widened to include the group which formed around Newman at Littlemore, and others from Cambridge. It seems possible that the controversy surrounding Newman's move from Oxford to Littlemore had unsettled Faber, and that this had contributed to his doubts about his vocation. Faber's two options, whether he was best suited to life in an Oxford College or life in a parish,[406] were joined by a third. He began to think in terms of his inclination towards becoming a poet, perhaps because of the friendship and influence of Wordsworth and Keble, both of whom had encouraged Faber's poetic ambitions. His letters to Morris during the final four months of 1842 are centred on their mutual interest in writing poetry;[407] they contain detailed discussions about poetic language, inspiration, and the poems on which they were both working. Faber had just published his second volume of poetry[408] and was writing *Sir Lancelot*, whilst Morris had also published a volume of poetry. Faber wrote of poetry as his 'chief, if not ... sole, gift'[409] and stated that 'my poems are less Catholic than I am'.[410] His inner conflicts were the result of having to choose between poetry and his other two options: all of these were unsatisfactory for Faber and he exhibited a profound sense of guilt because of this. He also stressed his sinfulness and 'wilfulness'[411] in not accepting his priestly vocation. He wrote, 'I feel that my chief rock of offence is ye subduing ye poet to ye priest',[412] and later, 'I have very sinfully permitted ye man of letters to overlay ye priest'.[413]

A further reason for Faber's rejection of Elton was that the geographical remoteness of a country parish in rural Huntingdonshire was uncongenial to him,[414] particularly 'the solitude of that lone place'.[415] Faber's phrase 'hatred of loneliness'[416] highlights a significant aspect of his life as a whole; his temperament was such that he was afraid of, and could not cope with, being alone. He was anxious always to have other people around him, whether or not they were particular friends, as he did not like to be deprived of the companionship and intellectual stimulus which they provided. This pattern was in evidence throughout Faber's life; he continued the corporate life of Harrow and Oxford into Ambleside, and formed a group of friends around him in the rectory at Elton, and, as we shall see later, in the Wilfridians and the Oratory. An important aspect of this side of Faber's nature was expressed via a concern that celibacy would become impossible because of it, and that he would be forced into marriage by loneliness.[417] Faber's dislike of the prospect of Elton is presented to Morris in a passage whose choice of words, such as 'buried', provides a good example of Faber's impulsive and dramatic literary style which invites a sympathetic response: 'O pray for me that buried in that village I may endeavour to live an apostolical life in church, parsonage and cottages.'[418] The incumbency at Elton was the first and last time that Faber would be in charge of a parish on his own.

In January 1843, Faber visited his uncle, G. S. Faber, at Stockton-on-Tees. This encounter highlighted the gulf between Faber's mature Tractarian sympathies and the evangelical Low Anglicanism of his uncle, who 'boasted he was a "stiff backed protestant"'.[419] This remark encapsulated the spirit of this type of Anglicanism for Faber, and from this time onwards 'protestant' was used by him as a term of opprobrium rather than as a technical term. In the same month, Faber wrote to Morris, perhaps with relief, that he was not sure when he would go to Elton, as the incumbent, P. C. Claughton,[420] had not yet left the parish.[421] However, three months later Faber resigned his Fellowship at Oxford, was appointed to the Living on 27 March, and read himself in on 2 April. The primary source for Faber's life at Elton is Tom Godwin's 1901 narrative, a revised version of that which was written during 1884, forty-one years after the events which it describes.[422] Godwin was one of Faber's servants and, despite his undisguised hero-worship of Faber, his writing is perceptive, interesting and intelligent. Before arriving in Elton, Faber had notified Morris that he had decided to run the parish along Tractarian lines, and begin weekly communions and services on saints' days.[423] Faber's innovations were new to his parishioners, and Godwin's narrative provides details such as Faber's two services on Sundays, saints' days, and regular communion services and confessions. Faber also increased the standard of church music, particularly the singing of the psalms, and installed an organ to replace the small group of musicians. He provided confraternities for the parishioners,[424] and his servants took part in daily spiritual exercises; indeed Godwin remarks that 'the parish became so well organised that the duties of the poor law officers became almost unnecessary'.[425] A further interesting aspect of this narrative is that it indicates names of Tractarian visitors who were invited to Elton, details which are not included in any other extant sources from Faber's life.[426]

Notes

1 F. A. Faber, *Brief Sketch*, p. 16. The Faber family were close, and Faber's brothers looked after him after his father's death. See R. F.

2 This date is noted in F. W. Faber to J. B. Morris, LO, Vol. 17, No. 111, St Peter Damian (23 February) 1847.

3 F. W. Faber to Lord John Manners, 16 May 1839, in Addington, *Faber: Poet and Priest*, p. 74.

4 Faber frequently indicates evangelical leanings. For example, see F. W. Faber to J. B. Morris, LO, Vol. 17, No. 3, 23 July 1833.

5 F. W. Faber to J. B. Morris, LO, Vol. 17, No. 11, 11 September 1834.

6 Ibid.

7 Ibid.

8 F. W. Faber to J. B. Morris, LO, Vol. 17, No. 3, 23 July 1833.

9 F. W. Faber to J. B. Morris, LO, Vol. 17, No. 11, 11 September 1834.

10 F. W. Faber to J. B. Morris, LO, Vol. 17, No. 8, 4 August 1834.

11 Ibid.

12 Ibid.

13 Ibid.

14 F. W. Faber to J. B. Morris, LO, Vol. 17, No. 11, 11 September 1834.

15 Ibid.

16 Ibid.
17 Ibid.
18 F. W. Faber to J. B. Morris, LO, Vol. 17, No. 9, 25 August 1834.
19 F. W. Faber to J. B. Morris, LO, Vol. 17, No. 11, 11 September 1834.
20 Ibid.
21 F. W. Faber to J. B. Morris, LO, Vol. 17, No. 10, 4 September 1834.
22 F. W. Faber to J. B. Morris, LO, Vol. 17, No. 11, 11 September 1834.
23 Ibid.
24 Ibid.
25 F. W. Faber to J. B. Morris, LO, Vol. 17, No. 10, 4 September 1834.
26 Ibid.
27 F. W. Faber to J. B. Morris, LO, Vol. 17, No. 8, 4 August 1834.
28 Ibid.
29 Ibid.
30 F. W. Faber to J. B. Morris, LO, Vol. 17, No. 9, 25 August 1834.
31 F. W. Faber to J. B. Morris, LO, Vol. 17, No. 10, 4 September 1834.
32 F. W. Faber to J. B. Morris, LO, Vol. 17, No. 8, 4 August 1834.
33 Anon (1834), 'Life in Oxford', in *The Oxford University Magazine*, Vol. 1, pp. 95–106.
34 Ibid. p. 99.
35 F. W. Faber to J. B. Morris, LO, Vol. 17, No. 5, 19 December 1833.
36 See Chapman's brief reference to Faber's Calvinism in Chapman, *Father Faber*, pp. 23–4.
37 F. W. Faber to J. B. Morris, LO, Vol. 17, No. 12, 23 September 1834.
38 Addington, *Faber: Poet and Priest*, pp. 12–13.
39 F. W. Faber to J. B. Morris, LO, Vol. 17, No. 12, 23 September 1834.
40 Ibid.
41 Ibid.
42 Ibid.
43 F. W. Faber to J. B. Morris, LO, Vol. 17, No. 12, 23 September 1834.
44 Ibid.
45 Ibid.
46 F. W. Faber to J. B. Morris, LO, Vol. 17, No. 8, 4 August 1834.
47 *The Oxford University Magazine*, Vol. 1: 1834, advertisement, no page number.
48 F. W. Faber to J. B. Morris, LO, Vol. 17, No. 8, 4 August 1834.
49 *The Oxford University Magazine*, Vol. 1: 1834, p. 475.
50 Ibid. p. 471.
51 Ibid. pp. 472–3.

52 Ibid. p. 474.
53 Ibid. p. 476.
54 Ibid. pp. 254–5.
55 F. W. Faber to J. B. Morris, LO, Vol. 17, No. 3, 23 July 1833.
56 F. W. Faber to J. B. Morris, LO, Vol. 17, No. 2, 22 June 1833 and LO, Vol. 17, No. 3, 23 July 1833.
57 F. W. Faber to J. B. Morris, LO, Vol. 17, No. 3, 23 July 1833.
58 F. W. Faber to J. B. Morris, LO, Vol. 17, No. 6, 1 January 1834 and LO, Vol. 17, No. 7, 4 January 1834.
59 F. W. Faber to J. B. Morris, LO, Vol. 17, No. 7, 4 January l834.
60 F. W. Faber to J. B. Morris, LO, Vol. 17, No. 6, 1 January 1834 and LO, Vol. 17, No. 7, 4 January 1834.
61 F. W. Faber (n.d.), *The Creator and the Creature*, new edn, London, Burns & Oates, p. 376.
62 Will of Thomas Henry Faber, Public Record Office, Kew, PROB 11/1815.
63 F. W. Faber to Lord John Manners, 16 May 1839, in Addington, *Faber: Poet and Priest*, p. 74. See also F. W. Faber to J. B. Morris, LO, Vol. 17, No. 1, 8 June 1833, in which he describes his return to Bishop Auckland for the first time since T. H. Faber's death.
64 University College Admissions Register, 6 December 1834.
65 Ibid., 11 December 1834.
66 Chapman also describes this trait in Faber, but does not draw conclusions from it: 'There was in his mental nature an element of waywardness and inconstancy … It manifested itself sometimes in a rapid change of opinion, from one extreme to another …' Roundell Palmer, Earl of Selborne, *Memorials, Family and Personal*, I, pp. 136–8, quoted in Chapman, *Father Faber*, p. 17.
67 F. W. Faber to Roundell Palmer, January 1835, in Bowden, *Life*, Letter III, p. 19.
68 Ibid.
69 F. W. Faber to J. B. Morris, LO, Vol. 17, No. 11, 11 September 1834.
70 F. W. Faber to Roundell Palmer, January 1835, in Bowden, *Life*, Letter III, p. 18.
71 F. W. Faber to J. B. Morris, LO, Vol. 17, No. 21, 15 October 1836.
72 F. W. Faber to Roundell Palmer, January 1835, in Bowden, *Life*, Letter III, pp. 16–19.
73 Ibid. p. 18.
74 Ibid.
75 Ibid. pp. 18–19.
76 Ibid. p. 19.
77 Ibid. pp. 18–19.
78 F. W. Faber, quoting J. H. Newman, in a letter to Roundell Palmer, January 1835, in Bowden, *Life*, Letter III, p. 18.
79 Ibid. p. 18.
80 F. W. Faber to Roundell Palmer, 21 August 1835, in Bowden,

Life, Letter V, pp. 24–5; and 21 December 1835, in Bowden, *Life*, Letter XV, pp. 37–8.

81 F. W. Faber to J. B. Morris, LO, Vol. 17, No. 1, 8 June 1833.

82 F. W. Faber to J. B. Morris, LO, Vol. 17, No. 2, 22 June 1833.

83 F. W. Faber to Roundell Palmer, 15 January 1835, in Bowden, *Life*, Letter IV, pp. 21–2.

84 F. W. Faber to Roundell Palmer, 21 August 1835, in Bowden, *Life*, Letter V, pp. 24–5; and 22 December 1835, in Bowden, *Life*, Letter XV, pp. 37–8.

85 Particularly in letters to J. B. Morris.

86 F. W. Faber to Roundell Palmer, 15 January 1835, in Bowden, *Life*, Letter IV, p. 21.

87 F. W. Faber to Roundell Palmer, 11 November 1835, in Bowden, *Life*, Letter XIII, p. 35.

88 Ibid.

89 Ibid.

90 R. Hooker (1890), *The Works of Richard Hooker, with an Account of his Life and Death by Isaak Walton*, 2 Vols, Oxford, Clarendon Press, Vol. I, p. 148.

91 J. Butler (1849), *The Analogy of Religion*, 2 Vols, Oxford, OUP.

92 Ker notes J. H. Newman's enthusiasm for the works of Butler in the context of his (Newman's) mature dislike of Evangelicalism. See I. Ker (1990), *John Henry Newman*, Oxford, OUP, pp. 113–4.

93 F. W. Faber to J. B. Morris, LO, Vol. 17, No. 9, 25 August 1834.

94 Ibid.

95 F. W. Faber to Roundell Palmer, 25 August 1835, in Bowden, *Life*, Letter VII, p. 26. See also letter to J. B. Morris, LO, Vol. 17, No. 8, 4 August 1834 and LO, Vol. 17, No. 9, 25 August 1834.

96 F. W. Faber to Roundell Palmer, 25 August 1835, in Bowden, *Life*, Letter VII, p. 26.

97 Ibid.

98 Ibid. pp. 26–7.

99 Ibid. p. 26.

100 F. W. Faber to Roundell Palmer, 29 August 1835, in Bowden, *Life*, Letter VIII, p. 29.

101 F. W. Faber to Roundell Palmer, 25 August 1835, in Bowden, *Life*, Letter VII, pp. 26–8.

102 Ibid.

103 F. W. Faber to Roundell Palmer, 29 August 1835, in Bowden, *Life*, Letter VIII, pp. 26–8.

104 F. W. Faber to Roundell Palmer, 21 August 1835, in Bowden, *Life*, Letter V, p. 25; and 20 December 1835, in Bowden, *Life*, Letter VI, pp. 25–6.

105 F. W. Faber to Roundell Palmer, 29 August 1835, in Bowden, *Life*, Letter VIII, p. 28.

106 St Peter in the East, Oxford: the first Tractarian Church.

107 F. W. Faber to Roundell Palmer, 11 October 1835, in Bowden, *Life*, Letter XIII, p. 33.

108 F. W. Faber to Roundell Palmer, 29 September 1835, in Bowden, *Life*, Letter X, p. 32.

109 Ibid.

110 Ibid.

111 Faber was writing *The Knights of St John*, a poem which he entered for, and for which he was awarded, the Newdigate Prize, on 15 May 1836. See F. W. Faber to Roundell Palmer, 11 October 1835, in Bowden, *Life*, Letter XII, p. 34.

112 F. W. Faber to Roundell Palmer, 11 November 1835, in Bowden, *Life*, Letter XIII, p. 34.

113 F. W. Faber to Roundell Palmer, Sexagesima Sunday 1836, in Bowden, *Life*, Letter XVI, pp. 40–2.

114 Ibid.

115 F. W. Faber to Roundell Palmer, 5 August 1836, in Bowden, *Life*, Letter XX, p. 46.

116 F. W. Faber to J. B. Morris, LO, Vol. 17, No. 18, 5 August 1836.

117 F. W. Faber to Roundell Palmer, Sexagesima Sunday 1836, in Bowden, *Life*, Letter XVI, p. 41.

118 Ibid. pp. 40–1.

119 Ibid.

120 Ibid. p. 41.

121 Ibid.

122 Ibid.

123 F. W. Faber (1836), Essay: *A Christian Ideal of Friendship*, UCO, 23 January. Unpublished MS in hand of F. W. Faber, LO.

124 F. W. Faber to Roundell Palmer, Sexagesima Sunday 1836, in Bowden, *Life*, Letter XVI, p. 40 and p. 42.

125 Ibid. p. 42.

126 F. W. Faber to J. B. Morris, LO, Vol. 17, No. 18, 5 August 1836.

127 Ibid.

128 Ibid. It is tempting to see some significance in the fact that although Faber had ample space left on the sheet of paper on which this letter was written, his handwriting became smaller and smaller when he was discussing a return to childlike obedience.

129 See, among others, F. W. Faber to J. B. Morris, LO, Vol. 17, No. 1, Monday 8 June 1833; LO, Vol. 17, No. 10, 4 September 1834; LO, Vol. 17, No. 15, 5 January 1836.

130 F. W. Faber (1836), Essay: *A Christian Ideal of Friendship*, UCO, 23 January. Unpublished MS in hand of F. W. Faber, LO.

131 F. W. Faber (n.d.), Essay: *The Idea of Man*. Unpublished MS in hand of F. W. Faber, LO.

132 Ibid.

133 Ibid.

134 Faber's continuing unhappiness with Tractarianism is implied in his letter to J. B. Morris, LO, Vol. 17, No. 16, 22 May 1836.

135 Ibid.

136 F. W. Faber to J. B. Morris, LO, Vol. 17, No. 21, 15 October 1836.

137 F. W. Faber to J. B. Morris, LO, Vol. 17, No. 6, 1 January 1834; LO, Vol. 17, No. 7, 4 January 1834; LO, Vol. 17, No. 13, 5 August 1835.
138 See p. 18.
139 F. W. Faber to J. B. Morris, LO, Vol. 17, No. 13, 5 August 1835.
140 Ibid.
141 Ibid.
142 We shall discuss this idea further in our discussion of Faber's sermons.
143 F. W. Faber (1836), Essay: *A Christian Ideal of Friendship*, UCO, 23 January. Unpublished MS in hand of F. W. Faber, LO.
144 Ibid.
145 Ibid.
146 F. W. Faber to J. B. Morris, LO, Vol. 17, No. 16, 22 May 1836.
147 F. W. Faber to Roundell Palmer, Whit Sunday, 22 May 1836, in Bowden, *Life*, Letter XVIII, p. 44.
148 Ibid. p. 45.
149 F. W. Faber to J. B. Morris, LO, Vol. 17, No. 16, 22 May 1836.
150 Ibid.
151 Ibid.
152 F. W. Faber to Roundell Palmer, 22 May 1836, in Bowden, *Life*, Letter XVIII, p. 45.
153 I. Williams (1838), Tract 80, *On Reserve in Communicating Religious Knowledge*, p. 68.
154 J. Keble (1840), Tract 89, *On the Mysticism Attributed to the Early Fathers of the Church*, p. 4.
155 *Tracts for the Times*, Vols 3–4 (1835–6) p. 23 and p. 24.
156 W.A.G. [*sic*], *J. B. Morris (1812–1880)*, in DNB (Oxford, OUP, 1921) Vol. 13, pp. 996–7.
157 F. W. Faber to J. B. Morris, LO, Vol. 17, No. 21, 15 October 1836.
158 Ibid.
159 F. W. Faber to J. B. Morris, LO, Vol. 17, No. 18, 5 August 1836.
160 F. W. Faber to Roundell Palmer, 22 August 1836, in Bowden, *Life*, Letter XXI, p. 47.
161 Ibid. p. 48.
162 Ibid. pp. 47–8.
163 Ibid.
164 F. W. Faber to J. B. Morris, LO, Vol. 17, No. 18, 5 August 1836.
165 Ibid.
166 F. W. Faber to J. B. Morris, LO, Vol. 17, No. 19, 17 September 1836.
167 Morris was ordained on Sunday 2 October 1836. See F. W. Faber to J. B. Morris, LO, Vol. 17, No. 20, 27 September 1836.
168 F. W. Faber to J. B. Morris, LO, Vol. 17, No. 19, 17 September 1836.
169 Ibid.
170 Faber discussed the circumstances of his examination in letters to

Roundell Palmer. See 18 November 1836, in Bowden, *Life*, Letter XXIV, pp. 50–1; and 21 November 1836, in Bowden, *Life*, Letter XXV, pp. 51–2.

171 Bowden, *Life*, pp. 42–3.

172 F. W. Faber to J. B. Morris, LO, Vol. 17, No. 23, 30 November 1836.

173 Bowden, *Life*, p. 51.

174 F. W. Faber to Roundell Palmer, 21 November 1836, in Bowden, *Life*, Letter XXV, pp. 51–2.

175 See p. 22.

176 Bowden, *Life*, p. 43.

177 F. W. Faber to J. B. Morris, LO, Vol. 17, No. 24, 24 December 1836.

178 F. W. Faber to J. B. Morris, LO, Vol. 17, No. 11, 11 September 1834.

179 F. W. Faber to Roundell Palmer, 26 January 1837, in Bowden, *Life*, Letter XXVII, pp. 53–6.

180 Ibid.

181 Longley was the first bishop of the 'newly created See of Ripon'. J. R. Garrard, *C. T. Longley (1794–1868)*, in DNB (Oxford, OUP, 2004) Vol. 34, p. 400.

182 F. W. Faber to J. B. Morris, LO, Vol. 17, No. 29, 17 April 1837.

183 Ibid.

184 Ibid.

185 F. W. Faber to Roundell Palmer, 21 November 1836, in Bowden, *Life*, Letter XXV, p. 51.

186 F. W. Faber to J. B. Morris, LO, Vol. 17, No. 25, 10 January 1837.

187 F. W. Faber to J. B. Morris, LO, Vol. 17, No. 26, 31 January 1837.

188 F. W. Faber to J. B. Morris, LO, Vol. 17, No. 25, 10 January 1837.

189 Ibid.

190 Ibid.

191 F. W. Faber to J. B. Morris, LO, Vol. 17, No. 23, 31 November 1836.

192 Published in January 1837.

193 F. W. Faber to J. B. Morris, LO, Vol. 17, No. 26, 31 January 1837.

194 Ibid.

195 Ibid.

196 Ibid.

197 F. W. Faber to J. B. Morris, LO, Vol. 17, No. 25, 23 January 1837.

198 F. W. Faber to J. B. Morris, LO, Vol. 17, No. 28, 31 March 1837.

199 Ibid.

200 F. W. Faber to J. B. Morris, LO, Vol. 17, No. 26, 31 January 1837.

201 His rooms were Staircase 5, Room 3. Letter to the Author from Dr R. Darwall Smith, 19 March 2001, Archives of University College, Oxford.

202 Bowden, *Life*, p. 43.

203 F. W. Faber to J. B. Morris, LO, Vol. 17, No. 27, March 1837.

204 J. H. Newman (1837), *Lectures on the Prophetical Office of the Church, viewed relatively to Romanism and Popular Protestantism*, London, Rivington, p. 154.

205 F. W. Faber to J. B. Morris, LO, Vol. 17, No. 27, March 1837.

206 Ibid.

207 See p. 32.

208 F. W. Faber to J. B. Morris, LO, Vol. 17, No. 28, 31 March 1837.

209 Ibid.

210 Ibid.

211 F. W. Faber to Roundell Palmer, 26 January 1837, in Bowden, *Life*, Letter XXVII, p. 53.

212 Ibid. pp. 53–4.

213 F. W. Faber to J. B. Morris, LO, Vol. 17, No. 31, 20 June 1837.

214 Ibid.

215 F. W. Faber to J. B. Morris, LO, Vol. 17, No. 25, 10 January 1837.

216 Optatus, *De Schismate Donatistarum* (AD 370). See F. W. Faber to J. B. Morris, LO, Vol. 17, No. 29, 17 April 1837.

217 F. W. Faber to J. B. Morris, LO, Vol. 17, No. 31, 20 June 1837.

218 Ibid.

219 Ibid.

220 Ibid.

221 Ibid.

222 F. W. Faber to J. B. Morris, LO, Vol. 17, No. 32, 26 June 1837.

223 F. W. Faber to J. B. Morris, LO, Vol. 17, No. 30, 19 June 1837.

224 See poem beginning: *I have a dread and glorious home* (n.d., probably 1837). Unpublished MS in hand of F. W. Faber, British Library [hereafter referred to as BL] Add MSS 58225: F. W. Faber: Poems and Letters 1837–1851.

225 Ibid.

226 Sonnet beginning: *The Springs of Silent thought and purpose high* (August 1837). Unpublished MS in hand of F. W. Faber, BL Add MSS 58225: F. W. Faber: Poems and Letters 1837–1851.

227 It is not certain why Faber was ordained within a different diocese to that in which he took up his curacy. The entry in the Bishop's Act Book reads: 'Frederic [*sic*] William Faber, BA, University College, Oxford.' Letter to the author from N. J. Harding, Ripon and Leeds Diocesan Archivist, 15 November 2004.

228 F. W. Faber to Roundell Palmer, January 1835, in Bowden, *Life*, Letter III, p. 17.

229 F. W. Faber to J. B. Morris, LO, Vol. 17, No. 34, 31 August 1837.

230 Ibid.

231 Faber, *Young England*, p. 29. R. Faber describes the church as

being 'set on a hilltop with commanding and intoxicating views
... [A] larger church was built in the valley a few years after Faber
left.' Ibid. p. 29.

232 F. W. Faber to J. B. Morris, LO, Vol. 17, No. 30, 19 June 1837.
233 F. W. Faber to J. B. Morris, LO, Vol. 17, No. 34, 31 August 1837.
234 Ibid.
235 Ibid.
236 F. W. Faber to J. B. Morris, LO, Vol. 17, No. 36, 24 July 1838.
237 F. W. Faber to J. B. Morris, LO, Vol. 17, No. 35, 18 July 1838.
238 Ibid.
239 Ibid.
240 F. W. Faber to A. J. Hope, 23 January 1839, in Addington, *Faber:
     Poet and Priest*, p. 70.
241 Ibid. p. 70.
242 F. W. Faber (n.d.), *Verses Sent to a Friend with a Copy of Froude's
     Remains*. Unpublished MS in hand of F. W. Faber, BL Add MSS
     58225: F. W. Faber: Poems and Letters 1837–1851. Also
     published in *Poems*, p. 197.
243 R. H. Froude (1838), *Remains of the Late R.H. Froude MA, Fellow of
     New College Oxford*, London, Rivington, Preface pp. xiv–xv.
244 F. W. Faber to Roundell Palmer, 7 May 1838, in Bowden, *Life*,
     Letter XXXIV, pp. 63–4.
245 F. W. Faber to J. B. Morris, LO, Vol. 17, No. 36, 24 July 1838.
246 F. W. Faber to J. B. Morris, LO, Vol. 17, No. 35, 18 July 1838.
247 J. H. Newman to F. W. Faber, 4 July 1838, in Newman, *Letters
     and Diaries*, Vol. VI, p. 260.
248 J. H. Newman to F. W. Faber, 25 September 1838, ibid. p. 320.
249 Ibid.
250 *Seven Books of St Optatus against the Donatists*. Unpublished MS in
     the hand of F. W. Faber, LO.
251 J. H. Newman to F. W. Faber, 4 July 1838, in Newman, *Letters
     and Diaries*, Vol. VI, p. 260.
252 Addington, *Faber: Poet and Priest*, p. 64.
253 Ibid. p. 11.
254 Faber, *Young England*, p. x.
255 R. Addington, *Faber: Poet and Priest*, p. 11.
256 C. Whibley (1925), *Lord John Manners and His Friends*, Edinburgh,
     William Blackwood and Sons, pp. 63–4.
257 B. Disraeli (1998), *Sibyl*, Oxford, OUP, p. 150.
258 Ibid. pp. 107–8.
259 Lord John Manners, Journal, 22 July 1838, quoted in C. Whibley
     (1925), *Lord John Manners and His Friends*, Edinburgh, William
     Blackwood and Sons, p. 65.
260 Lord John Manners, Journal, 22 July 1838, ibid.
261 F. W. Faber to J. B. Morris, Vol. 17, No. 36, 24 July 1838.
262 Addington, *Faber: Poet and Priest*, p. 69.
263 F. W. Faber to J. Manners, 19 January 1839, in Addington, *Faber:
     Poet and Priest*, pp. 69–70.

264 Ibid.
265 F. W. Faber to J. B. Morris, Vol. 17, No. 36, 24 July 1838.
266 See pp. 13–14.
267 F. W. Faber to J. B. Morris, LO, Vol. 17, No. 36, 24 July 1838.
268 Such as Matthew Arnold's retrospective description of the sermons that Newman preached in the University Church. See I. Ker (1990), *John Henry Newman: a Biography*, Oxford, OUP, p. 90.
269 26 May is also the feast day of St Philip Neri, the founder of the Congregation of the Oratory.
270 It is not clear why Faber, who had been ordained to the diaconate at Ripon, was ordained priest at Oxford. One reason for this may be that his family was from Yorkshire, whereas Faber was going to administer a living from University College, Oxford.
271 R. Bagot (1782–1854) BA, Christ Church, Oxford (1803), Fellow All Souls (1803), MA (1806), DD (1829), Rector of Leigh, Staffordshire (1806), Bluthfield (1806), Prebendary of Lichfield Cathedral (1812), Canon of Worcester (1817), Dean of Canterbury (1827), Bishop of Oxford (1829). See P. B. Nockles, *Richard Bagot (1782–1854)*, in DNB (Oxford, OUP, 2004) Vol. 3, pp. 240–2.
272 Ibid. p. 241.
273 F. W. Faber to J. H. Newman, LO, Vol. 2, No. 257, 25 May 1850.
274 Addington, *Faber: Poet and Priest*, p. 76.
275 Faber's travelling companions were 'Richard Church (1815–1890) and Arthur Penrhyn Stanley (1815–1881)'. S. Gilley, *F. W. Faber (1814–1863)*, in DNB (Oxford, OUP, 2004) Vol. 18, p. 872.
276 F. W. Faber to J. B. Morris, LO, Vol. 17, No. 38, 25 August 1839.
277 Ibid.
278 Ibid.
279 Ibid.
280 Ibid.
281 F. W. Faber to J. B. Morris, LO, Vol. 17, No. 39, 28 September 1840.
282 Ibid.
283 Ibid.
284 Christopher Wordsworth (1807–1885). See Christopher Wordsworth Jnr to F. W. Faber, 6 November 1840, Lambeth Palace Library, Wordsworth Papers, MS 2142, Letter 125.
285 For one example of this, see F. W. Faber, Sermon, Jude 3, Ambleside, St Anne's Day (26 July) 1840. Unpublished MS in hand of F. W. Faber, LO.
286 F. W. Faber to J. B. Morris, LO, Vol. 17, No. 42, 16 November 1840.
287 Ibid.
288 Ibid.
289 Ibid.
290 One example of this is the differences between the responses of Newman and Faber to Faber's *Life of St Wilfrid* in 1845. See p. 85.

291 F. W. Faber (1857), *Unkind Judging*, Sonnet LXXXVI, in *Poems*, p. 248.
292 Ibid.
293 Ibid.
294 F. W. Faber, *Admonition*, LXXXVII, in *Poems*, p. 249.
295 Ibid.
296 Ibid.
297 F. W. Faber, Sonnet LXXXV, in *Poems*, p. 248.
298 F. W. Faber, *Admonition*, LXXXVII, in *Poems*, p. 249.
299 F. W. Faber to J. B. Morris, LO, Vol. 17, No. 40, 21 October 1840.
300 Ibid.
301 Ibid.
302 Ibid.
303 Ibid.
304 F. W. Faber to J. Manners, 25 January 1839, in Addington, *Faber: Poet and Priest*, p. 71.
305 F. W. Faber to J. B. Morris, LO, Vol. 17, No. 41, 22 October 1840.
306 F. W. Faber to J. B. Morris, LO, Vol. 17, No. 40, 21 October 1840; and LO, Vol. 17, No. 45, 26 January 1841.
307 F. W. Faber to J. B. Morris, LO, Vol. 17, No. 40, 21 October 1840.
308 F. W. Faber to J. B. Morris, LO, Vol. 17, No. 45, 26 January 1841.
309 F. W. Faber to J. B. Morris, LO, Vol. 17, No. 40, 21 October 1840.
310 Ibid.
311 Morris's letter, to which Faber replied, is not extant.
312 F. W. Faber to J. B. Morris, LO, Vol. 17, No. 43, 25 November 1840.
313 W.A.G. [*sic*], *J. B. Morris (1812–1880)*, in DNB (Oxford, OUP, 1921–2) Vol. XIII, p. 997.
314 F. W. Faber to J. B. Morris, LO, Vol. 17, No. 43, 25 November 1840.
315 Ibid.
316 Ibid.
317 Ibid.
318 Ibid.
319 Ibid.
320 Ibid.
321 *The Oxford Concise Dictionary of the Christian Church* (London, OUP, 1996) p. 148. [Hereafter referred to as OCDCC.]
322 F. W. Faber to J. B. Morris, LO, Vol. 17, No. 43, 25 November 1840.
323 Ibid.
324 Ibid.
325 Ibid.
326 Ibid.

327 F. W. Faber to J. B. Morris, LO, Vol. 17, No. 42, 16 November 1840.
328 J. A. Möhler (1997), *Symbolism [Symbolik]*, New York, Crossroad Herder, introduction to the 1997 edition, p. xi.
329 F. W. Faber to J. B. Morris, LO, Vol. 17, No. 43, 25 November 1840.
330 F. W. Faber to J. B. Morris, LO, Vol. 17, No. 42, 16 November 1840.
331 F. W. Faber to J. B. Morris, LO, Vol. 17, No. 43, 25 November 1840.
332 F. W. Faber to J. B. Morris, LO, Vol. 17, No. 42, 16 November 1840.
333 See, for example, ibid.
334 Chapman, *Father Faber*, pp. 157–8.
335 F. W. Faber to J. B. Morris, LO, Vol. 17, No. 44, 1 January 1841.
336 Letter to the author from Dr John Hughes, 26 October 2001.
337 Ibid.
338 Ibid.
339 Ibid.
340 F. W. Faber to J. B. Morris, LO, Vol. 17, No. 42, 16 November 1840.
341 Ibid.
342 F. W. Faber, *Brathay Bridge*, XCI, in *Poems*, p. 254.
343 Ibid.
344 F. W. Faber to J. B. Morris, LO, Vol. 17, No. 42, 16 November 1840.
345 Ibid.
346 F. W. Faber to J. B. Morris, LO, Vol. 17, No. 42, 16 November 1840.
347 R. Bright (1937), *Original Papers of Richard Bright on Renal Disease*, Oxford, OUP, pp. 32, 45, 164 and others.
348 F. W. Faber to J. B. Morris, LO, Vol. 17, No. 44, 1 January 1841.
349 Ibid.
350 F. W. Faber to J. B. Morris, LO, Vol. 17, No. 44, 1 January 1841.
351 Ibid.
352 Letter to the author from Dr John Hughes, 26 October 2001.
353 F. W. Faber to J. B. Morris, LO, Vol. 17, No. 44, 1 January 1841.
354 Ibid.
355 F. W. Faber to J. B. Morris, LO, Vol. 17, No. 45, 26 January 1841.
356 Entry for Pilulae Hydrargyri: Mercurial, or Blue Pills, in R. Hooper (ed.) (1839), *Lexicon Medicum* (London, 7th edn) p. 1034.
357 F. W. Faber to J. B. Morris, LO, Vol. 17, No. 45, 26 January 1841.
358 Entry for Pilulae Hydrargyri: Mercurial, or Blue Pills, in R. Hooper (ed.) (1839), *Lexicon Medicum* (London, 7th edn) p. 1034.
359 He left England on 26 February.
360 F. W. Faber to J. B. Morris, LO, Vol. 17, No. 44, 1 January 1841.

361 F. W. Faber (1842), *Sights and Thoughts in Foreign Churches and Among Foreign Peoples* (London, Rivington). [Hereafter referred to as *Sights and Thoughts*.]

362 F. W. Faber to J. B. Morris, LO, Vol. 17, No. 46, 8 April 1841.

363 For an example of this, see *Sights and Thoughts in Foreign Churches and Among Foreign Peoples, in the Year of Our Lord MDCCCXLI*, Vol. 1, p. 37. [Hereafter referred to as *Sights and Thoughts MSS*.]

364 *Sights and Thoughts*, pp. 1–7.

365 *Sights and Thoughts MSS*, p. 127.

366 Ibid. pp. 109–11.

367 Ibid. p. 111.

368 Ibid. p. 109.

369 Extract from *Sights and Thoughts MSS*, in Bowden, *Life*, pp. 140–1.

370 *Sights and Thoughts*, p. 23.

371 *Sights and Thoughts MSS*, pp. 49–50.

372 Extract from *Sights and Thoughts*, in Bowden, *Life*, pp. 134–5.

373 Extract from *Sights and Thoughts*, in Bowden, *Life*, p. 84.

374 F. W. Faber to J. B. Morris, LO, Vol. 17, No. 46, 8 April 1841.

375 *Sights and Thoughts MSS*, p. 51.

376 Ibid.

377 Ibid. p. 57.

378 Ibid.

379 Ibid. p. 55.

380 Ibid. p. 57.

381 Ibid. p. 49.

382 Ibid. p. 60.

383 Ibid. p. 88.

384 F. W. Faber to J. B. Morris, LO, Vol. 17, No. 44, 1 January 1841.

385 F. W. Faber to J. B. Morris, LO, Vol. 17, No. 46, 8 April 1841.

386 F. W. Faber to Christopher Wordsworth Jnr, 18 November 1840, in Wordsworth Papers, Lambeth Palace Library, MS 2142.

387 F. W. Faber to J. B. Morris, LO, Vol. 17, No. 45, 1 January 1841.

388 Ibid.

389 F. W. Faber to J. B. Morris, LO, Vol. 17, No. 49, 31 January 1842.

390 F. W. Faber to J. B. Morris, LO, Vol. 17, No. 51, 27 September 1842.

391 R. Hoblyn (1892), *Hoblyn's Dictionary of Medical Terms* (London) p. 449.

392 *Churchill's Illustrated Medical Dictionary* (1991), (London, Churchill, Livingstone), entries for mercury poisoning, p. 1482 and stomatitis, p. 1789.

393 Entry for mercury, in R. Hooper (ed.) (1839), *Lexicon Medicum* (London, 7th edn) p. 889.

394 *Churchill's Illustrated Medical Dictionary* (1991) (London, Churchill, Livingstone), entry for erethism, p. 642.

395 Miscellaneous symptoms and signs of mercury poisoning gleaned from Bidstrup's book include: tiredness, irritation of mouth and

throat with blisters, general malaise, diarrhoea, anorexia, abdominal pain, insomnia, headaches, tremor, depression, unsteady gait, excitability and restlessness. (Anorexia and, possibly, tremor were the only symptoms from this list not suffered by Faber at some time during his life.) See P. L. Bidstrup (1964), *Toxicity of Mercury and its Compounds*, Amsterdam, Elsevier Publishing Company.

396 Ibid. p. 43.
397 Ibid.
398 J. H. Newman to J. W. Bowden, LO, Vol. 13, No. 113, n.d. 1841.
399 F. W. Faber 'Obituary', in *The Saturday Review*, 28 September 1863, p. 5.
400 F. W. Faber to J.B Morris, LO, Vol. 17, No. 56, St Lucy's Day (13 December) 1842.
401 F. W. Faber to J. B. Morris, LO, Vol. 17, No. 57, 16 December 1842.
402 Ibid.
403 Ibid.
404 Morris, like Faber, was frequently unwell. See W. A. G. [*sic*], *J. B. Morris (1812–1880)*, in DNB (Oxford, OUP, 1921–2) Vol. XIII, pp. 996–7.
405 F. W. Faber to J. B. Morris, LO, Vol. 17, No. 56, St Lucy's Day (13 December) 1842.
406 F. W. Faber to J. B. Morris, LO, Vol. 17, No. 57, 16 December 1842.
407 F. W. Faber to J. B. Morris, LO, Vol. 17, No. 51, 27 September 1842; LO, Vol. 17, No. 52, n.d. 1842; LO, Vol. 17, No. 53, 29 October 1842; LO, Vol. 17, No. 54, 11 November 1842; LO, Vol. 17, No. 55, 25 November 1842; LO, Vol. 17, No. 56, 13 December 1842; LO, Vol. 17, No. 57, 16 December 1842.
408 *The Styrian Lake and other Poems* (1840). (The first volume was *The Cherwell Water-Lily and Other Poems* (1840).)
409 F. W. Faber to J. B. Morris, LO, Vol. 17, No. 57, 16 December 1842.
410 F. W. Faber to J. B. Morris, LO, Vol. 17, No. 41, 22 October 1840.
411 F. W. Faber to J. B. Morris, LO, Vol. 17, No. 57, 16 December 1842.
412 Ibid.
413 Ibid.
414 Ibid.
415 Ibid.
416 Ibid.
417 F. W. Faber to J. B. Morris, LO, Vol. 17, No. 58, 21 December 1842.
418 F. W. Faber to J. B. Morris, LO, Vol. 17, No. 57, 16 December 1842.
419 F. W. Faber to J. B. Morris, LO, Vol. 17, No. 59, 31 January 1843.

420 The article on P. C. Claughton notes that he succeeded Faber at Elton, but does not mention that he held the post before Faber's arrival. C. W. Sutton, *P. C. Claughton (1814–1884)*, in DNB (Oxford, OUP, 1921–22) Vol. 4, pp. 458–9.

421 F. W. Faber to J. B. Morris, LO, Vol. 17, No. 59, 31 January 1843.

422 T. Godwin, *Personal Recollections of Father Faber* (1901) in *Various Memoranda Relating to London Oratorian History*, pp. 206–14. [Hereafter referred to as Godwin, *Personal Recollections*.]

423 F. W. Faber to J. B. Morris, LO, Vol. 17, No. 58, 21 December 1842.

424 Godwin, *Personal Recollections*, p. 208.

425 Ibid.

426 'Wordsworth, Manners, Beresford Hope, Watts Russell, Roundell Palmer ... J. B. Morris ... John Walker.' Ibid. p. 210.

Chapter 3

Conversion:
May 1843–November 1845

Stage Four of Faber's spiritual development

Between May and October 1843, Faber accompanied his pupil, Matthew Harrison,[1] on the second part of his Grand Tour.[2] Although these travels were premeditated, they were part of a pattern that constantly recurred during Faber's life; he took on a responsibility and then went abroad. There are two equally plausible, and possibly related, reasons for this character trait. Firstly, he hoped that travelling would improve his health. Secondly, Faber seems to have gone abroad during or after periods of stress, or prior to taking on responsibility, whether or not the change was congenial. It would seem that travel gave him space to become accustomed to changed circumstances.

During May and June, Faber was in Rome. He did not keep a journal of his impressions of this visit,[3] which was, from a spiritual and historical point of view, more important than that detailed in *Sights and Thoughts*. However, in a letter to Morris,[4] he described his impressions and responses to both city and Church, and, as we have come to expect from Faber, these were contradictory. Faber's aesthetic sense was concerned only with the spiritual, and he wrote that he had not visited any art galleries, museums or 'antiquities except such as are conse-crated by church traditions'.[5] Despite this ecclesiastical bias, Faber records that he was unimpressed by a number of the churches which he visited, writing that, 'repeated visits ... to St Peter's ... only keep up ye original feeling of disappointment'.[6] A significant part of Faber's positive response to Rome is an openness to Christian history, a trait which is present also in his poems and the journal *Sights and Thoughts*; and it is for historical reasons that he writes, 'it is quite impossible for any Christian to be disappointed in Rome'.[7] Rome was a continual reminder of the past, a trait that may represent, in Faber's case, an idealised historical world which contrasted with the unsatisfactory nature of nineteenth-century Christianity. This extends to the saints, martyrs and heresies which Faber mentions, all of which are products of either the Early Church or of the pre-Reformation Church.[8]

The influence of Roman Catholicism, which forms the fourth major stage of Faber's spirituality, began at this time; and although Roman Catholicism initially unsettled and disturbed him, it became increasingly important. Faber's primary attitude towards the contemporary Church of Rome was one of guarded dislike; in one example he refers to it as 'ye enemy'.[9] However, he seems to have realised that this response was conditioned by outside influences, such as upbringing, and not a true reflection of his increasing openness to the Church that he encountered whilst in Rome. This idea is reinforced by the revealing group of phrases in the following: 'I am anxious to keep my mind open to conviction, and to expel all rude unreasoning dislike out of my thoughts; for neither shame nor station nor interest would, I hope, prevent me from going where conscience leads.'[10]

Faber was reading Roman theology,[11] although he does not indicate the content of, or his responses to, his reading. It is probable that it was in order to discern his religious position, as he had been discussing the dogmatic differences between Anglicanism and Roman Catholicism with a number of clerics[12] from the English College. Their primary argument was that Faber would not be saved unless he converted to Rome, to which he replied that God would not refuse to save him if he genuinely believed in the moral and spiritual rightness of the Church of England. This was based on the idea that the Anglican Church was part of the primitive Church,[13] and Faber thought of this response in terms of an apologetic victory. Faber was suspicious of his own positive response to the welcome from the Roman clergy, writing, 'I find my attachment to ye Church of England growing in Rome, ye more I bewail our position.'[14] Also, 'I feel much benefited by my visit to Rome, and my allegiance to England quite unshakeable.'[15] It is interesting to note that the distinction between the Churches of England and Rome was national and political as well as spiritual.[16] Faber was writing of Oxford friendships as being one of the factors that tied him to the Church of England,[17] a point which is significant because of his frequently dismissive attitude towards people associated with the University of Oxford.

Perhaps because of these contrary impressions, Faber indicated to Morris that he had tried to simplify the arguments for and against Roman Catholicism.[18] He wrote, 'in reality ye one thing necessary to prove was that adherence to ye Holy See was essential to ye <u>being</u> of a church'.[19] In a letter to his brother, Faber discussed his interpretation of the situation regarding Anglicanism and Protestantism and wrote, 'You must remember that the Church of England is not Protestant.'[20] Faber anathematised Protestantism, characterising it as a 'diabolical'[21] and 'heretical'[22] system leading ultimately to 'blasphemy and unbelief'.[23] He was convinced that, if the Church of England was Protestant, his only alternative was to make the less than ideal transfer to the contemporary Church of Rome.[24] His primary reason for discounting this option was that he believed that Anglicanism was orthodox, and possessed apostolic continuity in both priesthood and Sacraments.[25]

On 17 June, Faber was introduced to Pope Gregory XVI. This meeting was a watershed in Faber's spiritual development and, from this time onwards, Roman Catholicism became as important a spiritual influence as the Church of England; one which overlaid, but did not dilute, his Anglican spirituality. Faber's response to the Church of Rome seems to have been motivated, to a great extent, by his emotional empathy, of which a prime example is kissing the Pope's foot.[26] In his critique of secrecy and Romeward tendencies in the Church of England, Walsh presents a detailed description of Faber's visit to Rome. Although he reserves his most pointed satire for the encounter between Faber and the Pope,[27] he also criticises Faber's enthusiasm for the churches, ceremonies, and saints associated with the Roman Church.[28] He also accuses Faber of hypocrisy and dishonesty, noting that 'he had gone so far away from the sound judgement of an English Churchman, that he was actually "persuaded to wear a miraculous medal"'.[29] Walsh's agenda was such that he did not attempt to empathise with Faber's position or try to understand his temperament. However, like Walsh, we cannot ignore, or dismiss as unimportant, such a blatantly Roman response from an Anglican clergyman; and the fragmentary nature of the historical evidence for this event presupposes more questions than it is able to answer. Faber had been fiercely evangelical just nine years earlier, and his reaction to his sojourn in Rome highlights the inherent difficulty of balancing Anglicanism, whether Low or High, and Roman Catholicism, a conundrum which was increasingly part of Faber's spiritual makeup from this point until his conversion. As our purpose is not to dismiss Faber but to unravel the complexities of his religious makeup, we can suggest that kissing the Pope's foot is a typically Faberian response, one which is theatrical, overdone and perhaps leaning towards bad taste. Faber qualified this act, and perhaps sought to give it legitimacy for himself, by writing 'there seems to be a mean puerility in refusing ye customary homage'.[30] This may mean that Faber knew what to do in a given situation for maximum effect, rather than that there was a spiritual motive for the act itself.

The problematic catholicity of the Anglican Church was put into focus for Faber on hearing himself described as Protestant,[31] with its implication, from both the Roman and Tractarian standpoints, of schism. The central reason put forward by Pope Gregory XVI as to why Faber should leave the Church of England, was that there was a lack of doctrinal unity within it; an idea which contradicts Faber's view, expressed in 1840, that the Anglican Church's claim to individuality was that it admitted more than one doctrinal stance. By 1843, Faber had realised that lack of doctrinal unity equated with lack of authority, and this idea was reinforced as one of the central ideas of his intellectual and religious makeup. Whilst abroad, Faber received news of a practical demonstration of the aforementioned ideas and, in a letter to Morris, discussed details of Pusey's 'suspension'[32] by the University of Oxford, 'for holding ye Catholic doctrine of ye Eucharist'.[33] Faber's views on this event underline his high sacramentality, particularly as he viewed the subsequent denial of the real presence as promulgating the 'heresy of Zwingli'.[34] However, Faber does not precisely define what his theology of the real presence consists of, and his primary concern was that these actions proved that the Church of England had 'no unity, no order, [*and*] no authority'.[35] This event, which was one of the pivotal moments in Faber's conversion process, was made more significant because of Pusey's long-standing influence on Faber's spirituality. It may also have been, for Faber, an ideal example of the heretical spirit of the age in which he lived.

In June 1843, Faber wrote to Morris expressing his dissatisfaction with Anglicanism: 'I hardly dare read ye articles; their weight grows heavier on me daily.'[36] However, despite this, and the lure of an idealised pre-Reformation Rome, he was concerned that to leave the Church of England would be a 'disobedient act of self will'.[37] The idea of self will, to which Faber returned throughout the timescale covered by this chapter, was, together with the fear of private judgement, one of his major reasons for not leaving Anglicanism before November 1845. Perhaps because of this, Faber frequently stressed his willingness to defer to others, and wrote to Morris that he had not invoked the saints for a year because Morris had said that to do so was un-Anglican.[38] This trait, which was necessary for Faber's spiritual morale from 1843 onwards, was relatively straightforward where Morris was concerned. It was less so with Newman, as Faber's relationship with Newman consisted of two completely contradictory sets of emotions. In one sense Faber was, like Newman's other Tractarian associates, dependent on him for advice; particularly in relation to their practical conduct as Tractarian priests. Thus, despite his doubts, Faber viewed Newman as a figurehead whose 'vision'[39] of Anglicanism was 'a consoling subject of thought'.[40] In another sense, Faber's mindset was so individual and independent of Newman's that the latter's influence was problematic; particularly as Faber was, at this time, going towards, but not yet over, the boundaries of Tractarianism.

Whilst in Florence, during August, Faber wrote to Morris and encouraged him to begin to read Roman theology. He indicated that he had been studying Thomas Aquinas, Albertus Magnus, Suarez, and assorted lives of saints,[41] but did not provide further details. This letter is notable because in it Faber displayed an enthusiasm for reading theology, a trait which had been almost totally lacking in his letters from 1840 until then. Faber was also meditating a group of lectures on 'ye sacred infancy and childhood of O[ur] S[aviour] J[esus] C[hrist]'[42] for his parishioners at Elton. This was Faber's response to the subject matter and controversy surrounding Pusey's sermon on the Eucharist. His intention was to make available to his parishioners, in a much simplified form, the theology regarding the divinity and humanity of Christ,[43] thereby educating them in order to lessen the impact of discussion of contested points of theology;[44] although it is impossible to say how much his parishioners were aware of theological controversy. In the same letter, Faber wrote that a number of Anglican clergy in Italy were worried by the excessive Romanising implied in Pusey's sermon.[45] Faber also noted that the sermon had been defined as heretical by several individuals in Rome. This was because it created a link between remission of sins and the Eucharist, thereby denying that they were two independent Sacraments.[46] Faber's response to the charge of Pusey's Romanism is interesting, as it indicates that he was still thinking of Rome in a particular sense. He wrote, 'it shows how little Pusey's theology is (in ye bad sense) Roman, and how, from its patristic spirit it ... unconsciously names Romanism even while travelling towards quite a different end'.[47]

From September 1843 onwards, Faber wrote to Newman for help with decisions in connection with the process of religious change; and Newman's replies exhibit a measured prudence which provides the perfect contrast to Faber's volatile rashness. He was sympathetic to Faber's concerns about the Church of England, primarily because his thoughts were running along similar lines. However, despite this, he was unwilling to give Faber specific advice, a stance which was interpreted by Faber as showing a lack of concern. Newman's advice, when given, was given warily and in the form of examples rather than in overt terms of praise or blame, although it is fair to say that he did not leave Faber in doubt as to his true feelings. Newman was not uncritical of Faber's methods at Elton, and his primary concern in September 1843 was that Faber was going too far towards Rome on his own, a stance which had overtones of private judgement.[48] Newman opined that the better option was to remain within the Church of England, and that, if the inspiration for change was divine, it was important to work for change as part of a group within the Church.[49]

A notable aspect of Faber's letters written during 1843 is their emotional intensity, an effect which is cumulative if they are read chronologically. A particular example of this is found in letters which Faber sent, during September from Switzerland, to Morris and Newman,[50] and which form an extended discussion of the Church of England. They are significant, not only because they represent a further stage in Faber's spiritual change, but because they highlight aspects of the mental, spiritual and physical[51] suffering which he was undergoing at this time. Although Faber did not yet doubt the validity of his priesthood, he questioned whether the rites and Sacraments which he performed were real, which may amount to the same thing. His confidence in the Church of England was weakened because of his questioning, and he was concerned whether he was in the true church. Faber had already indicated to Morris that he had contemplated converting to the Roman Church whilst in Rome,[52] and in this letter he wondered whether the true church had already been revealed to him at Rome, and whether he had ignored the revelation.[53] It is significant that Newman advised him not to convert, perhaps because he recognised Faber's impetuosity, and this advice gave Faber a sense of perspective. Faber wrote, 'It is a great comfort to me to see you recommending <u>delay</u> even in my state of mind.'[54]

Faber's return to England and Elton on Monday, 9 October 1843,[55] marked the beginning of a new phase in his practical and personal spirituality, which had been occasioned by the debate, correspondence and internal questionings that had taken place whilst he was abroad. Chapman wrote that Faber returned to England a Roman Catholic in all but name, and that this was a natural progression from his High Anglicanism.[56] However, Chapman's assessment is too simplistic, and it seems more likely that Faber was spiritually both an Anglican and a Roman Catholic. The primary evidence for this problematic spiritual state occurs in the sonnet *Two Faiths*,[57] in which Faber described himself as 'one in whose weak heart two faiths are lodged'.[58] He was aware that both Anglicanism and Roman Catholicism were an important and necessary part of his spiritual personality, and so was unable to distinguish, or choose, between the two.[59] This is a prime example of the blurring of distinctions between religious groups, which was a notable facet of Faber's religiosity leading up to his move to Roman Catholicism. Although Faber's eventual move to Rome undoubtedly originated in Rome, we can speculate that his spiritual crisis and struggle did not. It seems probable that Faber's unhappiness with Anglicanism predated Rome, and that it had its roots in criticisms of Anglicanism and the questioning of his vocation, which took place at Ambleside during 1841.

Whilst in Rome, Faber had bought a copy of the *Spiritual Exercises* of St Ignatius Loyola,[60] and, although he briefly mentioned them in correspondence on several occasions, he did not indicate their precise appeal. However, it seems probable that the spiritual discernment involved in their execution provided a framework for the process of spiritual change, and perhaps influenced, and appealed to, aspects of it, such as Faber's sense of moral scrupulosity and fastidiousness. On his return to Elton, Ignatian spirituality became an increasingly significant part of Faber's personal spirituality. The *Exercises* were important for his pastoral office, because the emphasis on practical spirituality provided Faber with a framework within which to instruct his parish.[61] After he became a Roman Catholic, Faber's spirituality remained fundamentally Ignatian, and it seems likely that the primary reason for this was that Ignatius' visual use of the imagination, which gauges its success by its emotional effect on the individual, suited Faber's temperament.[62] Several facets of Faber's mature literary style are a progression from his early use of the *Exercises*, in particular the creation of a secondary narrative around the events and individuals mentioned within written sources such as scripture, which is a notable facet of Faber's mature writings.[63] A number of passages in Faber's works resemble the Ignatian method of meditation on passages from scripture, particularly those recommended during the second and third weeks of the *Exercises*.[64] The uniqueness of Faber's treatment of scripture in his mature writings is that he blurred the distinction between imagination and fact, and was frequently unable to create a balance between the two, ideas which we shall return to later in this study.

From 15 December 1843, Faber noted saints' days in Latin as well as the date at the top of his letters. The fact that a number of these are in the Roman, rather than the Anglican, calendar points to his using the Roman breviary by this time.

During 1844, Faber suffered from a number of abscesses,[65] boils[66] and cowpox.[67] He enclosed a litany of symptoms in a letter to Newman, which included 'liver won't act – pains in the spine – cramps in the legs – constant sick headache'.[68] The seriousness of his symptoms and the elusiveness of relief are expressed in a letter to Morris in which he wrote that, once again, he was no longer taking quinine as it gave him headaches.[69] He had also been advised to use nitrate of silver as an alternative to 'grey powder and opium',[70] advice which he did not take. Once again, Faber is aware of a fundamental physical change taking place, as the passage ends: 'I begin to think there is something more wrong than a mere knock up. I have had a very hard year both of body and mind ... I have some funny inward feelings of giving way at times.'[71] The main ingredients of grey powder are chalk, and mercury[72] which was, as we have already noted, present in the blue pills which Faber had been taking since 1841. Faber had for several months been suffering from what he described as dysentery, which he thought that he had contracted whilst in Italy.[73] However, it is significant that mercury can also cause bowel disorders,[74] particularly 'violent purging, even of blood',[75] for which opium was also given;[76] and it seems probable that this could have been confused with the effects of dysentery. This scenario gives added weight to the hypothesis that Faber had mercury poisoning, and it seems probable that this caused his physical deterioration and, eventually, death. It also proves that Faber was, by this time, genuinely ill and not just oversensitive or suffering from hypochondria. Faber's writing deteriorated when he was ill, and a number of letters written to Morris during this time are almost unreadable.[77] Faber mentions, but does not dwell on, ill-health in his letters to Newman, perhaps because Newman's health was generally good; but only mentions his health in letters to Morris, who was himself frequently unwell.

At the end of March 1844, Faber sent Newman three of his saints' lives for the *Lives of the English Saints*, together with the information that he was working on a further three.[78] In a covering letter, Faber described to Newman the popularity of dissent in Elton and expressed his concern that his parishioners would be led astray by it.[79] However, Faber's spiritual emphasis had also moved away from the Established Church and he was leading his parishioners towards Rome; a direction opposite to, and as contentious as, that taken by the dissenters. Rome had become Faber's ideal church, a panacea that would solve all of his problems, both pastoral and personal. He wrote, 'I feel impatient, thinking I could do all things in my parish if I were roman [*sic*], and had not my feet in the stocks of our system.'[80] In one sense this vision was, at this time, a mirage. By introducing Roman practices into his parish he had created an idealised vision of Rome within Anglicanism which could not be the same as Roman Catholicism itself. However, he had now gone beyond Tractarian principles, and had reached the stage where Anglicanism and Romanism could not co-exist. From this point onwards Faber's spirituality moved more closely towards Rome.

In July 1844, Faber spent a few days with Morris in Oxford. His return to Elton intensified feelings of isolation, solitude, loneliness, and the lack of individuals with whom he could discuss intellectual and spiritual matters.[81] He also indicated that he was not reading literature or writing poetry, both of which he considered unprofitable when compared to spiritual reading.[82] Life in Elton contrasted unfavourably with the company of Morris and his circle, and Faber wrote to Morris, 'I was amazed at ... ye boisterous mirth of all of you when I have scarcely smiled for months.'[83] Faber's introspection also had a spiritual dimension, which was a symptom of a personal as well as a doctrinal spiritual change which manifested itself in an 'unsettling sadness ... and loathing of prayer'.[84] Because of this, he indicated a wish to ask Newman to allow him to use Marian devotions as an alternative to others, which were unprofitable.[85] He believed that his mental and physical sufferings were penance for his self will,[86] and coupled this with the notion that none of his spiritual problems could be solved within the Church of England. Two statements sum up his feelings: firstly, 'O that my wretched nature had ye yoke of S. [*sic*] Ignatius laid on it: there is nothing in our system to macadamize one.'[87] Secondly, 'I sometimes get a glimpse of a state of mind which would view my position as a parish priest as that of a man telling a lie to people.'[88] During this time, Faber decided that he needed a spiritual director,[89] presumably to help him with the process of discernment, as well as to provide an individual with whom to communicate.[90]

Newman's role in Faber's conversion was as complicated as his role during other periods of Faber's life. During the timescale of this chapter, Faber's letters to Newman are formal, and show a high regard for his opinion in spiritual matters, whilst Newman's letters are sympathetic, paternal, and exhibit an interest in Faber's affairs. From September 1843 onwards, Newman had actively dissuaded Faber both from converting to Rome and from using Roman devotional practices. However, in August 1844, Faber asked him for the second time to remove his prohibition concerning the invocation of Mary.[91] Faber was always concerned to have Newman's opinion on spiritual matters. However, his 'superstitious reverence for his [Newman's] discernment'[92] caused tension, particularly when it concerned something which was a highly personal and significant part of Faber's spirituality. It also indicates that Faber was advanced on his journey towards Rome, particularly as he wrote, 'I seem to grow more Roman daily, and almost to write from out the bosom of the Roman Church.'[93] Such sentiments contradict the idea, commonly held by historians, that Faber followed Newman to Rome.

Early in August, Faber sent Newman one of his saints' lives and began writing the *Life of St Wilfrid*;[94] St Wilfrid had been, and continued to be, important to Faber throughout his life. In a letter of acknowledgement, Newman wrote that he had found doctrinal inaccuracy and bad taste, and Faber gave him permission to alter the text so that it could not be misinterpreted.[95] Faber was concerned that the eccentric isolation of Elton had made him incapable of judging what was and was not acceptable, and for this reason was willing to defer to Newman's editorial judgement.[96] He was also in a morally, spiritually and pastorally complex position, because he was mentally thinking of himself as a member of the Church of Rome.[97]

By the end of November 1844, one year before his conversion, Faber was using the Office of the Roman Breviary as well as that of the *Book of Common Prayer*.[98] He informed Newman that he could 'give no good grounds for ... staying where I am',[99] and repeated his request for permission to invoke Mary, angels and saints.[100] Newman's reply[101] expressed ecclesiological, doctrinal, and personal misgivings about Faber's private or public use of Roman devotions at Elton. Newman was concerned not to present his thoughts in the form of a prohibition, and wrote, 'I am saying this by way of showing you the grounds of my opinion, and not as forcing it upon you.'[102] Newman began by stating his 'great repugnance at mixing religions or worship together'.[103] He thought that devotions were not transferable between denominations, and wrote: 'I do not like decanting Rome into England.'[104] Thus, the fact that a devotion was being used by one church did not automatically imply that it was acceptable in another, particularly one whose ethos was essentially different.[105] Newman was also concerned that Faber was committing the cardinal Tractarian sin of private judgement by employing Roman devotions, and that this was dishonest.[106] There may also be the implication that Faber was unfairly unsettling his parishioners by doing so. Newman was concerned that Faber was being disloyal by continuing to minister as a priest in one church whilst tacitly or overtly arguing for the moral and spiritual supremacy of another. He wrote, 'I am not satisfied that our church has not a claim in such observances on the obedience of her members to her directions.'[107] Newman's admonition reminded Faber of his own fears of private judgement and self will, and he wrote, 'I believe a wish to imitate the saints has been a great snare to me.'[108] Newman concurred with this evaluation, and remarked that the invocation of saints was a temptation.[109] This exchange encapsulates the conflict between Faber's personal, intellectual, and spiritual journey, and his need to have the approval of other people. He was now trying to convince himself that the only morally secure course was to wait for others to go to Rome, and then decide whether or not to go himself.[110] However, he was obviously not succeeding, as he wrote to Newman, 'Do what I will I cannot outgrow the fear of being "damned", as out of the church.'[111]

In January 1845, Faber articulated his dissatisfaction with

Tractarianism. His primary concern was that Tractarianism had created instability and disunity within the Church of England,[112] and because of this, he expressed misgivings that he had allowed himself to become involved with the Movement. In the same month, Faber wrote to Morris that Newman and F. Oakeley had distanced themselves from him, and that their example had been followed by other Tractarians.[113] They did so because of the extreme Roman leanings expressed by Faber in his *Life of St Wilfrid*,[114] a work which fostered the idea that he was about to become a Roman Catholic.[115] These rumours were not unfounded, as Faber had briefly discussed the possibility of moving to Rome in correspondence with Bishop Wareing, Vicar Apostolic of the Eastern District, who resided in Northampton.[116] The book has biographical overtones and there are several passages in which we learn as much, possibly more, about Faber as about St Wilfrid; particularly in the idealisation of the ecclesiastical unity within the Church of Rome,[117] which may have been intended to be, either covertly or overtly, a reference to the Church of England. In a letter to Morris, Faber wrote that he had been accused of Nestorianism,[118] but does not provide details of the precise reasons for this. Faber thought that he was being made a scapegoat by Newman and Frederick Oakeley, and opined that he had been following a Tractarian lead by becoming more Roman[119] and using 'extreme practices of Roman doctrine'.[120] He wrote, somewhat indignantly, 'I have done no more, nor ½ [*sic*] as much to Romanize men's minds and unsettle them, as others have done <u>unblamed</u> …'[121]

Newman's letters to Faber contradict the lack of perspective in the latter's interpretation of the aforementioned events, and refute any suggestion that Newman had abandoned Faber. *St Wilfrid* was one part of the controversy which surrounded the *Lives of the Saints* series, not its originator; and, despite complaints about Faber's occasional lapses in taste, Newman continued to support Faber's work. He was fully aware of the controversial nature of *St Wilfrid*,[122] and wrote, 'the public has got to realise the fact that the series has a Romeward tendency'.[123] Newman was mentally and physically robust enough to cope with his share of controversy, whereas Faber was not; and Faber's reaction was to decide not to contribute anything more to the Tractarian cause. It is indicative of Faber's mindset at this time that he was able to interpret this chain of events as divinely inspired, and an excuse for a more contemplative life, albeit one within his parish at Elton.[124]

Faber's health became progressively worse during 1845.[125] Several letters mention the symptoms[126] of Bright's disease, or mercury poisoning, such as 'pain in spine',[127] 'swollen feet',[128] problems with his heart, swollen ankles and pain when standing still.[129] He wrote to Morris, 'my feet will not bear the weight of my body'[130] and indicated that he was taking laudanum[131] and 'using alum baths'[132] in an effort to combat his symptoms. Faber became ill on a visit to Oxford, and this seems attributable to conflict within his spiritual life influencing his wider health, particularly as he remarked, 'I have grave fears that if I were to die, I should be lost.'[133]

The controversy surrounding Tract XC and W. G. Ward were important contributory factors to the process of spiritual change,[134] and the combination of all of these gave added urgency to Faber's wish to make a decision about his spiritual future. The period between New Year and October 1845 was characterised by a more intense experience of the scruples which had been part of Faber's religiosity since 1842. He fluctuated between being on the point of converting to Rome and pulling himself back, and his letters portray the frustration of an individual who is able to see reasons for staying and reasons for going but cannot take the decision to do either. Faber wrote, 'do what I will to Anglicanize myself, I may go over any day'[135] and, 'I seem more Roman than ever, yet more frightened than ever at going'.[136] Concern for the spiritual welfare of his parishioners at Elton was one of Faber's main reasons for wanting to remain an Anglican.[137] This is reminiscent of the evangelical fervour of his undergraduate years at Oxford, and underlines the seriousness with which he viewed his role as pastor. It is also noticeable that he seems to have lost his earlier misgivings about remaining in the parish, although this could have been an excuse to avoid making a decision. A further reason for staying was that Faber did not have any confidence in P. C. Claughton, his predecessor[138] and elected successor at Elton,[139] although he does not elaborate on these concerns.[140] Faber's reasons for moving to Rome were more theological in their emphasis, but still related to his position as leader. In June, he began to have scruples about the validity of his Orders,[141] and it seems significant that this concern became important to him whilst he was still an Anglican, rather than retrospectively. This shows how Roman Faber's mindset had become, and that he was already thinking along Roman lines.[142] Faber was also uncertain about the validity of his consecration of the sacrament,[143] a concern which provided the bargaining point of this phase of Faber's conversion. In June, he wrote that he was ready to leave the Church, both place and institution, if he sensed during the service that what he was doing was invalid, a scenario which did not happen at this time.[144]

On 5 October, Faber wrote Newman a letter in which he sought reassurance, and, although Newman still would not make any decisions for Faber, he did empathise with Faber's position. Faber had known for some time that Newman's conversion was imminent;[145] however, he did not realise that it was only five days away. Faber's letter was concerned with the pros and cons of Roman Catholicism and Anglicanism,[146] although any sense of balance is immediately compromised by the remark, 'my affections are with the Rom[an] Ch[urch] – my attractions towards Rom[an] Doctrine'.[147] Faber put forward several points for Newman's consideration, the first of which was that he was not convinced that the Church of England was schismatic as such, but thought that the toleration of heresy undermined its teaching.[148] His major reason for remaining within the Anglican Church was that he felt that the work he was doing at Elton was important, writing 'God seems to have been more with me since I came here, than ever he was before.'[149] However, Faber was concerned that the work had been carried out using Roman methods, such as the use of St Ignatius' *Spiritual Exercises*, and he asked Newman if this had been dishonest. Faber was using Ignatian methods of discernment to question his own spiritual motives, with the result that he had become concerned that his spiritual angst was a sign that the Church of Rome was a temptation[150] rather than an inspiration from God.[151] There was also tension in Faber's mind between the desire for Newman's approval, and advice which had already been given by Pusey, whose influence had always been more congenial to Faber than that of Newman. Pusey remained within the Church of England after the Tractarian exodus, and his advice that Faber should not leave the Church in which he had been born[152] provided Faber with a further layer of difficulty. It seems probable that Faber had already decided that he would not remain an Anglican, and therefore pushed Pusey's influence into the background and brought Newman's influence to the fore. Perhaps at one level he knew that Newman was more likely to convert than Pusey, and hoped that Newman's actions would crystallise his own thinking.

Newman became a Roman Catholic on 9 October 1845, and Faber reacted to the news with a profound sense of betrayal.[153] Faber was particularly affected by a phrase in Newman's circular letter in which he described Roman Catholicism as the 'one true fold'.[154] We have seen that Faber had been more or less convinced of this notion three years earlier, and had, from that time, been haunted by the possibility that the Church of England was schismatic. It is significant that it was separation from Newman, rather than any other doctrinal factor, which finally resolved Faber's three-year period of doubt about the nature of Anglicanism. Faber had described Newman as 'the greatest scholar and divine since St Augustine',[155] and he wrote to Morris, 'Surely, when <u>such</u> a man so words it, a sheep's 1st [*sic*] duty is to see if he has really wandered.'[156] However, Faber also felt that Newman had been spiritually and intellectually dishonest by keeping him from converting in both 1843 and 1844,[157] and he wrote, 'it was your staying with us which retained me ... and now that you are gone and I am left behind I feel as if I may have been doing wrong'.[158] The primary significance of Newman's conversion, from a wider historical point of view, was that it changed Faber's position from an individual who was part of the vanguard of potential conversions to Rome, to one in the rearguard, an imitator of Newman. However, as we have seen, it would be historically inaccurate and far too simplistic to think of Faber merely as an imitator of Newman, despite his excessive concern to have Newman's approval. It is possible that Newman prevented Faber from converting because he wanted to lead the move to Rome rather than follow younger more extreme individuals, such as Faber. However, it seems more likely that he wanted to be part of a movement which was based on intellectual reasoning rather than on impulsive whims, however doctrinally centred. Newman clearly understood, and possibly mistrusted, Faber's volatile and impulsive temperament, and wished to keep him from making an over-hasty decision which would lead to loss of his income and position in society. Faber replied to Newman's circular letter, but indicated to Morris that his letter had not been answered, and wrote: 'I suppose he thinks I have asked indelicate questions.'[159] This comment indicates that Faber had misunderstood and overreacted to Newman's silence by attributing it to coldness, despite Newman's closing words: 'believe the great affection I have for you'.[160] It is significant that a letter written by Newman later in November 1845 contains the line 'I should have spoken to you about your mistrusting me, had it gone on.'[161] Clearly, both men were equally capable of misunderstanding, and being misinterpreted by, the other.

Letters written by Faber between 9 October and 10 November 1845 are characterised by stress, nervous tension, and an overpowering sense of indecision. Faber was now reluctant to give the impression that he wished to convert only because Newman had already done so,[162] and he reminded Newman that he had been drawn towards Rome in 1844 and the early part of 1845.[163] The phrase, 'I have never had anything like permanent peace of mind upon the subject'[164] explains the uncharacteristic caution behind Faber's decision to give himself a further nine months, until June 1846, to decide what to do.[165] However, caution was not Faber's natural *modus operandi*, and at one level he had already decided what to do: 'I feel calmest when most resolved to go.'[166] He re-affirmed the idea that, as an Anglican, he had been dishonest by teaching his congregation using Roman devotions, and it seems possible that Newman's prompting had encouraged this decision.[167] However, Faber excused himself by saying that he did so because he was unable to find comparable devotions in Anglican literature. 'I was using the spiritual riches of, what is amongst us, a despised hated minority, and at the same time enjoying the temporal station and ease of the establishment.'[168] It is notable, and revealing of Faber's mindset at this time, that he was concerned that the process of moving to Rome would entail the renunciation of his priesthood, and carry the implication that the work which he had done as an Anglican was worthless; a scenario which he was reluctant to admit to himself or encourage in others.[169] Faber was not at this stage in his spiritual development concerned with argument, and questions such as whether the Anglican Church was Apostolic were secondary to his own personal concerns.

Faber's closeness to the Church of Rome was underscored by a general interest in post-Reformation theology, and subscription to the doctrines of the counter-Reformation Council of Trent.[170] He was now on a course which was theologically divergent from that taken by Pusey, and was impatient with Pusey's refusal to take any form of decision regarding the Church of Rome.[171] Towards the end of October, Faber discussed the Thirty-Nine Articles in a letter to Morris. Morris had indicated to Faber that he had scruples about converting because of the contents of six of the Articles; conversely, Faber wanted to convert because he could no longer give assent to the same six Articles, as well as to the Oath of Supremacy.[172] In the background to this debate is an idea which we discussed during Chapter 2, that is, that the Articles' main function is to negate the doctrines of the Church of Rome, rather than to provide a positive statement of Anglican orthodoxy.[173] Faber's difficulty was that he was now in a position to affirm the doctrines of Rome, and therefore he disagreed with a number of matters of Anglican doctrine in these Articles, such as the prohibition against invoking saints.[174] The idea of authority was a recurring theme during Faber's life, and it is notable that the majority of Articles in this group are concerned with the authority of the Church versus that of the State.[175]

At the beginning of November Faber travelled to Littlemore for a meeting with Newman.[176] Newman was not the only ex-Anglican at Littlemore,[177] and it seems probable that being in the presence of other individuals who had already moved to Rome was as important an influence on Faber as that of Newman. In a letter written after his return to Elton, Faber informed Newman of his concern that morale was low among Anglicans of his acquaintance,[178] such as his brother, Francis Atkinson Faber,[179] and Thomas Francis Knox, an undergraduate at Trinity

College, Cambridge, who had provided Faber with a view from Cambridge which complimented that from Oxford.[180] On Sunday, 9 November 1845, Faber gave Communion for the last time as an Anglican, as he had now concluded that both his priesthood and the Sacraments that he was giving had no intrinsic validity.[181] J. B. Morris was also critical of Anglicanism, and, because of his own situation, Faber expressed the hope that Morris would also move to Rome.[182] Morris's entry in the *Dictionary of National Biography* records that he converted in the wake of Newman;[183] however, it seems more likely that we can ascribe Morris's Romeward leanings mainly to the influence of Faber. It is noticeable that Faber had now ceased to be sympathetic towards Anglicanism, and the imminence of his departure gave him the freedom to leave rhetoric aside and be outspoken in his criticisms. He wrote, 'Poor Church of England! There will be a sliding, slippery treason in her camp henceforth to the end.'[184] On his return to Elton, Faber made the final decision to move to the Church of Rome. He wrote a positive letter to Newman in which he ascribed his newly-found resolve and calmness solely to the latter's influence.[185] The tone of this letter, and Faber's state of mind whilst writing it, are perfectly summed up by the following: 'I have been so very, very happy since my visit to you ... and intend to put all doubts away ... as ... temptations, which I am sure they are.'[186] Despite his resolve, Faber decided to put off the actual moment of change until Epiphany 1846,[187] a decision which underlines the intense psychological difficulties inherent within the process of change that was taking place.

On Tuesday, 11 November, the day after he promised that he would wait, Faber informed Newman that even discussing the move to the Church of Rome was incompatible with carrying on the duties of an Anglican clergyman,[188] and therefore he wished to move as soon as possible. We have noted Faber's indecision, and have seen that his inability to decide for himself when to convert was one of the factors in his becoming one of the last instead of one of the first to move. It is undoubtedly significant that the final decision was suggested by a letter received from an acquaintance in Italy, who opined that Faber should be received into the Roman Church at Ushaw.[189] This letter is not extant; however, it seems probable that the acquaintance was Wiseman, who had attended Ushaw.[190]

Although he did not follow the advice to the letter, Faber chose to interpret it as significant because of the association of his family with Durham. He also decided that he had been given permission to act: 'this will be a law to me; particularly as one likes to have such things suggested from without'.[191] There are Ignatian overtones in Faber's belief that the suggestion was divine in origin because it had come from outside himself, and he wrote, 'I feel very happy at the thought of so soon being, by God's mercy, where my sympathies have so long been.'[192] This charge also allowed Faber to disregard the fear of one of his most enduring sins, that of self will.

On Saturday, 15 November, Faber informed Newman that he had made arrangements to travel to Northampton on the following Monday, in order to be received into the Roman Church by Bishop Wareing, at Northampton. Faber was not alone, as his policy of introducing Roman devotions at Elton had resulted in seven of his parishioners wishing to convert with him;[193] and at one level, Faber's indecision had been replaced by the camaraderie and enthusiasm of plan-making with this group.[194] At a deeper and more personal level, Faber's physical illness was coupled with mental and spiritual turmoil. The depth of this is indicated by his phrase 'If I dared, I would pray God to take me to himself',[195] and, unlike previous occasions, there is no sense that Faber was exaggerating or choosing his words only for dramatic effect. He questioned whether he was able to cope with the emotional strain of his final service as an Anglican priest on the following day;[196] however, it seems probable that he was aware that he was only going through the motions of taking a service, and using it as a vehicle for saying goodbye to his parishioners. On Sunday morning, 16 November, Faber was unable to continue with his sermon, 'from the text Ruth 1:16–17 ... hastily descended from the pulpit, threw his surplice to the ground and quitted the church'.[197] The events of these two days underline the central problem and difficulty with the latter part of the process of Faber's spiritual change; he remained at Elton despite his doubts, rather than retiring in order to resolve them, as Newman had done at Oxford. Obviously Newman was a more public figure than Faber; however, both had influence, albeit at different levels and among different groups. Faber had involved his parishioners in his private spiritual indecision which was, even at this late stage, only partially submerged and imperfectly resolved. He wrote, 'I ... can see no reason for going, and such a horror of Roman people and things that it almost seems as if I should draw back at the last.'[198]

Faber left Elton on Monday, 17 November. He wrote to Morris of 'ye intense and fiery struggle which began on ye Tuesday and only ended in ye violent hysterical fits of ye Monday morning following'.[199] To Newman he described his hysteria and fear, caused primarily by the decision to move but exacerbated by harrowing scenes with his parishioners,[200] who were concerned only that he had been a good pastor, and not with the theological niceties of his position. On the same day, Faber travelled to Northampton, where he was received into the Roman Catholic Church.[201] He wrote: 'Arrived at Northampton at ten, and made our profession of faith; at night we made our general confessions and received conditional baptism, and on Tuesday [18 November] we were confirmed[202] and communicated.'[203] In the days that followed, Faber presented his move to Roman Catholicism as the attainment of an ideal and a resolution of his spiritual difficulties, after which 'every hour now seems to dispel doubts, and so to augment inward peace'.[204] He legitimised, rather than analysed, his indecision as to whether or not to go with the remark 'on looking back I see nothing in the step, or in the approaches to it, which I regret'.[205]

A number of Faber's acquaintances did not find it so easy to reconcile themselves to his conversion. Among these were Wordsworth, and Pusey who objected in particular to Faber's comment that 'ye very step I had taken implied ye highest disaffection, if not positive aversion to ye Engl[ish] Ch[urch]'.[206] The majority of Faber's former parishioners were favourable towards him.[207] However, he caused controversy in some circles because two of those who followed him were under twenty-one,[208] and this led to a certain amount of anti-Catholic polemic. Lord Carysfort was particularly displeased because one of Faber's converts was his grandson, Frederick Wells, an undergraduate at Trinity College, Cambridge, with T. F. Knox. Faber wrote to Newman, 'L[or]d Carysfort's steward has written to me to say that if I come to Elton just now, there would be an *auto da fe*, in which I should play a painfully conspicuous part.'[209]

In a letter to the *Northampton Mercury*, the Revd G. S. Robinson satirised the events leading up to Faber's conversion, and rebuked him for dishonesty because he had continued to minister as a clergyman despite his doubts about the Church of England.[210] Robinson expressed awareness of Faber's long-standing espousal of Tractarian Anglicanism, although he was clearly not aware that Faber had distanced himself from the Movement at the beginning of 1845. He wrote that the 'miserable Jesuitical shuffling of Tract XC'[211] had proved beyond doubt that the Tractarians had been, whilst Anglicans, supporters of the Roman Church; and that this had been proved by the secession to Rome of several of Faber's parishioners. Faber's language in reply[212] to this letter is significantly lighter in tone, more positive, assured and intellectually sophisticated than that which he used in his letters to Morris and Newman during this period. He vindicated himself in terms which caused Robinson to retract his criticisms of Faber's personal sincerity and of his conduct towards his parish, although he did not retract those of Tractarianism or of Roman Catholicism.[213] It is significant that although Faber admitted to being retrospectively aware of the Roman tendencies of 'Puseyism', he indicated that he had not been aware of it earlier.[214] He wrote, 'I acted bona fide, fully believing that what I taught was more in accordance with the prayer book than the opinions of any other Anglican party, and was for the good of the English Church.'[215] It is possible that Faber had been naive and short-sighted in making this assumption; however, he indicated that he was now convinced that his move to Rome had been the only natural progression from Tractarianism.[216] Faber excused his treatment of his parishioners by stating that, during the period leading up to his conversion, he had not shared his doubts with his parishioners, and would not allow them to confess to him because of them.[217] He also wrote that during this time he re-used sermons from 1837 and 1838, as he could rely on these being doctrinally orthodox and not betraying his spiritual doubts.[218] We saw earlier in this chapter that Faber went away from familiar surroundings whenever he had to make a difficult decision, and he seems to have thought that he had helped his parishioners by staying away from Elton during the week immediately preceding his conversion.[219] Faber also made the, possibly arrogant, assumption that other people would automatically agree with and follow whatever decision he made, a trait that returns at strategic moments throughout his life.

Our knowledge, particularly of Faber's interpretation of Anglicanism, and the blurring of distinctions between it and Roman Catholicism, shows that Anglicanism was not merely an unimportant preamble to Faber's Roman Catholic period; a point which proves beyond doubt that Anglicanism formed Faber's spirituality.

Notes

1 Moorman highlights an interesting connection with Wordsworth, in that Matthew Harrison's mother, 'Mrs Benson Harrison was Dorothy Wordsworth, daughter of Wordsworth's cousin Robinson Wordsworth of Whitehaven'. M. Moorman (1968), *William Wordsworth: A Biography* Vol. 2, Oxford, OUP, p. 479, n. 2.

2 The first part of this tour had taken place between February and September 1841.

3 See F. W. Faber to J. B. Morris, LO, Vol. 17, No. 62, 11 August 1843, in which he comments that he did not keep a journal, to 'keep myself from writing a book'.

4 F. W. Faber to J. B. Morris, LO, Vol. 17, No. 60, 20 May 1843.

5 Ibid.

6 Ibid.

7 Ibid.

8 Ibid.

9 Ibid.

10 Ibid.

11 Ibid.

12 Ibid.

13 Ibid.

14 Ibid.

15 Ibid.

16 F. W. Faber to J. B. Morris, LO, Vol. 17, No. 61, 17 June 1843.

17 F. W. Faber to J. B. Morris, LO, Vol. 17, No. 60, 20 May 1843.

18 Ibid.

19 Ibid.

20 F. W. Faber to F. A. Faber, 27 May 1843, in Bowden, *Life*, Letter XXXXVII, p. 160.

21 Ibid. p. 162.

22 Ibid. p. 161.
23 Ibid.
24 Ibid.
25 Ibid. pp. 161–2.
26 F. W. Faber to J. B. Morris, LO, Vol. 17, No. 61, 1st Sunday after Trinity (17 June) 1843.
27 W. Walsh (1897), *The Secret History of the Oxford Movement*, London, Swan Sonnenschein & Co. Ltd, p. 30.
28 Ibid. pp. 30–2.
29 Bowden, *Life*, p. 175, quoted ibid. p. 32.
30 F. W. Faber to J. B. Morris, LO, Vol. 17, No. 61, 1st Sunday after Trinity (17 June) 1843.
31 Ibid.
32 Ibid.
33 Ibid.
34 Ibid. Pusey's sermon *The Holy Eucharist* was written during 1843.
35 Ibid.
36 Ibid.
37 F. W. Faber to J. B. Morris, LO, Vol. 17, No. 60, 20 May 1843.
38 F. W. Faber to J. B. Morris, LO, Vol. 17, No. 61, 1st Sunday after Trinity (17 June) 1843.
39 Ibid.
40 Ibid.
41 F. W. Faber to J. B. Morris, LO, Vol. 17, No. 62, 11 August 1843.
42 Ibid.
43 Ibid.
44 See Faber's reference to the scandal that crises in the Church cause to 'plain thinking people' in letter to J. B. Morris, LO, Vol. 17, No. 31, 17 June 1843.
45 F. W. Faber to J. B. Morris, LO, Vol. 17, No. 62, 11 August 1843.
46 Ibid.
47 Ibid.
48 J. H. Newman to F. W. Faber, LO, Vol. 8, No. 7, Advent Sunday (1 December) 1844.
49 J. H. Newman to F. W. Faber, LO, Vol. 8, No. 5, 2 September 1843.
50 F. W. Faber to J. B. Morris, LO, Vol. 17, No. 63, 30 September 1843; F. W. Faber to J. H. Newman, LO, Vol. 8, No. 6, 30 September 1843.
51 F. W. Faber to J. B. Morris, LO, Vol. 17, No. 62, 11 August 1843; LO, Vol. 17, No. 63, 30 September 1843; LO, Vol. 17, No. 64, 15 December 1843, all of which mention the dysentery which he contracted whilst in Italy.
52 F. W. Faber to J. B. Morris, LO, Vol. 17, No. 62, 11 August 1843.
53 F. W. Faber to J. B. Morris, LO, Vol. 17, No. 63, 30 September 1843.
54 F. W. Faber to J. H. Newman, LO, Vol. 17, No. 63, 30 September 1843.

55 Exactly two years before Newman's conversion, on 9 October 1845.
56 Chapman, *Father Faber*, p. 82.
57 F. W. Faber, *Two Faiths*, LXXXIII, in *Poems*, p. 247.
58 Ibid.
59 Ibid.
60 The only evidence we have for this is Faber's copy of the *Spiritual Exercises*, which is dated Vigil of St Peter, 29 June (the day after Faber's 29th birthday) 1843.
61 See Faber's comments to Newman, LO, Vol. 1, No. 13, 5 October 1845.
62 In a wider historical context, it is significant that the spirituality of both Ignatius and Faber stressed the emotional effects of devotion.
63 This is particularly noticeable in *The Precious Blood* (London, 1860).
64 The retreatant is advised to imagine themselves in a particular scene from scripture and to formulate their responses to it. For an example of this, see the contemplation for Day One of Week Three of the *Spiritual Exercises*, in, J. A. Munitiz and P. Endean (1996), *Saint Ignatius of Loyola, Personal Writings*, London, Penguin, pp. 321–2.
65 F. W. Faber to J. B. Morris, LO, Vol. 17, No. 67, 17 April 1844; F. W. Faber to J. H. Newman, LO, Vol. 1, No. 4, 9 April 1844.
66 F. W. Faber to J. B. Morris, LO, Vol. 17, No. 71, 9 August 1844.
67 F. W. Faber to J. B. Morris, LO, Vol. 17, No. 74, 3 December 1844.
68 F. W. Faber to J. H. Newman, LO, Vol. 1, No. 9, 28 September 1844.
69 F. W. Faber to J. B. Morris, LO, Vol. 17, No. 73, 5 October 1844.
70 Ibid.
71 Ibid.
72 Entry for Gray [*sic*] Powder (Hydrargyrum cum creta) in R. Hoblyn (1892), *Hoblyn's Dictionary of Medical Terms* (London) p. 318.
73 F. W. Faber to J. B. Morris, LO, Vol. 17, No. 62, 11 August 1843. LO, Vol. 17, No. 64, 15 December 1843.
74 Entry for Pilulae Hydrargyri: Mercurial or Blue Pills, in R. Hooper (ed.) (1839), *Lexicon Medicum* (London, 7th edn) p. 1034.
75 Entry for mercury, ibid. p. 889.
76 Ibid.
77 A good example is his letter to J. B. Morris, LO, Vol. 17, No. 67, 17 April 1844.
78 Those completed were Ss Paulinus, Edwin and Ethelburga. Those in progress were Ss Oswald, Oswin and Ebba. F. W. Faber to J. H. Newman, LO, Vol. 8, No. 6, 27 March 1844.
79 Ibid.

80 Ibid.
81 F. W. Faber to J. B. Morris, LO, Vol. 17, No. 70, 17 July 1844.
82 Ibid.
83 Ibid.
84 Ibid.
85 Ibid. See also F. W. Faber to J. H. Newman, LO, Vol. 1, No. 5, 12 August 1844.
86 F. W. Faber to J. B. Morris, LO, Vol. 17, No. 70, 17 July 1844.
87 Ibid.
88 F. W. Faber to J. H. Newman, LO, Vol. 1, No. 5, 12 August 1844.
89 F. W. Faber to J. B. Morris, LO, Vol. 17, No. 70, 17 July 1844.
90 Faber's spiritual director was the Revd Michael Watts Russell, although Faber does not indicate precisely when he acquired him as director.
91 F. W. Faber to J. H. Newman, LO, Vol. 1, No. 5, 12 August 1844.
92 F. W. Faber to J. B. Morris, LO, Vol. 17, No. 68, 10 May 1844.
93 F. W. Faber to J. H. Newman, LO, Vol. 1, No. 5, 12 August 1844.
94 For the correspondence between Faber and Newman relating to the *Life* of St Wilfrid, see F. W. Faber to J. H. Newman, LO, Vol. 1, No. 7, 7 September 1844; LO, Vol. 1, No. 8, dated between 8 September and 27 September 1844; LO, Vol. 1, No. 9, 28 September 1844.
95 F. W. Faber to J. H. Newman, LO, Vol. 1, No. 5, 12 August 1844.
96 Ibid. See also F. W. Faber to J. H. Newman, LO, Vol. 1, No. 7, 7 September 1844.
97 F. W. Faber to J. H. Newman, LO, Vol. 1, No. 5, 12 August 1844.
98 F. W. Faber to J. H. Newman, LO, Vol. 1, No. 12, 12 December 1844.
99 F. W. Faber to J. H. Newman, LO, Vol. 1, No. 10, 28 November 1844.
100 Ibid.
101 J. H. Newman to F. W. Faber, LO, Vol. 8, No. 7, Advent Sunday (1 December) 1844.
102 Ibid.
103 Ibid.
104 Ibid.
105 Ibid.
106 Ibid.
107 Ibid.
108 F. W. Faber to J. H. Newman, LO, Vol. 1, No. 11, 3 December 1844.
109 F. W. Faber to J. H. Newman, LO, Vol. 1, No. 12, 12 December 1844.
110 Ibid.
111 Ibid.
112 F. W. Faber to J. B. Morris, LO, Vol. 17, No. 75, 29 January 1845.
113 Ibid.

114 F. W. Faber (1844) *Lives of the English Saints: St Wilfrid, Bishop of York*, London, Toovey.

115 F. W. Faber to J. B. Morris, LO, Vol. 17, No. 75, 29 January 1845.

116 F. W. Faber to Bishop Wareing, Feast of St Agnes (21 January) 1845, in Bowden, *Life*, Letter LIX, pp. 193–4.

117 F. W. Faber (1844), *Lives of the English Saints: St Wilfrid, Bishop of York*, London, Toovey, p. 5.

118 F. W. Faber to J. B. Morris, LO, Vol. 17, No. 82, 1 June 1845.

119 See also F. W. Faber to J. B. Morris, LO, Vol. 17, No. 87, 24 October 1845.

120 Ibid.

121 F. W. Faber to J. B. Morris, LO, Vol. 17, No. 75, 29 January 1845.

122 J. H. Newman to F. W. Faber, LO, Vol. 8, No. 9, 22 January 1845.

123 J. H. Newman to F. W. Faber, LO, Vol. 8, No. 10, 31 January 1845.

124 F. W. Faber to J. B. Morris, LO, Vol. 17, No. 75, 29 January 1845.

125 F. W. Faber to J. B. Morris, LO, Vol. 17, No. 78, Feast of St Scholasticae (10 February) 1845; LO, Vol. 17, No. 79, Tuesday after Passion Sunday (11 March) 1845; LO, Vol. 17, No. 87, 24 October 1845.

126 F. W. Faber to J. H. Newman, LO, Vol. 1, No. 15, 24 October 1845.

127 F. W. Faber to J. B. Morris, LO, Vol. 17, No. 91, n.d. – note in pencil reads 'before November 1845'.

128 F. W. Faber to J. B. Morris, LO, Vol. 17, No. 92, n.d. – note in pencil reads 'before November 1845'.

129 F. W. Faber to J. B. Morris, LO, Vol. 17, No. 83, 25 June 1845.

130 Ibid.

131 F. W. Faber to J. B. Morris, LO, Vol. 17, No. 93, n.d. – note in pencil reads 'before November 1845'.

132 F. W. Faber to J. B. Morris, LO, Vol. 17, No. 83, 28 June 1845.

133 Godwin, *Personal Recollections*, p. 212.

134 Ibid.

135 F. W. Faber to J. B. Morris, LO, Vol. 17, No. 77, Sexagesima Sunday (26 January) 1845.

136 F. W. Faber to J. B. Morris, LO, Vol. 17, No. 79, Tuesday after Passion Sunday (11 March) 1845.

137 Ibid.

138 The register of incumbents in Elton parish church records that P. C. Claughton (1814–1884) was Rector before Faber (1842–1843) and after Faber (1845–1860). This information is also given in R. F. Whistler (1892), *The History of Ailington, Aylton or Elton*, London, Mitchell & Hughes, p. 36. However, the information that Claughton was Rector before Faber is not given in either the

1924 or 2004 articles for P. C. Claughton in the DNB. Both arti-
cles state that he was based in Oxford as public examiner in
Classics (1842–1844) until his move to Elton to replace Faber,
and that he was at Elton from 1845 until 1859. See C. W. Sutton,
P. C. Claughton (1814–1884), in DNB (Oxford, OUP, 1921–22)
Vol. IV, pp. 458–9, and C. W. Sutton, revised Katherine Prior, *P.
C. Claughton (1814–1884)*, in DNB (Oxford, OUP, 2004) Vol. 11,
pp. 949–50. The parish of Elton was a living attached to
University College, Oxford. Whistler notes that the incumbents
of Elton, including Faber and Claughton, were all academically
competent, a direct result of the association of UCO with Elton.
See R. F. Whistler (1892), *The History of Ailington, Aylton or Elton*,
London, Mitchell and Hughes, p. 36.

139 F. W. Faber to J. B. Morris, LO, Vol. 17, No. 79, Tuesday after
Passion Sunday (11 March) 1845. P. C. Claughton (1814–1884)
was elected Faber's successor on 30 October 1844, because Faber
had informed his bishop that he was seriously contemplating
converting to Roman Catholicism.

140 Claughton's predecessor had been an absentee incumbent. See
Godwin, *Personal Recollections*, p. 208.

141 F. W. Faber to J. B. Morris, LO, Vol. 17, No. 82, 1 June 1845.

142 The controversy over Anglican Orders did not receive prominence until 1870.

143 F. W. Faber to J. B. Morris, LO, Vol. 17, No. 83, 25 June 1845.

144 F. W. Faber to J. B. Morris, LO, Vol. 17, No. 82, 1 June 1845.

145 F. W. Faber to J. H. Newman, LO, Vol. 1, No. 16, 28 October
1845.

146 F. W. Faber to J. H. Newman, LO, Vol. 1, No. 13, 5 October
1845.

147 Ibid.

148 Ibid.

149 Ibid.

150 For St Ignatius, unsettled emotions were a sign of temptation.
See Annotations 9 and 10 of the *Spiritual Exercises*, in J. A. Munitiz
and P. Endean (1996), *Saint Ignatius of Loyola, Personal Writings*,
pp. 284–5.

151 F. W. Faber to J. H. Newman, LO, Vol. 1, No. 13, 5 October
1845.

152 Ibid.

153 J. B. Morris was staying with Faber at Elton when Newman's
letter arrived. Godwin's narrative provides details of the shock
that affected him and Faber on reading the news that Newman
had converted. See Godwin, *Personal Recollections*, p. 210.

154 J. H. Newman to F. W. Faber, LO, Vol. 8, No. 11, 8 October
1845.

155 Godwin, *Personal Recollections*, p. 206.

156 F. W. Faber to J. B. Morris, LO, Vol. 17, No. 87, 24 October
1845.

157 Ibid.

158 Ibid.

159 F. W. Faber to J. B. Morris, LO, Vol. 17, No. 86, 21 October 1845.

160 J. H. Newman to F. W. Faber, LO, Vol. 8, No. 11, 8 October 1845.

161 J. H. Newman to F. W. Faber, LO, Vol. 8, No. 14, 22 November 1845.

162 F. W. Faber to J. H. Newman, LO, Vol. 1, No. 15, 24 October 1845; F. W. Faber to J. H. Newman, LO, Vol. 1, No. 16, 28 October 1845.

163 F. W. Faber to J. H. Newman, LO, Vol. 1, No. 16, 28 October 1845.

164 Ibid.

165 F. W. Faber to J. H. Newman, LO, Vol. 1, No. 14, 11 October 1845. 28 June 1846 was Faber's 32nd birthday.

166 F. W. Faber to J. H. Newman, LO, Vol. 1, No. 15, 24 October 1845.

167 J. H. Newman to F. W. Faber, LO, Vol. 8, No. 7, Advent Sunday (1 December) 1844.

168 F. W. Faber to J. H. Newman, LO, Vol. 1, No. 16, 28 October 1845.

169 F. W. Faber to Bishop Wareing, 14 October 1845, in Bowden, *Life*, Letter LXI, p. 196; and Bishop Wareing to F. W. Faber (no number), in Bowden, *Life*, n.d., p. 197.

170 F. W. Faber to J. B. Morris, LO, Vol. 17, No. 86, 21 October 1845.

171 Ibid.

172 Ibid. The Articles in question were: 14: *On Works of Supererogation*; 19: *Of the Church*; 21: *Of the Authority of General Councils*; 22: *Of Purgatory*; 24: *Of Speaking in the Congregation in such a Tongue as the People understandeth*; and 31: *Of the One Oblation of Christ finished upon the Cross.*

173 Ibid.

174 Article 22.

175 Article 21.

176 F. W. Faber to J. H. Newman, LO, Vol. 1, No. 18, 2 November 1845.

177 Other converts at Littlemore included J. B. D. Dalgairns (1818–1876), T. F. Knox (1822–1882), Ambrose St John (1815–1875), and Frederick Oakeley (1802–1880). The first three became Oratorians.

178 F. W. Faber to J. H. Newman, LO, Vol. 1, No. 19, 10 November 1845.

179 Revd Francis Atkinson Faber (1804–1876), remained within the Church of England.

180 F. W. Faber to J. H. Newman, LO, Vol. 1, No. 19, 10 November 1845.

181 Godwin, *Personal Recollections*, p. 212.
182 F. W. Faber to J. B. Morris, LO, Vol. 17, No. 97, 21 November 1845.
183 W. A. G. [*sic*] *J. B. Morris (1812–1880)*, in DNB (Oxford, OUP, 1921–22) Vol. XIII, pp. 996–7.
184 F. W. Faber to J. H. Newman, LO, Vol. 1, No. 19, 10 November 1845.
185 Ibid.
186 Ibid.
187 Ibid.
188 F. W. Faber to J. H. Newman, LO, Vol. 1, No. 28, 11 November 1845. See also Newman's reply to this letter: J. H. Newman to F. W. Faber, LO, Vol. 8, No. 13, 12 November 1845, in which he replied 'I do not see any objection to your acting at once as you propose'.
189 F. W. Faber to J. H. Newman, LO, Vol. 1, No. 28, 11 November 1845.
190 C. K. [*sic*] *N. Wiseman (1802–1865)*, in DNB (Oxford, OUP, 1922) Vol. XXI, p. 714.
191 F. W. Faber to J. H. Newman, LO, Vol. 1, No. 28, 11 November 1845.
192 Ibid.
193 F. W. Faber to J. H. Newman, LO, Vol. 1, No. 16, 28 October 1845. See also F. W. Faber to J. H. Newman, LO, Vol. 1, No. 28, 15 November 1845, in which he discusses the conversions of a number of members of his Elton parish.
194 F. W. Faber to J. H. Newman, LO, Vol. 1, No. 30, 15 November 1845.
195 Ibid.
196 Ibid.
197 R. F. Whistler (1892), *The History of Ailington, Aylton or Elton*, London, Mitchell and Hughes, p. 51.
198 F. W. Faber to J. H. Newman, LO, Vol. 1, No. 30, 15 November 1845.
199 F. W. Faber to J. B. Morris, LO, Vol. 17, No. 96, 19 November 1845.
200 F. W. Faber to J. H. Newman, LO, Vol. 1, No. 32, 19 November 1845.
201 Faber was received into the Roman Catholic Church with T. F. Knox (1822–1882) and one of his parishioners.
202 Faber took the name Wilfrid at his Confirmation. See Bowden, *Life*, p. 202.
203 F. W. Faber to J. H. Newman, LO, Vol. 1, No. 32, 19 November 1845.
204 F. W. Faber to J. B. Morris, LO, Vol. 17, No. 96, 19 November 1845.
205 F. W. Faber to J. H. Newman, LO, Vol. 1, No. 32, 19 November 1845.

206 F. W. Faber to J. B. Morris, in Bowden, *Life,* Letter LXIV, Feast of St Birinus (5 December) 1845, pp. 203–4. See also F. W. Faber to J. H. Newman, LO, Vol. 1, No. 36, 4 December 1845, in which Faber recalls his words to Pusey and the latter's reaction.

207 Godwin, *Personal Recollections*, pp. 212–14. See also R. F. Whistler (1892), *The History of Ailington, Aylton or Elton*, London, Mitchell and Hughes, p. 494.

208 The controversy between Faber and the father of William (17) and James (16) Pitts is detailed in the following letters: F. W. Faber to J. H. Newman, LO, Vol. 1, No. 34, 21 November 1845; LO, Vol. 1, No. 36, 4 December 1845; LO, Vol. 1, No. 38, 10 December 1845; LO, Vol. 1, No. 40, 12 December 1845; LO, Vol. 1, No. 41, 16 December 1845. See also J. H. Newman to F. W. Faber, LO, Vol. 8, No. 13, 12 November 1845; LO, Vol. 8, No. 14, 22 November 1845; LO, Vol. 8, No. 15, 15 December 1845; LO, Vol. 8, No. 18, 11 December 1845; LO, Vol. 8, No. 19, 14 December 1845; LO, Vol. 8, No. 16, 18 December 1845. See also letter from the Revd G. S. Robinson to *Northampton Mercury*, in 'Recent Secessions 1845–6, Mr. Faber', *Oxford and Cambridge Review* (1845) p. 61. [Hereafter referred to as *Recent Secessions*.]

209 F. W. Faber to J. H. Newman, LO, Vol. 1, No. 36, 4 December 1845.

210 Robinson was not the only individual to accuse Faber of dishonesty. See W. Walsh (1897), *The Secret History of the Oxford Movement*, London, Swan Sonnenschein & Co. Ltd, p. 41.

211 Revd G. S. Robinson to *Northampton Mercury*, in *Recent Secessions*, p. 61.

212 There are five letters in total: three from Robinson and two from Faber. See *Recent Secessions*, pp. 61–8.

213 Revd G. S. Robinson to F. W. Faber, in *Recent Secessions*, p. 64.

214 F. W. Faber to Revd G. S. Robinson, ibid. p. 62.

215 Ibid.

216 Ibid. pp. 66–7.

217 Ibid. p. 62.

218 Ibid.

219 Ibid. p. 63.

Chapter 4

Post conversion:
November 1845–September 1863

Stage Five of Faber's spiritual development:
December 1845–December 1847

After his conversion, Faber stayed at St Mary's College, Oscott, the Monastery of the Passionists[1] at Ashton Hall and St Chad's Cathedral, Birmingham. On 19 December, he moved to a house at 77 Caroline Street, Birmingham, to form a religious Order, the Brothers of the Will of God, or Wilfridians, with three individuals who had moved to the Church of Rome with him. In a letter written during the same evening, in which he informed Newman that six other individuals would be joining him on the following day, he wrote,

> I have this night taken possession of my little monastery ... Ye room which is to be ye chapel is full of filth, but we reared our dear Elton crucifix on a chair amid ye dirt, and recited ... ye prayers for England by way of an inauguration. [2]

Letters written by Faber, between November 1845 and early January 1846, are characterised by ebullient discussions of those who had recently joined the Roman Church;[3] and speculation as to whether individuals such as Pusey and J. B. Morris would also leave the Church of England.[4] Morris became a Roman Catholic in January 1846.

On 10 January 1846, Faber, who was now known as Brother Wilfrid of the Humanity of Jesus, published a pamphlet entitled *Grounds for remaining in the Anglican Communion: a letter to a High Church friend*.[5] Its title is somewhat ambiguous, as Faber

believed that there were no valid reasons for remaining an
Anglican. We can suggest that it functioned as an excuse for
him to express long suppressed feelings about the Church of
England, whilst underlining the rightness of the step that he
had just taken. The pamphlet is written in a style that is logical
and erudite; and the first question that he asks the individual
to consider is whether they can be saved within Anglicanism.[6]
He notes that although it is difficult to view the question objec-
tively, the salvation of the individual soul is more important
than questions relating to Church and loyalty towards a particular party within it. Faber asks the individual to choose
whether they can recognise the authority of the Church of
England,[7] and he highlights the freedom from the moral questions raised by Anglicanism, which is provided by the authority
of Rome. He demolishes the notion that any form of
Protestantism is valid, writing that the only two legitimate
options are Roman Catholicism or unbelief.[8] In contrasting
Roman truth with Anglican errors, he opines that arguments
for the validity of Anglicanism are 'profane and almost <u>blas-
phemous</u>'.[9] This pamphlet was written whilst Faber's doubts
about the Church of England were fresh, and he was both
enthralled and unsettled by the process of conversion that he
had recently undergone. Because of this, any triumphalism is
tempered by Faber's admission of the difficulties inherent
within his own decision to leave; and he concedes that the
argument for the individual's remaining in the Church of their
baptism has intrinsic validity, even if this necessitates remaining within Anglicanism.[10]

Faber's own Anglican life is highlighted by the observation
that there is an ever-present danger of unreality in Anglican
worship, which is particularly noticeable in the mixing of
Anglican and Roman religious practices.[11] He notes that the
Tractarians have the 'prettinesses of popery without its
worship, or its doctrine, or its structures',[12] and opines that it is
dishonest to use Roman devotions within the Anglican Church.
It is characteristic of Faber's thought that he viewed this as
being caused by pride, and refusal to submit to a religion that
had no social standing within England.[13] Faber criticised
Tractarians for comparing the English Church and the Church
of antiquity,[14] dismissing this as illogical, and writing that

Protestant Churches are not branches of the Catholic Church, but schismatic.[15] He noted that Anglicanism is inconsistent because of internal disagreements and the failure to build a systematic use of theology and doctrine; and opined that the fatal flaw of the English Church is its connection with nationality, national merit, and political importance.[16] He noted that Tractarians were obsessed with parties and personalities, and characterised by 'a profane, sickly, Puritanical mysticism',[17] rather than concern for the Church and doctrine; and characterised Anglicanism as a 'communion with nothing and with nobody, daily breeding new elements of subdivision, fierce, intolerant, and persecuting'.[18] Alongside this, Faber placed an almost utopian vision of Roman Catholicism whose 'spiritual vigour'[19] during the Reformation resulted in a significant number of important saints, an idea that he uses as proof of Roman orthodoxy.[20]

Newman was concerned that Faber's pamphlet would harm the cause of the Tractarians who had already moved to Rome, by providing ammunition for those who were hostile to their cause.[21] He also noted the names of Pusey and Keble as being two individuals who, because of Faber's pamphlet, would be unlikely to leave the Anglican Church.[22] Although he does not articulate his reasons for this, it is probably because Faber dismisses as myth the idea that Tractarianism leads inevitably to Rome. It also seems likely that Newman believed that Faber's scathing characterisation of Anglicanism was harmful. Newman's comments give an interesting insight into their relationship at this time and, despite his disapproval, Newman was one of the few individuals who empathised with, and supported, Faber.[23] This was because of his belief that Faber had not received sufficient spiritual direction and support since joining the Roman Church,[24] the result of his creating, rather than joining, a religious order, an idea with which we can concur.

Faber's post-conversion euphoria acted, for a time, as a shield from difficulties. However, he could not adjust to life as a Roman Catholic, and by the end of January he had misgivings as to whether he had been right to convert. A contributory factor was that Faber was responsible for the group who had moved to Rome with him, whose diverse educational backgrounds ensured that they could not remain together in a conventional religious community. The bulk of Faber's correspondence during January is concerned with the minutiae of his dealings with other people, rather than with personal spiritual matters. He wrote to Newman that the enthusiasm of the community was an inadequate substitute for an established programme of spiritual direction,[25] and added: 'There are daily fresh symptoms of ye work thawing away under my hands.'[26] At this early stage, Faber was looking for a way out rather than a resolution to his problems, a response that was, perhaps, somewhat naive. He was beginning to formulate the idea of being part of a religious community led by Newman, and had already decided that if the Wilfridians could not live together they should collectively become part of Newman's community at Oscott.[27] However, Newman's reply suggested that Faber should 'be a distinct centre of operation and collect people about you',[28] and one of the central tensions of this period is that Newman continually encouraged Faber to take on responsibilities that Faber was either unwilling or unable to.

Faber, together with Antony Hutchison,[29] a member of his Wilfridian community, left Birmingham on 2 February and spent February, March and April travelling through France and Italy. It is interesting to note, however, that this postconversion holiday should have been longer, but was shortened because of Faber's ill-health, particularly the recurrence of difficulty whilst walking and standing.[30] Faber's correspondence is mainly concerned with discussion of a few aspects of the situation in Birmingham. This journey was a response to stress, which was most probably the result of cumulative pressure leading up to his conversion, and he wrote from France, 'I am glad ... to get clear of England after all ye arrogance of ye last 3 [*sic*] months.'[31] Arrogance is used here as a euphemism for differences of opinion within the Wilfridian group, and between the Wilfridians and the church authorities.[32] It is indicative of the complex nature of Faber's character that he abandoned his new community at the worst possible time, both for their morale and for their formation as a group. Indeed, his letters to the Wilfridians in England[33] give the impression that he found it easier to encourage from afar, rather than actively making the community work by being part of it. This idea reinforces the notion that Faber expected other people always to concur with him despite his chronic indecisiveness, and this may be the root of why some individuals distrusted him. Faber's travels were also a reaction to the emotional and spiritual turmoil which preceded the move to Rome, and it becomes clear that he had not adequately realised that there would be difficulties after the change. Whilst abroad, Faber became increasingly nostalgic for Elton, and doubted not only his conversion and the wisdom of leaving, but also Christianity,[34] scruples which he attributed to 'the work of the devil'.[35] However, at one level, Faber clearly wished that he had not joined the Roman Church, a fact that is not mentioned by any of his biographers; and in a letter to the group that he had persuaded to leave Elton just three months earlier, he wrote: 'I must confess that my heart is always, always going back to Elton, and th[a]t the cross of leaving it grows heavier every day instead of lighter.'[36]

Faber's spiritual indecisiveness was particularly acute between 1846 and 1849, and his thoughts regarding his position in the Roman Church were frequently contradictory. We can therefore suggest that it took Faber several years, until his move to London during 1849, to achieve his full spiritual equilibrium.

The *Rule of the Brothers of the Will of God*, which has not previously been studied, was written at Sens, northern France, on 14 February 1846,[37] and subsequently sent to Wiseman and Pope Gregory XVI for approval. It consists of seven chapters, containing detailed descriptions of the private and public spirituality, and day-to-day administration of the Order; and is notable because it contains ideas that are of primary importance to Faber's spirituality. It is also distinctive because, unlike other nineteenth-century founders of small religious communities, Faber was sufficiently motivated to write a Rule. Faber's intention was to found a congregation of St Wilfrid, led by himself at Birmingham, which was part of a wider religious Order, the Brothers of the Will of God;[38] and from the tone of the Rule, it seems likely that Faber hoped that both of these would outlast his own lifetime. It is influenced by three saints who also founded religious orders: Philip Neri, John of God,[39] and Ignatius Loyola;[40] and patronised by two English saints, Wilfrid and Thomas of Canterbury.[41]

Faber intended that the Order should form a bridge between the monastic and secular clergy;[42] indeed, it is a sophisticated compromise, necessitated by the need to provide a vocation for the individuals who surrounded him. He stipulated that it was suitable for individuals who could not, for health reasons, enter a monastery or become secular priests,[43] a clause which was probably intended for his own situation. This may have been influenced by the Oratorians, a group of secular priests who are not bound by a Rule, as Faber wanted his Order to be more formal than a group of friends living together,[44] but informal, in that there were no discernible differences between the priests and lay brothers within the community.[45] The Rule does not create a definite diocesan role for the Order, and it seems possible that this policy ensured that the Wilfridians occupied a position in the diocese that did not impinge on the work of other religious orders. This is underlined by Faber's insistence on the importance of obedience to the local bishop as a point of reference for the community.[46] It seems probable that Faber also intended to provide insurance against any suspicion that the Wilfridians were new and so had the potential to be disloyal or contumacious. After Faber became a Roman Catholic, he stressed the idea that submission to authority was important. This idea was related to Faber's distrust of self, and the Rule promulgates an Ignatian emphasis on humility and obedience which is partly demonstrated by not replying to accusations.[47] There is no toleration of dissent within the community,[48] and very little room for error in that only 'three warnings'[49] would be given before the individual was asked to leave. It is interesting that one of the disagreements between Faber and J. B. Morris was caused by the latter's inability to be submissive.[50] Faber limited his Congregation to assisting the clergy in whatever it was asked to do, such as visiting the sick and the poor, and providing catechetical[51] instruction, particularly to young men.[52] Hospitality was also important, a trait which Faber draws from John of God; and he stipulated that the Houses, or Colleges, of the Order should contain either a hospice or an orphanage.[53] It is notable that Faber was concerned to bring together rich and poor, an idea which recurs throughout his life.

Faber's historical position is that of an individual whose

Ultramontanism contrasted with Newman's liberalism. This was apparent from 1846 onwards, and it is noticeable that, in contrast to Newman, Faber does not retain any of his Anglican personality; indeed, he provides us with a good example of the capacity of a certain type of convert to belittle what they previously believed. However, despite this, Faber retains many of the most important characteristics of his pre-Roman spirituality. Two of the central ideas in the Wilfridian Rule are reverence for Rome and obedience to the Pope, both of which underline the Ultramontane stress on the authority of Rome. The roots of Faber's Ultramontanism lie in the notion that he perceived the Roman Church abroad[54] as an ecclesiastical ideal, and it seems probable that he viewed his travels abroad as inspiration for his work in England, which was now not only Protestant, as it had been during his Anglican ministry, but also heretical.[55] Faber's intention was that the Wilfridians should engage in catechetical work in 'heretical countries',[56] because it was more difficult to be loyal to the Church of Rome in these circumstances.[57] He distrusted any spiritual stance that was excessively individualistic, primarily because of the danger that it would become eccentric and heretical, and depart from church teaching. From the outset of his Roman life, Faber was anxious to proclaim both his doctrinal orthodoxy and his loyalty to Rome, and on several occasions the Rule professes to be 'in harmony with ye mind of Holy Church'.[58] This is particularly apparent in the Prologue, during which Faber emphasised that he had written his Rule, 'after visiting ye relics of St Thomas of Canterbury',[59] a statement which illustrates his historical awareness of the advisability of ensuring that the Church remains free from State influence.[60] Faber's Roman notions of religion in England reinforced, rather than diluted, his Tractarian emphasis on the pre-Reformation ideal. The Prologue includes the phrase 'the England of the Saxon saints',[61] which echoes the saints' lives which he had read and written as an Anglican.

Study of the spirituality of the Wilfridian community provides an indication of the type of spirituality that Faber developed after he became a Roman Catholic. This was concerned with everyday spirituality rather than with spiritual high points, a notion which had been important to him whilst at Oxford, Ambleside and Elton. The influence of St Philip Neri is visible in the outward spirit of the Order, particularly in the idea that its members should be cheerful,[62] and observe 'playful ways and sweet manners'.[63] This aspect also ties in with Faber's lifelong antipathy towards aloofness, both in himself and in others, and he wrote, 'singularity ... impairs ye spirit of gaiety, wh[ich] is to animate ye community ... to represent ye amiable and winning aspect of Xtian strictness'.[64] He also wrote that members of the Congregation should encourage public prayers, such as the Rosary, and use of litanies.[65] The private devotional life of the Wilfridians was both practical and communal, a spirituality which encouraged wordy vocal prayers and group devotions[66] which were centred around 'submission to ye will of God'.[67] It was also incarnational in its devotion to the humanity of Jesus,[68] and contained references to the ordinariness of Jesus' early life, and aspects of the lives of Mary and Joseph.[69] The latter provides the first example of a devotion that was important to Faber for the remainder of his life.

As in Faber's Anglican period, this spiritual milieu is the antithesis of one which was ascetic, solitary, eremitical, or Apophatic. The central reason for this is that he believed that all of these could foster delusions and selfishness.[70] Faber wrote, 'Nothing is more rare in the Church than a true contemplative vocation.'[71] He was reluctant to allow individuals to espouse, or aspire to, any form of contemplative spirituality, and, until the later years of his life, remained profoundly distrusting of such a religiosity. This relates to an important idea in Faber's thought; his dislike of what he would describe as unreality, which stands for anything that might be illusory or untrue. He was concerned that individuals, both clerical and lay, would try to aim too high for their spiritual status and be encouraged to think that they were more advanced than they were. This does not mean that Faber was not acquainted with, or did not understand, the theory of the contemplative vocation, particularly as his works indicate that he had read the lives and writings of saints who were contemplatives, such as the Carmelite mystics St Mary Magdalene Pazzi, St Teresa of Avila and St John of the Cross. This indicates that Faber wrote for individuals who were spiritually similar to himself. Thus, in a later work, he contrasted his own spirituality with that of St John of the Cross, writing that he (Faber) wrote for the general Christian: individuals who needed spiritual consolations, and who, because of this, did not aspire to perfection.[72] In order to create his spiritual world, Faber frequently embroidered the scriptural facts at his disposal. This creativity enabled him to construct a complete narrative from very little historical evidence, thus creating a mental picture for those who may have been unable to create one for themselves. This technique has its origins in Faber's personal spirituality and poetic awareness, and the influence of the *Composition of Place* in the Ignatian method of meditation.

The notion 'spirit of the age' recurs in Faber's thought during 1846 and, as before, the contemporary world has negative connotations because it devalues God and does not recognise the certainty of future judgement.[73] Faber wanted the Wilfridians to be contrary to this spirit,[74] and there are Ignatian overtones in his notion that they should 'by an interior training abandon ye maxims of worldly prudence and morality'.[75] In the Wilfridian Rule, the Christian Church is in opposition to the world, which is engrossed in its own concerns: trade, commerce, vanity, the theatre and parties; all of which Faber considers to be the antithesis of religion. Several of these ideas are also an established part of his thought: 'subtle worship of self',[76] 'separation of sympathies between ye higher and lower classes',[77] 'morbidly protecting one's own reputation',[78] and 'depreciation of prayer'.[79] After he joined the Roman Church, the spirit of the age became identified with heresy,[80] and the Rule frequently returns to the eternal and temporal dimensions of heresy.[81] Faber stressed that heresy is found both inside and outside the Church of Rome, and writes of the 'outrages of heretics and indevout Catholics',[82] and the 'depravation of masses and prayers in heretical countries'.[83] Teaching was a central part of the Wilfridian vocation, and study occupied an important place in forming each member of the community.[84] This was not only the study of various branches of theology,[85] but also liturgy, as Faber was concerned about the low standard of liturgical practice in England.[86] The emotional centre of Faber's spirituality was Rome, and he thought it important that the Wilfridians should learn Italian, not just for purposes of study, but to imitate the minutiae of Italian devotional life.[87] It is typical of Faber's lack of differentiation between what others would consider important and less important, that at one level he does not distinguish between institutional theology and the private religious practice of Catholic individuals.

On 25 February 1846, eleven days after writing the Wilfridian Rule, Faber wrote from Florence of the contrast between his last visit abroad, during which he had been enthusiastic about plans for Elton, and his current state, which was one of deep depression, within which he could write 'life has nothing to offer'.[88] Faber's, revealing, response was to believe that, although he was unhappy in the Roman Church in England, he would not be unhappy if he moved to the same Church abroad.[89] This was because Faber's unhappiness was caused more by social factors than by spiritual ones, and brooding on the ease with which the clergy in Birmingham misunderstood and disliked each other, exacerbated his angst. Faber had now realised that the Roman clergy were as motivated by internal politics as those within the Church of England, and wrote of the 'difficulties and disturbances and enmities and evil speakings of England'.[90] Because of this, he doubted the long-term future of the Wilfridian community,[91] who were isolated within the diocese, and clinging to the hope that their move to the Roman Church had been the right decision.[92] Faber does not seem to have realised that the community, then at its most vulnerable, would need his personal support; and sentiments such as 'I am deeply pained at heart with ye disappointments I have received'[93] seem selfish, and to imply a lack of commitment. However, they may also be attributable to depression caused by a profound sense of being let down by what he had imagined to be an ecclesiastical utopia. Faber's unhappiness was increased by the knowledge that he had offended Newman, both by writing the pamphlet and by his irritability,[94] which was probably, like his depression, caused or exacerbated by Bright's disease, mercury poisoning, or medication. The undertones of this letter suggest that the Oxford converts were not well received by old Catholics, and that this was coupled with enmity from the clergy.[95]

One letter from this month is particularly significant as it is to an individual outside Faber's ordinary circle, and therefore perhaps written with more candour.[96] Faber wrote of his spiritual anguish because he thought that his life in the Church of England had been wasted. He described an overwhelming sense that starting again as a Roman Catholic was impossible because he was not physically strong enough to do so, but that his own accountability to God, and the reality of future judgement, made it necessary. As in his letters regarding the solitude of Elton, there is a sense of exaggeration and foreboding, almost of an impending martyrdom. However, it would be too simplistic to interpret this desperate plea for understanding purely as a Faber exaggeration.

Faber articulated his disquietude in a letter to Morris, and indicated that he still viewed the Jesuits as a spiritual ideal, a standpoint that underlines the continuing influence of Ignatian spirituality within Faber's spirituality.[97] This conundrum recurred throughout 1846, despite accompanying protestations that it was 'God's will'[98] that he should not become a Jesuit, principally because he wished to remain in England.[99] These questions illustrate a particular flaw in Faber's nature, which was that he always wanted to be doing what he was not doing, whilst being unable to do that which was expected of him. Also in the same letter is an example of another trait of Faber's, that of belittling something that he has already worked up and made a great show of. He expressed concerns about his community's internecine quarrels, and repeated the idea that he would give the venture only another eighteen months before applying to join Newman's group, who were now at Maryvale.[100] However, later he wrote, 'there were many <u>little</u> clouds gathering in a threatening way when I left England, but ... ye sky has cleared'.[101] Faber seems not to have been able to capitalise on his position within the diocese, despite Wiseman's favourable response to receipt of Faber's Rule, and notes about the first weeks of the Wilfridian community.[102] On 26 May, the Wilfridians moved from the house in Caroline Street to a larger house in Colmore Terrace, Summer Lane, Birmingham. In July, Faber suggested to Newman that the Wilfridians should join his community, but Newman refused. During the same month, the Wilfridians were asked by Lord Shrewsbury to administer the parish of Cheadle, Staffordshire, and were offered Cotton Hall, five miles from

Cheadle, as their monastery. On 26 July, the Sacrament was reserved in the Wilfridians' chapel for the first time,[103] and a member of the clergy of St Chad's Cathedral, Birmingham, visited in order to say the Eucharist for them. The chapel was 'decorated in the Gothic style, with red walls, a blue ceiling, and a handsome altar after a design by Pugin'.[104]

An ebullient letter written to L. Bartolommei, on 2 August, begins: 'I have been in the midst of battles.'[105] At this time, these seem to have been external rather than internal, as Faber continues with an idealistic presentation of the private devotional life of the Wilfridian community:

> I cannot describe to you, Leopoldo, the fervour and almost extatic [*sic*] love which is burning among my monks, the joyous spirit of penance, the delighted abnegation of self, the intense devotion to the Sacred Humanity of Jesus, the Happy [*sic*] servitude to Mary.[106]

There is no reason to suppose that this is not an accurate evaluation; however, it seems equally possible that Faber was, at least partially, employing his sense of rhetoric in order to impress his correspondent. Faber's letters to Bartolommei, all of which are written in the same flamboyant style, represent a selection from only a handful written during 1846 to include details of his personal spirituality. He now disliked discussing himself,[107] and passages in which he does so are disparaging of his efforts to be spiritual. One example of this highlights Faber's concern because he had been described as holy, and he writes of himself as 'a poor heretic whom Mary has rescued from the paths of darkness'.[108] It is, however, noticeable that Faber is describing a natural contrast between the youthful euphoria of his community and his own religiosity, which is less responsive because he is older and more mature. Faber's description of his sense of personal sin and unworthiness is expressed in terms the intensity of which hint at a heightened state of nervous tension, and phrases such as 'pray for one who is all ice, when he might be all fire'[109] have their origins in Faber's evangelical Anglicanism. They also hint that he was undergoing some sort of purgative spiritual experience,[110] which is not definable in purely Ignatian terms because it is outside its terms of reference. From August 1846 onwards, Faber's spirituality began to acquire a deeper contemplative strand, an undercurrent that is discernible although it is difficult to pin down. It never dominates, but remains part of Faber's private, as opposed to literary, spirituality, and rarely achieves prominence in published works. Where it does occur, it is identified with the Cross and with suffering, two ideas that become increasingly important during this period. It seems possible that this demonstrates the influence of Passionist spirituality, which is centred on devotion to the Passion, on Faber's private devotional life.

By 5 August, Faber had convinced himself that the Wilfridian venture had only been an experiment,[111] although we can presume that he would not have written the Rule had he thought so seven months earlier. This view was caused by the church politics which were an ongoing feature of this year, and which made him want to leave Birmingham. Faber gives several reasons for this. Firstly, he was being used as a pawn by the Bishop and could do nothing without the Bishop's approval, a scenario which disturbed him; and secondly, because of misunderstandings with old Catholics.[112] Friends who had moved to Rome with him also misunderstood him, and his relationship with J. B. Morris became less congenial as a direct result of Morris's profound, and chronic, unhappiness in the Roman Church. Faber responded to Morris's criticism that he had always been too unpredictable and changeable, both in his religious allegiances and by leaving Oxford rather than remaining as a Fellow,[113] with a detailed refutation, in which he wrote that his 'vacillation'[114] was not repeated untruthfulness or intellectual dishonesty, but part of an ongoing process of discovery.[115] It is part of Faber's distinctive and quirky mindset that he was able to reconcile the diverse movements of his spirituality; and Morris's observations highlight the dangers inherent in following another individual, especially one as volatile as Faber. As we have seen throughout this study, Faber did not compartmentalise religious ideologies, but frequently blurred the distinctions between his experiences of them in references to his personal spirituality. Because of this, he could draw parallels between past Evangelicalism and present Romanism, writing, 'ye more

Roman I get, ye more I seem to recover ... old boyish evangelical feelings'.[116]

On 21 August, Faber wrote a letter to Bartolommei in a style
which seems calculated to place himself firmly in the role of
spiritual inferior. He wrote, 'I am but a mere convert ... who
has spent 31 years in rebellion against Holy church.'[117] In
contrast to this, Faber came close to seeing himself as superior
to old Catholics in England, because a number had accused
him of being over enthusiastic in his devotions to Mary. In his
personal life, Mary represented a mother figure for Faber, who
had 'made a solemn vow ... to devote all my life, health,
strength, time and talents to the ardent devotion to Mary'.[118]
This devotion is one of the major distinguishing marks of
Faber's spirituality, and is discussed more fully in connection
with his sermons. Although it was present when he was an
Anglican, it was intensified by continental Roman models.

On 1 September, A. W. N. Pugin's Church of St Giles, at
Cheadle, Staffordshire, was opened.[119] The Wilfridians
accepted Lord Shrewsbury's offer of the parishes of Cheadle
and Cotton, and the community moved to Cotton Hall, which
was renamed St Wilfrid's, during the afternoon of Thursday,
10 September.[120] Bishop Thomas Walsh (1779–1849) invested
Faber with the minor orders in the chapel at Alton Towers[121]
on 12 October, the feast of St Wilfrid, and blessed the foundations of the new church of St Wilfrid on the same day. Faber
informed Bartolommei that St Wilfrid's was 'a wild and beautiful solitude among the hills of Staffordshire'.[122] He wrote to
Newman, 'Pugin says it will be "the only perfect church in
England", with "an east window he could die for"'.[123] Whilst an
article in *The Tablet*, noted:

> We shall not readily forget the scene that presented itself
> when the bishop knelt at his footstool before the Cross,
> behind him a group of kneelers in their surplices. Round
> the outside of the foundations were the people, bare
> headed, many of them apparently much moved.[124]

Correspondence between September and December is primarily concerned with day-to-day Wilfridian business. Early in
October, Faber received formal recognition of the Wilfridian

Order from Pope Gregory XVI; and on 13 October, he sent a long letter to Bartolommei in Florence, which contained details of the success of the parish at Cheadle. He wrote, 'Since Easter we have received about 200 poor heretics back into the fold of the Church.'[125] Faber writes of himself in terms which suggest that he thought of himself as having not only a mission to convert those who were not Catholics but to 'introduce Italian tones of feeling and devotion among ye cold Catholics of our native land'.[126] Not for the first time we see that England represented an unemotional religiosity, which, for Faber, gave rise to negative feelings. In a letter to Newman, one of Faber's community reported the case history of an individual received into the Church by Faber, who had 'died ... in despair'.[127] He commented, 'it looks as if he [Faber] were going on rather too fast receiving protestants without sufficient instruction'.[128]

The Wilfridian community took part in an Ignatian retreat given by Fr William Cobb (1804–1877), a Jesuit, between the end of October and the beginning of November. During the retreat, Faber became ill with symptoms which included complete paralysis, and was given the last Sacraments. Faber's mind was unaffected by the seriousness of his physical condition, and in a letter to Michael Watts Russell, he wrote of what we would recognise as a description of a Near Death Experience, which he described as follows: 'I seemed to pass thro' death; God was all around: I was inexpressibly happy, till I heard like an inward voice ... say I was to return to life, and I mourned.'[129] There is a characteristic sense of theatre and heightened emotionalism in Faber's description of his thwarted deathbed, which highlights his life-long penchant for describing such scenes in the lives of others. He wrote, 'I made my profession of faith, bade ye poor wretched Brothers goodbye, laid in ye arms of one of them, and received ye last benediction and papal indulgence, while Br Antony [Hutchison] thrust Pope Gregory's crucifix into my lifeless hands.'[130]

The retreat highlighted Faber's doubts, firstly about his own vocation (which were centred on whether he should become a Jesuit), and secondly, whether he had been right to move from the Church of England. It is tempting to ascribe to Faber some sort of unspoken wish that death in such idealised circumstances, within the Roman Church and in the presence of his community, would be the logical fulfilment of the experience of conversion. This encourages us to postulate that he may have believed, if only subliminally, that death would not only signify the end of decision-making, but would solve the problem of doubts over his present and future position.

Faber's letters to Michael Watts Russell, written immediately after the retreat, highlight the strain within the Wilfridian community; and Faber's descriptions of this retreat, and of their first weeks together, are so fervent and highly wrought emotionally that they frequently verge on being hysterical. In a letter written twelve days after the end of the retreat, Faber wrote that he had been subjected to 'awful temptations of the devil',[131] and that his community were experiencing, 'a most distressing disgust of spiritual things'.[132] Both Faber and other members of the community reported nocturnal demonic visitations in the form of a sense of evil presence, which was probably, but not necessarily, caused by their heightened sensitivity. Faber provides details of one individual's wish to leave the community, and interpreted the fits and repugnance towards the spiritual that accompanied this as being the result of temporary demonic possession.[133] Faber was clearly unwilling, or unable, to create a balanced spiritual environment, or to relieve the tension which had been created both by their conversion and by the retreat. This episode illustrates the extent to which Faber was formed spiritually by the psychological and emotional effects of the Ignatian *Exercises* and the Jesuit ethos. In a letter to Lord Shrewsbury, written later in the same month, Faber again referred disparagingly to his time as an Anglican; and within the context of a discussion of recent converts he highlighted the 'worship of <u>self</u> in which we young Protestant gentlemen have been brought up'.[134]

During December, Faber once again believed himself to be dying.[135] He ascribed this to spiritual 'agitation and anguish'[136] over the future of the Wilfridian community, rather than to physical causes, an example which illustrates how indivisible the physical and the spiritual were during his life.[137] In letters to Morris during this time, he frequently belittles his illness in a style of such defensiveness that it both invites and repels sympathy. It is notable that illness made Faber solitary and bad-tempered, and because of this only those contemporaries who could be personally loyal tried to be sympathetic towards him. On 19 December, Faber travelled to Oscott, where he was ordained to the sub diaconate.

At the beginning of January 1847, Faber took part in a second Ignatian retreat, which was given by the Passionist priest, Dominic Barberi. There is one extant copy of Faber's notes for the *Spiritual Exercises*,[138] although he used them more than once. His responses are formal, succinct, and provide little more than positive and negative reactions to the execution of the *Exercises*. Despite this, a number of significant points occur within them. Firstly, emotion was the central yardstick used by Faber to gauge his spiritual state; he wrote in terms of being 'distracted',[139] 'weary',[140] and described 'great sweetness'.[141] This contrasts with the distrust of emotion shown during his Anglican period. Secondly, Faber's meditations contain references to his health, particularly headaches and sickness,[142] a fact which, once again, illustrates how much the two were intertwined and affected one another. Thirdly, the relationship between poetry and theology, which caused scruples during the early 1840s, is revealed to be still part of Faber's mental makeup in the statement that he 'Felt compunction for past worship of natural scenery.'[143] Also extant is Faber's list of his spiritual faults and defects, which may or may not have formed part of the same retreat, but was certainly from this period.[144] These highlight Faber's self-knowledge, as three of his faults were 'exaggeration',[145] 'inconstancy of purpose'[146] and 'want of recollection'.[147] One of his spiritual defects was listed as 'aiming at high things',[148] a notion which became more prominent after he became a Catholic, and which consisted of a sense that it was important not to aim high so as to forestall any pursuit of holiness by thinking of it as an impossibility. It is particularly apparent in his later works, and will be discussed more fully in conjunction with them. As in August 1846, one of Faber's spiritual aims was the 'scrupulous ... concealment of my spiritual feelings or practices except to my director'.[149] However, given Faber's temperament, it seems unlikely that he would have been able fully to disguise his inner spirituality, and we can work from the premise that glimpses of Faber's inner life can, at one level, be seen in all of his writings. He also listed the 'abandonment of ridicule, jest or severity, as means of correction'.[150] This trait, which he did not completely abandon, is apparent in the majority of his mature works; it is the one facet of Faber's character that most leads the modern reader to be unsympathetic towards those passages in writings where it occurs.

During the retreat, Faber questioned whether he was following the correct vocation. He, once again, contemplated becoming a Jesuit, and wrote that had the retreat director suggested it, he would have done so immediately.[151] It seems unlikely that Faber would have been suitable for the Jesuits, because of his ongoing ill-health. However, in an ideal scenario, possible only with the benefit of hindsight, Faber might have been happier had he been able to go abroad as a Jesuit missionary, as his spirituality was such that it needed an enthusiastic response, which it was not in the English character to provide. There was also a conflict between Faber's personal spiritual desires and his responsibility for the Wilfridians; however, he gives the impression that he was most concerned about his own vocation, and that those nearest to him were expected to follow his decisions. In Chapter 2, we discussed Faber's hatred of being alone, and suggested that it was for this reason that he surrounded himself with a community.[152] Paradoxically, Faber never fitted in to the communities of which he was a part, and after he became a Catholic he remained as much on the outside as he had been at Oxford. There are also overtones that, as when he was thinking about joining the Roman Church, Faber wanted to be told what to do with the Wilfridian community, obedience being safe in terms of humility, and the surest way not to have to make a difficult decision.

In correspondence written prior to Ordination there is no sense that Faber still looked upon himself as an Anglican priest. He frequently noted his unworthiness to be ordained in the Roman Church, particularly in letters to Morris, which discuss the prospect of Ordination,[153] for which Faber was reading, unspecified, theology.[154] On 28 March, Faber travelled to Oscott for a pre-Ordination retreat;[155] and in a letter to Newman, written the day before his departure, Faber provided thoughts in response to Newman's plan to introduce the Oratory to England. What follows is highly significant for our historical awareness of the beginnings of the English Oratory, as Faber informed Newman that he had wanted to form an Oratory, and had suggested this to Wiseman, but had been rebuffed by him.[156] Faber wrote, 'It was rather curious that I had proposed to Dr. Wiseman to make an Oratory, but he discountenanced it, and we gave it up a little grumpily.'[157] The tone of this paragraph, together with Faber's, probably cynical, use of the word curious, implies that he suspected that Wiseman had thought it a better idea that an individual such as Newman should be responsible for such a venture, perhaps because he was more of a figurehead and well known. We can hypothesise that the idea of bringing the Oratory to England originated, not with Newman, but with Faber; and although we cannot say conclusively that Faber would eventually have intro-duced the Oratory to England, it seems probable that he would have done so. Newman was not well acquainted with St Philip,[158] whereas Faber had been devoted to the cultus of St Philip since he was an Anglican, and instigated Newman's devotion to the saint. The news reawakened Faber's doubts about continuing with the Wilfridian venture.[159] This was because the Wilfridian Order was an Oratory in all but name. It had, like the Oratory, been designed to work in large towns, and Faber was concerned that Newman's Oratorians would take over the work that another Wilfridian group might have done in Birmingham.[160] This highlights one problem with the Wilfridian Rule; its similarity to the charism of other orders makes it unworkable. It is also notable that Faber's affection for Newman showed itself in the idea that he should follow Newman's preference for founding a community within an existing religious order.[161]

Faber was ordained deacon on 30 March, and priest on Easter Saturday, 3 April,[162] by Wiseman in the Pugin church at St Mary's College, Oscott. The events remain private and he does not provide any details of his spiritual thoughts. He does, however, pinpoint several important associations: firstly, he thought it significant that he was ordained deacon on the Feast of St Cuthbert, as the saint was associated with Durham and with University College, Oxford; and secondly, that he was ordained priest on the anniversary of the death of his father.[163] On his return to Cotton, Faber's carriage was surrounded by villagers, who pulled it back to St Wilfrid's accompanied by 'fireworks and a brass band'.[164] He wrote to Newman, 'A series of ... tasteful triumphal arches were reared along the road, with illuminations and crosses on them; under each of these we stopped, for cheering and music.'[165]

Faber said his first Eucharist, at St Wilfrid's, on the morning of Easter Day. Correspondence during this time, particularly that to Newman, is concerned mainly with discussions which highlight the factions in the Roman Church at Birmingham. The major problem was a general distrust of Oxford converts, particularly Newman, and by association Faber, by old Catholics, clergy and bishops.[166] On his return to St Wilfrid's after Ordination, Faber indicated his surprise at the level of distrust which he had encountered in Birmingham, and wrote, 'ye priests at Birmingham are exceedingly irate and fierce with us; I think because they are more afraid of you than of us'.[167]One reason for this was the notion that converts had been influenced by personal loyalty to Newman, rather than by an attraction towards Roman Catholicism itself. In addition, Faber's style of devotion was, from the outset, widely misunderstood and disliked by groups of individuals within the church that he had elected to join.

During 1847, Faber translated and edited several volumes for the *Lives of the Saints* series. The *Life of Rose of Lima*,[168] which was translated by Faber and published during September, caused debate. Ullathorne was critical of Faber's hagiography in general, but his criticisms are expressed in a logical and balanced style that avoids becoming too emotionally involved. Ullathorne argued that its emotional and overwrought tendencies made it unsuitable for reading by the majority of English Catholics, who would be unable to distinguish between Faber's embroidering of historical facts and subjects for devotion, and the facts and devotions themselves.[169] Faber was not unduly worried by criticism, a reaction that was the opposite to that which surrounded his *Life* of St Wilfrid in January 1845, after which he had vowed to eschew controversy. The preface is particularly interesting as, despite the fact that it is undoubtedly addressed to individuals both inside and outside the Roman Church, it is written from the standpoint of an insider writing to those outside.[170] This is not as contradictory as it may at first seem, as Faber noted that he expected that the *Life* would be offensive, because individuals in England, whether or not they were Roman Catholics, would not be accustomed to hagiographical literature.[171] Faber published hagiography because he believed that people misunderstood, or had forgotten, the 'supernatural'[172] aspects of Catholic religion,[173] because of the cumulative effect of 'the daily dissonance of ... errors and unbelief around them'.[174] The latter was anathema to Faber, as was the 'habit of paring ... down the "unearthly" in order to ... lighten the load of the controversialist'.[175]

The *Life of Rose of Lima* is written in a manner which is hagiographical in its most undiscriminating sense, a style that clearly appealed to Faber, because of his reliance on the notion that sensation and religious phenomena were the primary gauges of authenticity. Faber revels in references to excessive bodily austerities and suffering, although he is not original in interpreting them as signs of holiness. There was undoubtedly a cruel streak in Faber's makeup, which is related to his use of sarcasm, and is illustrated in his major books by occasional examples of varying degrees of unpleasantness.[176] We can suggest that his intention was to provoke a reaction from people as an alternative to giving them, potentially forgettable, facts. However, this aspect makes some of his spiritual writing seem superficial; leaving the reader with the sense that he has somehow missed the point. Thus, Faber frequently used arguments that were unsubtle and over-simplified, as well as those which employed powerful psychological weapons, such as his suggestion that punishment would be applied by God to those who did not venerate saints.[177] In the *Lives* the individual saint symbolised the power both of God and the Church, as well as providing an antidote to heresy and disloyalty; thus, in order to stress the divine origin of hagiography, Faber wrote that the individual who rejects such literature is rejecting God.[178] He stated that the devil inspires individuals to misunderstand and be contentious about the *Lives*; and that these individuals do so only because they do not understand Catholic theology,[179] a stance which suggests intellectual arrogance on Faber's part, whether or not the statement had intrinsic validity.

Stage Six of Faber's spiritual development: December 1847–December 1849

In September 1847, the Passionist priest Dominic Barberi gave a retreat to the Wilfridians,[180] and in November, Faber sent Bishop Thomas Walsh the annual report on the Wilfridian community. He included details of their daily timetable, which extended from five o'clock in the morning until after nine o'clock in the evening. During this time, four hours were spent on meditation and prayer, such as the rosary, and seven hours in the study of 'moral theology ... dogmatic [theology] and ... Church History'.[181] He notes that four of the sixteen members of the community had had a university education,[182] that two of these were priests and two would soon be priests, and that of the remaining group, nine were lay brothers and six functioned as catechists.[183] The group provided their parish with the Eucharist, benediction, catechetics, and separate schools for boys and girls, a brass band and the Confraternity of the Precious Blood.[184] Faber noted that their parish consisted of one hundred Catholics,[185] and that they had 'received about 200 people into the Church during the past year'.[186]

Faber had experienced less remission from Bright's disease during 1847, and informed Morris, 'my feet are so bad again with ye heart complaint that even saying Mass is painful'.[187] At the beginning of December, and after two months' internal debate,[188] Faber decided to close the Wilfridian community[189] and, together with the other Wilfridians, join Newman's Oratory. He did so primarily because he had once again been *in extremis*.[190] This illustrates the extent to which Faber's plans were constantly interrupted by illness; leading us to the conclusion that, had he not been ill, his role in nineteenth-century history would have been as the founder of a religious community, such as the Wilfridians or the English Oratory, rather than of the London Oratory. We can also interpret this move as representing a further example of Faber's fickleness, which is illustrated by his expectation that the rest of his community would automatically follow him. Giving up the Wilfridian venture represented the next stage in the process of religious change; and, as at previous moments of change, Faber viewed his resolve to act as being God's will.[191] Faber also indicated to

Morris that he had been undergoing some sort of spiritual crisis, and 'much perplexity and doubt about ye will of God, and ye future'.[192] It is typical of Faber's nature that he made the decision at the last minute, and at the most insensitive time, during the preparation for the taking of the community's vows: indeed, Faber and Hutchison were to have visited Wiseman in London, in order to take their vows as Wilfridians, on 8 December.[193] Faber wrote, 'In my colloquy God distinctly called me to enter ye Oratory of St Philip, and ye instant he called there was an interior calm, very wonderful.'[194] This event is evangelical in its sense of sudden calling, and characteristic of Faber's spirituality because of the familiarity with which he refers to God, which occasionally leads to a sense of superficial ordinariness in writing of God.[195] There are Ignatian overtones in Faber's use of the colloquy, his interpretation of calm thoughts as being divine in origin, and in his certainty that God had ensured that there was no subsequent, outward, dissent in the community. Faber wrote to Morris of his happiness that he had at last made the decision;[196] however, it really represents an opting out of decision making, by transferring it to Newman. Faber was not an individual who could stand apart from others and, once again, he found security in accepting the will of another individual. He was aware that his change in position was potentially problematic, and wrote that he hoped to, 'sanctify myself by a simple and child-like aspect of surrender'.[197] Despite earlier reservations about inviting Faber to join the community at Littlemore,[198] Newman wrote: 'You may fancy the joy with which St John and I heard the news that you proposed we should be one.'[199]

Faber replied to this letter on the 1 January 1848, and reassured Newman of their suitability to be Oratorians in terms that present a contrary picture of the community from that given to Bartolommei in August 1846. The following passage highlights Faber's habit of demeaning himself and other people. He wrote: 'There is nothing ... ascetic or poetical about us now ... there were relics of ye <u>savagery</u> of Elton, but either prudence or lukewarmness or both have long since worn those away.'[200] The same sarcastic tone is exhibited in a letter to Ambrose St John, in which Faber described two individuals from a Rosminian parish who had joined, and subsequently left, the Wilfridian community: 'They are melancholy and grave, and apparently overawed by ye extreme spirituality of their own thoughts that I can't make them happy or love God with a bright face and natural manners.'[201]

The letter tells us as much, perhaps more, about Faber's dislike of inwardness and his mocking impatience with those who were not community people, as about the individuals in question. This leads us to question whether Faber's evangelical, Low Church, background had conditioned him to distrust such a spirituality, which he perhaps also equated with his antipathy towards Newman and the High Church style of Anglicanism whilst at Oxford. Faber's emphasis on natural expressions of spirituality also reveals the extent to which he had an affinity with the spirituality of St Philip Neri.

On 14 February, Faber and his Wilfridian community became Oratorians, and Faber viewed as providential the thought that this was the second anniversary of his writing of the Wilfridian Rule.[202] Faber informed Newman that the Wilfridians had been promulgating the cult of St Philip, whose picture was on 'every door of the house'[203] at St Wilfrid's, for some time, and that they now wished to 'apply the spirit of St Philip to England'[204] as Oratorians. Correspondence reveals the thoughts of T. F. Knox, one of Newman's community, about Faber's arrival: 'The discipline nights are quite terrible to contemplate in company with Faber's indurated community who perhaps are accustomed to chains and spiked disciplines besides hair shirts, chain girdles and such like.'[205]

On 21 February, Newman's 47th birthday, Faber left the other ex-Wilfridians at Cotton in order to begin his noviciate at Maryvale, Birmingham. Faber's correspondence during the following months is solely concerned with joining the Oratory, and does not contain any reference to his spiritual state. However, it is noticeable that, after the move to Rome, Faber became much less original, in the sense that he no longer had to strive intellectually to analyse his theological position or to think about his theological preferences, as he had done when he was an Anglican. Faber seems to have believed that the Church had set limits to the need for individual rational argument; he became more wary and in awe of the Church Establishment, and more willing both to conform and to advise others to conform. This is a development of Faber's dislike of private judgement, which ensured that he was happy to let others, such as Newman, make significant decisions for him. It seems probable that Newman recognised this as a defect in Faber's character, and that it was for this reason that he encouraged Faber to be independent.

Correspondence written during the first months of 1848 was dominated by illness, and Faber wrote, 'I was very ill yesterday, so ill that I could neither say Mass nor Office',[206] and 'No part of my past life has left such furrows in me as ye last 18 [*sic*] months.'[207] At the end of April, Faber sent Newman several letters which stated in graphic and minute detail information about his health, which was so bad that he was, once again, thought to be dying.[208] The symptoms of his illness were almost identical to those from which he had suffered throughout the 1840s, particularly the 'irritability of the mucous surface of the bowels'[209] which caused diarrhoea, and which he was certain had been caused by his supposed dysentery of 1842, but which was probably caused by mercury poisoning. Faber also complained of light-headedness and mental confusion, and wrote, 'I could not pray and had horrid temptations to blaspheme al[mighty] God.'[210] He informed Newman that 'ye increasing debility, ye clouded brain, ye loaded eye, ye continual going off in faints, and ye incessant feeling of vomiting ... get more distressing, and deject one'.[211] He also complained of nausea, headaches,[212] pain in his legs, which was so debilitating that he was unable to dress himself,[213] and swelling of his entire body.[214] It seems likely that the medication that Faber was given not only did not help his illness, but may have continued to make him considerably worse. He was prescribed anodynes and calomel,[215] colchicum, laudanum, opium, morphine, astringents, suppositories and arrowroot, and was covered with cod liver oil,[216] which became rancid.[217] A further side effect was Faber's bad temper, which seems to have been caused not only by Bright's disease, but also by a cumulative reaction to his medication, or by withdrawal symptoms when its effects were wearing off. This aspect is frequently commented on in the correspondence of other members of the community, which was disintegrating because of the increasingly intermittent character of Faber's leadership.[218]

Faber's awareness of how illness affects spirituality is expressed in a short series of notes[219] which reveal much about his personality and were, therefore, probably intended for his own use as much as for others. He creates a comfortable environment in which the individual is recommended to 'surround yourself with holy pictures and images'[220] and 'ask for ... ye gift of ye sensible presence of God'.[221] Faber notes that it is futile for the individual to engage in analysis of their spiritual state, or to keep a spiritual diary; and productive to use for meditation positive subjects, such as the incarnation, rather than negative, such as the four last things.[222] All of these are constant traits in Faber's thought and spirituality, as is the injunction 'to avoid solemnity of manner',[223] and the notion that 'inordinate desire for sympathy must be guarded against'.[224]

On the morning of Easter Tuesday, 25 April, St Wilfrid's Church was opened, with High Mass at which J. H. Newman preached the sermon.[225] During the afternoon, the Wilfridians provided a meal for the poor of the neighbourhood, which was followed, later that evening, by a service of benediction.[226] Faber's decision to join the Oratory was unpopular with the Earl of Shrewsbury and the parishioners at Cheadle, and in one sense, this event functioned as a farewell.[227] At the end of May, Faber became involved in a debate with A. W. N. Pugin and Ambrose Phillipps de Lisle. This controversy, regarding the necessity or otherwise of rood screens,[228] generated intense discussion and emotional outbursts on all sides, as Pugin considered them indispensable, whilst Faber believed that they were unnecessary. Its historical importance is due to its providing an indication of the lack of sympathy that Faber received from Roman Catholics, as de Lisle informed Newman that he hoped Faber would 'become less violent and excessive in his ways and ideas'.[229] At the same time, Faber delivered a paper concerning the first death of a member of the Wilfridian community, that of the lay brother Stanislas Besant,[230] an event which is given prominence in Chapman's biography.[231] It is significant for this study because of its detailed description of death,[232] a trait that recurs throughout Faber's later Roman Catholic writing. It also highlights an important Oratorian and Faberian devotion, to the 'childhood of the Eternal'.[233]

In June, Faber indicated that his health had improved, and whilst convalescing at Scarborough he wrote to Newman of his confidence that he would discover a permanent cure for recurrent headaches.[234] In July, on his return to St Wilfrid's from Scarborough, Faber discussed with Newman the latter's Superiorship of the Oratory, and unique powers as its founder; and it is significant that Faber intimated that he was content to be under obedience to Newman, and preferred this to being Superior of his own community.[235] Faber completed his noviciate on 22 July and was subsequently made Master of Novices. In August, he gave a retreat to the Oratory lay brothers on four days leading to the Feast of the Assumption.[236] This functioned as a review of the past year, and consisted of meditations on the vocation of the lay brothers and the life of Mary.[237] He also took part in an Ignatian retreat from 12 to 20 September. On 22 October, the forty members of the Oratorian community moved from Maryvale to St Wilfrid's, Cotton. In the following months, there was a resurgence of the controversy surrounding Faber's *Life of Rose of Lima*,[238] in the course of which Faber was accused of encouraging idolatry. He refuted this by stating that his was a translation of a book published in 1671, and therefore one that had been proved to be orthodox over a significant period.[239] This led to a discussion about the *Lives of the Saints* series as a whole,[240] and he informed Newman: 'These books were ye proximate cause of my conversion and I can hardly say now how strongly I feel about them or with what assiduity I have studied them.'[241]

There were also divisions within the Oratory, caused by those who wanted Italianate devotions and those who desired that the spirit of the Oratory should be English in character.[242] These factors later formed the basis of the distinction between the London and Birmingham houses of the English Oratory.

Correspondence between Newman and Faber during February and March 1849, discusses Newman's idea that the latter should found the London house of the Oratory; and it seems possible that Newman did so because of his awareness that the foundation of the English Oratory had originally been Faber's idea. However, Faber disagreed; firstly, because he thought that Newman was a more suitable leader[243] for the London house,[244] and secondly, because he disliked any form of singularity. Faber's attitude was also influenced by the profound distrust that existed between himself and his group from St Wilfrid's, who openly showed their disrespect for him;[245] a stance which was presumably caused by strong undertones of unexpressed resentment, because Faber had brought them so far before dismantling their vocation. Because of this, Faber felt that he would not have any authority if he were Superior in London,[246] particularly as the community automatically referred to Newman as arbiter for their problems. However, Faber's ex-Wilfridians also had misgivings about Newman's leadership; firstly, because they felt unable to be familiar with him,[247] an assessment which echoes Faber's own inability to relate to Newman whilst an undergraduate at Oxford, and secondly, because they believed that Newman's intense friendship with Ambrose St John exercised undue influence over Newman's judgement of both people and events.[248] Faber was unwell during the early part of 1849,[249] and it is characteristic of his temperament that he wrote of it as an excuse for a necessary period of mortification.[250] Here, as elsewhere, it seems probable that the causes of Faber's illness were both physical and mental, as he was apprehensive about the logistical difficulties of his responsibility for moving to London and forming the London Oratory.[251]

On 11 February, Faber wrote a long epistle, in which he discussed in detail his continuing sense that both he and the community were dependent on Newman. It is significant that Faber had allowed his life to be moulded by the influence and very different style of Newman's spirituality, and he believed that this was God's will despite its being difficult and unnatural.[252] Newman appreciated Faber's unconditional support, and wrote, 'God knows how I love you, and how grateful I feel to you.'[253] Once again, we see evidence of Faber's inability to work alone; he wrote, 'I think I am made to work under someone else.'[254] It is clear that confidence in his ability to make a religious community work had now been completely eroded, and because of this, there is a sense of emotional stress which borders on desperation at the thought of being separated from Newman. Newman provided a bulwark between Faber and those among the indigenous English Catholics, who resented the presence of Oxford converts because they formed

a self-contained group which had imported Tractarian principles.[255] Their antipathy was applied to Faber because of the
contrast between his residual Tractarianism, 'the leaven of
Puseyism',[256] and active Ultramontanism, and the more
subdued style of English Catholicism. Revealingly, he wrote
that it was the lack of acceptance offered to him by English
Catholics which led him to found the Wilfridians, an action
which he now described as a 'wrong and presumptuous inde-
pendence'.[257]

Despite his apprehension about the difficulties of moving to
London,[258] Faber was concerned to find somewhere which
would approximate to home, and wrote to Newman: 'When I
joined ye oratory I hoped for home and peace; I was tired of
unsheltered buffetings about.'[259] By mid-April, Faber was in
London and had found premises at 24–25 King William
Street,[260] which subsequently became the first house of the
London congregation.[261] This proved to be problematic,
because of hostility towards letting the property to Catholic
Priests[262] and doubts as to whether the lease allowed it to be
used as a Catholic Chapel.[263] On 28 April, the remaining fourteen[264] members of the community arrived at King William
Street, and the first Mass was said on the following day.[265]
Perhaps in order to underline his dislike at moving, Faber
informed Newman that the parishioners at St Wilfrid's had
described Newman as, 'ye old[266] gentleman who came here
and spoiled everything'.[267] This underlines a significant fact
about Faber; that he was always successful and popular with his
parishioners, who were, unlike members of the clergy, appre-
ciative of his style of spirituality. This contrasted with his
relationship with Lord Shrewsbury and Ullathorne, which
became increasingly acrimonious during 1849, because Faber
believed that St Wilfrid's was the property of the community
whilst Ullathorne viewed it as ecclesiastical property.[268] It
seems likely that the clause in the Wilfridian Rule, which disal-
lowed their being in charge of a district, was to ensure that they
would be able to remain independent from the ecclesiastical
control that Ullathorne was attempting to enforce. Faber
wanted to keep St Wilfrid's as an Oratory,[269] but was unable to
do so as it was a country parish and Oratorians were concerned
only with town parishes. These events are symptomatic of the

wider consequences of Faber's change of mind and vocation within the Roman Church and, once again, he did what he wanted to do without asking or thinking of the problems his actions might cause for others. This also represents a further example of Faber giving and quickly removing his obedience to authority; an attitude that highlights his lack of loyalty to other people, and betrays a deeply rooted singularity, despite his hatred of the same characteristic in his own nature and that of others. During May, Faber repeated the observation that his authority was not respected by the other Oratorians.[270] It is notable that Faber was distrusted for the style of his leadership and that, once again, this contrasts with the trust of his parishioners.

Mary occupied a central position in Faber's spirituality, and he wished to open the new Oratory before the end of May,[271] a month dedicated to Mary. His choice not only underlined the significance of this particular devotion, but also enabled him to begin by exhibiting his singular approach to Catholicism. Several of Faber's letters refer to the opening of the chapel. In one, he asked Newman to preach, and in an interesting reference to their past lives wrote, 'One Oxford man says he won't come, because your sermons took such hold of him in days of yore, that he is sure he should be converted if he heard you now.'[272] Another refers to his having written several hymns for the occasion,[273] and he informed Newman that he preferred writing hymns for general singing, as opposed to those which are 'clever'.[274] It is characteristic of Faber's spiritual world that he preferred hymns that created an emotional effect on those who read and sang them, rather than those which were purely doctrinal in character. Faber was always expectant that emotional involvement in worship would lead to religious experience, although it is not documented whether any individuals reported such experiences. This is demonstrated in Faber's report to Newman of the first performance of one of his hymns, 'you sh[oul]d hear a whole chapel full enjoying it with enthusiasm, to judge of it; I enclose you a copy, but it <u>reads</u> very tame'.[275] Faber sent Newman a manuscript volume of hymns,[276] and asked for his comments. The volume, *Jesus and Mary, or Catholic Hymns for Singing and Reading*, was published later in the same year.

Faber's correspondence during June presents the ecclesiastical climate in London as being one of disagreements between members of the clergy; acrimony that transferred itself to the Oratorians, fuelled by the large numbers of people attending services in their church.[277] It seems possible that this was initially caused by the novelty value of the new foundation; however, Faber wrote to Newman that the chapel was full, not only for Sunday services and during the week, but also for confessions[278] and for the annual Corpus Christi procession. He also noted that there had been a number of conversions.[279] Newman wrote to Faber, 'Everyone speaks of the Oratory',[280] and noted that individuals coming to Birmingham from London had praised Faber's foundation. Faber's success with the laity contrasted with difficulties within the community. In July 1849, there was a rebellion by the Brothers, who openly criticised his authority[281] and referred all of their grievances to Newman as though he were Superior. It is difficult to say whether this was caused by jealousy, or by Faber's lack of personal authority, or because illness made him a difficult person to live with. The climate of the Oratory was also unhealthy, as fleas, cholera and the dirt and smell of the poor had alienated the middle- and upper-class members of the congregation.[282] Faber and his community had been made ill by this, and he informed Newman, 'There are ... immovable belts of stink in ye chapel, no wonder people faint or go off in ... fits.'[283] In reply, Newman suggested that Faber should segregate his congregation by having two services at the same time, one for the poor and one for everyone else.[284] This is because, although the Oratory was popular with the poor, the central reason for its existence in England was to encourage rich individuals to become Catholics.

In correspondence written after they had settled in King William Street, Faber wrote of rheumatism, headaches and, unspecified, problems with his eyes.[285] He indicated to Newman that his physician believed that a stroke was likely, as he believed that part of Faber's brain had 'softened',[286] probably, in fact, due to the presence of mercury. Faber also noted that he continued to suffer from hemiplegia, or partial paralysis, and remarked, 'I ... lock my door when I feel it coming on; but it is merely transient.'[287] There was also a recurrence of 'inflammation of the bowels',[288] which was, again, probably caused by mercury poisoning. He wrote 'My health gets worse and worse, tho' I look so well',[289] and informed Newman, 'I am quite floored simply by having to endure ye pain, which is a cut above my usual power of pain bearing.'[290] Faber's medication at this time included laudanum, chloroform, hydrochloric acid, which made him more ill, and iron, which worsened his headaches.[291] He also noted the presence of cholera, within the Oratory and in the surrounding area.[292] He wrote to John Bowden: 'I never shall be well in London; I have 2 [*sic*] vocations, one for my body and one for my soul, and they happen to be incompatible.'[293]

The Jesuits, and particularly Jesuit theologians, were a major influence on Faber's thought at this time. On 5 August 1849, Faber preached at the Jesuit Church in Farm Street, which had been opened on 31 July,[294] St Ignatius' Feast. He noted that, in contrast to the Redemptorists and Oratorians, the Jesuit presence linked pre- and post-Reformation Catholicism.[295] Several characteristics of Faber's thought emerge in this sermon. He highlighted the immoral and amoral aspects of the London society which surrounded the new church, such as politics,[296] trade,[297] and poverty,[298] and stressed the 'anti-Christian bent of Literature and Philosophy'[299] and 'the power of evil in London'.[300] We have already noted the influence of St Igantius on Faber, and his characterisation of the Jesuit ethos used ideas which were particularly important to his private and public spirituality, namely, 'St Ignatius ye saint ... of common sense ... of boldness for truth, of carelessness for human respects.'[301] The dedication of the church, to the Immaculate Conception, took on a greater significance for Faber, because of the centrality of Mary to his spirituality.[302]

The spirituality of Faber's Oratory caused controversy, although this did not unduly concern him. He noted that critical articles occurred frequently in newspapers and periodicals, and that individuals whom he described as dissenters were concerned by the style of religion that was being preached by the Oratorians.[303] Such discord was not confined to inter-denominational relations, but was symptomatic of the climate within the Roman Church in which the clergy were jostling for the allegiance of individual members. Faber noted a particularly good example of emotional blackmail and control, 'persons come to say they can come here no more; because Revd. Mr. [*sic*] so and so says he won't see them when dying if they do'.[304] As a direct result of misquotation of his words, Faber was accused of heresy.[305] He informed Newman that he hoped that a closer association with Newman would lessen the amount of criticism that he received, although this did not happen, and the climate of controversy[306] continued into November and December.

During the autumn of 1849, Faber visited St Wilfrid's, in order to give a retreat to the Oratory lay brothers and a mission to Catholics in the surrounding villages. Although we can interpret Faber's movement away from St Wilfrid's as implying lack of commitment, this seems too simplistic; and we should not underestimate Faber's emotional attachment to the place and the people associated with it, particularly as he expressed an, ongoing, wish to be buried in the church and had decided precisely where his burial place should be.[307] It is also interesting to note that there is a likeness of Faber 'in habit and biretta kneeling at the feet of St Peter',[308] in one of the windows above the Lady Altar of the church.[309] In a letter to Lord Shrewsbury he wrote, 'I have had to mortify my affections about it [St Wilfrid's], and seem to feel as I did not feel',[310] and, in part of a long elegiac passage addressed to Newman, he opined,

> I cling to St Wilfrid's ... it is part of my own past life ...
> The place is so dear to me in absurd details that I can
> never settle in my own mind whether I love most the trees
> I found there or the trees I planted.[311]

It is noticeable that a well-developed sense of alienation and isolation from the society in which Faber lived, which is epitomised by his nostalgia for St Wilfrid's, became more marked from this time onwards. This is particularly noticeable in Faber's responses to illness and suffering, and the depression that they caused.[312] It is significant that 'change of temperament',[313] is a symptom of mercury poisoning. Faber's brother, Francis Atkinson Faber, noted that Faber's personality whilst at Oxford during the early 1830s was unrecognisable as that of the person whom he had encountered during 1849, after a four-year absence. In a revealing phrase he wrote, 'The identity was gone.'[314]

Stage Seven of Faber's spiritual development: 1850–1863

Stage seven of Faber's spiritual life began in 1850, the year in which Wiseman became the first Archbishop of Westminster; and, by this time, Faber had attained what is recognisable as the outward face of his mature Catholic spirituality. As we have already noted, Faber discountenanced the writing of a spiritual diary and, in correspondence written during the early 1850s, he made few references to his inner life. However, we can speculate that it was more complex than his outward religiosity. In a rare exception to this rule, he informed Newman of his devotion to the resurrection of Jesus,[315] and elsewhere he implied that the Carmelite devotion to Jesus' infancy,[316] childhood, and interior dispositions,[317] were an important preoccupation in his private spirituality.[318] He equated another favourite idea, that of the childishness of human nature, with his own experience of chronic illness, and reported that the latter had made spiritual discipline almost impossible.[319]

In the same year, the London Oratory became independent from the Birmingham Oratory; however, both communities discussed the idea of forming a College at St Wilfrid's, Cotton. The College was to be modelled on the universities of Oxford and Cambridge, and the education provided dominated by the study of Classics.[320] This is noteworthy, because of Faber's criticisms of his own education at Oxford, and his doubts whilst at Oxford about the moral validity of allowing young men to read such literature. This joint venture did not materialise; Newman founded the Oratory School near Birmingham[321] and the buildings at Cotton were sold to the Passionist Order.[322]

In January, Dalgairns informed Newman of his thoughts, and those of the other Oratorians, about Faber's leadership. He wrote, 'they know ... that they cannot possibly do without him ... without his energy and strength of character the London Oratory would go into ruin'.[323] The Oratorians were still the subject of rancour from the London clergy because of the number of individuals who became Catholics after attending their services.[324] However, for Faber, the novelty of being the cause of controversy had worn thin, and from 1850 onwards he wrote detailed notes for sermons and lectures so that he could prove what had been said in case of complaints.[325] Because of this, Faber often uses ideas from Catholic theology as an alternative to presenting his own views; a trait which is particularly noticeable in his Lent meditations on sin,[326] the particular judgement,[327] and separation from God.[328] Suarez influenced Faber throughout his Catholic period, more so than Aquinas, not only perhaps because of Aquinas's fundamentally intellectual approach to God, but also because Aquinas's theology had not attained the popularity which it achieved later in the nineteenth century. Faber wrote: 'I hardly ever preach without Suarez or De Lugo, and often translate expressions, especially about ye B[lessed] Sac[ramen]t, so as to be sure and accurate.'[329] Faber undoubtedly let his desire for orthodoxy and dread of criticism compromise his individuality of expression, and the tension between orthodoxy and originality was one reason why some projects, such as his lecture on the 'creation of man',[330] remained unfinished.

Faber always noted anniversaries in his letters. On 25 May, the day before St Philip's feast day and Trinity Sunday, he recalled, in a letter to Newman, his Anglican Ordination in Christ Church Cathedral, Oxford in 1839. This took place on a Sunday that combined the same two feasts,[331] and he mentioned that his devotion to Ss Philip Neri and Augustine of Canterbury stemmed from that day.[332] In one of the few letters between Faber and J. B. Morris written during the 1850s, Faber writes that the latter was 'wasting life'[333] because of his failure to obtain a permanent position within the Roman Church.[334] A note pencilled on this letter in Morris's almost illegible handwriting reads, 'still true 1863'.[335] Morris clearly blamed Faber for advising him to move to a Church that did not adequately compensate him for ruining a successful career at Oxford. Their friendship clearly suffered adversely because of this and Faber wrote few letters to Morris during the 1850s; however, the friendship revived during the late 1850s and early 1860s.

Vicarage of St Wilfrid's Church, Calverley, Yorkshire. Birthplace of Frederick William Faber.

Watercolour portrait of Frederick William Faber.
Probably painted to commemorate either his ordination to the
diaconate (1836) or priesthood (1839) in the Church of England.

Frederick William Faber in the Lake District (1839–40).
Colour miniature on ivory by Simon Rochard. Reproduced by
permission of Sir Richard Faber.

St Nicholas Church, Elton. Photograph by the author (2003).

St Wilfrid's, Cotton, Staffordshire (*c*.1900).

Cotton Hall is to the left of the picture. The extension to Cotton Hall and St Wilfrid's Church were both built for F. W. Faber by A. W. N. Pugin. The foundation stone of the church was laid on 12 October 1846 and the opening ceremony performed on 25 April 1848.

Interior of the first London Oratory Church at King William Street, Strand (c.1850).

The London Oratory House and original Church, Brompton Road,
designed by J. J. Scoles (1778–1863).

Frederick William Faber (1863).

The devotions which Faber instigated at the Oratory high-light his Ultramontanism. At the beginning of July, he informed Newman of his intention to set up a Confraternity devoted to the Precious Blood,[336] a feast that had been made universal in 1849.[337] Documents relating to the feast[338] highlight Faber's relationship towards Rome in phrases such as the 'sweetness of even our devotional life being under obedience to ye H[oly] See'.[339] In this context, the 'spirit of the age' is identified with disobedience towards the Church[340] and heresy.[341] Faber recognised that the instigation of the feast was not purely a devotional event, but one which restated the temporal and spiritual power of the pope in a spirit of triumphalism.[342] This aspect is also present in the latter part of Faber's year, which was concerned with controversy over points of theology.[343] Rumours of possible hostility towards Roman churches and individuals[344] was a localised reaction to the Restoration of the Roman Catholic hierarchy in England and Wales, which took place during September. The subsequent debate continued into October, and the public nature of the sermons of Faber[345] and other members of his community – especially those concerned with the jurisdiction of the papacy – made them vulnerable to attack. Faber explained this away as prejudice, made more culpable because it was theologically uninformed, and wrote with gleeful smugness, 'F[r] Bernard [Dalgairns] has been delated to the vic[ar] gen[eral] for a sermon on ye temporal power of ye pope, which was all out of Suarez.'[346]

During August 1850, Faber had visited St Wilfrid's for the last time,[347] and at the beginning of December, he noted that three years had elapsed since his decision to join Newman's Oratory.[348] The character of the London house was being formed at this time, and an exchange of letters between Faber and Newman is concerned with the intellectual character of the Oratory as a whole.[349] Newman believed that the Oratorians should be scholarly individuals, and advised of the importance of admitting only those individuals who satisfied educational requirements.[350] However, several members of the London community were concerned that they were presenting themselves as being too intellectual;[351] and one individual, R. A. Coffin, had already left the community because it was too much like an Oxford or Cambridge College.[352] The two Oratories were modelled on two quite different ideologies: the Birmingham Oratory on the Rome Oratory, and the London Oratory on the Naples Oratory. The latter is more rigorous than the former, and resembles a religious order in character.[353]

In January 1851, Faber was using chloroform to suppress the pain[354] caused by headaches and lumbago.[355] During the same month he began the practice of dedicating each year to a particular saint, beginning with St John of the Cross.[356] This idea seems to have been original to Faber, rather than one which he inherited, as one of his novice conferences[357] is concerned with the advantages of studying the virtues[358] and writings[359] of a saint over an extended period. The individual saint is not an obvious constant presence in Faber's writings for the whole of the particular year, but is an influence which surfaces occasionally. It seems likely that the choice of saint was left to the individual, as the novice is instructed to practise mortification and ask for a personal grace[360] associated with the particular saint.[361] As Faber was responsible for the foundation of a religious house, it is significant that six of his thirteen saints were founders of religious orders.[362] Three were archangels and, of the remaining eight men and two women,[363] all were from outside Britain. A significant proportion of these were from France and Spain, such as Bossuet and Suarez, a fact that underlines the substantial influence that saints and theologians from these countries had upon Faber's spirituality.

H. E. Manning was seven years older than Faber. Both individuals attended Harrow School and Balliol College, Oxford; and each moved from Evangelical to Tractarian Anglicanism, although Manning's family background was, unlike that of Faber, within the High Church tradition.[364] Manning's conversion to Roman Catholicism, on 6 April 1851, represents one of the most important conversions during this period, more so as Manning had held a prominent position within the Church of England. Faber, W. G. Ward and Frederick Oakeley were particular friends of Manning, who was ordained priest on 14 June 1851.[365] Faber's wider role in the diocese of Westminster, and friendship with Manning, are both illustrated by his being given responsibility for instructing and preparing Manning for his first Mass, at the Jesuit Church at Farm Street, on 16 June.[366]

During August, Faber wrote, 'I have been so ill ... that I can hardly keep my temper in ye confessional ... I have no appetite, and sleep badly',[367] and, 'I am so weak and have such odd sensations inside.'[368] It is significant, in the context of this study, that the 'unexplained outbursts of temper'[369] which he described, could also be attributable to mercury poisoning. There is considerable contrast between Faber's health and the amount of work that he achieved, and we can only speculate as to how much more he could have achieved had he not been ill. In September, he was diagnosed with gout for which he was taking iodine,[370] and noted that headaches were almost continuous.[371] He spent the period between October and December abroad; however, his correspondence, with Oratorians Hutchison and Strickson, is primarily concerned with illness, and there is no wider travelogue associated with this journey. Faber had not mentally left England, and his letters are so insular and involved with Oratory affairs that they could have been written in London.[372] From Marseilles, he wrote that travelling had not lessened his symptoms,[373] which he describes thus, 'I have a ... tendency to be lightheaded, when I awake ... but this goes off as ye day wears on.'[374] Letters from Malta show that he had not improved;[375] however, in Palermo he wrote, 'in the last few days all symptoms of illness have passed away, and I consider myself now quite well'.[376] This occasion was the last on which Faber hoped that he could return to some form of normality; however, this feeling did not last until his arrival in Naples, some twelve days later.[377] On his return to London, Faber informed Newman that the worst effect of his illness was his inability to function as a priest. He wrote,

> I can hardly ever say mass, people are near or they see my face, and I get flurried and break ye rubrics, I have left out Gloria's even and Credos ... and I am never very well when I haven't said mass.[378]

During 1852, Faber's health underwent a dramatic decline,

and it is impractical to record the sizeable number of references to illness that permeate his correspondence from this
year onwards. Because of this, 1852 was the first of three
outwardly uneventful years in Faber's life. Between January
and March he stayed in a rented house at Hither Green,
Lewisham, in order to convalesce,[379] and after its opening in
June, he spent a significant amount of time at the Oratorians'
private retreat, St Mary's, Sydenham Hill.[380] Faber's letters and
sermons demonstrate glimpses of an increased perception and
knowledge of himself, characterised by an awareness of his own
lack of progress towards holiness. It is revealing of his state of
mind that he also expressed doubts as to whether he would be
saved.[381] Faber's spirituality became more subtle, and more
contemplative from this year onwards.

Faber's year saint for 1852 was Francis de Sales, an individual who was closely associated with St Philip Neri, whose cult
was being actively promoted by the London Oratorians.
Several of Faber's letters during this time refer to the Achilli
trial,[382] which began on 21 June, and during the course of
which Newman stayed at the London Oratory.[383] In one of
these, Faber informed Newman of his intention to make the
saint's influence more pronounced than being centred only on
his feast day, 26 May.[384] In another letter, he informed
Newman of Wiseman's approval of the activities of the London
house. The latter had used his visit to the Oratory for St
Philip's feast to congratulate the Oratorians on creating a new
climate among the secular clergy of London, and for introducing and encouraging unfamiliar devotions and rituals.[385] In a
novena leading up to St Philip's feast, Faber explored ways in
which the charism of the Oratory founder could be used in
order to appeal to contemporary English society. In doing so,
he cited the positive achievements of the British Empire, and
those of the early 1850s: the construction of the Houses of
Parliament, the Crystal Palace and the railways. Among the
negative facets were journalism and public and private insular-
ity.[386]

At the end of August, Faber received the first of two letters
from the Reverend Edward Price. These functioned as an
apology for his review of Faber's *Life of Rose of Lima*, written
after its publication in 1850.[387] The second letter, of 1

September,[388] provides a retrospective illustration of the amount of opprobrium that was attached to Faber after his departure from Lord Shrewsbury's parish at Cheadle, which had been administrated by Faber and his Wilfridians. It is revealing that, because of Faber's sudden departure, Lord Shrewsbury had given Price a copy of Faber's book, with passages underlined, and had asked its reviewer to be particularly harsh, both in his condemnation of the book and of the selected passages.

On 26 September 1852, Faber's community decided to purchase Blemmell House, Brompton, as a site for the new Oratory. The house was demolished in early October, and building work began on the new house and temporary church. In November, Faber gave a five-day mission at the school at Dunne's Passage, Holborn, which was run as a joint venture by the Sisters of Compassion and the London Oratorians. He did so in order to evangelise the poor, non-practising, Catholics who lived in slums within the boundaries of his parish, and encourage them to attend the Oratory. The relish with which Faber describes the services demonstrates his ideal religious milieu, characterised by over-wrought and unashamed emotionalism and outward displays of fervour, which owes much to Evangelicalism. Although it is difficult to say conclusively whether this was the easiest or most difficult group to encourage to be emotional, Faber clearly succeeded, as he wrote of 'many most unhappy women ... on their knees before the crucifix, sobbing and beating their breasts'.[389]

During this year, Faber's correspondence exhibits a sense of melancholia and depression, a symptom of mercury poisoning,[390] and this becomes an embedded characteristic of his thought from this time onwards.[391] There is also, some eleven years before his death, an insightful awareness of personal mortality, which was undoubtedly strengthened by his experience of chronic illness and solitude, as it differed subtly from what we can describe as a general Christian awareness of death. These are both highlighted in a letter to the Countess of Arundel, in which Faber remarks that he has no earthly ties, and therefore nothing for which he has to remain alive.[392] He wrote, 'Today I made a meditation on giving up to God promptly, sweetly, and without a word, the soul he has given me.'[393] These themes continued during 1853, and the oppressive, stifling descriptions of symptoms within Faber's correspondence makes certain that the historian does not underestimate the extent to which their unpleasantness affected his morale.[394] He wrote to Newman, 'I find invalidism anything but sanctifying to <u>me</u> ... suffering doesn't make saints, but polishes them up when once made.'[395]

Faber's year saint for 1853 was St Vincent de Paul and, at Easter, he celebrated the seventh anniversary of his Ordination in the Roman Church.[396] Another anniversary, which occurred on 26 May, was fourteen years since his Anglican ordination; however, this event had been deleted from the public side of Faber's thought. Among the works written during 1853 was the *Essay on Catholic Home Missions*, which was published during August. The essay is concerned with the missionary activity of the Church, and the notion of the spirit of the age is represented by the distrust that exists between it and contemporary society.[397] Faber writes that the Church has an important role to play in persuading those who are not devout to be more serious, which it does by confraternities, the building of churches, schools, and poor relief.[398] We have already seen that authenticity in the spiritual life is important to Faber, and he notes that the majority need the missionary activity of the Church because of insufficient devotion.[399] It is characteristic of Faber's mind that he often exaggerates the distinction between active and contemplative spirituality, and by doing so, creates a distinctly compartmentalised view of spiritual experience. Here, he uses the experiences of female saints and religious to measure their authenticity and success.[400] He ascribes to this group 'ecstasies, visions, and unearthly heights of prayer',[401] and by linking these to sinlessness and 'weakness of sex',[402] epitomises the characteristic nineteenth-century Romantic idealisation of the female. He notes with surprise that such individuals are frequently interested in missionary activity, such as evangelisation.[403] In September, the London Oratorians closed the chapel in King William Street, and moved to Brompton.[404] Faber was at Sydenham for most of the autumn, and during October he wrote, 'I am very much out of spirits.'[405]

In January 1854, Faber noted that his invalid status was

common knowledge among critics of his book *All For Jesus*, writing, 'They say I send people to heaven lolling on a sofa.'[406] This comment leads us to question whether at least some of Faber's critics felt that his illness was an affectation, or caused by hypochondria, and therefore not entirely authentic. A letter to Newman, written during January 1854, contains one of Faber's few references to life outside the Oratory. He opined that Prince Albert would demand more constitutional power after the success of the Great Exhibition, and wrote wryly that public opinion would not allow this to happen.[407]

Twelve hundred people[408] attended the inaugural Eucharist for the opening of the new church and house of the London Oratory, at Brompton,[409] on Wednesday, 22 March.[410] Faber was so unwell on the opening day that he was unable to stand, and was still in bed at the beginning of the Gospel. In his dramatic account of the scene, Faber recalled that a message from Newman, who was sitting in the sanctuary with other bishops and clergy, persuaded him to leave his bed in order to preach. Faber arrived in the pulpit at the end of the Gospel[411] to give an address, which we will discuss later in this study. He wrote, 'I knew nothing more till I found myself in my room again'; however, he was well enough to preach at the afternoon service of Benediction, at which Newman presided.[412]

During the following month, Manning gave the sermon at the Oratory on St Philip's feast day, entitled *The Certainty of Divine Faith*.[413] Faber was 40 in June 1854, although his letters give the impression that he is much older, a trait that is reinforced by a cloying all-pervasive weariness with life. On 9 July, Pius IX created Faber Doctor of Divinity,[414] an event which demonstrated the pope's support for *All for Jesus* at both an official and an individual level. However, later in the year, Pius IX issued *Ineffabilis Deus*, the document which defined the doctrine of the Immaculate Conception. It seems possible that Faber's doctorate was awarded at least partially because the Pope thought that Faber would be enthusiastic about the latest devotion, and work to ensure its acceptance in England.

The reality of the situation was less simple, and Faber's correspondence shows that he too was able to see difficulties inherent within the definition. His acceptance of it was based not on emotional but on theological and ecclesiastical grounds, which were related to his Ultramontane acceptance of papal authority. However, it was the implications for increased papal authority, and not the theology surrounding the notion of the Immaculate Conception itself, which was problematic for the majority. In a letter to Newman, Faber recalled a conversation that took place in Wiseman's carriage, in which the latter indicated that several bishops, clergy, and lay people in London had been unsettled by the definition. He also noted that it had provided a common bond of discontent between indigenous Catholics and converts, primarily because a number of the latter had not realised the extent to which papal pre-eminence could be used. It is revealing of Faber's sensitivity to his position that he avoided arguing for the Ultramontane position in discussion,[415] a stance that illustrates that there were limits to Faber's espousal of Ultramontanism.[416] This controversy highlights the extent to which Wiseman and Faber supported each other, and shows that Faber was utilised as a link between Wiseman and Newman. In a letter to Newman, Faber indicates that he has been asked to persuade Newman to write on the Immaculate Conception, and suggests that doing so would necessitate writing at length on the development of doctrine.[417] Faber quotes Wiseman as saying, 'He is the only man to do it, and with his resources it will be easy to him, and people will listen to him.'[418] In *The Blessed Sacrament*, which was published on 24 March 1855, Faber described the definition of the Immaculate Conception as 'the irresistible and spontaneous outburst of doctrine and devotion, too hot to be longer pent within her mighty heart'.[419] This shows that, whatever his private thoughts and discussions with other clergy, Faber expressed support for the Church in literature for general consumption. Faber preached the sermon *The Living Church* on the first celebration of the feast within the Westminster Diocese,[420] and published a pamphlet entitled *An exploration of the doctrine and definition of the Immaculate Conception*.

During August 1855, Faber took part in the Second Synod of the Diocese of Westminster as part of a committee that was preparing a catechism. Bowden notes that Faber had been invited to take on a more active role, but was prevented from doing so by humility,[421] a stance which plausibly demonstrates Faber's dislike of drawing attention to himself. It seems equally probable, however, that Faber was too ill to have played a greater role, as by the end of the month he informed the Earl of Arundel that his health was unlikely to improve;[422] and, as we have noted throughout this chapter, it seems probable that medication was contributing to this process of decline. He stated, perhaps defensively, that he was not unduly depressed by the thought of suffering, as he accepted it as being divine in origin; however, he commented 'What I fear is my patience, temper, and the proper degree of unselfishness.'[423] Faber expressed concern that the large amounts of opium he was taking would affect his ability to write, and ensure that he would not produce any more books.[424] Although we cannot say, other than generally, to what extent fifteen years of taking opium affected Faber, it seems obvious that it would have affected his thought processes. It is interesting that, unlike a number of other individuals in the nineteenth century, such as Coleridge, he did not think that opium improved, or brought a new dimension to, creativity and the process of writing. We can postulate that this was because, by this time, Faber possessed an advanced contemplative spirituality, which was apophatic by nature. It seems reasonable to suggest that he did not want to endanger this authentic manifestation of spirituality by importing drug-induced, therefore inauthentic, experiences. Faber was clearly concerned that his spirituality would be compromised by the combined effects of medication, which had already caused the mental confusion that we noted during 1847.

Events that took place during November 1855 initiated the process of emotional detachment between the Oratories at London and Birmingham, which had become officially independent in 1850. The primary reason for this controversy was the responsibilities given by Wiseman to the London Oratorians, for schools and for the spiritual direction of female religious, and the fact that Newman did not believe that the latter was a specifically Oratorian task. The antipathy was fuelled by the geographical distance between the two houses, and Newman's misgivings were aroused by conversations reported by Ullathorne, the Bishop of Birmingham, on his return from a visit to London. These were articulated in a carefully worded, private, written *Statement to the Birmingham*

Fathers, which expressed concern that Faber had exercised the autonomy of the London Oratory to an excessive extent, and had lost touch with the views both of the Oratorians at Birmingham and of Newman, who was recognised as the figurehead of both houses. Newman was particularly concerned that Faber was exercising too much influence over Wiseman, and the Bishops of Southwark[425] and Birmingham, and that this would harm the reputation of the Birmingham house. It is significant that Newman had no confidence in Wiseman, and it seems possible that his distrust of Faber dated from Faber's friendship with Wiseman, which became more marked at this time.[426] There is a substantial element of anguish, and perhaps hysteria, in the *Statement*; particularly in the protestations that Faber was being secretive, and trying to gain moral supremacy over Newman.[427] The latter was perturbed by Faber's popularity and influence with the hierarchy in England and at Rome, and was concerned that Faber would be able to bring about changes that would be forced upon both houses of the English Oratory. He wrote, 'We may wake in the morning and find that the Fathers at Brompton have demanded a virtually new rule, and imposed it, through Propaganda, upon us.'[428] It would be true to say that, whereas Faber understood the Catholic mind better than Newman, Newman had a better understanding of the English mind, and approached it with far greater sensitivity than Faber was capable of doing. It seems probable that it was only now that Newman realised that Faber could act as an autonomous individual, and that he had previously thought that by sending Faber to London he would retain overall control. It is as though, at one level, Newman regretted not going to London himself, particularly now that Faber was at the centre of attention.

In a letter to Wiseman, Faber discussed the friction with Newman. He wrote that his aim was to assert the autonomy of the London house over Birmingham, although he revealed that several of his Oratory fathers had taken the part of Newman in the controversy.[429] The role of Dalgairns is particularly interesting, as he seems, at this time, to have had sympathy with Newman whilst residing in London, which is perhaps unsurprising as he had been at Littlemore with

Newman during 1845. In another letter, in which Faber writes
much but says very little, he notes that the debate with
Newman had exacerbated his headaches.[430] This highlights not
only that Faber was inept at the intrigue of church politics,
probably from choice rather than naivety, but was not, by this
stage, physically strong enough to enter fully into such discussions.

During the first week of January 1856, Faber confided in
Wiseman that their Christmas festivities had been overshadowed by the disagreement with Newman. He wrote: 'It is not
Fr. [*sic*] Newman's way to give opportunities of explanation
and in all ye years of our acquaintance I never knew an impression he had once got fairly removed from his mind.'[431] There is
a tremendous sense of anger and hurt feelings on both sides of
this correspondence. Newman's replies do not appreciate
Faber's concerns and he frequently fails, refuses, or is unable to
respond to them or to answer Faber's questions. This quarrel
presents us with the central difference between the two men:
that they each had a fundamentally different emotional, as well
as spiritual, vocabulary; and, because of the sense of intrigue
and the impasse that had built up, it is difficult to establish
precisely where the truth lies.[432] However, we should not
underestimate the depth of Faber's attachment to Newman, or
the extent to which the realisation that their friendship had
been irrevocably damaged affected his already low morale.
This is revealed in a letter written by Faber four months later,
which is almost unbearable to read in manuscript form because
of its overpowering intensity, epitomised in sentences such as
the one that follows:

> I cannot forget that to you I owe all that I most value in
> this life, and to you simply I owe my salvation, if I am
> saved; nor can I forget that I have once loved you as I
> have never loved a friend before.[433]

Faber notes that he is not sure of the precise nature of their
disagreement, but wrote: 'I do not doubt that you have had
much to bear from me ... but I have never been untrue to
you.'[434] The sense of pathos is increased by Faber's statement
that he used Newman's patron, John the Evangelist, as his year

saint in the hope that this would reunite them.[435] It is worth
noting that Faber had, since his time at Oxford during the
1830s, a contradictory and complex relationship with Newman.
He had not always agreed with Newman, and therefore, the
potential for disagreement between the two individuals was
much deeper than the crisis of 1855–6. Faber viewed Newman
primarily as a father figure, who had shared the experiences of
conversion and church politics within two denominations; and
it is probable that his apprehension was caused by forfeiting
this aspect, and not by losing Newman's leadership. Faber's use
of language hints at this, as he uses the notion that Newman's
attitude towards him was the culmination of past disagreements and 'jealousies'.[436] He also emphasises a reported
conversation between the Birmingham Oratorian Joseph
Gordon and Newman, in which the latter expressed his regret
at having allowed Faber's Wilfridians to become Oratorians
nine years previously.

The London Oratorians corresponded with Newman on 22
May, in order to try to end their disagreement by St Philip's
feast day, on the 26th.[437] The letter is carefully worded in
order to create the right impression on Newman: 'We are most
anxious to do all that lies in our power towards removing any
obstacle to the renewal of our old terms of cordiality and
charity.'[438] This formality is offset by being friendly and almost
affectionate, and by using phrases such as 'we had not the least
intention of wounding your feelings',[439] it highlights the sense
of their awareness that they have hurt Newman personally.
The letter, which was clearly written by the community as a
whole, constantly refers to the debt that they owe to Newman
as their founder. Newman replied to this letter later in the
month, and in another letter, to Faber, he indicated that it was
Dalgairns, a member of the London house, who had first
discussed the petition to Propaganda with Newman on a
private visit to Birmingham.[440] The reply from London, dated
5 June,[441] indicated, perhaps courteously, that they had misunderstood Newman's motives, and had assumed that he had
made the first move towards being antagonistic. Its writer,
probably Faber, argues that Newman had overreacted to the
application to Propaganda, which had been done only because
Wiseman had suggested that the London house should take on

responsibility for schools and spiritual direction[442] within the diocese. It seems that, by this time, the London Oratorians were convinced of the rightness of not living in Newman's shadow, and had decided to distance themselves from his influence. This is because the writer asserts that knowledge of Newman's views on the matter would not have changed the outcome of the situation, or led them to reconsider the amendment to the rule.

Faber's letters to Wiseman, which are prolific during the remainder of this year, describe illness and week-long headaches which caused him to be both unable to preach[443] or to function as Superior. Time spent recuperating at Sydenham,[444] during July, August and September, gave Faber the opportunity to reflect on the continuing débâcle with Newman,[445] and the relationship between the London Oratory and Rome.[446] In a letter concerned with domestic issues, which contains a substantial amount of point scoring, Faber thanked Wiseman for his kindness to the congregation, and recalled their past acquaintance in Birmingham,[447] during which Wiseman had encouraged the Wilfridian venture. Interestingly, Dalgairns informed Faber of his belief that the Oratory in London was more akin to St Philip's original conception of an Oratory than that at Birmingham.[448] Although this may have been intended to placate Faber after his behaviour with Newman, it becomes more significant if we remember that the idea of bringing the Oratory to England originated with Faber, not Newman. The Philipine ethos and character had been part of Faber's spiritual and intellectual makeup for far longer than it had for Newman, and was more deeply embedded in Faber's spirituality than in Newman's.

It is possible to gauge Faber's state of health from the style of his handwriting, which is small, neat and fairly upright when he is well and becomes sloping, and almost illegible, when he is ill. From 1856 onwards, it is almost solely the latter. In July, Faber moved away from London to Sydenham,[449] and at the beginning of October 1856 he resigned as Superior[450] because he was too unwell to continue, although his resignation does not seem to have been accepted. During the following four years, Faber spent long periods in bed.

The majority of Faber's sparse correspondence written

during 1857 is concerned with the day-to-day running of the Oratory. Likewise, his year saint was Mary Magdalene; but he does not indicate reasons for this, although it may be related to the altar to the saint, which had been erected in the Oratory church during the previous January. The common factor in Faber's letters is, unsurprisingly, illness, to which he was particularly susceptible after any form of exertion, such as the extra services during May and Lent.[451] The only extant letter to Morris for this year discusses Morris's move from Plymouth, and his inability to settle within the Church of Rome.[452] Once again, Faber's emphasis on Church authority did not allow him to wholly empathise with or understand Morris's position, and Faber believed that Morris's problems were caused primarily by his inability to be submissive towards authority.

Later in the year, Dalgairns published the third edition of his book on the Sacred Heart, and Faber petitioned Wiseman for DDs for Dalgairns and two other members of his community, whom he described as 'theologians and literary men':[453] Knox and Stanton.[454] This underlines Faber's constant willingness to promote and encourage the intellectual pursuits of members of his congregation. He opined that a writer should live in a large city, preferably the capital, because he thought that the group of intellectuals present in such an environment would be more varied, numerous, and exacting than was possible within the society of a small country town. He also warned against an individual becoming over confident of their ability prior to being tested by those who were intellectually superior. Despite such rigour, he indicated that he was no longer interested in criticism of his own work. He attributed this trait to the tutelage of the poet Wordsworth, some twenty years earlier, and noted that, because of this, he was able to formulate his own intellectual standards and targets for each book. In a rare example, he described the writing process, noting that he worked slowly and carefully so that he did not have to re-write before publication. It is interesting, and significant as we are judging Faber's literary output later in this study, that he believed that his ability to express ideas was of inferior quality to the ideas which he produced. Because of this, he opined that he hoped his work would be judged as a whole, rather than as individual books.[455]

In October 1857, Faber lost the use of one of his legs, and was confined to bed until February 1858. During November 1857, the London Oratorians became involved in debate with the editor of the *Union* newspaper, who accused them of heresy for a statement given in a public sermon during the previous year. Faber denied that the words 'to the sinner the name of Jesus was bitter and the name of Mary sweet'[456] had been used by anyone at the Oratory, and wrote that such a sentiment was heretical. This exchange of letters highlights the rightness of Faber's keeping a record of the contents of sermons.

By 1858, Faber inhabited a world that was mentally rather than physically active. He desired to write as much as was possible before his death, although he believed that he was hastening the event by working so hard.[457] In a letter to Hutchison, he wrote of the nine books and numerous sermons that he had written during the past five years, and of the three books in preparation. There is a desperate sense that he does not have time to write as much as he wants to, and he noted, 'my mind is now like a locomotive that has started with neither driver nor stoker'.[458] He wrote, 'a newspaper says of me, that the characteristic of my mind is that "it looks forward, not so much with horror, as with eagerness, to ... eternal glory!"'.[459] Faber's longing for death is expressed in emotional terms that parallel those of St Thérèse of Lisieux, who is Faber's natural heir in terms of the relationship between suffering, spirituality and the desire for God. This sense of anticipation is closely related to the eschatological strand that is present throughout Faber's mature thought, to the same extent both as an Anglican and as a Catholic.

Later in the year, Faber was sufficiently well to be present at the opening of St Wilfrid's Convent, Chelsea.

In the *Spiritual Conferences*, written in 1859, Faber divulged an important fact about himself, which is included here, rather than in discussion of the book, because it puts his life, intellectual development and style of working into a different perspective. Faber wrote that as a child he had been taught that it was wrong to be original, as originality was tantamount to showing off, and that this notion had remained with him throughout his life. Writing about his childhood love and enjoyment of poetry, Faber wrote of his parents:

> They showed ... their interest and their love by laying
> down this rule for me, that whenever any verse pleased
> me exceedingly, and appeared to me much better than
> the rest, I was to run my pen through it and concoct
> something less striking. It was a sharp discipline, but
> tolerably efficacious.[460]

This passage fundamentally alters the way in which historians
must assess Faber's life and thought, as it shows that he had
learned that it was better to be second best; and, because of
this, always held himself, and others, back. This idea permeates
every aspect of his mature thought. Thus, elsewhere in the
Spiritual Conferences he wrote, 'In devotion it is better to be safe
than to be original',[461] and he frequently intimates that it is
wrong to get above oneself, both spiritually and personally; an
idea which translates into Faber's belief that his best was
somehow wrong. This is coupled with legitimate spiritual ideas
such as humility, but it colours them with an element of sour-
ness that is related to Faber's well-developed sense of ridicule
and cynicism, which may have been caused originally by his
parents' attitude. Thus, although the notion of forgetfulness of
self shows the influence of scholasticism on his thought, the
Medievalist would have used his best work to glorify God, not
his second best, making this a perversion of such a tradition.
Another idea, present in the *Spiritual Conferences*, is the danger
of sickness in the spiritual life, and the equation of this with
lack of self-denial, to the detriment of the individual's spirituality.[462] We have already seen that meditation on death was an
important part of his spirituality throughout Faber's life,
particularly in the last ten years or so. In the *Spiritual
Conferences*, there is a marked preoccupation with death, which
mirrors the same preoccupation in his everyday life. Faber
notes that he had constantly expected the end of the world
when he was young, and this trait is linked to the eschatological
strand, which we discussed, during the previous year.[463] It
seems possible that this trait is a leftover from his early
Evangelicalism, and that it may stem, at least partially, from the
influence of the apocalyptic writings of his uncle, G. S. Faber.

In a letter to Morris, Faber discussed Newman's influence
over converts to Rome, writing 'now their work is his work,

and his success their success'.[464] Here, as elsewhere, Faber's response to Newman is contradictory; he seems unsure of whether to admire or to dislike him. An interesting, although almost illegible, endnote by Morris, provides the information that he had always believed Newman to be responsible for his own conversion. Morris does not indicate the extent to which Faber played a role in this event.

At the beginning of 1860, work started on building the South Kensington Museum adjacent to the Oratory. Several letters, from Faber and other Oratorians, discuss Queen Victoria's plan to ask them to move so that the museum could be larger; and they were advised that, should they wish to sell, their land was worth £42,000. Faber's room was on the first floor of the house, and he was distressed because the new building, which was only some thirty feet away, blocked the light and obliterated the view of fields from his window.[465]

Between December 1859 and May 1860, Faber was either in his room at the Oratory or at Sydenham. During this period he became more detached from, and dissatisfied with, the world around him. He wrote, 'You must all of you pray hard for me. I am breaking under my load',[466] which included sleeplessness, headache and sickness. In *Bethlehem*, which was published during 1860, he inserts, in passing, a notion which is almost certainly autobiographical:

> Then there are those who are always wishing life away. Our own hearts go along with these. We leave no place, however beautiful ... so much with regret as with the feeling wherewith a man turns away from an enemy he has beaten, and with whom he has no more to do.[467]

This passage highlights the detachment that was present within Faber's mental world, which combined a legitimate, positive, spiritual detachment with negative overtones of melancholia and lethargy. This, together with caring for the Oratorian Antony Hutchison, who was also unwell, used up his resources; and Faber wrote his Will some time during 1860, leaving his property and the copyright of his books to William Gordon and Charles Bowden, both of the London Oratory, who were also his executors.[468] There is a tangible sense of anguish, almost of claustrophobia, in Faber's correspondence, which is characterised by phrases such as, 'I have come to the end of my tether.'[469]

A number of Faber's letters are concerned with spiritual direction, and the majority of those that survive are addressed to both single and married women. These are essentially private documents and, because of the nature of Faber's personality, it is unsurprising that the most successful are to individuals who appreciate his own spiritual milieu. Thus, the group with whom he most empathises are those who share his own moral fastidiousness, devotional character, and serious-ness about religion; factors that are all present in the few letters to individuals who had entered contemplative religious orders.[470] Faber clearly regarded these individuals as being professional religious, and there is no sense that he viewed them as being inferior because they were women, or because they were not priests. Faber had a particular admiration for individuals who had a Carmelite vocation. His letters to Elizabeth Thompson,[471] who became a Carmelite in Paris in 1860, are characterised not only by enthusiasm and poetic ebullience, but also by theological awareness, as though Faber wished to demonstrate knowledge as well as piety, and reveal the deeper recesses of his own spirituality. The latter was now increasingly contemplative in character and, from 1860 onwards, Carmelite spirituality was the central facet of his spir-itual world. In letters written during this time, Faber encouraged others to practise both the practical spirituality that had always been part of his own experience, as well as a contemplative spirituality that was relatively new to him. This is underlined by Faber's choice of Teresa of Avila as his year saint, and by his note, 'I get more and more of a Carmelite in my affections; I wish I did so in spirit and in practice.'[472] In an official and businesslike letter to the Prioress of the Monastery that Thompson had joined, he wrote, 'It is a privilege of which I am quite unworthy, that God should have allowed me to send some of my spiritual children to Carmel.'[473] He also expressed the wish that there should be a Carmelite Monastery in London.[474]

Faber spent November and the first two weeks of December at Arundel with the Duke of Norfolk, who was dying. In a letter

to Wiseman, informing him of the Duke's death and arrangements for the funeral, Faber described himself as 'broken
down'[475] and wrote, 'I have been in pain myself most ye
while'.[476] The correspondence from Arundel underlines
Faber's moral and theological gravity with regard to death, and
the importance of being adequately prepared for it. It indicates
the seriousness with which Faber viewed his vocation as spiritual director and priest, and underlines his capacity for a
sympathetic, almost affectionate, compassion.

This empathy and enthusiasm is totally hidden in Faber's
dealings with other directees. These letters are dull, as though
he does not really care because he thinks that the individual
concerned is spiritually mediocre and unlikely to succeed,
perhaps because of some innate superficiality. This is apparent
in one letter, to the superior of a convent, which discusses an
individual's apparent lack of vocation.[477] Faber's cynical bitter-
ness and lack of sympathy with his subject is evident here, and
we can comment that he seems to have forgotten his own difficulties in the early stages of his vocation.[478] In another
example, Faber highlights the dangers inherent within the
experience of another individual, in this case the experience of
grief, because of negative associations of his own. In a, slightly
unsympathetic, letter written to a woman whose husband had
just died, he wrote: 'I ask our Lord to give you an increased
devotion to his passion … in order that you may not be
absorbed in this grief in the way in which our corrupt nature is
apt to be.'[479] Thus, our primary criticism of Faber's letters of
spiritual direction is that they can be excessively paternalistic,
and he seems occasionally to try to solve problems by discounting their existence.

Faber demonstrates the Philipine notion of not thinking of
any vocation as exclusive, so that a Christian life outside a
monastery is as important as one within it. He promulgated a
very simple view of religious observance, in which the moral
choices involved are expressed in terms of black and white,
such as his throwaway comment to Morris that it is equally
possible that he will be damned as saved.[480] Here, as elsewhere,
Faber is always aware of the propensity of the individual to
make excuses, whether caused by chronic illness, grief or
temporary sickness.[481] His most biting cynicism is reserved for

those whose spiritual endeavour is not sufficiently serious, and he is always aware of any form of insincerity, pride or self-interest.

During 1861, Faber spent several weeks on vacation at Filey, Yorkshire, and during this time illness manifested itself in the form of kidney pain, diarrhoea, and feelings of suffocation.[482] He wrote to Bowden, 'In all ye years I have been a Catholic I have never been so ill as I am now, nor so miserably depressed'[483] and, in a barely legible letter, informed Morris that he no longer experienced good days.[484] Tegart, his physician, attributed Faber's diarrhoea to the effect of kidney disease[485] but, as we have already seen, it could equally have been attributable to the mercury content of his medication. During December, Faber experienced the first of two final periods of remission from his illness, a recovery which he attributed to the intervention of God. There is a marked element of pathos in the joy and relief with which he asked those close to him for prayers of thanksgiving for the 'graces and spiritual sweetnesses'[486] experienced during the previous months.

Faber's year saints from 1861 until 1863, the year of his death, were Michael, Gabriel and Raphael. Overwork and illness remained two of the dominant themes of this period. His life became insular, concerned with Oratorian affairs, and impossible to define solely in outward terms. Overwork was caused by the success of the London Oratory apostolate, and Faber describes an ever-increasing flow of both male and female converts and of men applying to join the Oratory. He notes that he has no time to read literature for its own sake, or newspapers, and that he wrote only official and important personal correspondence.[487] Faber's choice of reading matter is also limited to what he considered essential, that is scripture, *The Imitation of Christ* and the works of St Teresa of Avila.[488] The latter provides an interesting balance between the detached contemplative spirituality of an individual such as St John of the Cross, and the realm of a more outward spiritual experience. This undoubtedly legitimised Faber's lifelong belief that spiritual experiences were important and necessary. His response to the latter also shows the distrust of the intellectual which had been a constant facet of his thought, and he wrote, 'The Teresian wish to die for ye least rubric of ye Church's least ceremony comes to me more natural than ever.'[489]

The level and style of Faber's Ultramontane intellectual deference to authority, which was alien to a liberal Catholic such as Newman, shows itself in his willingness to leave both fundamental and lesser questions solely to the church hierarchy to decide.[490] This notion is visible in several works of this period. In the pamphlet *Devotion to the Pope*, Faber notes the centrality to the Christian life of obedience to superiors, a notion which has two levels, personal and theological. In the first, obedience to the pope is part of a wider affection towards the person of Jesus,[491] whilst in the second the pope is presented as the earthly representative of Jesus.[492] He notes that the spiritual power of the papacy places it above earthly rulers, and reserves his greatest criticism for those who seek to deny or subvert it.[493] It is significant that the fundamental test of the piety of the individual Catholic is how much empathy they have towards the pope. This idea is expressed in uncompromising language as being a prerequisite of God's sympathy for the individual,[494] and therefore, those who reject the papacy are, like those who dishonour the saints, rejecting God.[495] Faber instructs his reader not to distinguish between the persona of the pope and the doctrine of the papacy, but to view both human and divine elements as being essentially the same.[496] The spirit of the age is present in *Devotion to the Church* as the notion that the Antichrist is present in the nineteenth century in the form of hostility towards the Church.[497] The sub-theme of this work is that to criticise the Church is to sin against Christ and the Holy Spirit,[498] and Faber notes that those inside, as well as those outside the Church, can be equally guilty of this. He expresses these notions in terms that reinforce the strand of apocalypticism, which is a consistent part of his thought. Thus, he writes that the age is like the 'last days',[499] 'evil … lawless … faithless … prayerless'.[500] Faber is concerned that those inside the Church do not have sufficient loyalty to the Church as a divine, rather than a human, edifice.

During the 1860s, Faber's private spiritual vocabulary differed considerably from that which still appeared within his books, a notion which is significant because his books are fairly uniform in character, despite being written over a period of ten years. We have already noted Faber's unwillingness to discuss spiritual matters; however, in a letter to Watts Russell, dated January 1862, he provides an uncharacteristically unguarded insight into his inner life. He noted that his spiritual life was unrecognisable from what it had been several years earlier, and the most noticeable difference is the pronounced contemplative strand that he had described during the previous year. He wrote, 'I can take little of ... interest in theological refinements, which once were the delight of my meditations',[501] and noted that these had been replaced by an awareness of the presence of God.[502] Although this reference is somewhat vague, it seems possible that he is describing an illuminative spiritual state, an idea that seems to be implied in the passage that follows:

> It seems as if God arrested me at the threshold, and so filled the <u>general</u> truth with surprising sweetness and the same time with vague misty intelligence, that I cannot proceed to details, and that I feel almost a dislike to having truths brought nearer or made clearer.[503]

The possession of such a spirituality may, at least partially, explain Faber's profound insight and ability to express spiritual notions, which at times was considerable. It seems likely, however, that the illuminative was not a constant spiritual state for Faber, but one that was intermittent; and here, as throughout Faber's life, his spiritual experience does not fit snugly into a precise category.

The letter also includes a discussion of French spiritual writers that Faber disliked, and those that he viewed favourably. The former are represented by Olier,[504] and his reasons are characteristic: namely, mannerisms and unreality, both of which he contrasted with the 'reverential familiarity, which belongs to Italian and Spanish saints'.[505] It is revealing that he is critical of French spiritual writers, noting that they are never entirely Catholic because they are unable to lose their national identity. Grignon de Montfort,[506] from whom Faber inherited his devotion to Mary, represents the latter. He wrote of his regard for the book *Vraie Devotion*, which he translated into English, but added that he was unable comfortably to make its contents part of his spirituality, as he considered its devotion to Mary to be difficult.[507] Faber also notes sympathy with St John Vianney,[508] and that he had translated the *Spiritual Doctrine of Fr Louis Lallemant* during 1855.

Faber preached at the Oratory Church during Lent 1863, and on Passion Sunday, 22 March, he preached his final sermon, upon the subject *Our Blessed Lord bowing his head upon the cross*. Its final paragraph is worth quoting in full, as a characteristic example of Faber's manner in both private and public expressions of spirituality.

> Dearest Lord! Why do we ever think of anyone but Him? How can we manage to love anyone but Him? Oh may we come to feel and to know that we have but one faith, one hope, one love, one consolation in weary painful time, and one reward in the grand, jubilant eternity – Jesus Christ and Him crucified![509]

We can also suggest that the chapters of Paul's first letter to the Corinthians, from which Faber's final extract comes, aptly sums up his own public apostolate, as shown by these words:

> I did not come proclaiming the mystery of God to you in lofty words or wisdom. For I decided to know nothing among you except Jesus Christ, and Him crucified.[510]

Faber presided at the Eucharist for the last time, in the Oratory Church, on Sunday 26 April.

The five months between May and September followed a characteristic pattern of illness and inaction, during which Faber became gradually weaker. In May 1863, Faber's illness once again went into remission, and John Bowden, in a letter to his mother, Elizabeth Bowden, wrote, 'nobody ever believes the Father's immense power of rallying until they see it'.[511] Faber was depressed by this period of remission, and wrote to the Duchess of Norfolk: 'I fear I am not going to die just now, and I feel how long and insufferable the time is till [*sic*] death comes.'[512] During this time, which was spent either in his room or in the garden at Brompton or Sydenham, Faber wrote valedictory letters to friends, a number of which contained reminiscences relating to the years since he had become a Roman Catholic.[513] However, it is notable that he destroyed the majority of letters that were sent to him during this period,[514] and few of those that remain are concerned with private spiritual matters. Later in June, Faber's health deteriorated, and on his 49th birthday, 28 June, he was thought to be dying. Wiseman visited Faber on 14 July and, on returning home, wrote a long epistle in which he praised Faber's contribution to the Roman Church abroad, in England, and in the diocese, both through his writings and in founding the London Oratory.[515] The letter is written in Wiseman's characteristically detached formal style, and reads almost as though he was already writing, or at least meditating, Faber's obituary. Newman also visited, on 20 July, and Faber's affectionate account of their final meeting contrasts with Newman's detached unsympathetic formality.[516]

On 3 August, Faber wrote of intense suffering which caused depression, and noted, 'I regret to say that yesterday I made the announcement that I neither would nor could bear the pain God was putting upon me.'[517] He believed that he had an unknown disease of the kidneys,[518] a diagnosis that was, in retrospect, correct. His physician believed that his illness was aggravated by heart disease and circulatory dysfunction,[519] which was the effect rather than the cause of his problem.

A series of letters from John and Charles Bowden, both members of Faber's community, to their mother, provides a comprehensive analysis of Faber's medical condition during the summer of 1863.[520] On 20 September John Bowden wrote, 'His whole state is very melancholy: getting more helpless and childish, not knowing people except at intervals, sometimes quiet and silent and sometimes very restless. One cannot wish it to last.'[521]

During the late evening of Friday 25 September, the day before Faber's death, the same correspondent opined,

> I think we must count by hours instead of days. A great change has come over the Father ... he is ... breathing hard, but quite conscious. His stomach is very much swelled, and he scarcely feels anything, neither the sores

from lying so long, nor even a large mustard plaster at the back of his neck.[522]

After writing this, John Bowden left Faber's room, returning at 6.15 on the following morning, at which time he observed, 'The dear Father is certainly in his agony now. This morning there are most of the signs of immediate death, and I shall not expect him to live more than an hour. Fiat voluntas tua.'[523] Faber died three-quarters of an hour later, at 7 o'clock, on the morning of Saturday 26 September:[524] 'Just after seven a sudden change came over the Father; his head turned a little to the right, his breathing seemed to stop; a few spasmodic gasps followed and his spirit passed away.'[525] The last of this series of letters, which contains a detailed description of Faber's death and its aftermath, contains the following: 'He lay quite still; his eyes open, but he saw nothing earthly, only looked marvellously beautiful. Could it have been St Philip's blessing?'[526]

Notes

1 During this time, Faber met Fr (now Blessed) Dominic Barberi (1792–1849). For references to Barberi, see F. W. Faber to J. H. Newman, LO, Vol. 1, No. 40, 12 December 1845; F. W. Faber to J. H. Newman, LO, Vol. 1, No. 41, 16 December 1845. Barberi labelled the Wilfridians 'Brothers of the will of Faber'. S. Gilley, *F. W. Faber (1814–1863)*, in DNB (Oxford, OUP, 2004) Vol. 18, p. 872.

2 F. W. Faber to J. H. Newman, LO, Vol. 1, No. 43, 19 December 1845.

3 F. W. Faber to J. B. Morris, LO, Vol. 17, No. 101, 4 January 1846. Also, F. W. Faber to J. H. Newman, LO, Vol. 1, No. 44, 9 January 1846, and LO, Vol. 1, No. 44, January 1846.

4 F. W. Faber to J. B. Morris, LO, Vol. 17, No. 101, 4 January 1846. For Faber's reference to Morris's conversion, see F. W. Faber to J. B. Morris, LO, Vol. 17, No. 101a, 27 January 1846.

5 F. W. Faber (1846), *Grounds for Remaining in the Anglican Communion*, London, Toovey.

6 Ibid. pp. 4–5.

7 Ibid. p. 4.

8 Ibid. p. 16.

9 Ibid. pp. 6–8.

10 Ibid. pp. 8–9.

11 Ibid. p. 16.

12 Ibid. p. 15.
13 Ibid. p. 21.
14 Ibid. pp. 10–11.
15 Ibid. pp. 22–3.
16 Ibid. pp. 31–3.
17 Ibid. p. 67.
18 Ibid. p. 37.
19 Ibid. p. 32.
20 Ibid.
21 J. H. Newman to A. St John, LO, Vol. 1, No. 47, 18 February 1846.
22 Ibid.
23 Ibid.
24 Ibid.
25 F. W. Faber to J. H. Newman, LO, Vol. 1, No. 45, 29 January 1846.
26 Ibid.
27 Ibid.
28 J. H. Newman to F. W. Faber, LO, Vol. 8, No. 20, 1 February 1846.
29 (William) Antony Hutchison (1822–1863).
30 F. W. Faber to L. Bartolommei, LO, Vol. 21, No. 70, 6 April 1846.
31 F. W. Faber to J. Strickson, Septuagesima Sunday (8 February) 1846, in Bowden, *Life*, Letter LCVII, pp. 220–2.
32 F. W. Faber to J. H. Newman, LO, Vol. 1, No. 45, 29 January 1846.
33 F. W. Faber to J. Strickson, LO, Vol. 16, No. 3, 14 February 1846.
34 Ibid.
35 Ibid.
36 F. W. Faber to Wilfridian Community, LO, Vol. 16, No. 2, 12 February 1846.
37 Faber provides this date in a letter to J. B. Morris, LO, Vol. 17, No. 122, 11 February 1848.
38 F. W. Faber, *Rule of Brothers of the Will of God.* Unpublished MS in hand of F. W. Faber, LO, Chapter 2.2. [Hereafter referred to as Faber, *Rule*.]
39 F. W. Faber to J. H. Newman, LO, Vol. 1, No. 50, 24 March 1847.
40 Philip Neri (1515–1595) (Oratory), John of God (1495–1550) (Brothers Hospitallers), Ignatius Loyola (1491/5–1556) (Society of Jesus).
41 Faber, *Rule*, Prologue.
42 Ibid. Chapter 1.3.
43 Ibid.
44 Ibid. Chapter 2.1. and 3.1.
45 Ibid. Chapter 2.8.

46 Ibid. Prologue.
47 Ibid. Chapter 2.3.
48 Ibid.
49 Ibid.
50 F. W. Faber to J. B. Morris, LO, Vol. 17, No. 137, 19 April 1852.
51 Faber, *Rule*, Chapter 1.5.
52 Ibid. Chapter 2.13.
53 Ibid. Chapter 4.2.
54 F. W. Faber to J. C. Strickson, LO, Vol. 16, No. 1, Septuagesima Sunday (8 February) 1846.
55 Faber, *Rule*, Chapter 1.1.
56 Ibid.
57 Ibid. Chapter 1.2.
58 Ibid. Prologue and Epilogue.
59 Ibid. Prologue.
60 Ibid. Chapter 3.4.
61 Ibid. Prologue.
62 Ibid. Chapter 3.4.
63 Ibid. Chapter 2.12.
64 Ibid.
65 Ibid. Chapter 3.4.
66 'The superior can hardly be too zealous of long vocal prayers as distinctive of ye Spirit of cheerfulness.' Ibid.
67 Ibid. Chapter 2.13.
68 Ibid. Chapter 2, Prologue, 2.13.
69 Ibid. Chapter 3.4.
70 F. W. Faber (n.d.), *Growth in Holiness: or the Progress of the Spiritual Life*, 3rd edn, London, Burns & Oates, p. 275.
71 Ibid. p. 199.
72 Ibid. p. 399.
73 F. W. Faber, Sermon, *On Frittering*, n.d. Unpublished MS in hand of F. W. Faber, LO, Packet 3, No. 65.
74 Faber, *Rule*, Chapter 2.4.
75 Ibid.
76 Ibid. Chapter 2.5.
77 Ibid.
78 Ibid.
79 Ibid.
80 Ibid. Chapter 2.2.
81 Ibid. Chapter 1.1, 2, Prologue, 3.4.
82 Ibid. Chapter 3.4.
83 Ibid.
84 Ibid. Chapter 7.3.
85 Ibid.
86 Ibid. Chapter 7.2.
87 Ibid. Chapter 7.1.
88 F. W. Faber to J. C. Strickson, LO, Vol. 16, No. 4, Ash Wednesday (25 February) 1846.

89 Ibid.
90 Ibid.
91 F. W. Faber to J. C. Strickson, LO, Vol. 16, No. 5, 27 February 1846.
92 F. W. Faber to J. C. Strickson, LO, Vol. 16, No. 6, 11 March 1846.
93 Ibid.
94 F. W. Faber to J. B. Morris, LO, Vol. 17, No. 103, 18 March 1846.
95 Ibid.
96 F. W. Faber to L. Bartolommei, LO, Vol. 21, No. 70, 6 April 1846.
97 F. W. Faber to J. B. Morris, LO, Vol. 17, No. 102, Easter Tuesday (14 April) 1846.
98 Ibid.
99 Ibid.
100 Ibid.
101 Ibid.
102 F. W. Faber to N. Wiseman, LO, Vol. 21, No. 127, n.d. 1846.
103 LO, Vol. *Oratory in London: Chronology 1845–1947*, n.p.
104 Bowden, *Life*, p. 254.
105 F. W. Faber to L. Bartolommei, LO, Vol. 21, No. 73, St Alphonso Ligouri (2 August) 1846.
106 Ibid.
107 Ibid.
108 F. W. Faber to L. Bartolommei, LO, Vol. 21, No. 74, St Jane Frances de Chantal (21 August) 1846.
109 F. W. Faber to L. Bartolommei, LO, Vol. 21, No. 73, St Alphonso Ligouri (2 August) 1846.
110 Ibid. Also, F. W. Faber to L. Bartolommei, LO, Vol. 21, No. 74, St Jane Frances de Chantal (21 August) 1846.
111 F. W. Faber to J. B. Morris, LO, Vol. 17, No. 106, 5 August 1846.
112 Ibid.
113 Morris's letter is not extant; however, his criticism can be gauged by Faber's reply. See F. W. Faber to J. B. Morris, LO, Vol. 17, No. 106, 5 August 1846.
114 Ibid.
115 Ibid.
116 Ibid.
117 F. W. Faber to L. Bartolommei, LO, Vol. 21, No. 74, St Jane Frances de Chantal (21 August) 1846.
118 Ibid.
119 Addington, *Faber: Poet and Priest*, p. 149.
120 F. W. Faber to A. Hutchison, 5 September 1846, in Addington, *Faber: Poet and Priest*, p. 149.
121 F. W. Faber to M. Watts Russell, LO, Vol. 21, No. 4, 5 October 1846.
122 F. W. Faber to L. Bartolommei, quoted in Addington, *Faber: Poet and Priest*, p. 149.

123 LO, Vol. *The Oratory in London*, p. 42.

124 *The Tablet*, 17 October 1846.

125 F. W. Faber to L. Bartolommei, LO, Vol. 21, No. 76, 13 October 1847.

126 F. W. Faber to L. Bartolommei, LO, Vol. 21, No. 77, trans. of St Thomas of Canterbury, 1847.

127 T. F. Knox to J. H. Newman, LO, Vol. 7, No. 81, 24 September 1847.

128 Ibid.

129 F. W. Faber to M. Watts Russell, LO, Vol. 21, No. 6, All Souls' Day (2 November) 1846.

130 F. W. Faber to M. Watts Russell, LO, Vol. 21, No. 6, All Souls' Day (2 November) 1846.

131 F. W. Faber to M. Watts Russell, LO, Vol. 21, No. 7, Feast of St Didacus (13 November) 1846.

132 Ibid.

133 Ibid.

134 F. W. Faber to Lord Shrewsbury, LO, Vol. 21, No. 18, 14 December 1846.

135 F. W. Faber to J. B. Morris, LO, Vol. 17, No. 110, November 1846. See also F. W. Faber to F. Lythgoe, LO, Vol. 21, No. 138, 12 January 1847.

136 F. W. Faber to F. Lythgoe, LO, Vol. 21, No. 138, 12 January 1847.

137 F. W. Faber to M. Watts Russell, LO, Vol. 21, No. 6, All Souls' Day (2 November) 1846.

138 This copy is undated, except for a heading that lists the meditation for Tuesday as taking place on the 'Feast of Our Lady's purity'. It is difficult to say which feast Faber is referring to; however, a letter to Newman written on 11 October (1848) is subtitled 'Feast of Our Lady's Purity', which was a Tuesday in 1853.

139 Meditations 2, 3, 4, 6, 7 (and others), in F. W. Faber, notes on the *Spiritual Exercises*, untitled, n.d. Unpublished MS in hand of F. W. Faber, LO, black box file, No. 8.

140 Ibid. Meditation 14.

141 Ibid. Meditation 17: Tuesday.

142 Ibid. Meditation 4 (headache), 20 (sickness).

143 Ibid. Tuesday.

144 Single sheet headed 'AMD Sitorum que Josephic et Wilfridi Gloriam'. Unpublished MS in hand of F. W. Faber, LO, black box file, No. 10.

145 Ibid.

146 Ibid.

147 Ibid.

148 Ibid.

149 Single sheet headed 'AMD Sitorum que Josephic et Wilfridi Gloriam'. Unpublished MS in hand of F. W. Faber, LO, black box file, No. 10.

150 Ibid.
151 F. W. Faber to F. Lythgoe, LO, Vol. 21, No. 138, 12 January 1847.
152 See p. 59.
153 F. W. Faber to J. B. Morris, LO, Vol. 17, No. 111, 23 February 1847.
154 F. W. Faber to J. B. Morris, LO, Vol. 17, No. 112, 26 February 1847.
155 F. W. Faber to J. H. Newman, LO, Vol. 1, No. 50, 24 March 1847.
156 Ibid.
157 Ibid.
158 J. H. Newman to F. W. Faber, LO, Vol. 8, No. 20, 1 February 1846.
159 F. W. Faber to J. H. Newman, LO, Vol. 1, No. 50, 24 March 1847.
160 Ibid.
161 Ibid.
162 The ceremonies lasted for five hours, after which Faber returned immediately to Cotton. See F. W. Faber to J. H. Newman, LO, Vol. 1, No. 52, Easter Monday (5 April) 1847.
163 F. W. Faber to J. B. Morris, LO, Vol. 17, No. 111, St Peter Damian (23 February) 1847.
164 F. W. Faber to J. H. Newman, LO, Vol. 1, No. 52, Easter Monday (5 April) 1847.
165 Ibid.
166 Ibid.
167 Ibid.
168 F. W. Faber (1847), *Saints and Servants of God: Rose of Lima*, London, Richardson & Sons.
169 W. Ullathorne to unspecified correspondent, 31 October 1848, in C. Butler (1926), *Life and Times of Bishop Ullathorne: 1806–1889*, London, Burns, Oates & Washbourne, p. 155.
170 F. W. Faber (1847), *Saints and Servants of God: Rose of Lima*, London, Richardson & Sons, p. vii.
171 Ibid. p. ix.
172 Ibid. p. x.
173 Ibid.
174 Ibid. p. ix.
175 Ibid. p. vii.
176 A mild example is the memo to himself, 'Remind them of a badly set limb'. In F. W. Faber, Sermon, *Proximate Occasions of Sin*, St Wilfrid's, 1848. Unpublished MS in hand of F. W. Faber, LO, notes from books folder, No. 146. The most unpleasant example occurs in F. W. Faber (n.d.), *Spiritual Conferences*, 9th edn, London, Burns & Oates, p. 184.
177 F. W. Faber, Sermon, *The Fear of ye Saints*. Unpublished MS in hand of F. W. Faber, LO, Packet 1, No. 101, n.d.

178 F. W. Faber (1847), *Saints and Servants of God: Rose of Lima*, London, Thomas Richardson & Son, p. xiii.

179 Ibid. p. vii.

180 F. W. Faber to Bishop T. Walsh, 24 November 1847, in Addington, *Faber: Poet and Priest*, p. 162.

181 F. W. Faber to Bishop T. Walsh, St John of the Cross, November 24, 1847, ibid. p. 161.

182 These were Faber, Antony Hutchison, Thomas Francis Knox and Austin Mills.

183 F. W. Faber to Bishop T. Walsh, St John of the Cross, November 24, 1847, in Addington, *Faber: Poet and Priest*, p. 161.

184 Ibid. pp. 161–2.

185 Ibid. p. 161.

186 Ibid.

187 F. W. Faber to J. B. Morris, LO, Vol. 17, No. 113, Corpus Christi (27 May) 1847.

188 F. W. Faber to J. B. Morris, LO, Vol. 17, No. 118, Second Sunday in Advent (5 December) 1847.

189 F. W. Faber to J. H. Newman, LO, Vol. 1, No. 64, St Chrysostom (27 January) 1848.

190 F. W. Faber to Lord Shrewsbury, LO, Vol. 21, No. 29, 3 November 1847.

191 F. W. Faber to J. B. Morris, LO, Vol. 17, No. 117, St Bibiana (2 December) 1847.

192 F. W. Faber to J. B. Morris, LO, Vol. 17, No. 118, Second Sunday in Advent (5 December) 1847.

193 F. W. Faber to M. Watts Russell, LO, Vol. 21, No. 10, 11 December 1847.

194 F. W. Faber to J. B. Morris, LO, Vol. 17, No. 118, Second Sunday in Advent (5 December) 1847.

195 F. W. Faber (1854), *All for Jesus*, 5th edn, London, Richardson & Sons, p. 113.

196 F. W. Faber to J. B. Morris, LO, Vol. 17, No. 117, St Bibiana (2 December) 1847.

197 F. W. Faber to J. B. Morris, LO, Vol. 17, No. 118, Second Sunday in Advent (5 December) 1847.

198 F. W. Faber to J. B. Morris, LO, Vol. 17, No. 118, Second Sunday in Advent (5 December) 1847.

199 J. H. Newman to F. W. Faber, LO, Vol. 8, No. 21, 31 December 1847.

200 F. W. Faber to J. H. Newman, LO, Vol. 1, No. 56, 1 January 1848.

201 F. W. Faber to A. St John, LO, Vol. 22, No. 60, St Agnes (28 January) 1848.

202 F. W. Faber to J. B. Morris, LO, Vol. 17, No. 122, 11 February 1848.

203 F. W. Faber to J. H. Newman, LO, Vol. 1, No. 56, 1 January 1848.

204 Ibid.
205 T. F. Knox to J. H. Newman, LO, Vol. 7, No. 85, 25 January 1848.
206 F. W. Faber to J. H. Newman, LO, Vol. 1, No. 82, 29 March 1848.
207 Ibid.
208 F. W. Faber to J. H. Newman, LO, Vol. 1, No. 96, end of April 1848.
209 F. W. Faber to J. H. Newman, LO, Vol. 1, No. 94, end of April 1848.
210 F. W. Faber to J. H. Newman, LO, Vol. 1, No. 96, end of April 1848.
211 F. W. Faber to J. H. Newman, LO, Vol. 1, No. 97, end of April 1848.
212 F. W. Faber to J. H. Newman, LO, Vol. 1, No. before 102, Thursday (5 May?) [*sic*] 1848.
213 F. W. Faber to J. H. Newman, LO, Vol. 1, No. 104, 19 May 1848.
214 F. W. Faber to J. H. Newman, LO, Vol. 1, No. 94, end of April 1848.
215 F. W. Faber to J. H. Newman, LO, Vol. 1, No. 100, 12 May 1848.
216 F. W. Faber to J. H. Newman, LO, Vol. 1, No. 94, end of April 1848.
217 F. W. Faber to J. H. Newman, LO, Vol. 1, No. 97, end of April 1848.
218 F. W. Faber to J. H. Newman, LO, Vol. 1, No. 98, after Easter 1848.
219 F. W. Faber, *Hints for Valetudinarians*, n.d. Unpublished MS in hand of F. W. Faber, LO, Packet 3, No. 89.
220 Ibid. 13.
221 Ibid. 14.
222 Ibid. 9.
223 Ibid. 16.
224 Ibid. 20.
225 F. W. Faber to J. H. Newman, LO, Vol. 2, No. 234, Lent (n.d.) 1850.
226 F. W. Faber to Lord Shrewsbury, LO, Vol. 21, No. 33, Ash Wednesday (8 March) 1848.
227 F. W. Faber to J. H. Newman, LO, Vol. 1, No. 64, St Chrysostom (27 January) 1848.
228 F. W. Faber to J. H. Newman, LO, Vol. 1, No. 108, 28 May 1848; A. Phillipps de Lisle to J. H. Newman, LO, Vol. 1, No. after 108 (No. 69 in Vol. 5, Birmingham Oratory Letters), 5 June 1848.
229 A. Phillipps de Lisle to J. H. Newman, LO, Vol. 1, No. after 108 (No. 67 in Vol. 5, Birmingham Oratory Letters), 29 May 1848.
230 F. W. Faber (1867), Lay Brothers Conference, *Bro Stanislas, Died 21 May 1848*, in *Notes on Community Life in the Oratory*, London, Richardson & Sons. Unpublished, pp. 90–3.
231 Chapman, *Father Faber*, pp. 181–2.

232 F. W. Faber (1867), Lay Brothers Conference, *Bro Stanislas, Died 21 May 1848*, in *Notes on Community Life in the Oratory*, London, Richardson & Sons. Unpublished, p. 91.

233 Ibid.

234 F. W. Faber to J. H. Newman, LO, Vol. 1, No. 116, Monday, 5 June 1848.

235 F. W. Faber to J. H. Newman, LO, Vol. 1, No. 119, 24 July 1848.

236 15 August. See F. W. Faber, *Lay Brothers Retreat before ye Assumption*, Maryvale, 1848. Unpublished MS in hand of F. W. Faber, LO, Packet 2, Part 3, No. 63.

237 Ibid.

238 F. W. Faber to J. Lewis, LO, Vol. 21, No. 80, 17 September 1848; J. H. Newman to F. W. Faber, LO, Vol. 8, No. 38, 4 October 1848; LO, Vol. 8, No. 40, 10 October 1848.

239 F. W. Faber to J. Lewis, LO, Vol. 21, No. 80, 17 September 1848.

240 J. H. Newman to F. W. Faber, LO, Vol. 8, No. 38, 4 October 1848 and LO, Vol. 8, No. 40, 10 October 1848.

241 F. W. Faber to J. H. Newman, LO, Vol. 1, No. 125, 5 October 1848.

242 F. W. Faber to J. H. Newman, LO, Vol. 1, No. 150, n.d. 1848.

243 See letters F. W. Faber to J. H. Newman, February–March 1849, LO, Vol. 1, Nos. 158–216.

244 F. W. Faber to J. H. Newman, LO, Vol. 1, No. 180, 17 February 1849.

245 F. W. Faber to J. H. Newman, LO, Vol. 1, No. 170, 10 February 1849.

246 Ibid.

247 F. W. Faber to J. H. Newman, LO, Vol. 1, No. 160, 5 February 1849.

248 F. W. Faber to J. H. Newman, LO, Vol. 1, No. 162, 8 February 1849.

249 In a letter to Newman, Faber wrote that he was suffering from flu and from two boils on his nose. See F. W. Faber to J. H. Newman, LO, Vol. 1, No. 234, 21 April 1849.

250 F. W. Faber to J. H. Newman, LO, Vol. 1, No. 224, Holy Saturday (7 April) 1849.

251 F. W. Faber to J. H. Newman, LO, Vol. 1, No. 220, 3 April 1849.

252 F. W. Faber to J. H. Newman, LO, Vol. 1, No. 172, 11 February 1849.

253 J. H. Newman to F. W. Faber, LO, Vol. 8, No. 47, Purification (2 February) 1849.

254 F. W. Faber to J. H. Newman, LO, Vol. 1, No. 184, 22 February 1849.

255 F. W. Faber to J. H. Newman, LO, Vol. 1, No. 178, 15 February 1849.

256 Ibid.

257 F. W. Faber to J. H. Newman, LO, Vol. 1, No. 172, 11 February 1849.

258 F. W. Faber to J. H. Newman, LO, Vol. 1, No. 220, 3 April 1849.
259 F. W. Faber to J. H. Newman, LO, Vol. 1, No. 196, 2 March 1849.
260 Due to the reordering of the streets in the area around The Strand, undertaken during the nineteenth and early twentieth centuries, King William Street roughly corresponds to the modern William IV Street. A plaque marks the position of the original Charing Cross Hospital, which was situated next door to the Oratory, but the site itself is impossible to discern.
261 F. W. Faber to J. H. Newman, LO, Vol. 1, No. 226, 16 April 1849. See also LO, Vol. 1, No. 225, 15 April 1849; LO, Vol. 1, No. 228, 18 April 1849; LO, Vol. 1, No. 230, 19 April 1849.
262 F. W. Faber to J. H. Newman, LO, Vol. 1, No. 238, 25 April 1849.
263 F. W. Faber to J. H. Newman, LO, Vol. 2, No. 27, Invention of the Cross (3 May) 1849.
264 Priests: F. W. Faber, J. B. D. Dalgairns, R. Stanton, W. A. Hutchison, T. F. Knox, F. A. Wells, R. A. Coffin. Novices: P. Gordon, J. E. Bowden. Lay brothers: J. Lewis Shepherd, J. C. Strickson, B. J. Deer, J. W. Radcliff, W. I. Rusher, W. F. Allan, H. Cheyne. See LO, Vol. *Oratory in London: Chronology 1845–1947.*
265 LO, Vol. *Oratory in London: Chronology 1845–1947.*
266 Newman was 48.
267 F. W. Faber to J. H. Newman, LO, Vol. 1, No. 228, 18 April 1849.
268 F. W. Faber to J. H. Newman, LO, Vol. 2, No. 5, 6 May 1849.
269 F. W. Faber to J. H. Newman, LO, Vol. 2, No. 11, 12 May 1849.
270 F. W. Faber to J. H. Newman, LO, Vol. 2, No. 26, before 18 May 1849.
271 F. W. Faber to J. H. Newman, LO, Vol. 2, No. 3, 2 May 1849.
272 F. W. Faber to J. H. Newman, LO, Vol. 2, No. 35, 25 May 1849.
273 F. W. Faber to J. H. Newman, LO, Vol. 2, No. 29, May 1849.
274 Ibid.
275 F. W. Faber to Lord Shrewsbury, LO, Vol. 21, No. 38, 23 March 1848.
276 F. W. Faber to J. H. Newman, LO, Vol. 2, No. 29, May 1849.
277 F. W. Faber to J. H. Newman, LO, Vol. 2, No. 41, 6 June 1849.
278 F. W. Faber to J. H. Newman, LO, Vol. 2, No. 40, 4 June 1849: and LO, Vol. 2, No. 41, 6 June 1849.
279 F. W. Faber to J. H. Newman, LO, Vol. 2, No. 42, 8 June 1849.
280 J. H. Newman to F. W. Faber, LO, Vol. 8, No. 114, 22 June 1849.
281 F. W. Faber to J. H. Newman, LO, Vol. 2, No. 61, 5 July 1849.
282 F. W. Faber to J. H. Newman, LO, Vol. 2, No. 69, 9 July 1849. See also LO, Vol. 2, No. 101, 14 August 1849.
283 F. W. Faber to J. H. Newman, LO, Vol. 2, No. 101, 14 August 1849.
284 J. H. Newman to F. W. Faber, LO, Vol. 8, No. 123, 19 July 1849.
285 F. W. Faber to J. H. Newman, LO, Vol. 2, No. 57, 26 June 1849; LO, Vol. 2, No. 73, 12 July 1849; LO, Vol. 2, No. 91, 19 July 1849.

286 F. W. Faber to J. H. Newman, LO, Vol. 2, No. 189, 3 January 1850.
287 Ibid.
288 F. W. Faber to J. H. Newman, LO, Vol. 2, No. 97, 3 August 1849.
289 F. W. Faber to J. H. Newman, LO, Vol. 2, No. 107, 7 August 1849.
290 F. W. Faber to J. H. Newman, LO, Vol. 2, No. 145, 20 November 1849.
291 Ibid.
292 F. W. Faber to J. H. Newman, LO, Vol. 2, No. 101, 14 August 1849.
293 F. W. Faber to J. E. Bowden, LO, Vol. 20, No. 6, St John's Day (27 December) 1849.
294 For date of this event, see Bowden, *Life*, p. 315.
295 F. W. Faber, Sermon, *Opening of ye Jesuits Church*, 1849. Unpublished MS in hand of F. W. Faber, LO, Packet 3, No. 103, 1 and 3:2.
296 Ibid. 1:1.
297 Ibid. 1:1–2.
298 Ibid. 1:4.
299 Ibid. 1:3.
300 Ibid. 1.
301 Ibid. 1:1, 4.
302 Ibid. 3:3 and final paragraph.
303 F. W. Faber to J. H. Newman, LO, Vol. 2, No. 121, 3 October 1849.
304 F. W. Faber to J. H. Newman, LO, Vol. 2, No. 127, 18 October 1849.
305 Ibid.
306 F. W. Faber to J. H. Newman, LO, Vol. 2, No. 158, 3 December 1849.
307 Faber wrote, 'If I lost it [St Wilfrid's] because others cared not to keep it, I should anyhow wish to be buried there ... in the place where my gravestone was laid down when the church was founded.' LO, Vol. *The Oratory in London*, p. 100.
308 Ibid. p. 101.
309 LO, Vol. *The Oratory in London*, p. 101. The buildings at Cotton have been empty since 1987. They are derelict at the time of writing (spring 2005), but Cotton Hall and Pugin's extension to Cotton Hall are to be saved, and the remainder of the site occupied by housing. The church of St Wilfrid is still used occasionally, but has been modified since 1846.
310 F. W. Faber to Lord Shrewsbury, *c*.11 October 1849, in Addington, *Faber: Poet and Priest*, p. 202.
311 LO, Vol. *The Oratory in London*, p. 100.
312 F. W. Faber to J. H. Newman, LO, Vol. 2, No. 175, 22 December 1849. See also F. W. Faber to J. H. Newman, LO, Vol. 2, No. 176, Christmas Eve (24 December) 1849.

313 P. L. Bidstrup (1964), *Toxicity of Mercury and its Compounds*, Amsterdam, Elsevier Publishing Company, p. 43.

314 F. A. Faber, quoted in R. F. Whistler (1892), *The History of Ailington, Aylton or Elton*, London, Mitchell and Hughes, p. 54.

315 F. W. Faber to J. H. Newman, LO, Vol. 2, No. 234, Lent n.d. 1850.

316 F. W. Faber, *O my infant Jesus*. Unpublished MS in hand of F. W. Faber, LO, maroon folder, No. 7.

317 F. W. Faber, Sermon, *Devotions for those who wish to lead an interior life, in honour of ye 18 hidden years of Jesus*, n.d. Unpublished MS in hand of F. W. Faber, LO, Packet 1, No. 35.

318 Ibid.

319 F. W. Faber to J. B. Morris, LO, Vol. 17, No. 130, 20 August 1850. See also F. W. Faber to J. H. Newman, LO, Vol. 2, no number (after No. 295) 2 October 1850, and F. W. Faber to R. Stanton, LO, Vol. 22, No. 8, 9 September 1850.

320 *St Wilfrid's*, LO, Vol. 2, No. 214, January 1850.

321 1859.

322 The Passionists resided at St Wilfrid's, Cotton, from January 1853 until 1855. Sedgley Park School acquired the buildings in 1868, finally completing its move to Cotton in 1873. The school, which became Cotton College, closed in 1987.

323 J. B. D. Dalgairns to J. H. Newman, LO, Vol. 6, No. 87, 31 December 1849 or 1 January 1850.

324 F. W. Faber to J. H. Newman, LO, Vol. 2, no number (after No. 212), 15 January 1850.

325 F. W. Faber to J. H. Newman, LO, Vol. 2, No. 225, 7 February 1850.

326 F. W. Faber, Meditations, Lent Retreat 1850, 4: *The Awfulness of Sin*. Unpublished MS in hand of F. W. Faber, LO, Packet 3, No. 83.

327 F. W. Faber, Meditations, Lent Retreat 1850, 8: *The Particular Judgement*. Unpublished MS in hand of F. W. Faber, LO, Packet 3, No. 118.

328 F. W. Faber, Meditations, Lent Retreat 1850, 9: *The Loss of God*. Unpublished MS in hand of F. W. Faber, LO, Packet 3, No. 122.

329 F. W. Faber to J. H. Newman, LO, Vol. 2, No. 225, 7 February 1850.

330 Ibid.

331 F. W. Faber to J. H. Newman, LO, Vol. 2, No. 257, 25 May 1850.

332 Ibid. The Feast of St Augustine of Canterbury, not St Philip Neri, is in the *Book of Common Prayer* on 26 May. See *Book of Common Prayer* (London, n.d.) p. 23.

333 F. W. Faber to J. B. Morris, LO, Vol. 17, No. 129, 21 June 1850.

334 For more discussion of J. B. Morris, see F. W. Faber to J. H. Newman, LO, Vol. 2, No. 269, 20 July 1850.

335 Note at end of F. W. Faber to J. B. Morris, LO, Vol. 17, No. 129, 21 June 1850.

336 F. W. Faber to J. H. Newman, LO, Vol. 2, No. 267, 12 July 1850.

337 OCDCC, p. 412.

338 F. W. Faber, *The Pope's Decree for ye New Feast of ye Precious Blood*, 1850. Unpublished MS in hand of F. W. Faber, LO, notes from books folder, No. 12. See also F. W. Faber, *The New Feast of ye Precious Blood*, 1850. Unpublished MS in hand of F. W. Faber, LO, notes from books folder, No. 22. These are two copies of the same document.

339 F. W. Faber, *The Pope's Decree for ye New Feast of ye Precious Blood*, 1850. Unpublished MS in hand of F. W. Faber, LO, notes from books folder, No. 12, 3:4.

340 Ibid. 2:1, 2.

341 Ibid. 2:4.

342 Ibid.

343 F. W. Faber to J. H. Newman, LO, Vol. 2, No. 277, 2 September 1850, for a report on Dr Grant's views of the quarrels within the Roman Church in England.

344 F. W. Faber to J. H. Newman, LO, Vol. 3, No. 7, 4 November 1850.

345 F. W. Faber to J. H. Newman, LO, Vol. 2, No. 277, 2 September 1850, which is concerned with a sermon preached at the LO during May by A. St John of the Birmingham Oratory.

346 F. W. Faber to J. H. Newman, LO, Vol. 3, No. 7, 4 November 1850.

347 Addington, *Faber: Poet and Priest*, p. 202. See also F. W. Faber to J. B. Morris, LO, Vol. 17, No. 130, 20 August 1850.

348 F. W. Faber to J. H. Newman, LO, Vol. 3, No. 18, 3 December 1850.

349 F. W. Faber to J. H. Newman, LO, Vol. 3, No. 42, 14 April 1851.

350 J. H. Newman to F. W. Faber, LO, Vol. 8, No. 122, 10 July 1849.

351 F. W. Faber to J. H. Newman, LO, Vol. 3, No. 42, 4 April 1851.

352 F. W. Faber to J. H. Newman, LO, Vol. 3, no number (after No. 13) 22 November 1850.

353 For discussion of the characteristics of the original Oratories at Rome and Naples, see P. Türks (1995), *Philip Neri: The Fire of Joy*, Edinburgh, T&T Clark, Chapter 15: 'New Foundations', pp. 87–94.

354 F. W. Faber to J. H. Newman, LO, Vol. 3, No. 30, 22 January 1851.

355 F. W. Faber to J. H. Newman, LO, Vol. 3, No. 37, 26 February 1851; see also LO, Vol. 3, No. 38, *c.*February 1851.

356 Faber's year saints from 1851–63 were: Ss John of the Cross, Francis de Sales, Vincent de Paul, Paul of the Cross, Dominic, John, Mary Magdalene, Joseph, Paul, Teresa of Avila, Michael, Gabriel, Raphael. See F. W. Faber, *Year Saints*. Unpublished MS in hand of F. W. Faber, LO, black box file, No. 37.

357 F. W. Faber (1867), *The Year Saint*, in *Notes on Community Life in the Oratory*, London, Richardson & Sons. Unpublished, p. 89.

358 Ibid. 1:4.
359 Ibid. 1:5.
360 Ibid. 3.
361 Ibid. 1:3.
362 These were, Ss John of the Cross (1542–91) (Discalced Carmelites) 1851; Francis de Sales (1567–1622) (Visitandines) 1852; Vincent de Paul (1580–1660) (Lazarist Fathers, Sisters of Charity) 1853; Paul of the Cross (1694–1775) (Passionists) 1854; Dominic (1170–1221) (Dominicans) 1855; Teresa of Avila (1515–82) (Discalced Carmelites) 1860.
363 The remaining individuals were: Ss John the Evangelist 1856, Mary Magdalene 1857, Joseph 1858, Paul the Apostle 1859, Michael 1861, Gabriel 1862, Raphael 1863.
364 H. E. Manning (1808–1892) Harrow School (1821–1827), Balliol College, Oxford (1827), BA (1830), Fellow Merton College, Oxford (1832), Deacon, Priest CoE (1832), MA (1833), Archdeacon of Chichester (1840), RC (April 1851), Priest (June 1851), DD (1854), Cardinal (1875). See D. Newsome, *H. E. Manning (1808–1892)*, in DNB (Oxford, OUP, 2004) Vol. 36, pp. 492–9.
365 A. W. Hutton (1892), *Cardinal Manning*, London, Methuen, p. 85.
366 Ibid.
367 F. W. Faber to J. H. Newman, LO, Vol. 3, No. 71, 8 August 1851.
368 F. W. Faber to J. H. Newman, LO, Vol. 3, No. 74, 25 September 1851.
369 P. L. Bidstrup (1964), *Toxicity of Mercury and its Compounds*, Amsterdam, Elsevier Publishing Company, p. 43.
370 F. W. Faber to J. H. Newman, LO, Vol. 3, No. 74, 25 September 1851.
371 F. W. Faber to J. H. Newman, LO, Vol. 3, No. 75, 30 September 1851.
372 F. W. Faber to A. Hutchison, LO, Vol. 16, No. 13, 16 December 1851 and F. W. Faber to Fr Rector, LO, Vol. 16, No. 14, 26 December 1851.
373 F. W. Faber to A. Hutchison, LO, Vol. 16, No. 9, 22 October 1851 (from Marseilles).
374 Ibid.
375 F. W. Faber to A. Hutchison, LO, Vol. 16, No. 10, All Saints' Day (1 November) 1851 (from Malta).
376 F. W. Faber to (J.) C. Strickson, LO, Vol. 16, No. 11, 29 November 1851 (from Palermo).
377 F. W. Faber to A. Hutchison, LO, Vol. 16, No. 12, 9 December 1851.
378 F. W. Faber to J. H. Newman, LO, Vol. 3, No. 83, 31 December 1851; see also F. W. Faber to J. H. Newman, LO, Vol. 3, No. 86, 18 January 1852, in which he mentions problems with his kidneys.
379 LO, Vol. *Oratory in London: Chronology 1847–1947*.

380 St Mary's was opened on 2 July 1852, and demolished almost exactly one hundred years later, in 1952. Part of its site is now occupied by housing.

381 F. W. Faber to Countess of Arundel, 29 November 1852, in Bowden, *Life*, Letter XCVIII, p. 335.

382 For an account of the events surrounding the Achilli trial, see I. Ker (1990), *John Henry Newman*, Oxford, OUP, pp. 372–5, 377, 398–9, 502, 503, 548.

383 F. W. Faber to J. H. Newman, LO, Vol. 3, No. 94, 4 June 1852.

384 For details of Faber's promotion of St Philip, see F. W. Faber to J. H. Newman, LO, Vol. 3, No. 88, *c*.April 1852.

385 F. W. Faber to J. H. Newman, LO, Vol. 3, No. 94, 4 June 1852.

386 F. W. Faber, *Novena of St Philip*, London, 1852, in Vol. *Father Faber: MSS of Sermons and on Spiritual Subjects*. Unpublished MS in hand of F. W. Faber, LO.

387 Revd E. Price to F. W. Faber, LO, Vol. 22, No. 136, Rose of Lima (30 August) 1852.

388 Revd E. Price to F. W. Faber, LO, Vol. 22, No. 138, 1 September 1852.

389 F. W. Faber to Countess of Arundel, 29 November 1852, in Bowden, *Life*, letter XCVIII, p. 335.

390 P. L. Bidstrup (1964), *Toxicity of Mercury and its Compounds*, Amsterdam, Elsevier Publishing Company, pp. 42–3.

391 For example, see F. W. Faber, Sermon, *How is it that life is short?*, Brompton, 1854. Unpublished MS in hand of F. W. Faber, LO, Packet 3, No. 57.

392 F. W. Faber to Countess of Arundel, 29 November 1852, in Bowden, *Life*, Letter XCVIII, p. 336.

393 Ibid. p. 335.

394 See, for example, F. W. Faber to J. H. Newman, LO, Vol. 3, No. 121, 24 October 1853.

395 F. W. Faber to J. H. Newman, LO, Vol. 3, No. 108, Easter Day (27 March) 1853.

396 F. W. Faber to J. H. Newman, LO, Vol. 3, No. 108, Easter Day (27 March) 1853.

397 F. W. Faber (1853), *Essay on Catholic Home Missions* (London, Richardson and Sons) p. 6.

398 Ibid. p. 22.

399 Ibid. p. 8.

400 Ibid. p. 11.

401 Ibid.

402 Ibid.

403 Ibid.

404 Faber wanted to build a larger church than was possible at King William Street. See Bowden, *Life*, pp. 333–4.

405 F. W. Faber to J. H. Newman, LO, Vol. 3, No. 121, 24 October 1853.

406 F. W. Faber to the Earl of Arundel, 2 January 1854, in Bowden,

Life, Letter XCIX, p. 341.

407 F. W. Faber to J. H. Newman, LO, Vol. 3, No. 129, 14 January 1854.

408 F. W. Faber to Lady Arundel, 23 March 1854, in Addington, *Faber: Poet and Priest*, p. 263.

409 The first letter from Brompton is F. W. Faber to J. H. Newman, LO, Vol. 3, No. 137, 2 March 1854.

410 F. W. Faber, Sermon, *Opening of Brompton*, 22 March 1854. Unpublished MS in hand of F. W. Faber, LO, Packet 3, No. 109.

411 F. W. Faber to Lady Arundel, 23 March 1854, in Addington, *Faber: Poet and Priest*, p. 263.

412 Ibid.

413 E. S. Purcell (1896), *Life of Cardinal Manning, Archbishop of Westminster*, Vol. 2, London, Macmillan & Co., p. 51.

414 F. W. Faber to J. H. Newman, LO, Vol. 3, No. 143, 12 August 1854.

415 F. W. Faber to J. H. Newman, LO, Vol. 3, No. 149, 16 March 1855.

416 We can concur with Addington's view, 'It is by no means certain that Faber would have agreed with all the extreme positions of this [Ultramontane] party.' In Addington, *Faber: Poet and Priest*, p. 270.

417 Ibid.

418 Ibid.

419 F. W. Faber, *The Blessed Sacrament*, p. 186, quoted in Bowden, *Life*, p. 362.

420 Bowden, *Life*, p. 363.

421 Ibid.

422 Extract from F. W. Faber to Lord Arundel, 31 August 1855, in Bowden, *Life*, no number, p. 357.

423 F. W. Faber to the Earl of Arundel, 11 September 1855, in Bowden, *Life*, letter CI, p. 357.

424 Extract from F. W. Faber to Lord Arundel, 31 August 1855, in Bowden, *Life*, no number, p. 357.

425 R. A. Coffin (1819–1885) became RC in 1845. Joined the London Oratory, and left in 1850 to join the Redemptorists. See Addington, *Faber: Poet and Priest*, note on p. 135.

426 After Wiseman's death, in 1865, Newman wrote, 'the two chief persons whom I felt to be unjust to me are gone – the Cardinal [Wiseman] and Faber'. He also recalled their 'cruelty' towards him. See J. H. Newman, 22 February 1865, quoted in Chapman, *Father Faber*, p. 344.

427 Newman's *Statement to the Birmingham Fathers*, LO, Vol. 3, No. 152, 9 November 1855.

428 Ibid.

429 F. W. Faber to N. Wiseman, Westminster Diocesan Archives, [hereafter referred to as WDA], AAW: W3/52: Letter 10, 18 November 1855.

430 F. W. Faber to N. Wiseman, WDA, AAW: W3/52: Letter 11, 15 December 1855.

431 F. W. Faber to N. Wiseman, WDA, AAW: W3/52: Letter 12, 5 January 1856.

432 It is interesting, in this context, to note Gilley's remark that 'Newman's difficulty in forgiving Faber remains the most signal objection to his [Newman's] canonization.' S. Gilley, *F. W. Faber (1814–1863)*, in DNB (Oxford, OUP, 2004) p. 873.

433 F. W. Faber to J. H. Newman, LO, Vol. 3, No. 153, 8 May 1856.

434 Ibid.

435 Ibid.

436 Ibid.

437 Congregation of the Oratory, London, to J. H. Newman (Letter No. 1 of 2), WDA, AAW: W3/16: Letter 13, 22 May 1856.

438 Ibid.

439 Ibid.

440 J. H. Newman to F. W. Faber, LO, Vol. 3, No. 157, 31 May 1856.

441 Congregation of the Oratory, London, to J. H. Newman (Letter No. 2 of 2), WDA, AAW: W3/52: Letter 14, 5 June 1856.

442 A school for boys, under the auspices of the London Oratory and the Sisters of Compassion, started in December 1856. See F. W. Faber to N. Wiseman, WDA, AAW: W3/52: Letter 34, 17 December 1856.

443 F. W. Faber to N. Wiseman, WDA, AAW: W3/52: Letter 15, 11 June 1856.

444 F. W. Faber to N. Wiseman, WDA, AAW: W3/52: Letter 18, 14 July 1856. See also F. W. Faber to J. B. Morris, LO, Vol. 17, No. 142, 17 July 1856.

445 F. W. Faber to N. Wiseman, WDA, AAW: W3/52: Letter 17, 28 June 1856.

446 F. W. Faber to N. Wiseman, WDA, AAW: W3/52: Letter 20, 19 August 1856.

447 F. W. Faber to N. Wiseman, WDA, AAW: W3/52: Letter 21, 23 August 1856. See also F. W. Faber to R. Stanton, LO, Vol. 22, No. 4, 23 August 1856, and F. W. Faber to R. Stanton, LO, Vol. 22, No. 5, 25 August 1856.

448 J. B. D. Dalgairns to F. W. Faber, LO, Vol. 24, No. 131, 28 August 1856.

449 F. W. Faber to J. B. Morris, LO, Vol. 17, No. 142, 17 July 1856.

450 F. W. Faber to N. Wiseman, WDA, AAW: W3/52: Letter 29, 13 October 1856.

451 F. W. Faber to K. Digby Best, LO, Vol. 22, No. 16, 25 July 1857.

452 F. W. Faber to J. B. Morris, LO, Vol. 17, No. 143, 13 February 1857.

453 F. W. Faber to N. Wiseman, WDA, AAW: W3/52: Letter 36, 8 June 1857.

454 T. F. Knox (1822–1882); R. Stanton (1820–1901). The latter was

the last surviving member of Faber's community.

455 F. W. Faber to E. H. Thompson, 23 August 1857, in Bowden, *Life*, Letter CXXXV, p. 410.

456 F. W. Faber (1857), *The London Oratory and the Union Newspaper: Being Three Letters on the Respect Due to our Blessed Lord*, London, Richardson & Sons, p. 5.

457 F. W. Faber to W. A. Hutchison, 2 February 1858, in Bowden, *Life*, Letter CII, pp. 358–9.

458 Ibid. p. 359.

459 F. W. Faber to W. A. Hutchison, 2 February 1858, in Bowden, *Life*, Letter CII, p. 359.

460 F. W. Faber (1858), *Spiritual Conferences*, 9th edn, London, Burns & Oates, p. 206.

461 Ibid. p. 223.

462 Ibid. pp. 171–2.

463 Ibid. p. 60.

464 F. W. Faber to J. B. Morris, LO, Vol. 17, No. 150, 14 June 1859.

465 F. W. Faber to J. E. Bowden, LO, Vol. 20, No. 55, 17 February 1860.

466 F. W. Faber to Philip Gordon, n.d., in Bowden, *Life*, Letter CIV, pp. 360–1.

467 F. W. Faber (n.d.), *Bethlehem*, London, Burns & Oates, p. 340.

468 F. W. Faber, *Last Will and Testament* (1860). Unpublished MS signed by F. W. Faber, LO, black box file, doc. 20.

469 F. W. Faber to Philip Gordon, n.d., in Bowden, *Life*, Letter CIV, p. 361.

470 F. W. Faber to 'Miss L' (Visitandine), 27 June 1857, in Bowden, *Life*, Letter CIX, p. 374; F. W. Faber to 'A penitent' (Carmelite), n.d., in Bowden, *Life*, Letter CXXII, pp. 388–9; and F. W. Faber to Elizabeth Thompson (Sr Mary of the B[lessed] Trinity), (Carmelite), St Vincent of Paul (19 July) 1860, in Bowden, *Life*, Letter CXXXI, pp. 396–8. Also, F. W. Faber to 'Sister M. P.' (Dominican), Whit Tuesday, n.d., in Bowden, *Life*, Letter CXXVIII, p. 394.

471 Sr Mary of the Blessed Trinity (Elizabeth Thompson) to F. W. Faber, LO, Vol. 21, No. 141, 25 March and LO, Vol. 21, No. 142, 27 March 1861.

472 F. W. Faber to Elizabeth Thompson (Sr Mary of the B[lessed] Trinity), St Vincent of Paul (19 July) 1860, in Bowden, *Life*, Letter CXXXI, pp. 396–8.

473 F. W. Faber to the Revd Mother Prioress, n.d., in Bowden, *Life*, Letter CXXX, p. 395.

474 F. W. Faber to the Prioress, Carmelite Convent, Paris, LO, Vol. 21, No. 88, n.d.

475 F. W. Faber to N. Wiseman, WDA, AAW: W3/52: Letter 45, 2 December 1860.

476 Ibid.

477 F. W. Faber 'To the Superior of a Convent', n.d., in Bowden, *Life*,

Letter CXXVI, pp. 392–3. For information on the involvement of Elizabeth Thompson in the foundation of the Carmelite monastery at Notting Hill, see Anon. (1964), *In the Silence of Mary*, London, Carmel, Notting Hill, Chapter 2.

478 F. W. Faber 'To the Superior of a Convent', n.d., in Bowden, *Life*, Letter CXXVI, pp. 392–3.

479 F. W. Faber to 'C', 17 September, n.d., in Bowden, *Life*, Letter CXIII, p. 377.

480 F. W. Faber to J. B. Morris, 30 August 1861, in Bowden, *Life*, Letter CXII, p. 376.

481 F. W. Faber to 'Mrs M.', 28 September 1854, in Bowden, *Life*, Letter CVIII, pp. 372–3.

482 F. W. Faber to J. E. Bowden, LO, Vol. 20, No. 65, 8 August 1861; see also F. W. Faber to J. E. Bowden, LO, Vol. 20, No. 66, 12 August 1861.

483 F. W. Faber to J. E. Bowden, LO, Vol. 20, No. 66, 12 August 1861.

484 F. W. Faber to J. B. Morris, LO, Vol. 17, No. 164, October 1861.

485 F. W. Faber to J. E. Bowden, LO, Vol. 20, No. 70, 18 September 1861.

486 F. W. Faber to M. Watts Russell, LO, Vol. 21, No. 14, St Nicholas (6 December) 1861.

487 F. W. Faber to J. B. Morris, LO, Vol. 17, No. 158, 30 August 1861.

488 Ibid.

489 F. W. Faber to J. B. Morris, LO, Vol. 17, No. 159, 30 September 1861.

490 Ibid.

491 F. W. Faber (1860), *Devotion to the Pope*, Epiphany 1860, London, Richardson & Sons, pp. 15–16.

492 Ibid. p. 16.

493 Ibid. pp. 16–18.

494 Ibid. pp. 18–19.

495 Ibid. pp. 20–1.

496 Ibid. p. 24.

497 F. W. Faber, *Devotion to the Church*, Feast of St Philip, 1861. LO, in Vol. *Miscellaneous Faber*, p. 9.

498 Ibid. p. 21.

499 Ibid. p. 27.

500 Ibid. p. 28.

501 F. W. Faber to M. Watts Russell, LO, Vol. 21, No. 15, 23 January 1862.

502 Ibid.

503 Ibid.

504 J. Olier (1608–1657).

505 F. W. Faber to M. Watts Russell, LO, Vol. 21, No. 15, 23 January 1862.

506 L. M. Grignon de Montfort (1673-1716).

507 F. W. Faber to M. Watts Russell, LO, Vol. 21, No. 15, 23 January 1862.

508 J. B. Vianney (1786-1859).

509 F. W. Faber, Sermon, *Our Blessed Lord Bowing His Head upon the Cross*, Brompton, Passion Sunday (22 March) 1863. Unpublished MS in hand of F. W. Faber, LO, Packet 1, No. 74.

510 1 Cor. 2:1–2. NRSV (Oxford, 1995).

511 J. E. Bowden to E. Bowden, LO, Vol. 22, No. 208, 19 May 1863.

512 F. W. Faber to Duchess of Norfolk, LO, Vol. 21, No. 57, 9 May 1862.

513 See, for example, F. W. Faber to Lady G. Fullerton, LO, Vol. 21, No. 126, 11 July 1863.

514 Addington, *Faber: Poet and Priest*, p. 16.

515 N. Wiseman to F. W. Faber, LO, Vol. 22, No. 217, 14 July 1863.

516 Newman, Letters and Diaries, Vol. XVII, Appendix 3, pp. 559–61.

517 F. W. Faber to J. E. Bowden, LO, Vol. 20, No. 87, 3 August 1862.

518 Ibid.

519 F. W. Faber to J. E. Bowden, LO, Vol. 20, No. 88, 2 September 1862.

520 J. E. Bowden and C. Bowden to E. Bowden, LO, Vol. 22, No. 212, 23 June 1863; No. 213, 24 June 1863; No. 214, 30 June 1863; No. 215, 3 July 1863; No. 216, 16 July 1863; No. 221, 20 September 1863; No. 230, 22 September 1863; No. 231, 23 September 1863; No. 232, 24 September 1863; No. 236, Friday Ev[ening] (25 September 1863); No. 238, 26 September 1863.

521 J. E. Bowden to E. Bowden, LO, Vol. 22, No. 226, 20 September 1863.

522 J. E. Bowden to E. Bowden, LO, Vol. 22, No. 236, Friday Ev[ening] (25 September 1863).

523 Ibid.

524 J. E. Bowden to E. Bowden, LO, Vol. 22, No. 237, 26 September 1863.

525 Bowden, *Life*, p. 442.

526 J. E. Bowden to E. Bowden, LO, Vol. 22, No. 238, 26 September 1863.

Chapter 5

Major Books: 1853–1863

All for Jesus

The books that make up Faber's mature spiritual writing contain two distinct literary styles: the first is theological and doctrinal, in which Faber writes of Catholic theology in the style of an academic essay, whilst the second is popular. Faber's first major book, *All for Jesus: or the Easy Ways of Divine Love*, belongs in the second category. Published in June 1853, the first edition sold out within one month, and 9,000 copies had been sold, at five shillings apiece, by the time the fifth edition was printed in 1855. It was subsequently translated into Flemish, French, German, Italian and Polish, and sold in America.

The style of *All for Jesus* is popular, emotional and sentimental.[1] It is characterised by fervent enthusiasm, which makes up for its lack of real profundity; and its most obvious fault is that occasional passages of good spiritual writing are submerged within a mediocre narrative. The book exhibits contradictions that mirror those within Faber's nature and personal spirituality, particularly the 'silliness' which is a lifelong presence in his thought.[2] Faber's intention in writing *All for Jesus*, was to make piety accessible to the 10,000 members of the Confraternity of the Precious Blood, and to individuals who could not aspire to the virtue demanded by saints and other spiritual writers because they lived in the world.[3] In the preface, Faber highlighted his own limitations as a writer on spiritual issues. He indicated that he was not writing spirituality of depth, or for individuals who wished for perfection,[4] and wrote, 'I am not trying to guide souls in high spirituality; God forbid I should be so foolish or so vain!'[5] Faber noted that this was because of his own inability to achieve great virtue, writing, 'I want to make piety bright and happy to those who need such helps [*sic*], as I do myself';[6] and later, 'What is the whole spirit of my book but making the best of a bad case.'[7] It seems plausible that, at one level, this disclaimer functioned as a calculated display of humility of the kind that he admired in others, a defence mechanism to forestall criticism, show his loyalty to the Church, and indicate that he knew his place.

The devotional style of *All for Jesus* is centred upon a spirituality that is intensely practical, one that is active rather than contemplative.[8] Faber indicates that he thought the former not only represented a higher ideal,[9] but also was more useful to the world. Indeed, he showed his lack of empathy with contemplative spirituality, during that period, by questioning why individuals should aspire to be contemplatives, and doubting their value to the Church as a whole.[10] In stating this, Faber demonstrates the temperamental characteristic whereby he diminishes his subject by use of ridicule and cynicism. The Jesuit influence is present throughout this book, and Faber notes that in seeing greater value in the active life he is imitating Jesuit theologians.[11] Despite this somewhat exaggerated distinction between active and contemplative spirituality, he cites a number of Carmelite saints who were also contemplatives: Mary Magdalene Pazzi, Teresa of Avila, and John of the Cross, all of whom he had studied during 1851.

The spirituality of *All for Jesus* exhibits ideas we have been discussing throughout this study, in the context of the relationship that the individual Christian has with Jesus. Faber treats intellectualism as negative, and gives at least one example that mocks what he considers to be the pretentiousness of intellectuals.[12] There is mean-spiritedness in this critique, which is the antithesis and perversion of the intellectual humility practised by an individual such as Aquinas. For Faber, the main function of theology was to provide an answer to the scientific questions[13] which were being debated in the 1850s, and we can assume that Faber believed that the answers provided by theology were superior to those provided by science. Faber highlights the childlike aspect of praising God,[14] although there is no sense that childishness is acceptable. The individual's sympathy for Jesus, and Mary, is presented as being the central part of the Christian's opposition to the world, the devil,[15] and sin.[16] Once again, Faber is concerned with the evil of countries which are not Roman, and which consequently allow heresy, such as America, India and China, and parts of the continent of Europe.[17]

All for Jesus illustrates the diversity of Faber's religiosity, and the seriousness with which he viewed every action in a religious life, as well as indicating the complexity of Roman Catholic devotion in the mid-nineteenth century. For Faber, every action, such as giving thanks after communion,[18] has a symbolic meaning and a particular prayer, medal, scapular, or rosary intention associated with it. In discussing these, he uses aspects of saints' lives in order to illustrate his point, and frequently refers to particular writings of individual saints, such as Catherine of Siena on Purgatory,[19] and Teresa of Avila on Hell.[20] He is always careful to show the distance between the ordinary Christian and the saint, writing, 'We read wonderful things in the lives of the saints ... which we dare not think of imitating.'[21] In *All for Jesus*, Faber brings the emotional side of the religiosity of saints to the fore. They are presented as in a constant state of rapture, and as partaking in a plethora of experiences that are closed to the average Christian. Faber was clearly familiar with a variety of saints with differing charisms. As well as Jesuit theologians and saints, he wrote of Franciscan saints such as Bonaventure and Angela of Foligno, and Dominicans Catherine of Siena, Aquinas, and Albertus Magnus.

Faber received mixed reviews regarding *All for Jesus*. Dr Newsham wrote from Ushaw College, Durham, of the 'great spiritual profit'[22] he had derived from it and of the 'great lights'[23] which he believed had been given by God to Faber.[24] V. Cardella, a Jesuit who admired Faber's writings,[25] wrote from Rome praising the 'unworldy spirit'[26] of the book, and enclosing several criticisms,[27] which Faber incorporated into the fourth edition.[28] He viewed Faber's works as being 'thoroughly English'[29] in character, containing sentiments that were not translatable into Italian.[30] This is significant because one of the most enduring comments about Faber's style is that it is fundamentally Italian, or at least continental, in its emphasis.

Ullathorne's primary criticism was of bad taste, because of what he called '"startling" expressions',[31] to which Faber replied, 'They evidently betoken some fault of taste, wh[ich] wants looking to.'[32] In the same letter, Faber wrote about another section of the book, 'The passage ... conveys more than I meant',[33] which highlights his tendency to allow his oratorical enthusiasm to adversely cloud his judgement. Indeed, Faber's innate 'silliness', which we have returned to throughout this study, means that he often has the opposite effect from the one that he clearly expected to have. Faber is capable of ruining a meditation by making a ridiculous remark or by using a fatuous example, both of which destroy the sense of profundity which he has created and compel the reader to ridicule a notion that would be serious in an author such as Newman. This is particularly apparent in his attitude towards God throughout this book, which sometimes seems irreverent. Faber also treats dubious ideas as being of equal merit with those which are of higher theological value, and is capable of bringing forth a ridiculous conclusion from an otherwise impeccable argument. This is fundamentally a matter of literary style, and certainly the language in which he presents spirituality and theology is highly idiosyncratic. It is, however, no longer historically adequate to write of Faber's use of language and imagery purely as demonstrating lack of taste, and it also seems possible that these swings of temperament were not within Faber's power to control, and that they were caused, or exacerbated, by his reliance on laudanum and other medication, or by the adverse effects of mercury.

Faber was still receiving criticism of *All for Jesus* in January 1854, six months after its publication. However, he observed that the book contained aspects of his own spirituality, such as encouraging individuals to be emotional in their religious observance, and he clearly felt that criticism of the book was also personal criticism. The tone of the letter contains more than a hint of flippant defensiveness and wounded feelings, and this is particularly apparent in the stance that he had decided to ignore criticism by thinking of it solely as an excuse for mortification, saying, 'The book may be all wrong ... but I wrote it to help souls, and to get our Lord some more love.'[34]

An anonymous article in the *Dublin Review* begins by noting that the popularity of *All for Jesus* makes it difficult to write an adequate critique of it;[35] however, despite this, the review manages to be both sympathetic and critical. The article characterises Faber as a writer who both understands the sentimentality[36] and fairly low 'devotional aspirations'[37] of the majority of Roman Catholics, whilst applauding him for being willing to advise them on spiritual matters.[38] The reviewer highlights one criticism that we have already noted independently of it: that is, Faber's disregard for contemplative spirituality, as he writes that Faber 'touches but cursorily ... upon the *purgative,* and is chiefly occupied with the branches of the affective life'.[39] The reviewer also highlights Faber's dislike of individuality, writing that he views the saints as an anonymous group with similar attributes rather than as individuals.[40] He also criticises Faber's habit of viewing those who are canonised and those who are not as being of equal importance.[41] The reviewer articulates contradictions within Faber's literary style by stating that although he 'invests ordinary subjects ... with the charm of glowing and poetic representation',[42] he also 'puts forth a view of spirituals which in some degree conflicts with the theories of existing writers'.[43]

Other individuals, such as the Jesuit provincial Waterworth, were less magnanimous about Faber's works. Waterworth described Faber's books as 'dangerous'[44] and informed Monsignor Talbot, in Rome, that both he and several unidentified bishops and theologians[45] believed that *All for Jesus* contained heresy. Faber's supporters believed that this was rooted in personal dislike, and that it was a criticism of taste[46] rather than concern for doctrinal orthodoxy. Wiseman described it as 'a party affair',[47] and Hutchison informed Talbot that the term 'heresy' was used not as a theological but as a political expression in the Roman Church in England.[48] Hutchison's letters to Talbot stress Faber's loyalty and willingness to retract anything unorthodox,[49] and he wrote somewhat dryly that the priests of the London Oratory were sufficiently theologically literate to have noticed the presence of heresy before the work was published.[50] Hutchison's strategy seems to have been to regain Faber's popularity in Rome, by illustrating how indispensable his books were to the cause of the wider Church. He stressed their popularity in America, France,

England and Ireland, and their indispensability in bringing about the 'conversions of bad Catholics'.[51]

Growth in Holiness

In October 1854, Faber published *Growth in Holiness*, his second book. The book contains Faber's collected thoughts on practical spirituality since his conversion, in 1845,[52] and is in one sense a continuation of *All for Jesus*. It represents the next stage in the spiritual life, and Faber makes an assumption that he did not make in *All for Jesus*, namely, that those who are reading it have a genuine desire to be spiritual. However, Faber constantly reminds his readers of their inability to make progress, because the fallen nature of humanity means that there is an inherent lack of response to God. The function of the book is to indicate faults present in the spiritual life, and to show how individuals can improve. Faber points out notions that limit the potential for holiness, a number of which are established in his thought. The 'spirit of the age' is once more associated with the idea that the Christian should be unlike the world.[53] Faber is concerned that Christians have a propensity to worldliness, and writes of an inordinate desire for human respect caused by 'building castles in the air and imagining heroic acts'.[54] A number of ideas have been used in sermons; for example, in writing of the importance of devotion to Mary, he re-uses ideas from his lectures on Mary.[55] Others include devotion to the infancy of Jesus, the centrality of prayer in the spiritual life, and the danger of misplaced solemnity. His reliance on Ignatian spirituality is shown in his use of Ignatian methods of meditation, and in encouraging his readers to be over loquacious in their prayer life.

The style of *Growth in Holiness* is mature and well written. Faber shows himself a good interpreter of spirituality, who is able to draw together ideas from the writings of diverse saints and theologians. In the preface, he writes that he wished to write for 'English Catholics in an English shape, translated into native thought and feeling'[56] and he succeeds in this aim. Faber is clearly happier with his subject matter than he was with *All for Jesus*. He is therefore less inclined to be flippant, although he frequently seems to want to discourage rather than encourage his reader. Despite this, Faber's deep sense of sarcasm and ridicule is never far below the surface, and his cynicism has been transformed into a cold realism about the worthlessness of life. Perhaps because of this, Faber can describe something profound in a way that is vaguely ridiculous, and this aspect represents the most fundamental contrast between himself and Newman. On one occasion, whilst discussing the holiness of heaven, Faber uses words and images that combine to be somewhat distasteful; and, although it is difficult to say precisely why, it seems probable that it is because the passage is banal. He writes, 'The strong angels tremble and are shaken; Our Lady is all abased; and the Sacred Heart of Our Lord Himself is flooded with reverential fear.'[57] This passage is an example of Faber's contradictions, in that there is a cosy familiarity that is off-putting, which is the direct opposite to the warning against over-familiarity with God that occurs later in the book.[58]

Faber clearly expected adverse criticism of *Growth in Holiness*, as he wrote in its preface of his intention to remove, in a later edition, any idea unacceptable to the church authorities.[59] Ullathorne wrote to Faber after the publication of each book, presenting positive thoughts and criticisms from himself and from other people. His fundamental criticism of *Growth in Holiness* was Faber's lack of 'theological prudence'.[60] He applied this to the substantial chapter on spiritual direction; writing that there should be a distinction between what is written for the clergy in a book on spiritual direction, and that written for general consumption.[61]

The Blessed Sacrament

Faber's third book, *The Blessed Sacrament*, was published on 24 March 1855. His intention was to stimulate a general interest in theology, and popularise it in the same manner as other sciences, such as geology.[62] In contrast to the hostility shown towards science in his parochial sermons, Faber sees no antipathy between the interests of the two subjects; this is because, for him, theology furnishes all scientific answers, and he wrote, somewhat naively, 'How many puzzles and perplexities would have been saved these writers, if they had been acquainted with ... Catholic theology.'[63] This book is more theological than the two that preceded it. Although it is not an academic work it illustrates that Faber had read a wide variety of theology, from the Fathers to theology written during the nineteenth century; and his studies of post-Reformation theology included both Roman and non-Roman theologians, the latter usually in the context of Apologetics. He also demonstrates a sophisticated and profound understanding of scholastic theology. However, although the book was, and continued to be, popular, it is ultimately unsatisfactory, as it is a hybrid which is too devotional to be a theological work and too theological to be a devotional work, fitting neither category convincingly. It is also unsuccessful because it does not distinguish between academic theology and saccharine pious anecdote, which is a characteristic Faberian trait. Its style does highlight, however, Faber's impressionistic poetic sensitivity and Ignatian use of the imagination. This, together with his creative ability to embroider historical and doctrinal facts, lends his writing the quality of a story or fictional narrative. It seems probable that Faber's true creative milieu lay in writing allegorical religious stories, as his short books for children, *The Last Children* and *Ethel's Book*[64] demonstrate. This trait is apparent in passages that draw their inspiration from nature, which are often recognisable as evocations of Northumberland and the Lake District. Much of Faber's nature imagery is nocturnal: thus he writes of Mary before the incarnation as 'a woody mountain lighted up with the gold of the yet unrisen sun'.[65]

Faber expected controversy, and before publication he informed Newman that three of the London Oratorians had read the manuscript in order to ensure that he had not written anything contentious or heretical.[66] He articulated his wish to avoid misunderstanding in the prefaces to each of the three editions,[67] and all quotes are in their original language, so that knowledgeable readers are aware that his sources are orthodox. It was, however, not Faber's considerable knowledge of theology that was problematic for critics among his contemporaries, but its mode of expression. Thus, although Ullathorne praised the book, he highlighted Faber's lack of theological discrimination, and criticised the book's style and manner for creating doubts in peoples' minds, leading to disbelief in its subject matter.[68] He did not confine these comments to himself, but wrote that several theologians, clergy and religious, in England, Rome and Germany had articulated them.[69] Ullathorne offered stabilising guidelines and amicable censorship, both of which ensured that Faber was kept within certain boundaries and knew what was expected of him. This is significant because it shows the extent to which Faber was perceived by his English contemporaries to be potentially troublesome. Ullathorne's first guideline was that Faber should write about doctrine rather than theological opinion, particularly in books intended for 'the general reader ... the uneducated, women, and young people'.[70] The second highlighted the danger of presenting for general consumption anything but the simplest forms of spirituality. He stressed that all theological opinion was unsuitable for those who were not theologically educated, as people would confuse Faber's poetical metaphorical embellishments with the point of doctrine which lay behind them.[71] Ullathorne did not think that *The Blessed Sacrament* was a suitable book for publication in England, because 'the mind of this country is too gross to apprehend the real sense of ... this divine mystery'.[72] He concluded his letter by expressing the wish that all books, such as Faber's, would be revised and re-written before publication in order to avoid such problems.[73]

The Blessed Sacrament contains all of Faber's major preoccupations, such as cynicism about the world, self-distrust, moral seriousness, and preparation for eternity, all of which are tinctured with a deeply-rooted cynicism. This is particularly noticeable in discussion of the worldly spirit of the age, which is mocked with a harshness that occasionally becomes ridiculous and loses the sympathy of the reader. In this context, Faber retreats from life outside the Roman Church, presenting it as irredeemable, and writes that Catholics should not subscribe to its frivolous and unspiritual values.[74] He uses as an example the hostility shown towards the Church after the definition of the Immaculate Conception, in 1854, and it is characteristic of Faber's thought that this was caused by fear of the truth. He is equally scathing of dissent from within the Church regarding the same definition, using the starkly uncompromising statement, 'the mother is ... like her son, set for the rise or fall of many who deemed themselves in Israel'.[75]

Faber's cynicism is also expressed in relation to the inability of the individual to live up to the high ideals of Christianity. He is concerned with the lack of spiritual commitment shown by the majority, and mocks and demolishes any sense that the individual has any possibility of acquiring spiritual merit, in language which is reminiscent of an evangelical preacher.[76] In a further development of the spirit of the age, he exposes the hypocrisy of personal relationships, and the dishonesty of popular society,[77] writing, 'Literature, philosophy, science, politics, and fashion ... are all striving to do without God.'[78] Several notions within the book contain an important insight into Faber's personal spirituality and role as a spiritual director. He wrote, 'Never keep a spiritual journal, a record of pious thoughts, or any vestige of a religious autobiography',[79] a notion that is related to that of the danger of unreality, which is central to Faber's thought. It is for this reason that Faber did not keep a diary, and he warned that the individual who did so would 'do and say follies, in order to write them down afterwards'.[80] Another, implied, objection is that it is unlikely that the average individual, however spiritual, will have anything worth writing about. In an example of Faber's deeply-rooted sarcasm, cynicism and, perhaps, realism, he wrote: 'If your visions and your ecstasies and ... sweet thoughts of God are a boon the world could hardly do without, God will send you a spiritual director to command you ... to write them down.'[81] As in his Anglican period, authentic spirituality is joyful,[82] never solemn or overly erudite. Here, Faber measures success by feelings, spiritual experiences and, in the case of the saints, showy miracles.[83] Towards the end of the book, he gives many examples of the Eucharistic phenomena experienced by saints and religious; and discussion of these brings forth Faber's most saccharine enthusiasm.

Poems

In June 1856 Faber published his complete *Poems*, the majority of which had been written at Oxford, Ambleside, and abroad, during the 1830s. In the preface, he wrote that he had been encouraged to re-publish because of popular demand, and the hope that a new generation would enjoy them, rather than for reasons of artistic vanity. Faber also indicated that, as he was primarily a priest and spiritual writer, rather than a poet, he wished the poems to be read in conjunction with the spiritual works.[84]

A number of Faber's poems, as well as his relationship with Wordsworth, have been discussed at some length by scholars of English Literature. We shall therefore confine ourselves to a brief mention of the major themes used in the poems, where these relate to those used elsewhere in Faber's thought. Several of Faber's poems are concerned with history, such as 'Chivalrous Times'[85] and 'Our Lady in the Middle Ages',[86] whilst others describe the relationship between the past and the present.[87] Those that provide retrospective portraits of Oxford, present Faber's own past in idealistic terms, which is notable in odes such as 'The Cherwell',[88] and the sonnets 'College Chapel'[89] and 'Absence from Oxford'.[90] Poems which present Faber's travels, frequently view the towns which he visited as stage sets for scenes from medieval or ancient history, as though he failed, or decided not, to grasp the present individuality of the town through which he had passed. On other occasions, Faber uses the place visited as a metaphor for something else; thus, Rome always represents the unity of the Church. The Church is, unsurprisingly, one of the central images in Faber's poetry. He writes of saints, feasts, individual churches, as well as theology, such as God's judgement of the world.[91] The nineteenth-century ideal of Christian manliness is also present, particularly in Faber's exhortations to one subject to follow Christ.[92] This is contrasted with complaints about the softness of the individual and the age, which are identified with anticipation of seasons of purification, such as Lent and Eastertide.[93] Another aspect of Faber's poems in general is that he is always concerned that the writing of poetry is inferior to his priestly work, and is unable to resolve this.

There is a pronounced streak of melancholy in Faber's poetry, which is apparent in poems in which he displays emotion personal to himself. This includes nostalgia for his family, home and childhood,[94] grief for his mother,[95] and his adult awareness of his lack of wife and children. Faber also uses melancholy as a poetic device; indeed, at one level sorrow suits his Romantic temperament better than joy.[96] This assists in the creation of atmosphere, particularly in those poems in which a solitary walker addresses objects in nature, such as the rivers, water,[97] mountains, and the hills of Northumberland and the Lake District. It is also noticeable that places outside those where he resides, such as Durham, Ambleside, Oxford, or Elton, always correspond unfavourably with, and are inferior to, his current home. Faber's most successful images are nocturnal, and concerned with the moon, darkness, and twilight. Here, the narrator is a solitary figure undertaking prayer at night, viewing, or imagining, the interior of a church at night,[98] or contrasting night with day.[99] Poems that address another individual, such as his brother, sister, friend, or niece, provide a contrast to those that are solitary.

Faber's writings and poems always have a piquant sense of the supernatural, in which the world of ghosts, souls, and angels runs parallel to, and is closely related to, the earth.[100] Thus, he writes:

> Hast thou ever felt in thy lonely room,
>   *   *   *
> When the walls of the world seem about to melt,
>   And to lay the weird realms of spirit bare, –
> Hast thou ever at such high seasons felt
>   What seemed like the waving of wings in air?[101]

Faber also possessed an acute awareness of atmosphere, in which the events and individuals of the past haunt the present; thus, in a sonnet written after visiting Penshurst Place, he wrote, 'there is a spirit and a presence there of one departed'.[102] The dead are often recognised or perceived to be present, but are rarely addressed, and are always just out of the reach of the narrator.[103]

Like all of Faber's writings, the poems received a mixed reception from critics. The *Dublin Review* published a long article entitled 'Living English Poets',[104] which mentioned the works briefly and favourably, although it is interesting to note that, in the aforementioned article, Faber received less attention than did other poets. The reviewer declined to present a detailed study of the contrast between the 'varied beauties and power ... of the poet with the deeper ... productions of the great aesthetic and devotional writer'.[105] Faber's poetry was known to poets a generation younger than himself, particularly those who came, like him, from Oxford. Gerard Manley Hopkins (1844–1889) wrote of Faber as a member of the Lakeland school of poets,[106] and the Anglican, Digby Dolben (1848–1867), read them during the 1860s with great admiration, whereas the poet Robert Bridges was indifferent towards them.[107] Another enthusiast contributed a privately printed article about Faber's life and poetry,[108] in which he noted Wordsworth's admiration for Faber,[109] particularly Faber's appreciation of nature.[110] He wrote, approvingly, that Faber was 'excessive ... in feeling and in language',[111] and that several of his sonnets were particularly good examples of the genre.[112] He admitted, however, that Faber's poetry was marred 'by deplorably weak ... absurd lines',[113] and opined that the, unspecified, 'defects and merits of his intellect and character'[114] were the primary reason for his suitability for the Roman rather than for the Anglican Church.[115]

The Creator and the Creature

Faber's fourth book, *The Creator and the Creature,* was written during the autumn of 1855, published in 1856, and translated into French and German during 1858. It is more philosophical and academic than his earlier books, and as such is the antithesis of *All for Jesus.* The book illustrates the significant volume of theological knowledge possessed by Faber who had read, among others, Scotus,[116] Tauler, Vázquez, Suarez and Aquinas during its preparation. This is also noticeable in the footnotes, and he clearly expected his reader to engage with the works that he gives as examples in them.[117] The style of the book is analytical and logical, particularly in its first two-thirds, and reminiscent of essays and shorter works written as an Anglican, at Oxford and thereafter. It provides an interesting example of the work that Faber might have produced had he chosen to write academic works rather than popular spirituality.

The Creator and the Creature is concerned with predestination, nature, and grace. Faber's central premise is that individuals do not acknowledge their relationship as creatures to the creator with sufficient seriousness.[118] In discussing this, he uses the notion that the spirit of the age actively distrusts, and is antagonistic towards, God,[119] and notes that each century has its own individual way of expressing this.[120] Faber contrasts the corrupt and immoral society outside the Church with the Church itself, and views Rome as, ideally, having a unifying influence upon international affairs.[121] He also enters into an elaborate discussion of predestination, and illustrates the various theological opinions regarding the number of Catholics who are saved.[122] In doing so, he constantly highlights the division between Christians inside and outside the Church, and between society and the Church.[123] On several occasions, he characterises the English as Protestant heathen,[124] whose company and influence is dangerous to Roman Catholics.[125] This is primarily because Britain is a State that has no loyalty towards Rome, and is therefore, in Faber's terms, worldly.[126]

Faber preaches distrust of everything that is not God-centred, and, in an example of a positive view of the intellect, writes that the study of religion and theology is fundamentally at variance from the spirit of the world. He is concerned that science, philosophy and theology have become over systematised and ignore the presence of a creator,[127] and writes: 'Philosophically speaking, things can be managed at Berlin without God.'[128] This is related to Faber's notion of unreality, in which individuals use the concept of God either in order to impress[129] or to manipulate other people.[130] Faber's inherent cynicism is present here, particularly when writing of the changing fashions of society. His language in *The Creator and the Creature* is calculated to provoke an immediate emotional response from the reader.[131] Like St Ignatius Loyola, the yardstick by which he measures the effectiveness of spirituality is outward displays of emotion, such as weeping, feelings, and inward sensations.[132] In the latter third of the book, which is more stylistically popular than the first two-thirds, the devotional style that he aims to inculcate is one that is essentially happy,[133] unquestioning, childlike[134] and dependent on God and the Church, a style that ties in with his personal spirituality. Within this scheme, Faber is always wary of physical, mental and moral softness.[135] Here, as elsewhere, he can be starkly uncompromising, primarily because he believed that the only real security is offered in heaven after death;[136] this is apparent in statements such as, 'there is no class of Christians to whom hell is not an assistance'.[137]

An anonymous reviewer of *The Creator and the Creature*, in the *Dublin Review*, begins by praising Faber, both for bringing the Oratory to London and for popularising theology.[138] He silences critical opposition by writing that those who criticise Faber's books frequently do not possess his wide-ranging knowledge of theology.[139] The writer is the perfect apologist, one who is aware of, but not unduly concerned by, his characterisation of Faber as an 'outspoken'[140] 'writer of ... much peculiarity'.[141] For him, Faber is a poet[142] who writes 'rhetoric rather than strict theology'[143] therefore his faults, such as stating the obvious,[144] lax use of words, and failure to articulate his thoughts in the most effective way, are not seen as detracting from the brilliance of the whole.[145] The reviewer writes that *The Creator and the Creature* distils the central notions of Faber's thought,[146] although we can add that not all of his characteristic notions are present here. He cites Faber's critique of worldliness[147] as being particularly effective. Interestingly, he writes that Faber was influenced by Ignatian methods of spiritual direction,[148] something which we have noted, independently, throughout this study. Chapman's review is too short and superficial to be of much use. However, despite the fact that the book is not the most characteristic of his works, he writes that it 'contains the essential Faber',[149] and recognises Faber's poetic qualities.[150] Gilley describes the book as 'Faber's greatest work in its vision of life as a work of the divine creative love'.[151]

The Foot of the Cross

Faber's original intention had been that *The Foot of the Cross* should form part of a series of books on the Passion,[152] but this scheme was not completed. *The Foot of the Cross* is concerned with the role of Mary, not only in the Passion itself but also in seven incidents in her life, which are collectively known as the Seven Dolours. This was an important devotion for members of the Order of Servites, of which Faber had been a tertiary since 1847,[153] the year in which he began writing this book. It was not completed until the spring of 1855, and publication was further delayed until autumn 1856. This was so that he could be certain that his Mariology was orthodox,[154] and in his text, he writes that the Church hierarchy approved of devotion to the Seven Dolours because it was inspired by scripture.[155] The book demonstrates Faber's empathy with Mary and provides an insight into the centrality of her position within his spirituality. It is significant that Faber does not promulgate an extreme Marian devotion, and his inclusion of a section on the, limited, extent to which Mary can be described as co-redeemer,[156] proves that he does not wish to appear excessive. *The Foot of the Cross* was subsequently translated into Italian (1856), French (1858), and German (1859).

Because of its concentration solely on the person of Mary, *The Foot of the Cross* is unlike any other of Faber's books; however, its nine chapters form narrative pictures that are stylistically reminiscent of *Bethlehem* and *The Precious Blood*. In *The Foot of the Cross,* Faber combined the writings of saints and spiritual writers with his own personal meditations, and, in doing so, created the most subdued, and intensely personal, book that he wrote. As elsewhere in Faber's literary output, the primary limitation of the book is the amount of material that has to be read through before coming to Faber's insights into, and interpretations of, his subject. In one example, Faber writes for twelve pages before beginning to discuss the point of his chapter, which is the meeting of Jesus and Mary during the events leading up to the Crucifixion.[157] Despite this fault, which is a characteristic of the majority of Faber's works, the best of his insights are rarely trite or commonplace. The content of the book is sentimental and emotionally exhausting, and the reader occasionally senses that hysteria is not far below the surface.[158] This is particularly noticeable in those passages that dwell on the bodily and mental pain and interior sufferings of Jesus and Mary, which are stated and re-stated with a force and depth which, occasionally, borders on mawkishness.[159] In its sense of the drama of suffering, Faber's work is reminiscent of meditations on the Passion by St Alphonso Ligouri and Sr Anne Emmerich. Occasionally, the taut, overblown intensity of his style inclines the reader to be sceptical about Faber's use of his subject matter. This is the same trait which we have discussed in connection with Ullathorne's criticisms of *The Blessed Sacrament*, in particular the idea that Faber's writings encourage scepticism rather than acceptance by his readers.

This book contains few of the facets we have come to recognise as an essential part of Faber's literary style. His cynicism about the failure of the individual to be spiritual is present on several occasions but is never dominant,[160] and is often coupled with the important place which devotion to Mary has within the life and death of the individual Christian.[161] Also present is Faber's sense that he is writing devotional literature for the ordinary Christian, rather than for potential saints. One passage, throughout which he discusses mystical theology, ends by stating Mary's appeal to this group; he writes, 'We breathe more fully, than when awhile ago we were straining up these high hills which were not meant for such as we are.'[162] This is a perfect example of Faber reminding individuals of their low level of spiritual attainment, with a degree of cynicism that has the effect of creating the subliminal sense that he is actively trying to hold them down. It seems possible that Faber possessed a genuinely mystical sense of his own lack of attainment, coupled with an intuition which applied this to others, but this is not certain. Perhaps the most significant element of this book is what it reveals about the changes that have taken place within Faber's personal spirituality. In contrast to earlier works, there are numerous examples of a distrust of sentimental religious practice,[163] and he promulgates the idea that spiritual experiences and feelings are unimportant.[164] Faber also uses the notion, which is dominant in the writings of St John of the Cross and others, that it is advisable to cultivate both worldly and spiritual detachment, and that the latter is less easy to achieve than the former.[165]

The Foot of the Cross received a mixed reception from critics. In a letter to J. B. Morris, Faber wrote for more information regarding Morris's comment that he had misrepresented the role of St John; and Faber replied that, on reflection, he agreed with Morris's criticism.[166] This highlights the extent to which other individuals noticed potentially problematic areas which Faber had failed to realise, primarily because he did not edit his works with the requisite detachment. In his *Life*, Bowden highlighted Faber's use of mystical theology. He also remarked that a reviewer in the *Civiltà Cattolica* for January 1867 had characterised Faber's works as being those which 'unite the most mystical devotion to the most profound theological learning'.[167] Bowden also highlighted the aforementioned reviewer's comment that *The Foot of the Cross* was 'one of the best books ever published on the Dolours of Mary'.[168] Chapman, writing almost a century after Bowden, wrote that the book was 'much less satisfactory'[169] than others written by Faber. He was particularly concerned that the book was overlong, and wrote that Faber 'squeezes so much devotion from each Dolour that the reader is stunned and ... discouraged'.[170]

Spiritual Conferences

Faber completed his sixth book, the *Spiritual Conferences*, early in 1858.[171] It comprised his lectures on the spiritual life given at the Oratory during May, Advent and Lent over a period of several years.[172] It is stylistically closer to Faber's early Roman writings and sermons than to the books which surround it chronologically; although, as we have seen, the actual chronology of Faber's works bears little resemblance to their order of publication. Faber delayed publishing the *Conferences* until August 1859,[173] because he was apprehensive that they would be widely misunderstood. He noted in the preface that some points would be clearer to those who knew his preaching style and mannerisms than they appeared on paper; and intimated, somewhat defensively, that the book was intended only for those who were sympathetic towards him.[174]

Bowden wrote of Faber's book as 'one of the most brilliant that ever proceeded from his pen'[175] whilst Chapman, in a review which is, at nine lines, too short to be useful, characterised it as a mélange of varied quality.[176] Both of these assessments have something of the truth about them. The

Conferences lends itself to being listened to rather than read, and, although its buoyant style is reminiscent of Faber's early works, it seems probable that there has been an under-edited transition between sermon and published work. Occasionally Faber's thought is not taut enough to keep the reader's interest; he employs too many generalisations to be completely successful, particularly when describing spiritual states, with the result that it is often inconclusive. The *Conferences* is not a comfortable book, and, although this is not a fault in itself, it is problematic because Faber often fails to engage the reader emotionally or gain their confidence in his opinions and teaching, a trait that is caused by the sarcasm that dominates the narrative. This was intentional,[177] as Faber worked from the, dubious, premise that 'An honest humorous sense of ridicule is a great help to holiness.'[178] It is particularly noticeable in pithy statements such as, 'Many people like to be ill, especially ill in mind.'[179]

The primary task of the *Conferences* is to illustrate the distinction between grace and nature, and between authentic and inauthentic forms of spirituality. In writing of the former, Faber puts forward an essentially Pauline Christian, who demonstrates simplicity, lightheartedness, humility, and kindness; and Faber is concerned that individuals should not try to stand out, or to draw attention to themselves. He writes, 'A kind man is ... genial ... sympathetic ... brave',[180] a description which is reminiscent of St Philip Neri, whose joyful approach to spirituality Faber admired. It is noticeable that all of these attributes are expressed here in the same spirit as in earlier writings, such as the Wilfridian Rule.

In the *Conferences*, the 'spirit of the age' is used as an example of human nature, and here it takes exactly the same form as his Anglican sermons, namely, a critique of the spirituality and religious practices of the mid-nineteenth century.[181] Faber's idealisation of history is noticeable here; the past has authenticity because its outcome is known, whereas the present is morally suspect. For Faber, the only solution to the 'spirit of the age' is a return to the spirituality of an earlier age, such as the Desert Fathers;[182] and in this he seems to be seeking to reform the Roman Church using a Tractarian model of a return to pre-Reformation spirituality. In Faber's works there is often cynicism, anger, and frustration, which is either implied or expressed openly.[183] This becomes more prominent as he matures, and here it is caused by Faber's concern that the dominant spirit is one of ease,[184] characterised by shallowness[185] and low spiritual standards[186] among the majority. In the *Conferences*, popular entertainment is portrayed as inherently sinful, and Faber writes that those who attend the theatre are putting themselves in moral danger by not putting their religious duties first.[187] Faber's antagonism towards family life, which is also related to the 'spirit of the age', always recurs in the same form in his thought, namely, that the majority of individuals have too high an estimation of themselves, which stems from childhood and the 'idolatry of domestic affections'.[188] The *Conferences* frequently reveal much about Faber's inner world and, in discussions of family life, there is the ever-present sense of regret for the early death of his parents. Perhaps because of this, Faber is always cynical, writing that the praise and love contained within the family encourages people to think themselves better than they really are. This hinders the practice of Christianity, ensuring that the majority only pretend to be spiritual,[189] a trait which is carried into their spiritual from their everyday life. Faber's essentially practical, unesoteric, spirituality is present here, particularly in the idea that mysticism is unsafe[190] because it can bolster delusions. He is also concerned that it is dangerous for the individual to read spiritual books which are in advance of their spiritual attainment.[191]

The 'spirit of the age' is also highlighted in the chapter on death, which analyses the differences between popular and Christian approaches to the subject. Faber is critical of popular sentimentality, mawkishness about death and deathbeds,[192] and of the literary view,[193] which has a tendency to put forward an overly erotic or sensual view of death. He is also critical of dramatisation and unreality of the death of the individual, by themselves or those close to them.[194] Here, indifference and unreality are particularly dangerous when applied to death,[195] and he writes, 'Alas! Few men die more than half awake.'[196] Descriptions of individual deaths are commonplace in Faber's later letters and writings, whilst exemplary, Roman Catholic, deaths frequently bring out the strong sense of empathy which is always a strand in Faber's thought. He always notes with relish those which have been particularly devotional, and which have inspired him, such as the death of Suarez.[197]

Ethel's Book

During 1858, Faber wrote a series of four stories for children entitled *Ethel's Book*[198] *or Tales of the Angels*. These stories, which are stylistically simple and naive, are concerned with the practical assistance of the individual's Guardian Angel in situations such as the illness and death of siblings, and the end of the world. The author of an article in the *Dublin Review*,[199] a journal that was usually, because of its Ultramontane leanings, favourable to Faber, was scathing about its publication. He believed that it would damage, and cause disappointment to, 'susceptible'[200] unformed minds because it gave undue prominence to the practical, conversational nature of the relationship, rather than emphasising its rarefied spiritual character. It seems probable that also in the background is the concern that the readers will place themselves in physical danger, believing that they will be rescued by their Guardian Angel. The significance of this review is threefold. Firstly, it demonstrates Faber's inability to judge the capabilities of his audience. Secondly, there are overtones that the reviewer is anxious that individuals must not be allowed to think themselves qualified to receive spiritual experiences to which they are not entitled. However, thirdly, it could be posited that Faber is not saying anything that is any more problematic than a catechism which teaches children the idea that hell is a reality, and putting forward the possibility that they could go there.

The Precious Blood

In July 1856, Faber preached eight sermons for the octave of the Feast of the Precious Blood. These were used as the basis for the book *The Precious Blood*, which was published during Lent 1860 and translated into French and German in the same year. The book is a manual for the 38,000 individuals of the

Confraternity of the Precious Blood, and it is significant that Faber wrote for a group that was sympathetic towards him. The Confraternity was based at the London Oratory, and had been formed shortly before the publication of *All for Jesus* in 1852.[201] It is indicative of the popularity of Faber's piety that the group had grown so large in so short a time.

The Precious Blood exhibits the positive and negative sides of Faber's literary style. Its most positive characteristic is that he creates a world which is recognisable as a synthesis of his poetic sensitivity and an Ignatian use of the imagination, an attribute which we also noted in relation to *The Blessed Sacrament*. The blood of Jesus is used as a motif around which Faber presents an extended meditation in the form of a series of narrative pictures. This is coupled with a series of secondary notions, such as 'the life of God is very vast',[202] used to unify chapter three. Faber imagines the scene before him, and the conversations and thoughts of those concerned,[203] in a manner which resembles the composition of place in the *Spiritual Exercises*; and, because of this, Faber's thought takes on the character of myth in its colourful presentations of ideas, a number of which are almost cinematic.[204] Thus, the Fall, the incarnation, the life of Jesus, and subsequent history, are always expressed as a type of dramatic pageant. It seems plausible that Faber developed this technique as a result of being ill and spending extended periods of time thinking about, rather than reading, theology. However, we do not know to what extent laudanum and other medication over a long period of time affected his imagination and intellectual capabilities.

The style of the book has several negative attributes. It is full of a sugary emotionalism which appeals to a folksy, rather than a sophisticated or intellectual, approach to religion. Faber occasionally writes about something which, although fundamentally orthodox, is expressed in such a way as to be banal, vulgar, and, in some cases, strange.[205] This is particularly noticeable when he employs a very physical image to describe the relationship of an historical individual with Jesus.[206] Faber's use of material is often too credulous and undiscriminating, particularly when he is discussing a particular devotion of a pious, but uncanonised, individual.[207] Chapman wrote of Faber, 'Whatever his musical powers his poetic imagination was visually weak ...'[208] and cited this as being the key to the ultimately unsatisfactory nature of Faber's writing. We can concur, but only to a certain extent, as Faber's ability to create a mental image is limited[209] rather than weak; he fails to allow his readers to create their own imaginative scheme, and this becomes tiresome. Chapman wrote that, 'Faber relies on the evocative rather than the visual connotation of words.'[210] This is also accurate, although it seems probable that Faber used this as a stylistic device, and that creating an impressionistic effect which moved, angered, or made his reader thoughtful, was more important to him than the example used. The fatal flaw in much of Faber's spiritual writing is that he can weary his reader, fail to engage them emotionally, and actively repel them.[211] This idea is linked to the sense of ridicule which we have noted in relation to the *Spiritual Conferences*, and it always leads us, perhaps unfairly, to question the depth of Faber's spirituality.

The Precious Blood exhibits Faber's considerable ability to present difficult concepts in a style which is accessible to those who are not theologically educated. In the preamble, he uses words such as 'easy'[212] 'little'[213] and 'simple'[214] to describe the book, a device that also functions as a display of humility corresponding to that in the preface to other works. The piety of the book is, like Faber's own spirituality, personal rather than remote,[215] and its style tells us much about Faber's perception of his audience. This is particularly noticeable in relation to Faber's evangelical sense of the personal nature of salvation.[216] Several sections read as though written for children, such as: 'Sin came. With sin came many fearful consequences. This beautiful earth was completely wrecked.'[217] These are stylistically reminiscent of *Ethel's Book*, and it seems plausible that they may have been catechetical in origin.

The Precious Blood illustrates several ideas which are central to Faber's thought. The expectation of the end of the world, important to his later writings, is used here, and the language used to describe it is similar to that of the Book of Revelation.[218] It is linked to Faber's critique of worldliness, and Faber mentally transplants the scriptural image to England, in order to suggest the end of Catholic persecution and to increase morale among English Catholics. Faber also exhibits a clearly defined notion of sin and punishment, which is related to worldliness, writing, 'what if the sinner's first awakening should be from the first touch of fire that burns beyond the grave?'.[219] Theology occupies a higher place here than in Faber's earlier writings.[220] Its study is equated with the love of the individual for God,[221] and, in an almost classical reference, he writes, 'In a simple and loving heart theology burns like a sacred fire.'[222] Despite what we have written about the simplicity of Faber's literary style, it is noticeable that the language used to describe God is more complex and subtle than in other works.[223] It is noticeable that Carmelite spirituality, particularly that of French Carmelites, both canonised and uncanonised, is important in this work.[224]

Bethlehem

Faber preached a series of sermons on the infancy of Jesus at the church in Spanish Place, London, during Advent 1852. By July 1857, he had collected these into his final book, *Bethlehem*, which is comprised of nine chapters, each of which is concerned with different aspects of devotion to the Trinity, Mary and Jesus. He did not publish it until November 1860, primarily because he was concerned about generating controversy with what he described as 'a wildish Faberian book'.[225] In the preface, Faber wrote that there was always a danger that parts of the book would be misunderstood if taken in isolation.[226] However, these scruples were outweighed by the sense that, by publishing, he was demonstrating his loyalty to the Church and, more importantly to him, to the Pope at a time of unpopularity.[227]

French spirituality was a consistent influence on Faber's thought throughout his life, and he frequently notes that he had read French translations of a number of books of theology and devotion. Because of this, and Faber's study of Carmelite spirituality, we can hypothesise that he inhabited a similar spiritual world to that of the French Carmelite, St Thérèse of Lisieux, some twenty-five years later.[228] In *Bethlehem*, Faber writes of the importance attached to devotion to the infant Jesus by the French Carmelites,[229] and Thérèse's original dedication, to the infant Jesus and the Holy Face, underlines this. It seems possible that St Thérèse had read Faber's books, as they had all been translated into French, and they may have influenced her, particularly as a number of aspects of the spirituality of these two individuals point either to influence, or to a shared spiritual, literary and cultural vocabulary. In one sense, this is part of the highly emotional expression of spirituality that we associate with this genre of nineteenth-century Roman Catholic piety; however, both Thérèse and Faber were capable of a more intellectual apprehension of theology than is visible in *Autobiography of a Saint*[230] and *All for Jesus*. There is a parallel between the attraction for St Paul, which is part of the intellectual world of Faber and St Thérèse. There is also a marked similarity between Faber's writing that 'a cloistered life … may cover the whole earth with its activity, if it be a life of worship',[231] and St Thérèse's wish to be a missionary.[232] Secondly, the chronic illness of both individuals leads to a sense of longing for an eternal life with God, an idea that is expressed in the letters and writings of both St Thérèse and Faber. The latter writes of life as 'an enemy he has beaten, and with whom he has no more to do',[233] and from the late 1850s onwards, the idea that heaven is his 'native land'[234] was central to Faber's thought.

In *Bethlehem*, the 'spirit of the age' is connected to Faber's cynicism regarding human knowledge, primarily because the incarnation embodies the wisdom of God. For him, popular science and the theological speculations of the majority, are part of a misplaced human desire to penetrate divine mysteries; and here, as elsewhere, this is presented as the direct result of the Fall.[235] In Faber's thought, the pursuit of knowledge, whether scientific or philosophical, is valid only when it is aligned with theology;[236] and likewise Christian art is important solely inasmuch as it conforms to the teachings of the Roman Church.[237] Faber dwells on the idea that his age has lost reverence for God, and he denounces theologians who make religion seem hazy and over-complicated. In a critique of private judgement he criticises those who reduce the doctrines of religion to personal opinion, writing that they 'talk in the empty, pedantic grandiloquence of the day'.[238] The tone of Faber's thoughts on this subject foreshadows Pope Leo XIII's critique of modernism.[239]

We have already suggested that Faber was fundamentally a storyteller, and *Bethlehem* illustrates this more than any other work we have considered in this chapter so far. In the preface, Faber writes of his indebtedness to W. A. Hutchison of the London Oratory, a particular friend of his,[240] who, during 1857–8, had visited places associated with the life of Jesus. Faber writes that Hutchison furnished him with an imaginative sense of the area, and that the scenery encountered during a holiday in Scotland provided other inspiration.[241] He indicated that he was concerned not only to convey this sense to his readers, but also to translate it into an easily accessible devotional format.

Chapman opined that, although *Bethlehem* is equal to Faber's best work, it includes nothing that is significantly new.[242] Faber's characteristic stylistic unevenness is present in this work. However, its most positive aspect is that Faber creates an impressionistic sense of mood and atmosphere by means of an almost symphonic development of ideas and images, the fluid intensity of which frequently conveys a sense of exaltation in the process of writing. It is also interesting to note the frequency with which Faber conveys the impression that he is looking at the earth,[243] or the English landscape, from above. This results in one of the most successful passages in the book, a descriptive tour around the churches, cathedrals, and native saints of Britain, which manages, in a few words, to capture the character of each place. The passage is historical, as it also functions as a lament for the loss of a once vibrant ecclesiastical heritage.[244] In *Bethlehem*, Faber does not think like a scripture scholar, or allow himself to be burdened by reliance on historical facts, but engages in colloquy with his subject matter in order to build up a narrative which is limited only by his imagination. In this way, he resembles the twentieth-century writer C. S. Lewis, particularly in his allegorical writings. This is particularly apparent in the following passage, part of an extended meditation on the world, and the impact of the incarnation:

> What is the whole world but a polar sea, a wilderness of savage ice ... a restless glacier creeping onwards with its huge talons, but whose progress is little better than spiritual desolation? The ... babe of Bethlehem has come to be the vast central fire of the frozen world.[245]

From a reader's point of view, there are several negative aspects to this book. The abundant imagery and loquaciousness of Faber's writing is occasionally tedious and overdone,[246] and he frequently labours his point with the result that the reader becomes bored. Also, he occasionally puts ideas together randomly, which disorientates the reader. The 'silliness' we have been discussing throughout Faber's life is also present, and occurs in several different guises. In the first, Faber gives an example that is incongruous because he focuses so finely on the minutiae of his meditations; in this case, his description of the infant Jesus' awareness of his postural confinement on the journey into Egypt.[247] In the second, Faber describes a profound example in language that has the opposite effect to that which is intended, thereby making us smile at its incongruity, which is caused because he has used the example literally rather than as an analogy.[248] In the third example, present throughout Faber's works, Faber has little sense of proportion or of the capabilities of his readership. Thus, he starts with an innocuous image, which he follows by a theological explanation too complex for the majority.[249]

Complete Hymns

In 1861 Faber published his sixth,[250] and final, book of hymns, a collection which included fifty-six new compositions, together with those from the previous books. The primary reason for re-publishing the hymns was to undo alterations made by other writers, particularly those from outside Roman Catholicism, who had changed the theological sense of Faber's original. The book is in seven parts, and contains 150 hymns. These are concerned with God, Jesus, Mary, angels and saints, Sacraments, the spiritual life and the last things, as well as several that fall into none of these categories. Faber's intention was to provide spiritual reading[251] and popular vernacular hymns for English Catholics, similar to those available in Germany, Italy and France.[252]

It is characteristic of the piety which Faber promulgated that the hymns were to be as simple as possible in form and metre, and contain easily understandable sentiments. He underlined this by highlighting his indebtedness to the influence of saints whom he viewed as presenting an essentially practical religiosity, such as Ss Philip Neri, Teresa of Avila, and Ignatius.[253] The most revealing part of the preface is Faber's statement that, in writing the hymns, he had purposely limited himself.[254] It is as though the intention to present easily intelligible piety had led him into an inauthentic sense of compromise, which involved neglecting his ability to write good poetry. This is also apparent at the end of the preface, in which Faber presented his hymns to his reader in terms which underline his acceptance that their popularity will be short-lived.[255]

The contents of Faber's hymns demonstrate the lack of reserve which dominates all of his writings. He was clearly aware of the emotional power of language to elevate or subdue his congregation or reader, and possessed the ability to create an ebullient sense of atmosphere, which is apparent in a number of the hymns for processions and feast days. The most effective of Faber's hymns are the few in which devotion and intelligent knowledge of theology combine with an almost mystical awareness of God. The most notable of these are 'The Sacred Heart',[256] with its hypnotic verse and refrain, and 'The Eternal Word'.[257] Several present an Ignatian sense of involvement with his subject matter, such as the second verse of 'Our Lady's Expectation'.[258] As in the poems, Faber is occasionally autobiographical, and this is apparent in the hymn entitled 'The God of my Childhood',[259] which functions as a significant insight into Faber's early religiosity. His hymn to St Michael is, in metre, structure and sentiment, almost identical to Newman's hymn 'Praise to the Holiest in the Height', which it predates, and could be sung to the same tune. The hymns contain several of the central ideas of Faber's thought. Thus, the 'spirit of the age' is present, both in the idea renouncing worldliness,[260] and in the sense that Mary is a refuge from the world.[261] 'St Martha'[262] underlines Faber's view that the active spirituality is superior to that which is contemplative, and shows that this idea was still present in his thought. His identification with Irish immigrants, who are presented as remaining faithful to Catholicism, returns in several hymns, notably 'St Patrick'[263] and 'Faith of our Fathers'.[264]

Faber's hymns which are unsuccessful do not all fail for the same reason. A number were obviously hurriedly written for a particular occasion, and these ephemera do not always bear close scrutiny. One which is particularly ineffective is written in the style of a folk song, and begins:

> Oh! Balmy and bright as a moonlit night,
>   Is the love of our Blessed Mother;
> It lies like a beam
>   Over life's cold stream,
> And life knows not such another,
>   O life knows not such another![265]

'Jesus, my God my all',[266] displays the ordinariness and trite sentiments which are possessed by a number of Faber's four-line hymns. Lines such as those which follow display no literary talent or theological sophistication, and their sentiments could be part of a music hall ballad.

> I love thee so, I know not how
>   My transports to control;
> Thy love is like a burning fire
>   Within my very soul.

It is, of course, debatable whether Faber intended to blur the distinction between sacred hymn, secular poem, and popular song; particularly as this is an artificial, and historically recent, distinction, both musically and theologically.

The hymn 'Blood is the price of heaven'[267] fails because Faber manages to make us instinctively uneasy, and promotes embarrassed hilarity at his imagery; despite our realisation that this is the opposite effect from his intention. Thus, in verse eight we read of Jesus,

> Ah me! His soul is fled;
>   Yet still for my great needs
> He bleeds when He is dead;
>   He bleeds,
> My Saviour bleeds!
>   Bleeds!

Several articles present critical appraisal of Faber's hymns. An anonymous *Dublin Review* article that is concerned with the 1848 edition,[268] provides an interesting insight into their reception by one of his contemporaries. Its writer views the majority of the hymns as being more suitable for private devotion than public singing[269] because of their individuality, and writes that the majority expressed 'sentiments ... which on the lips of the casual worshipper would be unreal'.[270] He notes, 'they are the expressions of ... a particular mind, which will find responses in many a devout heart, but which could not be introduced into a mixed congregation without danger of forcing the feelings ... into an unnatural state'.[271] The author's primary reservation towards Faber's hymns springs from his concern that all hymns are potentially dangerous, as they can provide incitement to rebellion and heresy. He is particularly concerned with those which express, in his terminology, Protestant doctrines.[272] Writing of those which are concerned with Catholic doctrine, he writes, 'The province of direct doctrine is so sacred and so slippery, that we should be for leaving it exclusively to the Church herself.'[273] Despite this caution, the reviewer is sympathetic to Faber's hymns, and, in writing of 'The Creation of the Angels', opines, 'We are not sure that in the whole range of sacred ... poetry we have ever met with any thing more simply sublime than the earlier stanzas of this hymn.'[274]

The 1858 edition of the Liberal Catholic journal, *The Rambler*,[275] includes a critique of the music written for Faber's hymns by Wilhelm Schulthes. This is included here because its poised acerbic prose provides the perfect antithesis to those reviews which are favourable to Faber's writings. The article begins by describing the music as 'compositions of some merit, and more pretension'.[276] It then proceeds to present an overview of their faults, such as, among others, changing the music of Beethoven without the requisite genius,[277] and 'confounding the childish with the childlike'.[278]

Chapman provides a well-balanced critique of the hymns. He begins by stating that 'Faber is popularly remembered as a writer of bad hymns',[279] and that he 'has been dismissed as an entirely mediocre hymn writer'.[280] Chapman does not view this as being an accurate assessment of Faber's capabilities,

although for him Faber's main flaw was that he tried, unsuc-
cessfully, to combine poetry and hymn writing.[281] He also
notes Faber's 'atrocious carelessness',[282] writing of the hymns
that, 'He had no pretensions as to their merit and therefore
took far less trouble than he should have done.'[283] We can
comment that this dangerous contentment, and inability to be
self-critical, is the central flaw in all of Faber's writings, one
which may have been caused by being too ill to be more exacting with himself. Chapman presents an important insight into
the positive side of Faber's hymnody, which he views as epito-
mising the evangelical style of hymn writing.[284] He highlights
what we have already, independently, characterised as an
authentic mystical strand in Faber's writing, by opining that
'Faber's poetic "blindness", compensated for by a heightened
aural and tactile awareness, accounts for his successes in sacred
poetry if not in hymnology. It enables him in a unique way to
describe the mysterious, the unusual, the almost indescrib-
able.'[285]

The continuing popularity of Faber's hymns

A number of Faber's hymns have remained in print from 1863
up to the present day. Their use is not confined to hymn books
used in the Roman Catholic Church, but extends to Anglican
and other Christian Churches.[286] In a random selection of nine
hymn books, four each from the Anglican and Roman Catholic
Churches and one from the Baptist Church,[287] twenty-seven
different Faber hymns were published between 1931 and 1979,
whilst thirteen were included between 1980 and 1999. The
Faber hymn that appears in each of the selected books is 'O
come and mourn with me awhile'. 'My God, how wonderful
thou art' is included in eight of these books, 'Sweet Saviour,
bless us ere we go' in seven, 'Jesus, gentlest Saviour' in six, and
'Faith of our Fathers' in five. Twenty-two other Faber hymns
are included in one or more of the selected books.[288] Sixteen of
these take God, Jesus or the Holy Spirit as their subject, four
are Marian, three are concerned with the Christian life and
four with angels and saints. They range from the sentimentality of 'Jesus, gentlest Saviour', to those that are particularly

stirring when sung, such as 'Faith of our Fathers' and 'There's a wideness in God's mercy'.

The language of Faber's hymns ensures that they do not always successfully translate from their original milieu.[289] Subjects selected for twentieth-century hymn books reflect changes in piety, and the hymns have been adapted by editors in several distinct ways. Firstly, to make them available in a more modern phraseology; thus, 'Sweet Saviour bless us ere we go' in the *Parish Hymn Book* becomes 'O Saviour bless us ere we go' in the *Baptist Hymnal*. Secondly, for reasons that are obviously doctrinal; thus, in the hymn 'Faith of our Fathers', 'Mary's prayers shall win our country back to thee' becomes 'God's great power shall soon all nations win for thee'.[290] Thirdly, one change, in the hymn 'O come and mourn with me awhile', reflects a more sensitive, and less dogmatic, late twentieth-century approach towards history; as 'while soldiers scoff and Jews deride' becomes 'while soldiers scoff and men deride'.[291] Faber's hymns seem to have been chosen by editors for their popular appeal, and it is noticeable that several of Faber's hymns that are most successful from a literary or theological point of view, are not included in modern hymn books.

Notes

1 F. W. Faber (1855), *All For Jesus*, 5th edn, London, Richardson & Sons, p. 3.
2 See Faber's story concerning the Jesuit priest, ibid. p. 113.
3 Ibid. p. ix: also pp. x and xi.
4 Ibid. pp. ix and xi.
5 Ibid. p. xi.
6 Ibid.
7 Ibid, footnote on p. 191.
8 For Faber's comparison of the two vocations, see ibid. p. 335.
9 Ibid. p. 177.
10 Ibid., footnote.
11 Ibid.
12 Ibid. p. 113.
13 Ibid. p. 283.
14 Ibid. p. 288.
15 Ibid. p. 6.
16 Ibid. p. 79.
17 Ibid. pp. 80–1.
18 Ibid. p. 257.

19 Ibid. chapter 9.
20 Ibid. p. 41.
21 Ibid. p. 3.
22 Dr Newsham to F. W. Faber, 28 July 1853, in Bowden, *Life*, no number, p. 339.
23 Ibid.
24 Ibid.
25 W. A. Hutchison to F. W. Faber, WDA, AAW: W3/52: no number, 29 July 1856.
26 V. Cardella SJ to F. W. Faber, 31 December 1853, in Bowden, *Life*, no number, p. 340.
27 Ibid. pp. 339–40.
28 F. W. Faber (1855), *All For Jesus*, 5th edn, London, Richardson & Sons, p. ix.
29 W. A. Hutchison to Mgr G. Talbot, WDA, AAW: W3/52: Letter 50, n.d. (probably September 1856).
30 Ibid.
31 F. W. Faber to W. Ullathorne, LO, Vol. 22, No. 55, 20 August 1853.
32 Ibid.
33 Ibid.
34 F. W. Faber to the Earl of Arundel, 2 January 1854, in Bowden, *Life*, Letter XCIX, p. 341.
35 Anon. (1854), '*All for Jesus, or the Easy Ways of Divine Love*. By Frederick William Faber, Priest of the Oratory of St Philip Neri', in *Dublin Review*, Vol. XXXVI, No. LXXI, March, p. 194.
36 Ibid. p. 196.
37 Ibid. p. 199.
38 Ibid. p. 200.
39 Ibid. p. 206.
40 Ibid. p. 200.
41 Ibid. p. 210.
42 Ibid. p. 195.
43 Ibid.
44 W. A. Hutchison to N. Wiseman, WDA, AAW: W3/16: Letter 8, 15 September 1856.
45 W. A. Hutchison to F. W. Faber, WDA, AAW: W3/52: no number, 29 July 1856.
46 Ibid.
47 Ibid.
48 Ibid.
49 W. A. Hutchison to Mgr G. Talbot, WDA, AAW: W3/52: Letter 50, n.d. (probably September 1856).
50 Ibid.
51 Ibid.
52 F. W. Faber (n.d.), *Growth in Holiness*, 3rd edn, London, Burns & Oates, pp. viii–ix.
53 Ibid. Chapter X.

54 Ibid. p. 128.
55 Ibid. p. 49.
56 Ibid. p. viii.
57 Ibid. p. 35.
58 Ibid. p. 94.
59 Ibid. p. ix.
60 W. Ullathorne to F. W. Faber, LO, Vol. 22, No. 169, 16 September 1856.
61 Ibid.
62 F. W. Faber (1861), *The Blessed Sacrament*, 3rd edn, London, Burns & Oates, p. vii.
63 Ibid. p. 301; see also pp. 296–7.
64 F. W. Faber (1858), *Ethel's Book or Tales of the Angels*, London, Burns & Oates.
65 F. W. Faber (1861), *The Blessed Sacrament*, 3rd edn, London, Burns & Oates, p. 156.
66 F. W. Faber to J. H. Newman, LO, Vol. 3, No. 150, 17 March 1855.
67 F. W. Faber (1861), *The Blessed Sacrament*, 3rd edn, London, Burns & Oates, pp. ix–x.
68 W. B. Ullathorne to F. W. Faber, LO, Vol. 22, No. 169, 16 September 1856.
69 Ibid.
70 Ibid.
71 Ibid.
72 Ibid.
73 Ibid.
74 F. W. Faber (1861), *The Blessed Sacrament*, 3rd edn, London, Burns & Oates, p. 199.
75 Ibid., note on p. 162.
76 Ibid. p. 216.
77 Ibid. pp. 215–7.
78 Ibid. p. 218.
79 Ibid. p. 222.
80 Ibid.
81 Ibid. pp. 222–3.
82 Ibid. p. 192.
83 Ibid. pp. 492–3.
84 F. W. Faber (1857), *Poems*, 3rd edn, London, Richardson & Sons, Preface.
85 Ibid. pp. 519–20.
86 Ibid. p. 522.
87 F. W. Faber, 'Thoughts while reading history', ibid. No. CLXXVII, pp. 516–26.
88 Ibid. No. CLXIX, p. 467.
89 Ibid. No. XIX, p. 147.
90 Ibid. Nos. XXIII and XXIV, p. 149.
91 'Memorials of a happy time: No. 3: The Vision', ibid. p. 49.

92 'To a Friend', ibid. No. LX, p. 209.
93 'Lent', ibid. No. LXXIX, pp. 235–6, and 'The Litany', ibid. No. LXXXI, pp. 239–40.
94 'Birthday Thoughts: At a grave in Somersetshire, 1839', ibid. No. XXXVI, pp. 183–4.
95 'Softly the Ships do sail: To my Mother', ibid. No. CVI, pp. 266–8.
96 'Where the pinewoods wave', ibid. No. CXXII, p. 329.
97 'On Revisiting the River Eden: in Westmoreland, 1836', ibid. No. VIII, p. 113.
98 'St Mary's at Night', ibid. No. XVIII, pp. 145–6.
99 'Sunlight and Moonlight', ibid. No. CXV, p. 292.
100 'The Mourner's Dream: 3: The World's Edge', ibid. pp. 67–80.
101 Ibid. p. 75.
102 'The Groves of Penshurst', ibid. No. XLIV, p. 192.
103 'The Haunted Place Revisited', ibid. p. 56. Also, 'A Dream', ibid. p. 57.
104 Anon. (1860–61), Review: 'Living English Poets' in *Dublin Review*, Vol. XLIX, No. XCVIII, pp. 503–42.
105 Ibid. p. 540.
106 G. M. Hopkins to R. W. Dixon, 16 December 1881, in C. Phillips (ed.) (1991), *Gerard Manley Hopkins: Selected Letters*, Oxford, OUP, p. 168.
107 R. B. Martin (1992), *Gerard Manley Hopkins: A Very Private Life*, London, Flamingo, p. 83.
108 D. Milnes Gaskell (1890), *Frederick William Faber*, in Duff, *Addresses*, London, n.p., pp. 3–23.
109 Ibid. p. 3.
110 Ibid. p. 5.
111 Ibid. p. 3.
112 Ibid. pp. 5–6.
113 Ibid. p. 7.
114 Ibid. p. 20.
115 Ibid.
116 F. W. Faber (n.d.), *The Creator and the Creature*, new edn, London, Burns & Oates, p. 146.
117 Ibid., footnote on p. 327.
118 Ibid. Preface, p. x.
119 Ibid. Preface, pp. vii–viii.
120 Ibid. p. 354.
121 Ibid. p. 11.
122 Ibid. p. 297.
123 Ibid. p. 15.
124 Ibid. p. 96.
125 Ibid. p. 17.
126 Ibid. p. 367.
127 Ibid. p. 5.
128 Ibid. p. 12.

129 Ibid. p. 6.
130 Ibid. p. 7.
131 Ibid. p. 25.
132 Ibid.
133 Ibid. pp. 84–5.
134 Ibid. p. 103.
135 Ibid. p. 360.
136 Ibid. p. 381.
137 Ibid. p. 293.
138 Anon. (1857), '*The Creator and the Creature, or, the Wonders of Divine Love*. By Frederick William Faber, DD, Priest of the Oratory of St Philip Neri', in *Dublin Review*, Vol. XLIII, No. LXXXV, September, p. 236.
139 Ibid. p. 237.
140 Ibid.
141 Ibid.
142 Ibid. p. 241.
143 Ibid. p. 243.
144 Ibid.
145 Ibid. p. 242.
146 Ibid. p. 239.
147 Ibid. p. 240.
148 Ibid. p. 238.
149 Chapman, *Father Faber*, p. 309.
150 Ibid. p. 309.
151 S. Gilley, *F. W. Faber (1814–1863)*, in DNB (Oxford, OUP, 2004) Vol. 18, p. 873.
152 F. W. Faber (1858), *The Foot of the Cross*, London, Richardson & Sons, Preface, p. vii.
153 Ibid.
154 Ibid.
155 Ibid. p. 66.
156 Ibid. pp. 447–51.
157 Ibid., beginning of Chapter 5.
158 Ibid. Chapter 2: The First Dolour: The Prophecy of St Simeon.
159 Ibid. p. 37.
160 Ibid. p. 226.
161 Ibid. pp. 333 and 340.
162 Ibid. p. 221.
163 Ibid. p. 392.
164 Ibid. p. 386.
165 Ibid. pp. 431–2.
166 F. W. Faber to J. B. Morris, LO, Vol. 17, No. 190, n.d.
167 Bowden, *Life*, p. 416.
168 Ibid.
169 Chapman, *Father Faber*, p. 310.
170 Ibid.
171 F. W. Faber to J. B. Morris, LO, Vol. 17, No. 148, 17 July 1858.

172 F. W. Faber (n.d.), *Spiritual Conferences*, 9th edn, London, Burns & Oates, Preface, p. vii.

173 F. W. Faber to J. E. Bowden, LO, Vol. 20, No. 50, 5 August 1859.

174 F. W. Faber (n.d.), *Spiritual Conferences*, 9th edn, London, Burns & Oates, Preface, pp. vii and ix.

175 Bowden, *Life*, p. 417.

176 Chapman, *Father Faber*, p. 310.

177 For an example, see F. W. Faber (n.d.), *Spiritual Conferences*, 9th edn, London, Burns & Oates, p. 167.

178 Ibid. p. 160.

179 Ibid. p. 172.

180 Ibid. p. 15.

181 Ibid. p. 150.

182 Ibid. p. 334.

183 Ibid. p. 307.

184 Ibid. p. 333.

185 Ibid. p. 347.

186 Ibid. p. 351.

187 Ibid. p. 335.

188 Ibid. p. 164.

189 Ibid. p. 252.

190 Ibid. p. 352.

191 Ibid. p. 165.

192 Ibid. p. 105.

193 Ibid. p. 124.

194 Ibid. p. 116.

195 Ibid.

196 Ibid. p. 220.

197 Ibid. p. 99.

198 Ethel was the daughter of the Duke of Norfolk.

199 Anon. (1858), 'Ethel's Book or Tales of the Angels by the Very Rev. F. W. Faber' in *Dublin Review*, Vol. XLV, December, pp. 532–3.

200 Ibid. p. 532.

201 Membership had increased by 28,000 since 1853.

202 F. W. Faber (1959), *The Precious Blood*, 3rd edn, Philadelphia, p. 79.

203 Ibid. pp. 204–5.

204 Ibid. pp. 141–3.

205 Ibid. p. 163.

206 Ibid. p. 169.

207 Ibid. p. 163.

208 Chapman, *Father Faber*, p. 316.

209 F. W. Faber (1959), *The Precious Blood*, 3rd edn, Philadelphia, p. 67.

210 Chapman, *Father Faber*, p. 316.

211 F. W. Faber (1959), *The Precious Blood*, 3rd edn, Philadelphia, pp. 146–7.

212 Ibid. p. 7.

213 Ibid.
214 Ibid.
215 Ibid. p. 15.
216 Ibid. p. 17.
217 Ibid. p. 22.
218 Ibid. p. 47.
219 Ibid. p. 16.
220 Ibid. p. 17.
221 Ibid. p. 37.
222 Ibid. p. 87.
223 Ibid. p. 82.
224 Ibid. p. 167.
225 F. W. Faber to J. B. Morris, LO, Vol. 17, No. 148, 17 July 1858.
226 F. W. Faber (n.d.), *Bethlehem*, new edn, London, Burns & Oates, Preface p. ix.
227 Ibid. p. x.
228 Thérèse of Lisieux (1873–1897).
229 F. W. Faber (n.d.), *Bethlehem*, new edn, London, Burns & Oates, pp. 168–9.
230 Ronald Knox, (trans.), (1958), Thérèse of Lisieux, *Autobiography of a Saint*, London, The Harvill Press, p. 234.
231 F. W. Faber (n.d.), *Bethlehem*, new edn, London, Burns & Oates, p. 74.
232 Ronald Knox, (trans.), (1958), Thérèse of Lisieux, *Autobiography of a Saint*, London, The Harvill Press, p. 233.
233 F. W. Faber (n.d.), *Bethlehem*, London, Burns & Oates, p. 340.
234 Ibid.
235 Ibid. p. 25.
236 Ibid. p. 48.
237 Ibid. p. 222.
238 Ibid. p. 275.
239 Leo XIII, Encyclical *Rerum Novarum* (1891).
240 It is interesting to note that whereas Newman's particular friend, Ambrose St John, remains in the background and provides no theological competition for Newman, Hutchison was an intelligent theologian, one whose opinion Faber valued.
241 F. W. Faber (n.d.), *Bethlehem*, London, Burns & Oates, p. viii.
242 Chapman, *Father Faber*, p. 311.
243 F. W. Faber (n.d.), *Bethlehem*, London, Burns & Oates, p. 43.
244 Ibid. pp. 49–51.
245 Ibid. pp. 132–3.
246 Ibid. chapter 1.
247 Ibid. p. 381.
248 See Faber's note regarding Mary and the prophecy of Simeon, in F. W. Faber (n.d.), *Bethlehem*, London, Burns & Oates, p. 371.
249 F. W. Faber (n.d.), *Bethlehem*, London, Burns & Oates, p. 412.
250 Faber had previously published volumes of hymns in 1848, 1849, 1852, 1854 and 1857.

251 F. W. Faber (n.d.), *Hymns*, London, Burns & Oates, Preface, p. viii.
252 Ibid. Preface, pp. xvi–xvii.
253 Ibid. Preface, p. xv.
254 Ibid. Preface, p. xiii.
255 Ibid. Preface, p. xviii.
256 'The Sacred Heart', ibid. No. 37, pp. 110–18.
257 'The Eternal Word', ibid. No. 12, pp. 30–3.
258 'Our Lady's Expectation', ibid. No. 44, p. 135.
259 'The God of my Childhood', ibid. No. 11, pp. 26–8.
260 'Lent', ibid. No. 24, pp. 76–8.
261 'A Daily Hymn to Mary: for the children of St Philip's home', ibid. No. 58, pp. 168–70.
262 'St Martha', ibid. No. 74, pp. 213–5.
263 'St Patrick's Day', ibid. No. 77, pp. 220–21.
264 'Faith of our Fathers: for Ireland', ibid. No. 93, p. 265.
265 'O Balmy and Bright', ibid. No. 52, p. 155.
266 'Jesus, My God My All', ibid. No. 14, pp. 35–7.
267 'Blood is the Price of Heaven', ibid. No. 28, p. 86.
268 Anon (1849), 'Jesus and Mary; or Catholic Hymns, by Frederick William Faber, Priest of the Oratory of St Philip Neri', in *Dublin Review*, Vol. XXVII, No. LIII, pp. 163–81.
269 Ibid. p. 178.
270 Ibid. p. 174.
271 Ibid.
272 Ibid. p. 176.
273 Ibid.
274 Ibid. p. 177.
275 Anon (1858), '*Oratory Hymns* by the Very Rev. F. W. Faber. Set to Music by Wilhelm Schulthes', in *The Rambler*, NS, Vol. IX, pp. 421–2.
276 Ibid.
277 Ibid. p. 422.
278 Ibid.
279 Chapman, *Father Faber*, p. 313.
280 Ibid. p. 314.
281 Ibid. p. 315.
282 Ibid.
283 Ibid.
284 Ibid. p. 314.
285 Ibid. p. 318.
286 For a comprehensive survey of the number of hymn books which contain versions of Faber's hymn 'Souls of men why will ye scatter', see A. J. MacGregor (1999), 'There's a Wideness in Variety – F. W. Faber Reassessed' in *Ushaw Library Bulletin*, 10, December, pp. 32–8.
287 *Songs of Praise* (London, OUP, 1931) [CoE, 4 Faber hymns]; *The English Hymnal* (Oxford, OUP, 1933) [CoE, 10 Faber hymns];

Hymns Ancient and Modern (London, Wm Clowes and Sons, 1939) [CoE, 12 Faber hymns]; *The Baptist Hymn Book* (London, Novello and Co., 1964) [Baptist, 6 Faber hymns]; *The Parish Hymn Book* (London, L. Carey and Co., 1968) [RC, 17 Faber hymns]; *Hymns Ancient and Modern* (London, Wm Clowes and Sons, 1972) [CoE, 7 Faber hymns]; *Celebration Hymnal* (Essex, Mayhew Macrimmon, 1986) [RC, 12 Faber hymns]; *Hymns Old and New* (Suffolk, Kevin Mayhew Ltd, 1991) [RC, 8 Faber hymns]; *Laudate* (Suffolk, Decani, 1999) [RC, 7 Faber hymns].

288　These are: 'By the blood that flow'd from thee'; 'Dear angel ever at my side'; 'Hail Jesu hail'; 'Hail holy Joseph hail'; 'Hark, hark my soul'; 'Holy ghost, come down upon thy children'; 'Have mercy on us God most high'; 'Jesus is God'; 'Jesus my Lord my God my all'; 'Most ancient of all mysteries'; 'Mother Mary at thine altar'; 'Mother of mercy, day by day'; 'My God, my God and can it be'; 'O come to the merciful saviour'; 'O God, thy power is wonderful'; 'O it is hard to work for God'; 'O paradise, O paradise'; 'O purest of creatures'; 'Sing, sing ye angel bands'; 'Souls of men, why will ye scatter'; 'There's a wideness in God's mercy'; 'Workmen of God'.

289　A. J. MacGregor has demonstrated that, on the various occasions where Faber's words have been changed in order to reflect twentieth-century taste, the changes have not always been successful. See A. J. MacGregor (1999), 'There's a Wideness in Variety – F. W. Faber Reassessed' in *Ushaw Library Bulletin*, 10, December, pp. 36-7.

290　Compare 'Faith of our Fathers', verse three, lines 1–2, No. 130 in *Hymns Old and New* (Suffolk, 1986) with verse three, lines 1–2, No. 466 in *The Baptist Hymn Book* (London, 5th edn, 1964) p. 546.

291　Compare 'O come and mourn with me awhile', verse two, line 2, No. 113 in *Hymns Ancient and Modern* (London, William Clowes and Sons, 1972) with No. 383 in *Hymns Old and New* (Suffolk, Kevin Mayhew Ltd, 1986).

Chapter 6

Sermons: 1837–1863

Anglican sermons, 1837–1845

Faber preached twice weekly[1] as curate at Ambleside between August 1837 and March 1842, and thereafter as Rector of Elton, until November 1845. In the first part of this chapter, we shall look at a selection of these sermons, in order to indicate ideas that were not only important to Faber's Anglican thought, but also remained important after his conversion to Roman Catholicism.

Faber's sermons all follow the same pattern, starting with a quotation from scripture and then developing one or two points from, or related to, this text. Subjects include: scripture, doctrine, morality, the practice of religion and the 'spirit of the age'. The sermons are also influenced by the theology, rubric, services, and articles of religion contained within the *Book of Common Prayer*. These were not the only literary influence on Faber, and his conscientious method of filing and retaining information, from the wide variety of books that he had read, is illustrated by an indexed book.[2] This contains a number of definitions of terms and ideas from theology, scripture, ecclesiastical history and the Fathers, for use in sermons. The variety of reading presented therein is an indication of the breadth of Faber's scholarship.

The sermons written at Ambleside represent Faber's first attempts to communicate his personal spirituality and reading of theology to a public that is wider than his tutors and friends. They are written in the formal, unemotional, preaching style practised by the majority of Anglican and Protestant clergy; and, in accordance with this tradition, they were read, rather than preached from brief notes. It is notable that sermons from Ambleside are stylistically the same as his academic essays, but those written at Elton show the development of a style that is more mature and personal. Faber's writing style is neither particularly learned nor over-simplified; and in a rare example of his thoughts on sermon writing, he noted that he aimed to be 'as easy as I can without being trashy, but I do hate easy sermons'.[3] His tone fluctuates between encouragement and admonishment, and his message is spiritually demanding, despite being written for an audience whose knowledge and spiritual attainment was undoubtedly mixed. This is high-lighted in a sermon on the Christian priesthood. Faber writes that he is writing for individuals who are not familiar with theology, and therefore he is not going to dwell on the acade-mic discussions of theologians, before presenting detailed, intellectual, ideas from the ordination service.[4] There is little poetry in Faber's early sermons and, although recognisably Faberian in style, the over-emotional and highly-wrought style of the Roman sermons and books is not present at this stage. Although he sometimes uses emotion for effect, Faber's language is generally formal and restrained, and his style is tailored to providing definite, practical ideas that could be practised by his hearers. It seems probable that one reason for this was that Faber was hoping that people would be able to become, albeit in a rudimentary way, apologists for their Anglican beliefs and, in his early sermons, for Tractarianism. He wrote, 'my duty is to teach not to argue. I will never prove out of the pulpit what I have taught in it',[5] and it seems proba-ble that this was one of the reasons why he did not present abstract concepts, or ideas whose meaning was ambiguous.

The primacy of scripture in Faber's thought is illustrated by its use as the basis for several sermons. Article VII states: 'The Old Testament is not contrary to the New: for both in the Old and New Testament everlasting life is offered to mankind by Christ.'[6] Faber's use of the Old Testament follows this rule, and starts from the premise that Christ was prefigured in all of the events and individuals within it.[7] He does this in order to tie the two halves of scripture together, because, 'we should not . . . have expected that . . . the only revelation from God to man . . . should have been in so large a portion of it merely historical'.[8]

Faber's use of Jewish history always makes a Christian point; thus, Eli is a representative of a type of Christian whose religion exists only on the surface.[9] We should not conclude from this that Faber's reading of Jewish history was unsympathetic. It is, however, always based on the belief that the whole of scripture is from God and therefore infallible, and is therefore ultimately Christian.[10] The idea that scripture is infallible leads Faber to teach his congregation about the importance of valuing the whole of scripture[11] as 'containing all things necessary to salvation'.[12] Faber contrasts the Anglican and Roman Catholic uses of scripture, writing, 'we are in full, unreserved enjoyment of the Holy Scriptures, which our brethren of the Roman Church are not'.[13] However, Faber also asks whether Anglicans have used the Bible any better than Roman Catholics have, 'not by a superstitious fear of its light, but by an impatient familiarity therewith'.[14]

Childhood innocence is an ever-present and recurrent strand in Faber's thought and sermons. In one of these he uses the idea in relation to scripture, writing that 'childlike credulity'[15] is needed to understand scripture properly. 'Bible history is not a common history – not to be handled with indecent roughness or philosophical criticism ... but read after a childlike fashion.'[16] In a revealing statement which contains more than a hint of Wordsworth's line 'the child is father of the man',[17] Faber wrote that, in retrospect, the individual will conclude of childhood reading of scripture, that 'he ... understood it then ... far better and far deeper than he understands [it] now'.[18] It is noteworthy that Faber contrasted childlike with its obverse, childish; and his use of the phrase 'laying aside our childish notions'[19] indicates that he was not advocating an immature or thoughtless approach to scripture, but one in which humility was apparent. It seems probable that his promulgation of childlike humility, which was scriptural in its inspiration, was a natural development of Faber's earlier idea that there were dangers evident in an excess reliance on human philosophy and reason. We can put forward the hypothesis that Faber did not wish to be an academic theologian because he saw this as being linked to church politics and personality, which he had encountered, disliked and distrusted at Oxford. A more sophisticated version of these notions, that humanity is not capable of comprehending the mysteries of God, is well developed in Faber's thought by 1839.[20] This represents a change of intellectual and religious direction, because admitting religious mysteries to his worldview is part of a more sophisticated religiosity, which is the opposite of the simplicity of a straightforward evangelical view of religion.

Faber contrasted the innocence of early childhood with notions of the dangers, vices and sinfulness which gradually become part of the makeup of adolescents.[21] This is a strand of Faber's criticism of humanity, an attitude which recurs in his thought, and which is typical of the early nineteenth-century presentation of humanity as sinful and depraved as the result of original sin.[22] In a sermon which may have been preached to undergraduates at Oxford, he wrote: 'are not boys old enough to be filled with anger and rage, with pride, uncleanness and lust?'[23] The latter is particularly associated with original sin as 'the flesh lusteth ... contrary to the spirit'.[24] Other sins associated with youth include 'vanity, deceit, quarrelling, [and] disobedience'.[25] Faber develops these facets by putting forward the notion that sinfulness becomes ingrained: 'each year you will sadly grow in sin',[26] and because of this, perfection becomes more difficult in adulthood.[27] Adulthood is often presented by Faber as a less than ideal state, and he asserts that sinfulness committed during adulthood, like that in childhood, has consequences beyond the sin itself, saying, for example, 'we have a few short years to live here; but on those years depends eternity'.[28] Because of the emphasis on sin, Faber's worldview also accentuates the four last things: death and judgement, heaven and hell.[29] In this group of sermons, Faber's presentation of the aforementioned notions is unsophisticated. The devil is presented as a figure which interacts with the individual personality, rather than being a figurative idea: 'does not the devil enter into boys and fill them full of all impurity?'[30] Faber's language in writing of hell was calculated to have an immediate sobering impact on his congregation, and his description of 'ye bitter heat and raging agonies of hell'[31] is of a world which has a physical, rather than a spiritual or mental reality. It is difficult to ascertain whether this was Faber's personal belief, or whether it represents a presentation to a particular type of audience.

In a sermon given four times in different churches between August and November 1839, Faber criticised Christians 'of the house of Eli',[32] a group which he contrasted with those 'of the house of the Apostles'.[33] The former are Christians whose 'religion does not ... go beneath the surface',[34] whose faith and works possess neither seriousness nor substance. He wrote of this type of religious practice, 'their soul remains amid it all like a cold quiet pool in a shady place'.[35] Later, he questioned 'how much arises from their naturally active and officious turn of mind, and how much from the love of Christ'.[36] From our perspective, we can interpret this sermon as an oblique criticism of the shallowness of the faith practised by the Anglican evangelicals: 'they have been living in excitement. They have laid nothing by in the way of solid religious habits. Their holiness is a shadow, not a substance.'[37] These phrases echo Faber's earlier criticism of his own Evangelicalism, and they serve to underline his personal progression away from a religiosity that is measured by emotional experience alone. Because of this, Faber continually preaches a distrust of emotion in religious matters; he uses phrases such as 'excited feelings'[38] to correspond to the false, ultimately shallow, mirth of the world. Despite this, Faber remains an individual for whom emotion is important.

Like his contemporaries, Faber believed that the world was created four thousand years before the birth of Jesus.[39] The idea of worldliness brings forth from Faber a similar set of criticisms to those associated with the 'spirit of the age'. He noted that the world is ultimately 'ye devil's world',[40] and criticised Christians for being 'at peace with the world',[41] rather than aloof from it. Worldliness was undesirable for Faber, because he saw it as an attitude of mind that leads ultimately to the profaning of the components of religion, such as scripture. He writes, 'mirth doth unto folly glide and folly on to sin'.[42] This may also be a sign of subliminal or residual Calvinism in Faber's thought. In one sermon, meditation is necessary for preventing temptation and for contradicting excessive worldliness;[43] whilst in another, it is used in the context of the contrast between worldly and Christian lifestyles, the first of which leads ultimately to hell and the second to heaven.[44] This sermon is also concerned with the seriousness of sin, and of the reality of God's judgement.[45]

One sermon in particular, that for Easter Day 1839, is Calvinistic in its emphasis on the unworthiness of humanity, and unremitting in its curtailment of the notion that it is legitimate to rejoice in the Resurrection. He wrote, 'We must be afraid of being too glad ... afraid to ask any blessing of Him.'[46] Faber draws a parallel between sinfulness and the Church's 'distrust'[47] of festivals, indicated by the 'preponderance of fasts over feasts'.[48] For Faber, even when the Church is rejoicing during Eastertide, there is the possibility that individuals will be led into moral danger; thus, 'Either we are cold and dead and full of worldliness; or our affections are so moved as to be ... scarcely reverent.'[49] Pessimism extends to the lack of success for the average Christian in practices such as keeping the commandments. He writes, 'when they involve self-denial and a sacrifice of their own wills and ways, then men go no further'.[50] All of these ideas are present in a sermon which Faber preached at St Mary's Church, Oxford on the eighteenth Sunday after Trinity,[51] in which he also stressed the sin of self will, and the undesirability of weakness in religious observance.[52]

Faber's presentation of religious practice was sombre, restrained and austere; and he exhibited a well-developed understanding of the necessity of the Cross.[53] He wrote, 'Catholicism is not one among the many ingeniously framed intellectual systems which gather about the cross; but that cross' home.'[54] These were coupled with the notion that self-denial, mortification, and adversity were necessary components of an authentic Christian life.[55] Faber was also concerned that fasting was an important tradition, and he commended the practice of it to his fellow Anglicans, particularly in the context of ordination, baptism and before receiving the Sacraments.[56] It is notable that he felt that he had to point out and reassure his parishioners that fasting was not a forbidden Roman ritual[57] but one that was orthodox, because it was included in the prayer book, central to scripture and part of the practice of the Early Church.[58] Faber's emphasis on presenting ideas that were central to the early Christians, such as fasting, is an indication of how far Tractarian ideas had worked themselves into his thought. The Early Church is increasingly presented as an ideal expression of unified Christianity, one which contrasted with the Church of his contemporaries in which 'the primitive fires have burnt out'.[59] Writing of Easter, Faber wrote, 'The primitive Christians did not kneel to pray at Easter; but stood up as obedient sons in favour with their Father. These privileges are not for us.'[60] By the late 1830s, Faber's intellect exhibited a profound, almost 'Froudeian' dissatisfaction with the post-Reformation Church. This was expressed in different contexts in a number of sermons, but the idea which links them together is the seriousness of factions and schism, indeed anything which affects the unity of the wider Church. He wrote, 'we are living in a time when low views, cold faith, that most sad and fearful sin of dissent and disobedience to the Church ... abound everywhere'.[61] His warnings extended to preaching against using doctrines or the Scriptures as tools to reinforce differences of sect, party and group.[62]

Perhaps because of his cynicism with regard to lack of authority in contemporary Anglicanism, Faber developed an increasingly high view of the authority of the Church within his sermons. In doing so, he supplanted the view that Anglicanism was a Protestant sect, with the belief that it was part of the Catholic-Apostolic lineage, and therefore Apostolic in its traditions, rites and rituals.[63] In a sermon based on the text *There is one Body and one Spirit*, Faber preached that it is important to obey the Church in its interpretation of doctrine and scripture because of its authority.[64] Authority stems from Apostolicity; therefore, 'the church tells us what the bible means ... and so we believe it. And there is no difficulty about the facts or the meanings of the words.'[65] This emphasis on doctrinal and ecclesiastical authority had also replaced the reliance on emotional experience, in Faber's vocabulary, as an assessment of religious matters. This is apparent both in Faber's personal religious life and in his sermons, and it seems probable that the emphasis on authority was one of the first signs of what would develop into his Ultramontane stress on authority as a Roman Catholic.

The Eucharist is presented by Faber as representing the one remaining strand of unity in the Church, one which was constant despite sectarian divisions.[66] He does not qualify this by saying whether he is referring to the Christian Church as a whole or to Anglicanism; but we can presume that the latter was intended. It is notable that Faber's treatment of the Eucharist is dependent upon, and influenced by, the *Book of Common Prayer* to a greater extent than other ideas which are treated in these sermons. The Eucharist was an important part of Faber's ecclesiology, one which is presented as forming a link between Christ, the Christian Church and the individual.[67] Despite several references to the Eucharist, these sermons yield only one example of an explicit reference to the manner of its reception; the phrase 'we spiritually eat His Flesh and drink His Blood'[68] indicates a form of receptionist position conforming to Article 22, 'The Body of Christ is given, taken, and eaten in the supper, only after an heavenly and spiritual manner.'[69] This statement underlines Faber's compliance with the post-Reformation emphasis on the importance of not implying adoration of the Sacrament, as adoration is condemned as 'Romish'[70] in the Articles. Here, as elsewhere, Faber does not dwell on theology, but presents a sacramentality that is easy for his congregation to comprehend. Thus, the Eucharist is portrayed as a vital part of the individual Christian's duty to God, and for this reason, he underlined the necessity of receiving it more than the statutory once or twice a year.[71] It is notable that Faber demonstrates an awareness of the problems inherent in persuading people to receive the Eucharist, particularly when they had little or no feeling for it due to lack of use.[72] Following the spirit of the *Exhortation* in the Communion service,[73] Faber's sermons aim to persuade his parishioners to adopt a higher appreciation of the value of the Eucharist. This is particularly apparent in a sermon which discusses it in the context of confirmation, in which he wrote of 'the privilege and the duty of coming to this holy sacrament'.[74] These sermons continually refer to and stress the importance of receiving the Eucharist in the spirit of penitence. This notion, which has its origins in the rubric given before the Communion Service in the *Book of Common Prayer*, stresses the importance of reconciliation between those who are to receive the Eucharist. Reconciliation in this manner is a central part of the relationship between the individual and God, as the worthy reception of the Eucharist ensures that individuals do not 'eat and drink their own damnation'.[75] Thus, reception of the Eucharist contains within it the forgiveness of sin and absolution. Faber wrote, 'Come to the H[oly] table with humility and an earnest desire to be cleansed from your sins.'[76]

Several of these sermons contain an eschatological dimension within them, although this was used by Faber as an oratorical device, rather than as a presentation of a particular strand of theology. Its purpose was to encourage his congregation with thoughts of 'the celestial Jerusalem',[77] or to end demanding or excessively sombre sermons on a positive note, such as 'we are one day to have thrones with Christ'.[78] The notion of the Church militant as a community of like-minded individuals worshipping God together[79] was important to Faber, and a number of his sermons contain phrases such as 'as we kneel together at ye earthly altar'.[80] This is frequently contrasted with the Church in heaven, which is presented as a state that is attained after a necessary period of suffering and endurance[81] on earth. God's judgement,[82] of the Church and of the individual, is a necessary part of the transition from earth to heaven. He used the notion of judgement to encourage his parishioners to be stricter in their Christian observance, and to take up a moral stance that would lessen the impact of God's judgement; and preached on the necessity of cultivating a sense of mystery, awe and adoration, as the opposite of the profanation of religious mysteries.[83] As in other examples from Faber's homilies, the world itself is unimportant: 'what is this world ... to the one thought of being brothers ... in our one common Father's house in Heaven'.[84]

Roman Catholic sermons, lectures and novice conferences, 1846–1863

Between 1846 and 1848, Faber preached to his Wilfridian parish, St Wilfrid's, at Cotton and Cheadle, Staffordshire.[85] Faber joined the Congregation of the Oratory in April 1848 and, in April 1849, founded the London Oratory. He preached at the two sites occupied by the London house: at King William Street, Strand, between 1849 and 1854, and at Brompton between 1854 and 1863. After the restoration of the Catholic hierarchy, during 1850, the London Oratorians, encouraged by Cardinal Wiseman, played a significant role in developing the Ultramontane strand of Catholicism within the Diocese of Westminster, through sermons, liturgy, catechetics and education. Faber also preached at other Roman churches in London: at Farm Street,[86] Spanish Place,[87] Bayswater[88] and Fulham;[89] and outside London, at Oscott (Staffordshire), Arundel[90] (Sussex), and St Edmund's College, Ware (Hertfordshire).

The congregations to whom Faber preached consisted variously of educated and uneducated, lay and clerical, and representatives of all social strata. His sermons can be divided into two literary styles. The first presents ideas that are easily understandable, and simple enough to be applied by his congregation to their everyday lives. These exhibit Faber's strong sense of theatre, and his skill in creating a mental picture, a product of the poetic sensitivity developed by his association with the Lakeland poets during the 1830s, and his Ignatian spirituality. Their emotion does not necessarily exclude profundity; and an example of this is the tangible, intense sense of pain and weariness in the meditations on the Passion, the subject of Faber's final sermon, preached on Passion Sunday 1863.[91] Faber advised the priests of his Oratory to follow his example, and wrote, 'You must cultivate a simple style. You must see that y[ou]r points pass by an easy and natural transition into each other. You must never extemporize.'[92] He also stated, 'Be enthusiastic, affectionate and very simple and soul saving in your course.'[93] The second style is more erudite, presenting theological ideas which are less straightforward, and potentially problematic for uneducated members of this congregation, such as the meditations on the relationship between the persons of the Trinity, for Trinity Sunday 1858.[94]

The lectures are stylistically reminiscent of Faber's writings whilst at Oxford during the 1830s, and the Anglican sermons. They reveal his ability to use theology in an academic context, and illustrate the diversity of theologians and spiritual writers that he had read, such as Vazquez, Aquinas, Suarez and Scotus. Faber was conscientious and thorough in preparing lectures; he studied the subject, wrote his lecture, and then kept the manuscript for several months, after which he read the information again, re-appraised, and re-wrote before preaching and publishing.[95] The lectures were more controversial than the sermons, as they were open to an audience wider than that of his parishioners; however, Faber's attitude to debate was contradictory. The Ultramontane nature of his Catholicism intensified as his Roman period progressed, and he does not mind causing controversy where his main concern is to present orthodox doctrine and to stress the authority and infallibility of the Church. At other times, Faber abandoned projects, either because he was uncomfortable with the controversy generated by them, or because they were too scholarly for the capabilities of his congregation;[96] whilst on one occasion he wrote, 'ye lectures are very prolific of anonymous letters ... I am fairly tired of them'.[97] The conferences for the instruction of novices and priests of the London Oratory are akin to his lectures in both style and content. They present a sophisticated view of God, which demonstrates Faber's writing for professional religious who have been initiated into the technicalities and subtleties of theology.

Faber's Roman Catholic sermons exhibit thematic continuity with those that he wrote as an Anglican. However, whereas the Anglican sermons are concerned with expressing doctrine within the context of a text from scripture, the Roman Catholic sermons are concerned primarily, but not exclusively, with Roman doctrine. Their structure is straightforward, moving from what is unknown to what is known, or vice versa, and between past, present and future. These documents have not been the subject of discussion, probably because they exist only as detailed notes. However, several of Faber's books written from 1854 onwards are constructed, either wholly or partially, around sermons or lecture series; and comparison of sermon notes with the relevant chapters indicates that the sermon notes contain the core of his thought and its development.[98] There is marked continuity in the central notions of Faber's thought between 1845 and 1863; however, this does not imply intellectual stasis, as the ideas contained within them develop, often considerably. We shall assess the most important recurring themes in order to present a fuller picture of Faber's preaching style, theological preoccupations, and the notions which he considered most important.

The 'spirit of the age'

The 'spirit of the age'[99] is, as we have seen throughout this study, a dominant and recurring motif in Faber's thought; and, in his sermons, the term functions as an umbrella term for a number of ideas. In the first of these, the 'spirit of the age' is one that does not value religion, and the lectures on Mary characterise the 'spirit of the age' as the distance between Church and State.[100] This is epitomised in the relationship between members of the Roman Catholic Church and British society, which is, for Faber, anti-Catholic at both an individual and an institutional level. He cites the Ecclesiastical Titles Act of 1851[101] as an example of this propensity, and, rather than seeking for a basis for this wariness in the historical indivisibility of religious, political, and national allegiance, he refers to anti-Catholic notions as being irrational. He did not shrink from being openly critical of England, and placed the ideas that the country was both Protestant[102] and schismatic at the forefront of his thought.[103] Faber also applied this notion to the presence of the British Empire in India,[104] writing dismissively, 'ye heartless pomp of ye state church simply goes as part of ye Englishman's bag and baggage'.[105]

Both as an Anglican and as a Roman Catholic, Faber used the word 'Protestant' as a term of opprobrium, rather than as a straightforward defining term. It is significant that he viewed other religions as being of greater interest than other Christian denominations and, in a letter to Newman, he wrote, 'I am up to my ears in infidel transcendentalism … it is a great deal more interesting than Protestantism.'[106] Faber completed a series of seven lectures on Protestantism;[107] and, because the term includes Anglicanism, the lectures can be read as functioning as a retrospective view of his Anglican period, as they refer to ideas such as Tractarianism[108] and the Anglican reading of Antiquity.[109] Faber's critique highlights notions which had remained a central part of his thought, such as that Protestantism encourages both worldliness[110] and private judgement,[111] and that it is not supernatural.[112] As we have seen, emotion was an essential component of Faber's makeup and, in contrasting Roman Catholicism with Protestantism, he characterised the latter as cold,[113] undevotional[114] and irreverent.[115] In the lecture on Protestant devotion, Faber 'compared an Anglican clergyman doing the afternoon service ... with ... a knot of poor Irish hugging ye feet of our big crucifix'.[116] He wrote to Newman 'ye old Catholics were very grave ... but ye converts behaved shockingly',[117] but does not elaborate on this. At the end of January 1848 Faber delivered a lecture on conversion.[118] In this lecture, which exists only as notes, Faber takes as background the conversion of Paul, and then discusses the attitudes of Protestants towards post-Tractarian converts to Rome, via a discussion of 'three hundred years experience of Protestantism'.[119] The lecture also progresses from the general to the personal, and several passages have autobiographical overtones in their emphasis on the spiritual and temporal problems associated with conversion.[120]

After his move to Rome, Faber placed an Ultramontane stress on the unity of Catholic countries,[121] which he contrasted with Protestant Britain.[122] Whilst in Ireland, during 1852, Faber presented both England and Scotland as representing a Protestant empire that contrasted unfavourably with Ireland.[123] The sermons preached there show that he was careful to create a favourable impression on his listeners; he had read Irish history, and provided illustrations from More and Bede, and saints associated with Ireland, such as Patrick and Columba. It seems likely that he underlined this because several of his sermons were presented to the Jesuits and the Christian Brothers, both of which were engaged in education; and for Faber, the primary importance of education for the general population was so that individuals could study Roman Catholicism. In a passage that illustrates his poetic nature, appreciation of the past, and his classical education, Faber described Ireland as being 'A sacred island, like Samothrace',[124] and described the Irish people as apostles,[125] who had propagated Roman Catholicism through their emigration.[126] From his experiences in London, he stressed their importance to English Catholics,[127] writing, 'England, triumphant Empire carries <u>not</u> ye gospel; Ireland ... is dispersed and carries it.'[128] These examples illustrate how little sympathy Faber had for England, and several of his comments may be interpreted as disloyal.

Faber presents Roman Catholics as passive onlookers,[129] who

have a duty to isolate themselves from 'Low principles and ...
daily intercourse with unbelievers and heretics.'[130] Faber's
language in discussing heresy is that of contamination which
compromises the purity of the Church. In his lectures on Mary
he dwells on the 'evils of living among heretics',[131] and writes
of Mary that 'devotion to her preserves men from infection'.[132]
Faber believed that Roman Catholics should not live in countries which were not Catholic,[133] despite the admission that the
latter are frequently more prosperous than Catholic countries.[134] This is related to the dualistic theological idea that
'hatred of ye world is a token of ye true church',[135] a stance
which leads him, occasionally, into a slightly distasteful smugness and triumphalism.[136] This is apparent in the sermon for
the closing of the King William Street Oratory, during which
Faber employs his sense of theatre by writing negatively of the
'blot'[137] of earth as seen from the perspective of the beatific
vision.[138] This image is also interesting because it views the
earth from above, and it is a stylistic trait of Faber to give an
aerial view of his subject, which he may have acquired through
study, or personal experience, of mystical experiences. Faber
uses the idea that suffering and persecution are indicators of
the elect,[139] and uses Suarez' theology of congruence and its
conclusion that Roman Catholics are predestined to salvation.[140] Because of this, any enemy of the Roman Church is the
enemy of God,[141] and Faber frequently cites powerful arguments such as 'God is attacked in us'.[142] He also uses this idea
in another context by writing that those who question the
authority of the Church are not only heretics but are defying
God.[143] The faith of the individual is reinforced by 'infallible
certainty and absence of all doubt',[144] and phrases such as
'private and personal marks of favour from him',[145] show the
continuance of Faber's evangelical sense of the relationship
between the individual and God in this context. This is particularly apparent in the overtones of singularity with which he
describes the indicators of predestination in the life of the individual.[146] He writes of God's 'eternal choice'[147] of the
individual soul, and describes God's love as being 'a sign of
predestination'.[148]

Faber always transplants ideas from history, unchanged and
unchallenged, into the contemporary Church. Thus, a number

of sermons draw parallels between the early Christians and Roman Catholics in mid-nineteenth-century England.[149] In one such sermon, his co-religionists are portrayed as occupying the same position as first-century Christians, that is as isolated and out of place in a society which has an irrational and innate fear of their religion.[150] In another, both groups are contrary to the spirit of the society in which they live, both socially and doctrinally.[151] In Faber's thought, life on earth is always presented as a state of exile,[152] which is contrary to the unseen world, which contains the only reliable truth.[153] He characterises the spiritual and moral desert,[154] which is life outside the Roman Church, as being engaged in conflict with the world inside it.[155] This notion is underlined in a sermon preached at the closing of the King William Street Oratory,[156] in which Faber contrasts the unchangeability and perfection of God with the changeability of earth, symbolised by their imminent move to Brompton. In this sermon,[157] as in others, Faber gives the impression that he is endeavouring to weave a cocoon with which to insulate his congregation from the world. He also employs the notion that devotion to God insulates the individual from worldliness,[158] an idea which he also develops in several novice conferences.

These ideas are also highlighted in Faber's lectures for Epiphany 1851, which were concerned with aspects of the history and practice of the Roman Church.[159] The lectures caused debate, and Faber informed Newman: 'My lectures have made rather a commotion; some are offended; on the other hand <u>several</u> conversions are coming of them.'[160] The real purpose of Faber's lectures was to be an apologetic with which to challenge those who had disagreed with the restoration of the hierarchy during the previous year, and a number of his, occasionally pointed, remarks underline this. Here, the 'spirit of the age' is identified with the changeability and discord of the world outside the Church, which is contrasted with the Roman Church, which 'survives enemies'[161] and outlives heresies.[162] These ideas recur on other occasions. In a sermon for Corpus Christi 1851, Faber distinguished between members of the Roman Church and the 'spirit of the age', which is equated both with heresy and with individuals who are antagonistic towards Rome.[163] In a sermon for the feast of the

Assumption, Faber again highlighted antagonism towards Rome, in order to show the extent to which the world had distanced itself from God.[164] He contrasted this with the 'humility' of God, manifested in the creation of Mary, and in the incarnation.[165]

A paper on journalism,[166] presented to the Brothers of the London Oratory, provides a perfect example of Faber's mind at its sharpest and most penetrating in his condemnation of the anti-Catholic 'spirit of the age'. Journalism, particularly that exhibited in *The Times,* is 'a powerful, tyrannical and triumphant scoundrelism',[167] because it was directly responsible for creating and sustaining 'popular delusions'[168] and anti-Catholic propaganda.[169] Journalism is also 'ungodly',[170] a product of the Antichrist,[171] because of its preoccupation with finances and with circulation figures.[172] It is also a form of trade, which is always negative in Faber's thought, a symbol of the 'world in its badness'[173] because of its dubious morality.[174]

A further form of the 'spirit of the age' is Faber's concern, also voiced by other mid-nineteenth-century churchmen, that scientific advances would have a detrimental effect upon the general understanding of religion and theology.[175] In this context, Faber treats the intellect negatively as being one of the root causes of scepticism and cynicism towards the tenets and practice of religion. This is summed up in an aside to Morris, in which he wrote 'I think you w[oul]d get further into ye spiritual life if you had less of ye critic, ye innovator, [and] ye reformer ... about you.'[176] In another sermon, he describes the 'spirit of the age' as, 'partly material and partly intellectual: science, commerce, discovery'.[177] Faber did not engage fully with the society of which he was part and, although he shared their capacity for hard work, he contrasted with the innovators of the nineteenth century in that he was not curious about, or excited by, knowledge. This trait, which is particularly noticeable from 1853 onwards, may have been the residue of the cynicism that he acquired after leaving Oxford, and of the alienation that he described at Elton. Whatever its cause, it is the continuation of Faber's life-long notion that self-limitation is a virtue, and that individuals should not strive to change their status in life. This idea is in the background of several of the sermons, although it is less marked here than in Faber's

books or life. Despite a wide reading of Patristic theology, and
of the works of theologians such as Suarez, Aquinas, and
Scotus, Faber rarely mentions the contribution of intellectuals
to the Church, and in a lecture for Epiphany 1851 wrote that
the Church was not fundamentally intellectual in character.[178]
There are only two situations in which Faber encourages study.
Firstly, in those who were not clergy, so that they could become
apologists for the Roman Church.[179] Secondly, in priests, who
should be theologically literate so that they can instruct their
congregation, and be an antidote to the unchristian 'spirit of
the age'.[180] During his Roman period, Faber became increasingly anxious to proclaim his own orthodoxy and loyalty to the
Church, and noted that the Church as a whole was more
important than the individual was. It is not surprising, therefore, that in passages where Faber writes of the 'conversions of
intellectual men'[181] he also underlines the necessity of their
submission to church authority. He also noted that any form of
individualism, particularly that of the intellect, would lead
almost inevitably to heresy, and countered this by citing St
Teresa of Avila as an example of loyalty coupled with originality.[182] Faber consistently highlights the 'Anti Christian bent of
literature and philosophy',[183] and describes journalism as
representing the worldly aspect of the human intellect.[184] One
sermon describes the reaction of *educated* first-century Jews to
the Baptist's[185] preaching of unfashionable ideas such as
penance.[186] This is a slightly different idea from what we have
been discussing, as the latter exhibits a moral attractiveness,
possessed by saints[187] in Faber's thought, which is related to
the possession of divine, rather than human, wisdom;[188] and it
is the possession of divine wisdom, rather than straightforward
knowledge, which Faber applauds. In a sermon preached on St
Philip's Feast 1861, Faber noted that St Philip was not primarily intellectual,[189] and, in a sentence which reminds us of Faber
himself, wrote that he practised an 'enthusiastic unadventurous
simplicity'.[190] It is indicative of the individual working of
Faber's mind that he suggests countering heresy not by use of
the intellect, which is often 'antagonistic'[191] to the Church, but
by practical means such as Confraternities,[192] prayer, the
rosary and the use of scapulars and medals.[193]

Several sermons refer to the clergy in relation to the 'spirit of the age'. The division between those inside the Roman Church, and those outside it, is mirrored by a similar distinction between clergy and congregation,[194] and he wrote of lay people, 'they love to listen as inferiors'.[195] He underlined the personal and corporate authority of clergy in an admonitory sermon which forbids the congregation to enter into dispute with their parish priest,[196] and noted that 'punishment and curse'[197] are the outcome in situations where dispute has occurred. Faber wrote several meditations and sermons referring to the priesthood and the Church. These are illustrative of the extent to which there was continuity in his thought, as a number of ideas had been present since his Anglican period. A conference written for the London Oratorians[198] follows a pattern which is familiar in Faber's writings, in that he starts with history, on this occasion that of the secular clergy, and makes a hierarchical distinction between them and priests who are members of religious orders. Faber highlighted the same distinction in a sermon preached before an assembly of clergy of the Diocese of Westminster, writing that the former are seen as being superior to the latter, principally because he characterises Jesus as a 'founder and member of the secular clergy'.[199] Despite this distinction, Faber wrote in a conference for the London Oratorians of the danger that individuals within his community would become insular, and that this would affect their relationship with the religious orders and secular priests of London.[200] In another conference for the London Oratorians, Faber is concerned with the particular circumstances of priests who work in England.[201] He affirms the idea that England is defined by its 'absence of faith',[202] and notes that Catholic purity is compromised by exposure to other forms of religion.[203]

Faber frequently highlights attributes of St Philip, which are part of his own spiritual and mental world. A number of these are concerned with being contrary to the 'spirit of the age', and, during 1852,[204] he explored ways in which the Oratorians could use the charism of the Order as part of their relationship with their parishioners, and with the wider society of London. Faber concluded that this would be best served by fostering a spirit of inclusiveness, and wrote, 'St Philip w[oul]d have no one excluded from his world. Men and women, old and young, priest or lay; all may bear their part in it.'[205] In a sermon for the vigil of St Philip's Feast 1854, Faber wrote that he admired the ordinariness of St Philip's life, and closeness to God.[206] Faber's constant concern, to present heaven as the only reality, is mirrored in the notion that the saint practised a perfectly balanced detachment from the world. He wrote, 'His was a beautiful mind – full of bright things and fair pictures – ye zeal of an apostle in ye repose of a hermit.'[207] In a sermon for St Philip's Day 1861, Faber dwelt on the idea that St Philip had been contrary to the spirit of the sixteenth century, and noted that the London Oratorians should be contrary to that of the nineteenth century.[208]

Other themes in Faber's Roman Catholic sermons, lectures and novice conferences

In sermons, lectures and novice conferences, we gain an insight into Faber's role in forming the devotional character of his parishioners and community; and it is noticeable that Faber uses the same metaphors and examples when expressing ideas relating to the spiritual life, whether he is writing for parishioners or the clergy.

For Faber, God is the most important consideration in life; and therefore prayer, and contemplation where applicable, is the only use of time that is not wasted.[209] In novice conferences, Faber inculcates the importance of cultivating an interest in private and public devotions, and observance of feast days.[210] He notes that a characteristic of saints is their 'taste for God, and for celestial things',[211] and encourages the novices to acquire this orientation. This is part of Faber's emphasis on the importance of a well-spent life,[212] characterised by the disciplines of spiritual reading, mental prayer, examination of conscience and confession.[213] Faber often discusses the moral and spiritual seriousness expected of priests; and writes that the fundamental aspects of the priesthood are teaching, sacrifice, suffering and unworldliness, the model for which is the ministry of Jesus.[214] He stresses the personal attributes required of the priest, such as the pursuit of spiritual excellence, selflessness, and the centrality of mental prayer.[215] Prayer is also discussed in a sermon preached at the

Quarant 'ore of Lent 1855, which dwells on its importance at a historical, as well as a personal level,[216] whilst a novice conference discusses difficulties associated with prayer.[217] Another, undated, conference is concerned with the recitation of the Office.[218] Several important ideas are expressed here: the importance of history and tradition, the notion that the devil is always working against the Church, and the constant movement of the individual towards death and eternity.[219] Characteristically for Faber, 'sweetness'[220] and emotion are the two fundamental markers of whether God's grace has been given to the individual member of the clergy.[221] Faber's personal spirituality is also evident in a conference on the Eucharist, which discusses the importance of ceremonial and of devotion to Mary.[222] This conference contains one of very few examples in Faber's sermon writing of a sense of numinousness and realisation of divine presence, rather than straightforward emotion.

Despite his emphasis on spiritual perfection, Faber did not possess one of the fundamental instincts of the spiritual genius, the ability to encourage individuals to a higher level of attainment. The sermons on the spiritual life are austere, as Faber was pessimistic about the ability of Christians to arrive at the high expectations inherent within certain strands of Christianity. He consistently highlighted the propensity of the individual to avoid effort in the spiritual life,[223] and frequently returned to the idea that individuals cannot be sufficiently religious, holy, or serious about God.[224] Thus, although he frequently encourages the individual to aspire to 'higher perfection',[225] he always counters this by emphasising the ever-present possibility of self-delusion. Faber's pessimism stemmed from a considerable apprehension of God, the supernatural,[226] and the invisible world,[227] which was, at one level, mystical, although the authentic contemplative strand, which was in the ascendant during the final five or so years of Faber's personal spiritual life, remained undeveloped in his sermons and lectures. This is not surprising as, throughout his Roman period, he felt uncomfortable with presenting deeper aspects of theology and spirituality to his congregation, and never discussed mysteries before those whom he thought would not be receptive.[228] This is interesting, as during his Anglican period he criticised the Tractarians for their doctrine of reserve in communicating mysteries. The mental world of his Roman sermons inhabits the same hierarchical structure as his Anglican sermons, which is composed of earth and humanity, heaven, God, angels and saints, hell, devils and the inhabitants of hell. These strata are always present; indeed earth is frequently presented as being intrinsically less real than the others.

A pensive sermon, for New Year's Eve 1849, is concerned with the contrast between the spiritual life as practised by the saints, the ordinary Christian, and the worldly 'spirit of the age'.[229] Faber applied concepts such as unreality, falsehood, and delusion[230] to the spiritual state of the majority,[231] particularly those who failed to acknowledge the reality of the supernatural.[232] Following the particular judgement, Faber stated, the eternal destination for this group is hell,[233] which is expressed in Ignatian terms as, 'filling hourly'.[234] Hell is also discussed in relation to original sin in a way which underlines Faber's overpowering sense of the seriousness of both mortal and venial sin;[235] whilst meditation on the reality of hell is recommended in a novice conference for Lent 1862, which begins: 'It is not certain that I may not be one of ye damned in hell.'[236] The latter highlights a fear which was present throughout Faber's life, and which is often expressed in connection with death. It is notable that he shared his contemporaries' preoccupation with death, and often recorded precise details of deaths of those who were important to him, both personally and historically. The powerful admonition *Bad deaths of those who have once been good*,[237] is concerned with individuals who go to hell after an unsatisfactory death, as a result of 'self trust'[238] and 'hidden covetousness',[239] and he highlights earthly wisdom[240] among his list of traits which lead to an unsatisfactory death. Loss of God and consignment to hell is also used in connection with the notion of excessive worldliness.[241] This has a public as well as a private dimension, and Faber employs the Pauline distinction between faith and works in order to remind his congregation of their responsibility to ensure that no individuals are separated from God because of their lack of good works.[242] Thus, self-denial[243] is important so that religion is not merely 'a ... sofa of sweet soft thoughts for conscience to lie down upon'.[244] On the Feast of the Sacred Heart 1855, Faber preached to the children of the poor school, warning them of the dangers of materialistic London, and presenting the possibility that, if they embrace its worldliness, they will eventually go to hell.[245]

Faber's lifelong preoccupation with the superficial, untruthful and unsatisfying[246] nature of life percolated through to his sermons. In those written from 1860 onwards,[247] this is joined by cynicism about his own life, and Faber writes that although life is often made unsatisfactory by our own actions, it is spoiled primarily by the actions of other people.[248] Faber considered that human nature is essentially childish.[249] During the 1850s, discussion of childishness is related to the theology of the Fall, and he writes that individuals content themselves with low, worldly, pastimes such as 'amusement',[250] 'dancing',[251] and 'dreaming over novels'[252] rather than aspiring towards God.[253] As an antidote to this behaviour, Faber writes of the necessity of purging oneself of 'evil habits',[254] and of atoning for past sin,[255] which is, in Faber's thought, always remembered by God. The sermon *How is it that life is short?* develops one of Faber's most important themes, the danger of wasting time in life, because of its shortness when compared with eternity.[256] Another notion, that life is profoundly unsatisfactory, is also present in the background of this sermon, and he underlines the futility of anything unnecessary, such as any form of entertainment.[257] In an Easter sermon for 1848, Faber draws parallels between his text, from John's Gospel,[258] and the worldly spirit of the 1840s,[259] which is characterised by 'Care of reputation. Esteem of greatness ... Spirit of ... management. Attachment to wills and ways. Pursuit of pleasures. Worship of comforts.'[260] Faber also highlights things that waste time, such as sleeping, pain and illness; ideas which clearly have autobiographical overtones, as Faber's letters repeatedly refer to time spent ill in bed. In a sentence which echoes the language of Newman, he wrote, 'So much of life is already gone ... we have got fixed in our groove.'[261] He writes, 'Love alone makes up for lost time',[262] a phrase which refers to God's love and grace for the individual, and the love of the individual for God, which shows itself as a willingness to change, despite negative associations connected with the past. The contradictions in

Faber's character are evident here, as on other occasions he seems dangerously content to keep individuals in a state of childishness, by frequently presenting sermons that are senti-mental, and appeal primarily to the emotions of his congregation.

The Roman sermons, like those that he wrote as an Anglican, exhibit a deeply-rooted pessimism about family life which, arguably, tells us more about Faber's own experiences than about his subject. This is related to Faber's idea that the Church supplants family ties, because heaven, rather than earth, is centrally important.[263] His main emphasis is on a lack of truthfulness inherent within families, and he writes that, 'family traditions are often ye strongholds of sin'.[264] In the same sermon, praise is viewed as being intrinsically wrong, as are the 'foolish fondnesses'[265] expressed by parents towards children 'as if they were dogs or cats'.[266] Although this sermon begins with a discussion of parents, it ends by discussing mothers, which is significant because in his mature writings Faber uses the idea of mother far more than that of father.[267]

In his sermons, Faber expresses ideas relating to God the Creator on several different levels. The first employs a rela-tively simple logic to explain a concept such as God's patience with humanity,[268] or the presence of the Holy Spirit,[269] in terms that are colloquial and easily digested by his congrega-tion. One example of this takes the form of a meditation on the eternal mercy of God,[270] whilst in another, God, as creator and redeemer, is presented in the context of God's personal involvement with the individual.[271] Faber's sermons are emotional and empathetic, rather than esoteric, and because of this he occasionally describes God in a manner which is cloying and unsatisfactory, such as 'Is he not sweet!'[272] He writes of 'omnipotence embracing, fondling'[273] creation, an idea which is echoed by G. M. Hopkins' 'Father and fondler of heart',[274] written fourteen years later. It is also noticeable that Faber usually characterises God as mother, and in sermons always uses maternal imagery in writing of the creator.[275] The second level of discussing God is more sophisticated, and reliant on the listeners' knowledge of at least the catechetical rudiments of doctrinal and sacramental theology.[276] Faber's poetic nature is present on both levels, and is apparent in descriptive

passages, such as that which describes the destiny of the individual as the 'magnificence ... of ye golden heavens'.[277] These
are undoubtedly rooted in Faber's personal spiritual experience, and the intensity of their expression highlights the
evangelical strand inherent within his spirituality.[278] In
another sermon, Faber underlined the personal nature of God
in evangelical terms, writing of 'private and personal marks of
favour from Him',[279] received in the Oratory Church. Thus,
God is a constant everyday presence, not one which is esoteric
or aloof, and he noted, 'we love ye place where He spoke –
listened – appeared'.[280] This leads us to the, unanswerable,
question as to whether Faber's preaching created a climate in
which the congregation or priests of the London Oratory
expected, and therefore experienced, religious phenomena
such as ecstasies or visions.

The sermon *The Eye of God* is an example of Faber's thought
at its most well balanced, logical and straightforward. He
begins with the concept of the individual's need for solitude,
even from the presence of those closest to them, a concept
understandable to his congregation. The world is also present,
as an unreal and claustrophobic presence. These thoughts are
a preamble to the real point of the sermon: the movement
towards God, the ultimate reality, by virtue of God's omnipotence and omnipresence.[281] God's 'continual recorded
judgement of us'[282] is the antidote to the ever-present possibility that individuals will delude themselves. Faber follows this
rather oppressive build-up by stating the positive aspects of this
presence, as 'joy and consolation'[283] and 'support in temptation'.[284] It is characteristic of Faber's thought that he concludes
by reminding his congregation of the incarnation, and by
stating that Jesus is the ultimate judge of the individual.[285]

The reality of future judgement, and the unwillingness of
individuals to meditate upon it, is the subject of Faber's sermon
The Judgement of ye reprobate. Faber presents a minute analysis of
the judgement of the individual, starting with areas of the life
of the subject, such as sins, motives and works, and moving
through accusers, such as the devil; witnesses, such as the
guardian angel; assessors, such as apostles and martyrs; and
executioners, such as demons, and instruments of torture.[286]
This sermon is uncompromisingly stark, particularly in its

exhortation that his congregation should view their judgement as the only thing of significance throughout their lives. It is the perfect counterpoint to Faber's lighter style, and the antithesis of the style of the book *All for Jesus*, written during the same year.

Faber's spirituality was fundamentally Christocentric, and several sermons are concerned with the second Person of the Trinity.[287] Two sermons, the first[288] of which was probably preached during the final weeks of Lent, and the second on Palm Sunday,[289] underline the incarnational nature of Faber's spirituality. God is identified with Jesus and Mary, rather than being presented as a remote, intellectual or esoteric creator; indeed, on a number of occasions, Faber is perhaps too informal in speaking of God. These sermons present a personal spirituality expressed in popular language, such as 'If life be bright and smiling, Jesus is ye brightness and ye smile.'[290] Faber tailored his presentation of Jesus to the situation and aspirations of his congregation, as being amiable and amicable,[291] thus: 'he comes to satisfy his insatiable longing for human love by haunting ye company of men'.[292] Faber also discussed Jesus in the context of spiritual and worldly poverty.[293] In one sermon, he wrote of three types of poverty: the voluntary poverty of Jesus, the clergy, and the involuntary poverty of his parishioners.[294] Faber observed that the world, and the 'spirit of the age', are indifferent towards poverty, but that there are 'supernatural motives for patience, supplied by ye choice of Jesus'.[295] In another, he expresses the notion that the 'comforts of poor men in general'[296] are greater than the, by implication, more authentic poverty of Jesus.[297] The major problem with both of these sermons is that Faber's preference for poverty removes any responsibility for bringing about change in the lives of his parishioners. He also transferred attributes of Jesus to his congregation. Thus, a sermon for Christmas Day 1855 used the humility of the infant as an example,[298] whilst another described the latter as being, like the individual Christian, reliant on Mary.[299] Faber drew parallels between the parent–child relationships in his congregation and the early life of Jesus, and sentiments such as 'let no rude word, no rough oath ... awaken ye sleeping babe'[300] were unmistakably intended as social teaching. The notion of worldliness is explored in the sermon *Without Jesus in ye world*, which characterises those inside and outside the Church as those who possess and those who reject Jesus.[301] Faber also encouraged his parishioners to practise devotions, such as those to the Sacred Heart.[302] In other sermons, Faber used more complex ideas, such as the importance of acquiring holiness modelled upon the example of the Cross,[303] the incomprehension shown by Jesus' contemporaries,[304] and the idea that Jesus is the judge of the individual.[305]

The Passion of Christ was a particularly important facet of Faber's spiritual life, lectures[306] and sermons, and he informed Morris that he possessed one hundred books on the subject.[307] This Pauline emphasis is highlighted in a sermon written during Eastertide 1854, in which he declared that the Passion should be an all-year-round devotion and personal mortifica- tion, rather than one that was confined to the weeks of Lent. In a novice conference, Faber instructs the individual to ask for 'compunction'[308] and 'tears'[309] as part of their meditations on the Passion, and he writes, 'Do not take any of this up lightly – but with great seriousness'.[310] For Faber, the emotional effects of this meditation were the most significant, as the antidote to cynicism, the world, and the 'spirit of the age'. He demon- strates a tremendous sense of sin, and of the fallen state of humanity, and writes that for the majority there is 'so little striving after perfection, and consequently little knowledge of our own vileness'.[311] As we would expect, Faber highlights the redemptive nature of the sufferings of the Passion, and views the individual as, among other things, a potential execu- tioner.[312] Faber wrote of the 'hatred of our own sins which caused it',[313] and employs a psychological approach which would undoubtedly have affected all but the least impression- able members of his congregation. Here, as elsewhere, Faber puts his listener at the centre of the action, in a way which recalls the composition of place of the Ignatian exercises, particularly in his dwelling on the head[314] and face[315] of Jesus on the Cross. It is significant that Faber had set limits to the type of devotions which he allowed; Morris wrote to Faber asking if he could popularise a devotion to the tongue of Jesus, but Faber thought it unwise, writing, 'It requires a theological mind to keep it delicate and reverent.'[316] In another sermon, he concludes by linking the past, present and future in the person of Christ, and in the Sacrament,[317] and by doing this links the Passion to all other actions in the devotional life of the individual.

During Lent 1854, Faber began the devotion of the Stations of the Cross at Brompton. The sermon preached on this occasion begins by ensuring that his parishioners understand that the devotion had the authority of the Church,[318] and places the devotion in its historical context by writing of pilgrimages in the Middle Ages.[319] Faber was concerned that people should not think that this was just a whim of his own, an action which shows his loyalty and, perhaps, insecurity. He creates a sense of place which is Ignatian, and highlights the importance of Mary by dwelling on her rather than on Jesus, and presenting her as the instigator of the devotion on Good Friday.[320]

On Easter Sunday, 16 April 1854, Faber preached a sermon entitled *The Resurrection – A Mystery of Calmness*.[321] The subtleties of the development of ideas within this sermon, all of which are well established in Faber's thought, and its complex structure, make this possibly his most impressive extant sermon from a structural point of view. We have already stated that Faber's sermons move from that which is known to his congregation, to that which is unfamiliar. Here, this is joined by the regression from the present to the past. Faber begins by using the natural image of sunrise and the supernatural silence of the Resurrection. He then moves from the spiritual body of Jesus to the specific historical presence of Jesus,[322] and notes the 'calmness of ye adorable body lying separate in ye tomb'.[323] We can compare this image with Ignatius' idea that the dead body represents a model of detachment; and Faber's idea, expressed in other sermons, of God's silence, despite sin. The calmness of the Resurrection is, for Faber, contrary to the worldly 'spirit of the age',[324] and emphasises the distance between the two. From Faber's own, essentially personal, meditation on the person of Jesus, he moves to the scriptural past, and Jesus' effect on other people – his mother,[325] the disciples, and Mary Magdalene.[326] In this sermon, that which is unfamiliar to his congregation is also unworldly, and is represented by abstract ideas about God and Jesus; for example, Faber opines that the latter's unworldliness and calmness after the

Resurrection is a mirror of the incomprehensibility of God.[327] Faber unifies visible and invisible by using the theological idea of electionism in reminding his congregation of the slow progression of individuals within the Church militant towards the status of Church triumphant. Thus, the future – heaven – is the ultimate reality because of its unchangeability, an idea which reminds us of Newman's epitaph (taken from St Francis de Sales): 'Out of shadows and images into the truth'. The influence of Paul, which is common to all of Faber's writings, is present here, as he closes the sermon by reminding his congregation that the peace of God 'surpasses all our under-standing'.[328]

Faber's spirituality is fundamentally Marian in character. A number of sermons discuss Mary, and those that do not frequently include discussion of her. The relationship between Jesus and Mary is one of the central motifs in Faber's sermons and lectures; it recurs in several different formats, the first of which characterises them as almost spousal co-redeemers.[329] For Faber, Mary is always a pivotal figure between God the Father, Jesus as Lord and humanity,[330] and he regularly high-lights Mary's unique closeness to the Trinity.[331] This idea is emphasised in Faber's description of the rosary as being central to the devotional life of members of the Roman Church,[332] and the idea that the devil inspires individuals to be disparaging about the rosary is a favourite device in Faber's thought.[333] Secondly, Faber also highlights the parental aspect of their relationship:[334] Jesus' dependence on Mary as mother, and as the facilitator of the incarnation.[335] Thirdly, Faber highlights the relationship between Jesus and Mary and the individual Christian,[336] and does not differentiate between the love and concern of either for the individual.[337]

Faber opined that Marian devotions[338] were one of the most important characteristics of the Roman Church of the mid-nineteenth century. He was not original in this observation; however, in order to illustrate it he wrote seven lectures enti-tled *Mary and the Modern Church*.[339] The tone of the lectures is, at times, somewhat defensive. It would have divided his audi-ence between those who agreed and those who disagreed with his Mariological stance, and here, as elsewhere in Faber's writ-ings, there is no middle way. It is characteristic of Faber's thought to opine that individuals are unsympathetic to Marian devotion only because they do not properly understand it, and he warns that in speaking against it they are going beyond their place.[340] He wrote, 'Men speak beyond their growth just as they venture to pray beyond their growth.'[341] In order to forestall criticism, Faber stated that Marian devotion was a component part of the spirituality of all members of the Church,[342] not just of a few eccentrics like himself. He underlined this by writing that the devotion was a dogmatic instruction from the church hierarchy,[343] and given further official approval by being practised by those who had recently been canonised.[344] These lectures, like all works of Faber's maturity, exhibit an impressive repertoire of saints, both well known and obscure. Lecture Six is wholly concerned with the Marian devotions practised by different categories of saint, such as mystics,[345] martyrs, and Doctors of the Church, and Faber underlines their importance in propagating this devotion.[346] Characteristically, Faber reminds his congregation of the moral strictness required to imitate saints, and the gulf between them and the average Christian.[347]

A notable feature of these lectures is what they disclose of the amount of theology read by Faber in preparation for their delivery. He was influenced by Jesuit theologians and by French spirituality: the works of the Spanish theologian Vazquez on the intercession of Mary,[348] and those of the French spiritual writer de Montfort on Marian devotion,[349] were both read by Faber. He also noted orthodox and heretical doctrines concerning Mary,[350] feasts devoted to Mary,[351] and religious orders which are particularly Marian in character.[352] It seems likely that Faber was familiar with, and had studied, a work such as Butler's *Lives of the Saints*, as he used a similar stylistic idiom in his writing of hagiography. This stylistic similarity is particularly apparent if we compare Butler's account of the Immaculate Conception with that of Faber.[353] Faber wrote a series of three lectures[354] and preached four sermons in commemoration of this doctrine, which was not new at the time of its definition in July 1854; and its importance in Jesuit and Carmelite spirituality underlines the importance of these orders in Faber's spiritual milieu. His acceptance illustrates both his loyalty to the Church and his readiness to accept without hesitation any doctrine that came from Rome. He viewed the definition as one that would unify the Church against the world outside it, and wrote, perhaps somewhat defensively, that the members and hierarchy of the Church were completely unconcerned about any criticism which arose from it.[355]

Other sermon writers compared with F. W. Faber

In order to place Faber within the context of mid-nineteenth-century sermon writing, we shall look briefly at the content and style of a small sample of the sermons of three of his contemporaries: Wiseman, Newman and Oakeley.

The sermons of Faber and Wiseman are concerned with similar subjects: doctrine, theology, issues of morality, such as death and judgement, aspects of the spiritual life and sacramentality, whilst several are concerned with specific services, such as the forty hours' devotion. Wiseman's[356] sermons contain a more rigid sense of structural development, and are more polished, stylistically academic, and reserved than those of Faber. There is less poetry or spontaneity in Wiseman's style, and, whereas his sermons can be admonitory, devotional, uplifting, and possess a profound sense of innate spirituality, they are not as passionate and excessively emotional as a number of those of Faber. Unlike Faber, Wiseman's emotions seem always to be controlled by his mind and regimented by Church doctrine, and he remains conscious of his position as an ecclesiastic. This is particularly noticeable in sermons concerned with doctrine, which, unlike Faber's wordy and ebullient style, are frequently statements of fact, void of embellishment or spare emotional weight. It seems possible that Faber was aware of this in another context, as his letters to Wiseman are reserved, polite rather than effusive, and the reader is unsure of the precise depth of their friendship. However, as Faber's nature inclined towards excessive ebullience, this does not necessarily imply criticism.

Murray, writing of Newman's sermons, stated that no 'other collection of liturgical homilies ... composed in the last century and a half ... could compare with them in quality and quantity'.[357] Newman's Anglican and Roman sermons are concerned with the same spiritual preoccupations as those of Wiseman and Faber, such as doctrine and instruction in the spiritual life.[358] Newman's Anglican sermons are interesting, scholarly, well written, emotional but restrained, and similar in style to the Anglican sermons of Faber, whom he may have influenced. Murray writes that not only are Newman's Anglican sermons 'dogmatic ... using the traditional patristic theology of the Incarnation, Redemption and the Trinity',[359] they are also 'highly liturgical, arising ... out of the liturgical celebration and keeping in mind the assembled congregation'.[360] He describes an essential difference between the Anglican and Roman Catholic sermons of Newman, which he ascribes to Newman's desire 'to fall into line with Catholic practice, even where no principle of faith or discipline was involved'.[361] We can concur with this statement, noting that it is particularly visible in the earliest Roman Catholic sermons, written during 1847.[362] The best of these demonstrate Newman's ability to create atmosphere, they are erudite and move logically and smoothly from one point to another.[363] However, other sermons in this group have the self-conscious, stilted character of an individual who is anxious not only to demonstrate his own Catholic orthodoxy, but is aware that his words are being judged,[364] leading to a certain flatness in his use of language.

Oakeley's Anglican sermons, like those of Faber and Newman, are written in a style which is highly academic in its structure, use of argument and display of knowledge, a trait which makes them interesting to read.[365] In contrast, Oakeley's Roman Catholic sermons are self-consciously Catholic; the majority of those studied contain references to church authority and doctrine, and their flow is occasionally interrupted by references to heresy which are surplus to his argument. In these sermons, Oakeley's writing style is formal and less effusive than Faber's,[366] and, although it is perhaps more learned, it contains little variation of tone and is therefore less interesting. There is not the same personal involvement in Oakeley as in Faber, and the sermons read as though he was dispassionate and detached from his congregation.[367] Oakeley's *Popular Lectures* are more paternalistic than Faber's sermons.[368] They demonstrate three similarities between Oakeley and Faber, namely concern for the poor, disgust of the worldliness of popular society,[369] and a desire to break down barriers between classes.[370] Oakeley's *Parochial Sermons* share the same concerns as those we have been discussing, such as the Christian life and doctrine, Mary, Jesus and the Trinity. Like those of Faber, Wiseman and Newman, they were extemporised rather than read, although, unlike Faber's sermons, they were originally written out. Oakeley's sentences are short and his style is reserved and unemotional, more like Wiseman's sermons, or Newman's university sermons minus their oratorical power, than the excessive flamboyance of Faber.[371] Each sermon contains only two or three ideas, which are not over-developed. He does not share Faber's sense of visual imagery or poetic imagination, and references to items taken from nature, such as flowers or scenery, are inert examples, devoid of individuality.[372]

From this brief survey of the sermons of Wiseman, Newman and Oakeley, it is clear that, both as an Anglican and as a Roman Catholic, Faber was typical for the style of, and concerns expressed within, his sermons, but atypical in his ebullient emotionalism and involvement with his subject matter.

Notes

1 F. W. Faber to J. B. Morris, LO, Vol. 17, No. 34, 31 August 1837.
2 Untitled notebook, LO.
3 F. W. Faber to J. B. Morris, LO, Vol. 17, No. 36, 24 July 1838.
4 F. W. Faber, Sermon, St John XX.21.22.23, Elton, Third Sunday in Advent (17 December) 1843. Unpublished MS in hand of F. W. Faber, LO, light brown box, No. 77.
5 F. W. Faber to J. B. Morris, LO, Vol. 17, No. 34, 31 August 1837.
6 *The Book of Common Prayer* (London, Eyre and Spottiswoode Ltd, n.d.) p. 377.
7 F. W. Faber, Sermon, Exodus XXIII.20.21, 22 July 1838. Unpublished MS in hand of F. W. Faber, LO, Packet No. 4, bundle 1, no number.
8 Ibid.
9 F. W. Faber, Sermon, 1 Sam. III.13, 4 August 1838. Unpublished MS in hand of F. W. Faber, LO, Packet No. 4, bundle 1, no number.
10 F. W. Faber, Sermon, Exodus XXIII.20.21, 22 July 1838. Unpublished MS in hand of F. W. Faber, LO, Packet No. 4,

bundle 1, no number. He also discusses the reading of scripture, and refers briefly to the infallibility of scripture in Sermon, Revelation XXII.18.19. Unpublished MS in hand of F. W. Faber, LO, Packet No. 4, bundle 1, no number.

11 F. W. Faber, Sermon, Revelation XXII.18.19. Unpublished MS in hand of F. W. Faber, LO, Packet No. 4, bundle 1, no number.

12 Article VI, *Of the Sufficiency of the Holy Scripture for Salvation.*

13 F. W. Faber, Sermon, Exodus XXIII.20.21, 22 July 1838. Unpublished MS in hand of F. W. Faber, LO, Packet No. 4, bundle 1, no number.

14 Ibid.

15 Ibid.

16 Ibid.

17 *The Collected Poems of William Wordsworth: Poems Relating to the Period of Childhood* No. 1, (Hertfordshire, Wordsworth Editions, 1994) p. 79.

18 F. W. Faber, Sermon, Exodus XXIII.20.21, 22 July 1838. Unpublished MS in hand of F. W. Faber, LO, Packet No. 4, bundle 1, no number.

19 Ibid.

20 F. W. Faber, Sermon, Ephesians IV.4.5.6. August 1839. Unpublished MS in hand of F. W. Faber, LO, Packet No. 4, bundle 1, no number.

21 F. W. Faber, Untitled Sermon, n.d. Unpublished MS in hand of F. W. Faber, LO, Packet No. 4, bundle 1, no number.

22 Ibid.

23 Ibid.

24 Article ix, *Of Original or Birth-sin*, in *The Book of Common Prayer* (London, Eyre and Spottiswoode Ltd, n.d.) p. 377.

25 F. W. Faber, Sermon, 1 Cor. IX.25. Ambleside, 10 September 1837. Unpublished MS in hand of F. W. Faber, LO, Packet No. 4, bundle 1, no number.

26 F. W. Faber, Untitled Sermon, n.d. Unpublished MS in hand of F. W. Faber, LO, Packet No. 4, bundle 1, no number.

27 Ibid.

28 Ibid.

29 Ibid.

30 Ibid.

31 Ibid.

32 F. W. Faber, Sermon, 1 Sam. 3:13. 4 August 1838. Unpublished MS in hand of F. W. Faber, LO, Packet No. 4, bundle 1, no number.

33 Ibid.

34 Ibid.

35 Ibid.

36 Ibid.

37 Ibid.

38 Ibid.

39 F. W. Faber, Sermon, Luke II.14, n.d. Unpublished MS in hand of F. W. Faber, LO, light brown box, No. 128.

40 F. W. Faber, Sermon, Ezekiel XLIII.12.13. Elton, 10 December 1843. Unpublished MS in hand of F. W. Faber, LO, light brown box, No. 76.

41 F. W. Faber, Sermon, John XX.17. St. Aldate's, Oxford, Easter Sunday 1839. Unpublished MS in hand of F. W. Faber, LO, Packet No. 4, bundle 1, no number.

42 Ibid.

43 F. W. Faber, Sermon, Gen. XXIV.6.3. Elton, 26 May 1844, evening. Unpublished MS in hand of F. W. Faber, LO, light brown box, No. 5.

44 F. W. Faber, Sermon, Romans VIII.4. Elton, 27 October 1844. Unpublished MS in hand of F. W. Faber, LO, light brown box, No. 4.

45 Ibid.

46 F. W. Faber, Sermon, John XX.17. St. Aldate's, Oxford, Easter Sunday 1839. Unpublished MS in hand of F. W. Faber, LO, Packet No. 4, bundle 1, no number.

47 Ibid.

48 Ibid.

49 Ibid.

50 F. W. Faber, Sermon, Romans XIV.17. (possibly unfinished), n.d. Unpublished MS in hand of F. W. Faber, LO, Packet No. 4, bundle 1, no number.

51 F. W. Faber, Sermon, John 1 IV.17. St Mary's, Oxford, 18 Sunday after Trinity (15 October) 1843. Unpublished MS in hand of F. W. Faber, LO, light brown box, No. 103.

52 Ibid.

53 F. W. Faber, Sermon, 1 Sam. 3:13. 4 August 1838, evening. Unpublished MS in hand of F. W. Faber, LO, Packet No. 4, bundle 1, no number.

54 F. W. Faber to J. B. Morris, LO, Vol. 17, No. 37, 19 October 1838.

55 F. W. Faber, Sermon, 1 Sam. 3:13. 4 August 1838, evening. Unpublished MS in hand of F. W. Faber, LO, Packet No. 4, bundle 1, no number.

56 F. W. Faber, Sermon, 1 Cor. IX.25. Ambleside, 10 September 1837. Unpublished MS in hand of F. W. Faber, LO, Packet No. 4, bundle 1, no number.

57 Ibid.

58 Ibid.

59 F. W. Faber, Sermon, John XX.17. St. Aldate's, Oxford, Easter Sunday 1839. Unpublished MS in hand of F. W. Faber, LO, Packet No. 4, bundle 1, no number.

60 Ibid.

61 Ibid.

62 F. W. Faber, Sermon, Revelation XXII.18.19. Unpublished MS

in hand of F. W. Faber, LO, Packet No. 4, bundle 1, no number.

63 Ibid.

64 F. W. Faber, Sermon, Ephesians IV.4.5.6. Sandford, August 1839. Unpublished MS in hand of F. W. Faber, LO, Packet No. 4, bundle 1, no number.

65 Ibid.

66 F. W. Faber, Sermon, Revelation XXII.18.19. Unpublished MS in hand of F. W. Faber, LO, Packet No. 4, bundle 1, no number.

67 F. W. Faber, Sermon, 1 Cor. IX.25. Ambleside, 10 September 1837. Unpublished MS in hand of F. W. Faber, LO, Packet No. 4, bundle 1, no number.

68 F. W. Faber, Sermon, Ephesians IV.4.5.6. St Aldate's, Oxford, 6 October 1839. Unpublished MS in hand of F. W. Faber, LO, Packet No. 4, bundle 1, no number.

69 Article XXVIII, *Of the Lord's Supper*, in *The Book of Common Prayer* (London, Eyre and Spottiswoode Ltd, n.d.) p. 380.

70 Article XXII, *Of Purgatory*, ibid. p. 379.

71 F. W. Faber, Sermon, untitled, n.d. Unpublished MS in hand of F. W. Faber, LO, Packet No. 4, bundle 1, no number.

72 F. W. Faber, Sermon, Ephesians IV.4.5.6. 6 October 1839. Unpublished MS in hand of F. W. Faber, LO, Packet No. 4, bundle 1, no number.

73 Communion Service, *The Book of Common Prayer* (London, Eyre and Spottiswoode Ltd, n.d.) pp. 171–4.

74 F. W. Faber, Sermon, Ephesians IV.4.5.6. 6 October 1839. Unpublished MS in hand of F. W. Faber, LO, Packet No. 4, bundle 1, no number.

75 Communion Service, *The Book of Common Prayer* (London, Eyre and Spottiswoode Ltd, n.d.) p. 174.

76 F. W. Faber, Sermon, Ephesians IV.4.5.6. 6 October 1839. Unpublished MS in hand of F. W. Faber, LO, Packet No. 4, bundle 1, no number.

77 F. W. Faber, Sermon, 1 Cor. IX.25. Ambleside, 10 September 1837. Unpublished MS in hand of F. W. Faber, LO, Packet No. 4, bundle 1, no number.

78 F. W. Faber, Sermon, 1 Sam. 3:13. Ambleside, 4 August 1838. Unpublished MS in hand of F. W. Faber, LO, Packet No. 4, bundle 1, no number.

79 F. W. Faber, Sermon, untitled, n.d. Unpublished MS in hand of F. W. Faber, LO, Packet No. 4, bundle 1, no number.

80 Ibid.

81 F. W. Faber, Sermon, 1 Sam. 3:13, Ambleside, 4 August 1838. Unpublished MS in hand of F. W. Faber, LO, Packet No. 4, bundle 1, no number.

82 F. W. Faber, Sermon, Exodus XXIII.20.21. Ambleside, 22 July 1838. Unpublished MS in hand of F. W. Faber, LO, Packet No. 4, bundle 1, no number.

83 F. W. Faber, Sermon, Ps. 57:12, Matt. XXVII.45. Elton, Good Friday 1844. Unpublished MS in hand of F. W. Faber, LO, light brown box, no number.

84 F. W. Faber, Sermon, untitled, n.d. Unpublished MS in hand of F. W. Faber, LO, Packet No. 4, bundle 1, no number.

85 M. J. Wilkinson, *An Exploration of the Roman Catholic Sermons, Lectures and Novice Conferences of F. W. Faber: 1846–1863*. Paper for the Catholic Record Society Conference (3 August 2004).

86 F. W. Faber, Sermon, Feast of St Francis Xavier, Farm Street (3 December) 1857. Unpublished MS in hand of F. W. Faber, LO, Packet 1, No. 100.

87 F. W. Faber, Sermon, *The Spirit of devotion to ye sacred infancy*, Spanish Place, 1852. Unpublished MS in hand of F. W. Faber, LO, notes from books folder, No. 65.

88 F. W. Faber, *Panegyric of St Charles on his Feast*, Bayswater, 1861. Unpublished MS in hand of F. W. Faber, LO, Packet 1, No. 96.

89 F. W. Faber, Sermon, *Anniversary of St Thomas Church, Fulham*, 1848. Unpublished MS in hand of F. W. Faber, LO, notes from books folder, No. 134.

90 F. W. Faber, Sermon, *The Epiphany*, 1861. Unpublished MS in hand of F. W. Faber, LO, Packet 1, No. 31.

91 This sermon contains what are probably autobiographical references based on Faber's experience of chronic illness and headaches. See F. W. Faber, Sermon, *Our Blessed Lord Bowing His Head on the Cross*, Passion Sunday (22 March) 1863. Unpublished MS in hand of F. W. Faber, LO, Packet 1, No. 74.

92 F. W. Faber to K. Digby Best, LO, Vol. 22, No. 12, 27 November 1858.

93 Ibid.

94 F. W. Faber, Sermon, *The Three Epochs of the Holy Trinity*, Brompton, Trinity Sunday (30 May) 1858. Unpublished MS in hand of F. W. Faber, LO, Packet 1, No. 1.

95 F. W. Faber to J. B. Morris, LO, Vol. 17, No. 148, 17 July 1858.

96 F. W. Faber to J. H. Newman, LO, Vol. 2, No. 225, 7 February 1850.

97 F. W. Faber to J. H. Newman, LO, Vol. 2, No. 158, 3 December 1849.

98 Compare F. W. Faber, *The Life of Prayer*. Unpublished MS in hand of F. W. Faber, LO, notes from books folder, No. 148, with F. W. Faber (n.d.), *Growth in Holiness*, 3rd edn, London, Burns & Oates, pp. 217–9.

99 To date, I have been unable to discover whether Faber had read William Hazlitt's book *The Spirit of the Age* (1825) or Richard Hengist Horne's *A New Spirit of the Age* (1844).

100 F. W. Faber, Lectures, *Mary and the Modern Church: 5: The Church at war with sin*, 1851. Unpublished MS in hand of F. W. Faber, LO, Packet 3, No. 12, 2:1.

101 F. W. Faber, Sermon, *Opening of Brompton*, 22 March 1854.

Unpublished MS in hand of F. W. Faber, LO, Packet 3, No. 109, 2:IV.

102 F. W. Faber, Sermon (not preached), *St John ye Baptist's Day* (24 June) 1849. Unpublished MS in hand of F. W. Faber, LO, Packet 1, No. 93.

103 F. W. Faber, Sermon, *Thankfulness that we are Catholics*, London, 1852. Unpublished MS in hand of F. W. Faber, LO, Packet 3, No. 10.

104 F. W. Faber, Sermon, *Ireland (I): Glance at the Irish people.* Unpublished MS in hand of F. W. Faber, LO, maroon folder, No. 42M.

105 Ibid.

106 F. W. Faber to J. H. Newman, LO, Vol. 2, No. 238, n.d. March 1850.

107 F. W. Faber, *Lectures on Protestantism*: 1. *Its rise and present condition*, 2. *Protestantism considered as a theological system*, 3. *The effects of Protestantism on ye individual character*, 4. *Its effects upon ye social welfare of men*, 5. *The connection of Protestantism and infidelity*, 6. *The character of Protestant devotion*, 7. *Protestant notions of our Lord.* Unpublished MS in hand of F. W. Faber, LO, Packet 3, No. 39.

108 Ibid. Lecture 3:3.3.

109 Ibid. Lecture 2:4.4.

110 Ibid. Lecture 3:3.2.

111 Ibid. Lecture 3:2.1.1.

112 Ibid. Lecture 3:3.3.

113 Ibid. Lecture 6:3.7.

114 Ibid. Lecture 6:3.3.

115 Ibid. Lecture 6:3.4.

116 F. W. Faber to J. H. Newman, LO, Vol. 2, No. 158, 3 December 1849.

117 Ibid.

118 F. W. Faber, *Lecture on Conversion*, St Wilfrid's, Conversion of St Paul (28 January) 1848. Unpublished MS in hand of F. W. Faber, LO, Packet 3, No. 40.

119 Ibid.

120 Ibid.

121 F. W. Faber, Sermon, *Thankfulness that we are Catholics*, London, 1852. Unpublished MS in hand of F. W. Faber, LO, Packet 3, No. 10, 2:4.

122 Faber had tried to go to Ireland during April 1852, but had been thwarted by illness. See F. W. Faber to Mrs J. (E.) Bowden, LO, Vol. 21, No. 51, Good Friday (9 April) 1852.

123 F. W. Faber, Sermon, *Ireland (2): Pagan Ireland.* Unpublished MS in hand of F. W. Faber, LO, maroon folder, No. 42H.

124 Ibid. This may indicate that he had read G. S. Faber's book, *A dissertation on the Mysteries of the Cabiri, or the Great Gods of Phoenicia, Samothrace, Egypt, Troas, Greece, Italy and Creete* [*sic*], 2 vols. (1803).

125 F. W. Faber, Sermon, *Christian Brothers*, Limerick. Unpublished MS in hand of F. W. Faber, LO, maroon folder, No. 42J.

126 F. W. Faber, Sermon, *England, triumphant Empire carries not ye Gospel*, 1852. Unpublished MS in hand of F. W. Faber, LO, maroon folder, No. 42F.

127 F. W. Faber, Sermon, *Ireland (I): Glance at the Irish people*. Unpublished MS in hand of F. W. Faber, LO, maroon folder, No. 42M.

128 F. W. Faber, Sermon, *England, triumphant Empire carries not ye Gospel*, 1852. Unpublished MS in hand of F. W. Faber, LO, maroon folder, No. 42F.

129 F. W. Faber, Sermon, *The View ye Saints Take of ye World as a Howling wilderness compared with the view ordinary good men take of it*, New Year's Eve 1849–50. Unpublished MS in hand of F. W. Faber, LO, Packet 1, No. 30, Section 3.1–2.

130 F. W. Faber, Sermon, *Opening of ye Jesuits Church*, 1849. Unpublished MS in hand of F. W. Faber, LO, Packet 3, No. 103, 1:7.

131 F. W. Faber, Lectures, *Mary and the Modern Church: 4: The Church at war with heresy*, 1851. Unpublished MS in hand of F. W. Faber, LO, Packet 3, No. 12, Section 6.

132 Ibid.

133 Ibid.

134 Ibid. Section 5.

135 F. W. Faber, Sermon, *Thankfulness that we are Catholics*, London, 1852. Unpublished MS in hand of F. W. Faber, LO, Packet 3, No. 10, 3:4.

136 F. W. Faber, Sermon (not preached), *St John ye Baptist's Day* (24 June) 1849. Unpublished MS in hand of F. W. Faber, LO, Packet 1, No. 93.

137 F. W. Faber, Sermon, *Closing of King William Street*, 11 September 1853. Unpublished MS in hand of F. W. Faber, LO, Packet 3, No. 108.

138 Ibid.

139 F. W. Faber, Sermon, *Opening of Brompton*, 22 March 1854. Unpublished MS in hand of F. W. Faber, LO, Packet 3, No. 109, 3:v.

140 F. W. Faber, Sermon, *The strangeness of God's love for us*, n.d. Unpublished MS in hand of F. W. Faber, LO, Packet 1, No. 16. Also F. W. Faber, Sermon, *God's love of single souls*, n.d. Unpublished MS in hand of F. W. Faber, LO, Packet 1, No. 15, and F. W. Faber, *The life of Jesus in ye bosom of ye Eternal Father*, Advent Meditations, St Wilfrid's, 1848. Unpublished MS in hand of F. W. Faber, LO, Packet 1, No. 27.

141 F. W. Faber, Sermon, *Opening of Brompton*, 22 March 1854. Unpublished MS in hand of F. W. Faber, LO, Packet 3, No. 109, 3:v.

142 F. W. Faber, Sermon, *Thankfulness that we are Catholics*, London,

1852. Unpublished MS in hand of F. W. Faber, LO, Packet 3, No. 10, 3:6.

143 F. W. Faber, Epiphany Lectures 1851:1: *The history of ye Church*. Unpublished MS in hand of F. W. Faber, LO, Packet 3, No. 1, 3:7.

144 F. W. Faber, Sermon, *Thankfulness that we are Catholics*, London, 1852. Unpublished MS in hand of F. W. Faber, LO, Packet 3, No. 10, 2:1.

145 F. W. Faber, Sermon, *Closing of King William Street*, 11 September 1853. Unpublished MS in hand of F. W. Faber, LO, Packet 3, No. 108, 2:2.

146 Ibid. 2:4.

147 F. W. Faber, Sermon, *God's love of single souls*, n.d. Unpublished MS in hand of F. W. Faber, LO, Packet 1, No. 15.

148 F. W. Faber, Sermon, *The strangeness of God's love for us*, n.d. Unpublished MS in hand of F. W. Faber, LO, Packet 1, No. 16.

149 F. W. Faber, Sermon, *Opening of Brompton*, 22 March 1854. Unpublished MS in hand of F. W. Faber, LO, Packet 3, No. 109.

150 F. W. Faber, *Lectures on Protestantism*, 1849. Unpublished MS in hand of F. W. Faber, LO, Packet 3, No. 39, Lecture 1: final paragraph.

151 F. W. Faber, Sermon, *Opening of Brompton*, 22 March 1854. Unpublished MS in hand of F. W. Faber, LO, Packet 3, No. 109, 1:v, vi.

152 F. W. Faber, Sermon, *Devotions to the Omnipotence of God*, 1860. Unpublished MS in hand of F. W. Faber, LO, Packet 1, No. 3, 1:1. See also F. W. Faber, Sermon, *The three epochs of the Holy Trinity*, Trinity Sunday (30 May) 1858. Unpublished MS in hand of F. W. Faber, LO, Packet 1, No. 1, 2:3.

153 This idea is also used in F. W. Faber, Sermon, *The Blood of Jesus Christ, His Son, cleanseth us from all sin*. London, May 1852. Unpublished MS in hand of F. W. Faber, LO, notes from books folder, No. 5.

154 F. W. Faber, Sermon, *The Sacred Heart*, 1850. Unpublished MS in hand of F. W. Faber, LO, Packet 1, No. 50.

155 F. W. Faber, Novice Conference, *What sort of men were ye saints?*, Eve of All Saints 1861. Unpublished MS in hand of F. W. Faber, LO, Packet 2, No. 40.

156 F. W. Faber, Sermon, *Closing of King William Street*, 11 September 1853. Unpublished MS in hand of F. W. Faber, LO, Packet 3, No. 108.

157 Ibid.

158 F. W. Faber, Sermon, *Devotion to the Omnipotence of God*, 1860. Unpublished MS in hand of F. W. Faber, LO, Packet 1, No. 3, 3:1. See also F. W. Faber, Sermon, *A taste for God*, 1859. Unpublished MS in hand of F. W. Faber, LO, Packet 1, No. 21.

159 F. W. Faber, Epiphany Lectures 1851:1: *The history of ye Church*, 2: *The vicissitudes of ye Church*, 3: *The empire of ye Church*, 4: *The Church*

at war with ye world, 5: *The conversion of England*, 6: *The last age and ye reign of Anti-Christ* [*sic*]. Unpublished MS in hand of F. W. Faber, LO, Packet 3, Nos. 1–6.

160 F. W. Faber to J. H. Newman, LO, Vol. 3, No. 30, 13 January 1851.

161 F. W. Faber, Epiphany Lectures 1851:1: *The history of ye Church.* Unpublished MS in hand of F. W. Faber, LO, Packet 3, No. 1, 1:5.

162 Ibid. 3:4.

163 F. W. Faber, Sermon, *Corpus Christi: ye triumph of ye Church* (12 June) London, 1851. Unpublished MS in hand of F. W. Faber, LO, notes from books folder, No. 31.

164 F. W. Faber, Sermon, *The Assumption* (15 August) London, 1851. Unpublished MS in hand of F. W. Faber, LO, Packet 1, No. 87.

165 Ibid.

166 F. W. Faber, *On journalism*, Orat[orium] Parv[um]. May 1852. Unpublished MS in hand of F. W. Faber, LO, Packet 3, No. 41.

167 Ibid.

168 Ibid. 1:2.

169 Ibid. 1:3.

170 Ibid. 3.

171 Ibid. 4:4.

172 Ibid. 3:7.

173 F. W. Faber, Sermon, *The Secular Clergy*, 1850. Unpublished MS in hand of F. W. Faber, LO, Packet 3, No. 107, 3:5.

174 F. W. Faber, Sermon, *Opening of ye Jesuits Church*, 1849. Unpublished MS in hand of F. W. Faber, LO, Packet 3, No. 103, 1:2.

175 F. W. Faber, Sermon, *The Secular Clergy*, 1850. Unpublished MS in hand of F. W. Faber, LO, Packet 3, No. 107, 3:4–5.

176 F. W. Faber to J. B. Morris, LO, Vol. 17, No. 168, n.d.

177 F. W. Faber, Sermon, *Feast of St Francis Xavier*, Farm Street, 1857. Unpublished MS in hand of F. W. Faber, LO, Packet 1, No. 100.

178 F. W. Faber, Epiphany Lectures 1851:1: *The history of ye Church.* Unpublished MS in hand of F. W. Faber, LO, Packet 3, No. 1, 2:8.

179 F. W. Faber, *Lecture on Conversion*, St Wilfrid's, Conversion of St Paul (28 January) 1848. Unpublished MS in hand of F. W. Faber, LO, Packet 3, No. 40, 3.5.

180 F. W. Faber, Novice Conference, *Beatific Vision consists chiefly in ye knowledge of God,* n.d. Unpublished MS in hand of F. W. Faber, LO, Packet 2, No. 45.

181 F. W. Faber, Epiphany Lectures 1851:1: *The history of ye Church.* Unpublished MS in hand of F. W. Faber, LO, Packet 3, No. 1, 2:9.

182 F. W. Faber, Sermon, *Thankfulness that we are Catholics*, London, 1852. Unpublished MS in hand of F. W. Faber, LO, Packet 3, No. 10, 4:5.

183 F. W. Faber, Sermon, *Opening of ye Jesuit's Church*, 1849. Unpublished MS in hand of F. W. Faber, LO, Packet 3, No. 103, 1, 3.

184 F. W. Faber, *On Journalism*, Orat[orium] Parv[um] May 1852. Unpublished MS in hand of F. W. Faber, LO, Packet 3, No. 41, 3.

185 F. W. Faber, Sermon (not preached), *St John ye Baptist's Day* (24 June) 1849. Unpublished MS in hand of F. W. Faber, LO, Packet 1, No. 93, Section 1.

186 Ibid. Section 2:1–5.

187 F. W. Faber, Sermon, *Feast of St Francis Xavier*, Farm Street, 1857. Unpublished MS in hand of F. W. Faber, LO, Packet 1, No. 100.

188 F. W. Faber, Sermon (not preached), *St John ye Baptist's Day* (24 June) 1849. Unpublished MS in hand of F. W. Faber, LO, Packet 1, No. 93.

189 F. W. Faber, Sermon, St Philip's Day (26 May) 1861. Unpublished MS in hand of F. W. Faber, LO, Packet 1, No. 99, 3:1.

190 Ibid.

191 F. W. Faber, Lectures, *Mary and the Modern Church: 5: The Church at war with sin*, 1851. Unpublished MS in hand of F. W. Faber, LO, Packet 3, No. 12, 2:2.

192 Ibid. 5:4.

193 F. W. Faber, Lectures, *Mary and the Modern Church: 4: The Church at war with heresy*, 1851. Unpublished MS in hand of F. W. Faber, LO, Packet 3, No. 12, 7.

194 F. W. Faber, Sermon, *On ye influence of Catholic priests over their congregations*, n.d. Unpublished MS in hand of F. W. Faber, LO, Packet 3, No. 26.

195 F. W. Faber, Sermon, *Lay Piety*, n.d. Unpublished MS in hand of F. W. Faber, LO, Packet 3, No. 90.

196 F. W. Faber, Sermon, *On ye influence of Catholic priests over their congregations*, n.d. Unpublished MS in hand of F. W. Faber, LO, Packet 3, No. 26.

197 Ibid.

198 F. W. Faber, Paper, Ordinandi, Sydenham: *What we commit ourselves to in ye priesthood*, Sydenham, 1852. Unpublished MS in hand of F. W. Faber, LO, Packet 2, No. 23.

199 F. W. Faber, Sermon, *The Secular Clergy*, 1850. St Edmund's College, n.d. Unpublished MS in hand of F. W. Faber, LO, Packet 3, No. 107.

200 F. W. Faber, *Selfishness a temptation of ye Congregation*, Cong. Culp., 8 January 1851. Unpublished MS in hand of F. W. Faber, LO, Packet 2, No. 10. Also in *Notes on Community Life in the Oratory*, London, Richardson and Son, 1867, unpublished.

201 F. W. Faber, Paper, Ordinandi, Sydenham: *What is to sanctify priests in England*. Unpublished MS in hand of F. W. Faber, LO, Packet 2, No. 24.

202 Ibid.

203 Ibid.
204 F. W. Faber to J. H. Newman, LO, Vol. 3, No. 88, c.April 1852.
205 F. W. Faber, *Novena of St Philip*, London, 1852. Unpublished MS in hand of F. W. Faber, LO, in Vol. *Father Faber MSS of sermons and on spiritual subjects.*
206 F. W. Faber, Sermon, *First Vespers of St Philip*, Brompton, 1854. Unpublished MS in hand of F. W. Faber, LO, Packet 2, No. 20. See also F. W. Faber, Sermon, St Philip's Day (26 May) 1861. Unpublished MS in hand of F. W. Faber, LO, Packet 1, No. 99, in which the same idea is expressed in section 2:1.
207 F. W. Faber, Sermon, *First Vespers of St Philip*, (25 May) Brompton, 1854. Unpublished MS in hand of F. W. Faber, LO, Packet 2, No. 20.
208 F. W. Faber, Sermon, *St Philip's Day*, (26 May) Brompton, 1851. Unpublished MS in hand of F. W. Faber, LO, Packet 1, No. 99.
209 F. W. Faber, Sermon, *How is it that life is short?* Brompton, 1854. Unpublished MS in hand of F. W. Faber, LO, Packet 3, No. 57, 3.
210 F. W. Faber, Novice Conference, *Taking an interest in divine things*, January 1862. Unpublished MS in hand of F. W. Faber, LO, Packet 2, No. 33.
211 F. W. Faber, Novice Conference, *What sort of men were ye saints?* Eve of All Saints 1861. Unpublished MS in hand of F. W. Faber, LO, Packet 2, No. 40.
212 F. W. Faber, Sermon, *On frittering*, n.d. Unpublished MS in hand of F. W. Faber, LO, Packet 3, No. 63.
213 F. W. Faber, Sermon, *The horrible condition of a man who leads no inward life – between whom and his God there is no privacy*, n.d. Unpublished MS in hand of F. W. Faber, LO, Packet 3, No. 91. See also F. W. Faber, Sermon, *The Life of Prayer*, n.d. Unpublished MS in hand of F. W. Faber, LO, notes from books folder, No. 148.
214 F. W. Faber, Paper, Ordinandi, Sydenham: *What we commit ourselves to in ye priesthood*, (Sydenham, 1852). Unpublished MS in hand of F. W. Faber, LO, Packet 2, No. 23.
215 F. W. Faber, Paper, Ordinandi, Sydenham: *What is to sanctify priests in England*. Unpublished MS in hand of F. W. Faber, LO, Packet 2, No. 24.
216 F. W. Faber, Sermon, Lent *Quarant' ore*, 1855. Unpublished MS in hand of F. W. Faber, LO, Packet 1, No. 49.
217 F. W. Faber, Novice Conference, 29 March 1862. Unpublished MS in hand of F. W. Faber, LO, Packet 2, No. 53.
218 F. W. Faber, Paper, Ordinandi, Sydenham: *Office*. Unpublished MS in hand of F. W. Faber, LO, Packet 2, No. 25.
219 Ibid.
220 Ibid.
221 Ibid.
222 F. W. Faber, Paper, Ordinandi, Sydenham: *Mass*. Unpublished MS in hand of F. W. Faber, LO, Packet 2, No. 26.

223 F. W. Faber, Sermon, *Childishness*, n.d. Unpublished MS in hand of F. W. Faber, LO, Packet 3, No. 81.3.

224 F. W. Faber, Sermon, *How is it that life is short?* Brompton, 1854. Unpublished MS in hand of F. W. Faber, LO, Packet 3, No. 57, 4.3.

225 F. W. Faber, Sermon, *Thankfulness that we are Catholics*, London, 1852. Unpublished MS in hand of F. W. Faber, LO, Packet 3, No. 10, 4:4.

226 F. W. Faber, Sermon, *Personal Holiness*, n.d. Unpublished MS in hand of F. W. Faber, LO, Packet 3, No. 59, Section 1.

227 F. W. Faber, Sermon, *On frittering*, n.d. Unpublished MS in hand of F. W. Faber, LO, Packet 3, No. 65.

228 F. W. Faber, Sermon, *Easter Sunday*, 1855. Unpublished MS in hand of F. W. Faber, LO, Packet 1, No. 42.

229 F. W. Faber, Sermon, *The View ye Saints Take of ye World as a Howling wilderness compared with the view ordinary good men take of it.* New Year's Eve 1849. Unpublished MS in hand of F. W. Faber, LO, Packet 1, No. 30.

230 F. W. Faber, Sermon, *The horrible condition of a man who leads no inward life – between whom and his God there is no privacy*, n.d. Unpublished MS in hand of F. W. Faber, LO, Packet 3, No. 91.

231 F. W. Faber, Sermon, *The Strangeness of God's love of us*, n.d. Unpublished MS in hand of F. W. Faber, LO, Packet 1, No. 16.

232 Ibid.

233 F. W. Faber, Sermon, *On frittering*, n.d. Unpublished MS in hand of F. W. Faber, LO, Packet 3, No. 65.

234 F. W. Faber, Sermon, *God so little loved*, n.d. Unpublished MS in hand of F. W. Faber, LO, Packet 1, No. 18.

235 F. W. Faber, Sermon, *Meditations, Lent Retreat, 1850*, 4: *The awfulness of Sin*. Unpublished MS in hand of F. W. Faber, LO, Packet 3, No. 83.

236 F. W. Faber, Novice Conference, March 1862. Unpublished MS in hand of F. W. Faber, LO, Packet 2, No. 53.

237 F. W. Faber, Sermon, *Bad deaths of those who have once been good*, Brompton, 1856. Unpublished MS in hand of F. W. Faber, LO, Packet 3, No. 117.

238 Ibid. 2:2.

239 Ibid. 2:6.

240 Ibid. 1:4.

241 F. W. Faber, Sermon, *On frittering*, n.d. Unpublished MS in hand of F. W. Faber, LO, Packet 3, No. 65. Also F. W. Faber, Sermon, *Personal Holiness*, n.d. Unpublished MS in hand of F. W. Faber, LO, Packet 3, No. 59.

242 F. W. Faber, Sermon, *Meditations, Lent Retreat 1850: The loss of God*. Unpublished MS in hand of F. W. Faber, LO, Packet 3, No. 122.

243 F. W. Faber, Sermon, *Self-denial ye essence of religion*, n.d. Unpublished MS in hand of F. W. Faber, LO, Packet 3, No. 58.

244 F. W. Faber, Sermon, *God so little loved*, n.d. Unpublished MS in hand of F. W. Faber, LO, Packet 1, No. 18.

245 F. W. Faber, Sermon, *For ye poor schools*, Sacred Heart, 1855. Unpublished MS in hand of F. W. Faber, LO, Packet 3, No. 110.

246 F. W. Faber, Sermon, *The View ye Saints Take of ye World as a Howling wilderness compared with the view ordinary good men take of it.* New Year's Eve, 1849. Unpublished MS in hand of F. W. Faber, LO, Packet 1, No. 30, Section 2:1–4.

247 F. W. Faber, Sermon, *The one drawback of life*, Brompton, June 1861. Unpublished MS in hand of F. W. Faber, LO, Packet 3, No. 56.

248 Ibid.

249 F. W. Faber, Sermon, *Childishness*, n.d. Unpublished MS in hand of F. W. Faber, LO, Packet 3, No. 81.

250 Ibid. 2:1.

251 Ibid. 2:3.

252 Ibid.

253 Ibid. 1:1–5.

254 F. W. Faber, Sermon, *How is it that life is short?* Brompton, 1854. Unpublished MS in hand of F. W. Faber, LO, Packet 3, No. 57, 3.1.

255 Ibid. 3.2.

256 Ibid. 1.1.

257 Ibid. 2.1.

258 John XVII.14: 'I have given them Thy word, and ye world hath hated them, because they are not of ye world.'

259 F. W. Faber, Sermon, *The Sacred Heart*, John XVII.14. London, 1848. Unpublished MS in hand of F. W. Faber, LO, Packet 1, No. 51.

260 F. W. Faber to J. H. Newman, LO, Vol. 1, No. 91, St Richard (3 April) 1848.

261 F. W. Faber, Sermon, *How is it that life is short?* Brompton, 1854. Unpublished MS in hand of F. W. Faber, LO, Packet 3, No. 57, 2.2:3.

262 Ibid. 3.5.

263 F. W. Faber, Sermon, *The View ye Saints Take of ye World as a Howling wilderness compared with the view ordinary good men take of it.* New Year's Eve, 1849. Unpublished MS in hand of F. W. Faber, LO, Packet 1, No. 30.

264 F. W. Faber, Sermon, *Duties of Parents to Children*, n.d. Unpublished MS in hand of F. W. Faber, LO, Packet 3, No. 86.

265 Ibid.

266 Ibid.

267 Ibid.

268 F. W. Faber, Sermon, *God's patience with us*, n.d. Unpublished MS in hand of F. W. Faber, LO, Packet 1, No. 10.

269 F. W. Faber, Sermon, *Docility to ye Holy Ghost*, Whit Sunday (31 May) 1857. Unpublished MS in hand of F. W. Faber, LO, Packet 1, No. 26.

270 F. W. Faber, Sermon, *The mercy of God*, n.d. Unpublished MS in hand of F. W. Faber, LO, Packet 1, No. 6.

271 F. W. Faber, Sermon, *The Strangeness of God's love of us*, n.d. Unpublished MS in hand of F. W. Faber, LO, Packet 1, No. 16, 3:2–3.

272 F. W. Faber, Sermon, *The one drawback of life*, June 1861. Unpublished MS in hand of F. W. Faber, LO, Packet 3, No. 56.

273 F. W. Faber, Sermon, *Devotion to ye omnipotence of God*, 1860. Unpublished MS in hand of F. W. Faber, LO, Packet 1, No. 3, 2:5.

274 G. M. Hopkins, *The Wreck of the Deutschland*, Stanza 9, in W. H. Gardner and N. H. MacKenzie, (eds) (1988), *The Poems of Gerard Manley Hopkins*, 4th edn, Oxford, OUP, p. 54.

275 F. W. Faber, Sermon, *The Fall of ye Angels*, 1860. Unpublished MS in hand of F. W. Faber, LO, Packet 3, No. 97, 1:3.

276 F. W. Faber, Sermon, *The Three epochs of the Holy Trinity*, Trinity Sunday (30 May) 1858. Unpublished MS in hand of F. W. Faber, LO, Packet 1, No. 1.

277 F. W. Faber, Sermon, *The mercy of God*, n.d. Unpublished MS in hand of F. W. Faber, LO, Packet 1, No. 6, final paragraph.

278 F. W. Faber, Sermon, *Our Blessed Lord bowing His head upon the Cross*, Passion Sunday, 1863. Unpublished MS in hand of F. W. Faber, LO, Packet 1, No. 74.

279 F. W. Faber, Sermon, *Closing of King William Street*, 11 September 1853. Unpublished MS in hand of F. W. Faber, LO, Packet 3, No. 108.

280 Ibid.

281 F. W. Faber, Sermon, *The Eye of God*, London, 1853. Unpublished MS in hand of F. W. Faber, LO, Packet 3, No. 55.

282 Ibid.

283 Ibid.

284 Ibid.

285 Ibid.

286 Ibid.

287 F. W. Faber, Sermon, Sunday in ye Octave of Corpus Christi, 1860. Unpublished MS in hand of F. W. Faber, LO, Packet 1, No. 47.

288 F. W. Faber, Sermon, *The Legacies of Jesus*, London, 1848. Unpublished MS in hand of F. W. Faber, LO, Packet 1, No. 76.

289 F. W. Faber, Sermon, *The Person of Jesus Christ*: John 17.3. London, Palm Sunday (16 April) 1848. Unpublished MS in hand of F. W. Faber, LO, Packet 1, No. 36.

290 F. W. Faber, Sermon, *The Legacies of Jesus*, London, 1848. Unpublished MS in hand of F. W. Faber, LO, Packet 1, No. 76.

291 F. W. Faber, Sermon, *Personal Holiness*, n.d. Unpublished MS in hand of F. W. Faber, LO, Packet 3, No. 59.

292 F. W. Faber, Sermon, Sunday in ye Octave of Corpus Christi, 1860. Unpublished MS in hand of F. W. Faber, LO, Packet 1, No. 47.

293 F. W. Faber, Sermon, *Our Lord's Choice of poverty*, London, 1852. Unpublished MS in hand of F. W. Faber, LO, Packet 1, No. 37. Also F. W. Faber, Sermon, *Poverty ye choice of Jesus*, n.d. Unpublished MS in hand of F. W. Faber, LO, Packet 1, No. 38.

294 F. W. Faber, Sermon, *Our Lord's Choice of poverty*, London, 1852. Unpublished MS in hand of F. W. Faber, LO, Packet 1, No. 37.

295 Ibid. 3:3.

296 F. W. Faber, Sermon, *Poverty ye choice of Jesus*, n.d. Unpublished MS in hand of F. W. Faber, LO, Packet 1, No. 38, 2:4.

297 Ibid.

298 F. W. Faber, Sermon, Christmas Day, 1855. Unpublished MS in hand of F. W. Faber, LO, Packet 1, No. 28.

299 F. W. Faber, Sermon, *Mary the mother of sinners*, n.d. Unpublished MS in hand of F. W. Faber, LO, Packet 1, No. 80.

300 F. W. Faber, Sermon, *The Epiphany*, n.d. Unpublished MS in hand of F. W. Faber, LO, Packet 1, No. 33.

301 F. W. Faber, Sermon, *Without Jesus in ye world*, 1856. Unpublished MS in hand of F. W. Faber, LO, Packet 1, No. 57.

302 F. W. Faber, Sermon, *Personal Holiness*, n.d. Unpublished MS in hand of F. W. Faber, LO, Packet 3, No. 59, 4.3.

303 F. W. Faber, Sermon, *Self-denial ye essence of religion*, n.d. Unpublished MS in hand of F. W. Faber, LO, Packet 3, No. 58. See also F. W. Faber, Sermon, *The mystery of Jesus being thought mad,* 1850. Unpublished MS in hand of F. W. Faber, LO, Packet 1, No. 40, 2:2.

304 Ibid.

305 F. W. Faber, Meditations, Lent Retreat 8: *The Particular Judgement*, 1850. Unpublished MS in hand of F. W. Faber, LO, Packet 3, No. 118. See also F. W. Faber, Sermon, Octave of Corpus Christi, 1860. Unpublished MS in hand of F. W. Faber, LO, Packet 1, No. 47.

306 F. W. Faber, Sermon, *Calvary*, Lent 1857. Unpublished MS in hand of F. W. Faber, LO, Packet 1, No. 60.

307 F. W. Faber to J. B. Morris, LO, Vol. 17, No. 148, 17 July 1858.

308 F. W. Faber, Novice Conference, beginning of Lent 1862. Unpublished MS in hand of F. W. Faber, LO, Packet 2, No. 57.

309 Ibid.

310 Ibid.

311 F. W. Faber, Sermon, *The Passion, our devotion, ye whole year round*, Brompton, 1854. Unpublished MS in hand of F. W. Faber, LO, Packet 1, No. 75, 2.8.

312 Ibid. 3.1–7.

313 F. W. Faber, Sermon, *The Face of Jesus*, 1859. Unpublished MS in hand of F. W. Faber, LO, Packet 1, No. 68.

314 F. W. Faber, Sermon, *Our blessed Lord bowing His head upon the Cross*, Passion Sunday, 1863. Unpublished MS in hand of F. W. Faber, LO, Packet 1, No. 74.

315 F. W. Faber, Sermon, *The Face of Jesus*, 1859. Unpublished MS in

hand of F. W. Faber, LO, Packet 1, No. 68.

316 F. W. Faber to J. B. Morris, LO, Vol. 17, No. 149, 13 October 1858.

317 F. W. Faber, Sermon, *The Passion, our devotion, ye whole year round,* Brompton, 1854. Unpublished MS in hand of F. W. Faber, LO, Packet 1, No. 75, 4.1–4.

318 F. W. Faber, Sermon, *Setting up ye Stations,* Brompton, 1854. Unpublished MS in hand of F. W. Faber, LO, Packet 1, No. 77.

319 Ibid. 2.4.

320 Ibid. 2.2.

321 F. W. Faber, Sermon, *The Resurrection – A Mystery of Calmness,* Brompton, 1854. Unpublished MS in hand of F. W. Faber, LO, Packet 1, No. 46.

322 Ibid. 1.2.

323 Ibid.

324 Ibid. 1.7.

325 Ibid. 2.1.

326 Ibid. 2.2.

327 Ibid. 3.3.

328 Phil. 4:7. Ibid. Conclusion.

329 F. W. Faber, Sermon, *Setting up ye Stations,* Brompton, 1854. Unpublished MS in hand of F. W. Faber, LO, Packet 1, No. 77.

330 F. W. Faber, Sermon, *The three epochs of the Holy Trinity,* Trinity Sunday (30 May) 1858. Unpublished MS in hand of F. W. Faber, LO, Packet 1, No. 1. See also F. W. Faber, Sermon, *Mary ye safety of souls,* Triduo at Islington, 1853. Unpublished MS in hand of F. W. Faber, LO, Packet 1, No. 81. See also F. W. Faber, Sermon, *Closing of King William Street,* 11 September 1853. Unpublished MS in hand of F. W. Faber, LO, Packet 3, No. 108.

331 F. W. Faber, Sermon, *The three epochs of the Holy Trinity,* Trinity Sunday (30 May) 1858. Unpublished MS in hand of F. W. Faber, LO, Packet 1, No. 1, 2:3.

332 F. W. Faber, Sermon, Rosary Sunday (7 October) 1851. Unpublished MS in hand of F. W. Faber, LO, Packet 1, No. 89.

333 Ibid.

334 F. W. Faber, Sermon, *The Epiphany,* 1861. Unpublished MS in hand of F. W. Faber, LO, Packet 1, No. 31. See also *The Epiphany ye feast of converts,* 1856. Unpublished MS in hand of F. W. Faber, LO, Packet 1, No. 32.

335 F. W. Faber, Sermon, *Dependence on Mary,* Lent 1856. Unpublished MS in hand of F. W. Faber, LO, Packet 1, No. 82.

336 F. W. Faber, Sermon, *The Sacred Heart,* 1852. Unpublished MS in hand of F. W. Faber, LO, Packet 1, No. 50.

337 F. W. Faber, Sermon, *Mary ye safety of souls,* Triduo at Islington, 1853. Unpublished MS in hand of F. W. Faber, LO, Packet 1, No. 81.

338 F. W. Faber, Epiphany Lectures 1851, 1: *The history of ye Church.* Unpublished MS in hand of F. W. Faber, LO, Packet 3, No. 1, 2:8, Nos. 3–5.

339 F. W. Faber, Lectures, *Mary and the Modern Church*, 1: *Mary's place in the modern Church*, 2: *The Church in Intercession*, 3: *The Church in thanksgiving*, 4: *The Church at war with heresy*, 5: *The Church at war with sin*, 6: *The Church making saints*, 7: *Mary magnifying God*, See F. W. Faber to J. H. Newman, LO, Vol. 3, No. 49, 30 April 1851.

340 F. W. Faber, Lectures, *Mary and the Modern Church*, 1: *Mary's place in the modern Church*, 1851. Unpublished MS in hand of F. W. Faber, LO, Packet 3, No. 12, 3:5.

341 Ibid. 3:5.

342 Ibid. 2:1.

343 Ibid. 3:2.

344 Ibid. 2:4.

345 F. W. Faber, Lectures, *Mary and the Modern Church*, 6: *The Church making saints*, 1851. Unpublished MS in hand of F. W. Faber, LO, Packet 3, No. 12, 2:3.

346 Ibid. 1:1–3.

347 Ibid. 5:6.

348 F. W. Faber, Lectures, *Mary and the Modern Church*, 2: *The Church in intercession*, 1851. Unpublished MS in hand of F. W. Faber, LO, Packet 3, No. 12, 2:1.1.

349 Ibid. 2:2.7. The latter was probably his *Traite de la vraie devotion de la Sainte Vierge*. See *OCDCC* p. 225.

350 F. W. Faber, Lectures, *Mary and the Modern Church*, 4: *The Church at war with heresy*, 1851. Unpublished MS in hand of F. W. Faber, LO, Packet 3, No. 12, 3:1–10.

351 Ibid. 2:1 Section 5:1–9.

352 Jesuits, Passionists, Redemptorists, Sulpicians, Conceptionists, Oratorians. See F. W. Faber, Lectures, *Mary and the Modern Church*, 5: *The Church at war with sin*, 1851. Unpublished MS in hand of F. W. Faber, LO, Packet 3, No. 12, 4:2 Section 1–6.

353 B. Kelly (ed.) (1954), *Lives of the Fathers, Martyrs, and Other Principal Saints*, London, Virtue & Co. Ltd, Vol. 4, pp. 1558–62.

354 F. W. Faber, Four Lectures, *The Immaculate Conception*, Brompton, 1854. Unpublished MS in hand of F. W. Faber, LO, Packet 3, Nos. 133–6.

355 F. W. Faber, Sermon, *The living Church: Thanksgiving for ye definition of ye Immaculate Conception*, 1855. Unpublished MS in hand of F. W. Faber, LO, Packet 3, No. 8.

356 T. E. Bridgett (ed.) (1898), *Characteristics from the Writings of Nicholas Cardinal Wiseman, Archbishop of Westminster*, London, Burns & Oates.

357 P. Murray (1969), *Newman the Oratorian*, Dublin, Gill & Macmillan Ltd, p. 32.

358 J. H. Newman (1840), *Parochial and Plain Sermons*, Vol. 1, 4th edn, London, Rivington.

359 P. Murray (1969), Newman the Oratorian, Dublin, Gill & Macmillan Ltd, p. 31.

360 Ibid.

361 Ibid. p. 39.

362 J. H. Newman (1957), *Catholic Sermons of Cardinal Newman*, London, Burns & Oates.

363 Ibid. Sermon 2: *Preparation for the Judgement* (1847) p. 33.

364 This is particularly apparent in the general tone used in ibid. Sermon 5: *Surrender to God*. See also the general tone of Sermon 1: *The Omnipotence of God, the Reason for Faith and Hope*.

365 Compare the style of F. Oakeley, *Christ Manifested to the Faithful through his Church*, Margaret Chapel, twenty-fifth Sunday after Trinity 1839 (Oxford, 1839) with his Roman Catholic sermons.

366 Ibid. p. 6.

367 See the general tone of ibid. Lecture 2: *Personal Reminiscences of the Oxford Movement*.

368 F. Oakeley (1855), *Popular Lectures Addressed to the Islington Catholic Popular Club*, London, Henry Teulon, p. 11, pp. 13–14.

369 Ibid. pp. 13–14, 21.

370 Ibid. p. 6.

371 See the general tone of Sermon 1: *The Sanctity of the Christian Vocation*, St Edmund's College, Ware, Feast of All Saints, 1847, in F. Oakeley (1848), *Practical Sermons Preached in 1847–8*, London, James Burns.

372 See the general tone of Sermon XV: *The Month of Mary*, ibid.

Chapter 7

Conclusions

One of the most important conclusions that we can draw from this study is that knowledge of Faber's health is fundamental to understanding his life, personality and spirituality; and, in demonstrating this, we have contradicted the over-simplistic apprehension of Faber's health which is currently available. In his biography of Newman, Ker writes at length about the disagreements between Newman and Faber, during which Newman dismissed Faber's ill-health as an affectation, principally because of his propensity for moving between being dangerously ill and completely well in a short time.[1] In another biography of Newman, Trevor writes of Faber's ill-health as a hysterical response to disagreements with contemporaries, such as Newman, which was fundamentally psychosomatic in origin.[2] This is part of Trevor's wider agenda, which is to depict Faber as a foolish individual who Newman's saintly genius had to endure. Newman's interpretation of Faber's constitution has been widely used by historians; and, because Newman witnessed at least some of Faber's periods of illness, it is impossible to judge conclusively whether his judgements were accurate, or inaccurate – the result of a broader dislike of Faber. Despite this, it seems certain that it is dangerous for the historian to rely too heavily on Newman's view of Faber's health: firstly, because during the mid-nineteenth century there was a lack both of clear medical diagnosis and of knowledge of the effects of substances on the individual; and secondly, because of Newman's own lack of medical knowledge, which ensured that he was unaware of the precise nature of Faber's illness.

We have demonstrated that Bright's disease affected Faber

from an earlier date than has been assumed by those historians who mention his health; and suggested that medication caused more harm to Faber than disease. Indeed, it seems certain that much of Faber's eccentric temperament and chronic illness, particularly in the second half of his life, stemmed from his response to medication, as well as to the effects of Bright's disease. We have hypothesised that because this medication contained a high concentration of mercury, Faber actually suffered from undiagnosed mercury poisoning, which ruined his health, personality and mature intellectual development. It seems possible, in fact, that the original diagnosis of Bright's disease was incorrect, and that he simply had mercury poisoning; this is, however, impossible to prove conclusively. This knowledge adds considerably to our understanding of Faber's life, temperament and spirituality, his undoubtedly complex temperament, and the reaction of contemporaries towards him.

In the course of this study, we have explored the complex spiritual and intellectual processes that marked the progression in Faber's spirituality from evangelical Anglicanism to Roman Catholicism; and, in our Preface, we stated that we would divide his life into seven stages, noting that each of these possessed a definite character of its own. In Chapter 1, we looked briefly at the evangelical influences on Faber's spirituality before 1833, and in Chapter 2, we studied his spiritual development between 1833 and 1836. Stage One was concerned with Faber's life as an evangelical between January 1833 and December 1834, and we observed that after his arrival in Oxford he remained on the periphery of the religious life of the university. Faber's dissatisfaction stemmed from his evangelical background, which showed itself in an unwillingness to accommodate ideas dissimilar to his own. The primary influences on Faber's early university life were student contemporaries rather than tutors or individuals such as Newman or Pusey. We discovered that, although his responses to spirituality were theologically simplistic at this time, his view of what spirituality should consist of formed part of his own spirituality for the remainder of his life. Faber believed that religion should be presented in a style that was practical, and not be excessively intellectual, in order to be accessible to those with limited education; and that it should avoid obscure notions or any form of mysticism. Perhaps because of this, his spirituality was highly emotional, stressing the centrality of spiritual experiences such as conversion. We also noted the primacy of scripture in Faber's thought, and that, despite its emotionalism, his spirituality possessed an overriding austerity that leaned towards pessimism. We discussed the response to Tractarianism made by Faber during 1835, examining his belief that the Tractarian ideal of Anglicanism was heretical. We also noted that he was unhappy with Newman's influence over the Movement, viewing him as promulgating an over-intellectual reading of Anglicanism, which was more dependent on the cult of personality than the principles of religion. Another notable dimension of this period was Faber's unhappiness with his Classical Studies, as he came to believe that its subject matter was morally unsuitable for discussion amongst undergraduates. Faber became more didactic during this period, seeking to be a leader of his contemporaries in order to promulgate his ardent belief in evangelical teaching.

Stage Two concerned Faber's movement away from Low Church Anglicanism during 1836, due to his growth in maturity and awareness that his religion was limited because it was based on feelings alone. In looking at this stage, we illustrated his movement towards some of the principles of the Oxford Movement, which manifested itself in an increasing awareness of the importance of doctrine, greater variety in reading, and sophistication in his response to theology. We also briefly included the influence of individuals such as John Keble, E. B. Pusey, R. H. Froude, William Palmer and Isaac Williams on Faber's intellect and spirituality. The characteristic tensions and contradictions, which, as we have seen, are always present in Faber's intellect, appear at this time.

Stage Three, which lasted from 1837 until 1843, is not only interesting in a prosopographical context, but is also important in a wider historical context. This is because, in discussing Faber's acceptance of the principles of the Oxford Movement, we see how these principles were applied within the life of an individual. In Faber's case, it is significant that he passed rapidly over them, and that here, as throughout his life, he followed his own path rather than simply copying other people. Changes during this period reorganised Faber's emotional belief structure and the intellectual thought processes concerned with religion, in a manner that was both subtle and revolutionary. Faber no longer identified with Evangelicalism, Low Church Anglicanism, or the reformers; and his thought shows a preoccupation with intellectual distinctions between heresy and orthodoxy, and distrust of Rome. We characterised the period as one during which Faber noted the beginnings of his dissatisfaction with Anglicanism, which was caused, and influenced, by Newman's historical reading of Anglicanism and patristic theology. The influence of Pusey became less prominent during 1842, as Faber realised that Newman, rather than Pusey, was moving in the direction in which he wished to move. We discussed these changes of emphasis within the context of Faber's preparation for ordination to the diaconate and priesthood, and the first years of his ministry. During this time, Faber suffered from depression and dissatisfaction with Oxford and the Church of England.

Chapter 3 was concerned with the period between 1843 and 1846. During this chapter, we presented a detailed account of the spiritual, emotional, and moral processes through which Faber progressed during the three years leading up to his conversion. This was the fourth stage of his spiritual life and, during its first year, Faber made his first visit to Rome. We discussed the minutiae of his responses to Roman Catholicism, and the blurring of distinctions between the Churches of Rome and England, which was an important facet of Faber's spiritual world from this point onwards. We also noted the effects that this indecision had on Faber's intellect and spirituality, and discovered that Faber used the *Spiritual Exercises* of St Ignatius of Loyola whilst an Anglican. We also discussed Newman's influence at this time, which served primarily to keep Faber within the Anglican Church, and noted that, although he had moved to Littlemore in 1842, Newman did not discuss his own doubts about Anglicanism with Faber. In a wider historical context, it is significant that Faber was one of the first individuals to go over the boundaries of Tractarianism into Romanism. It is notable that Newman, Dalgairns and Oakeley viewed Faber as dangerous, and distanced themselves from what they saw as excessive leanings towards Rome, primarily because of his use of Roman devotions. We highlighted that Faber's contemporaries, both inside and outside the immediate Tractarian circle, viewed Faber as dishonest and disloyal to the Anglican Church; and we concluded from this that he represented an extreme, rather than a typical, follower of Tractarianism. We can say that Faber was not an archetypal follower of any of the spiritual phases through which he passed, as his temperament was such that he always inclined towards excess. During this phase, Faber's position highlights the inherent difficulties of an extreme following of the Tractarian position.

In Chapter 4, we discussed Faber's life as a Roman Catholic, from his conversion, in December 1845, until his death, in 1863. Stage Five of his spiritual life lasted from 1845 until 1847. In our discussion of this stage, we presented a detailed view of the Wilfridian Order and its Rule, during which we noted that the spirituality within the Rule highlights the religiosity that Faber began to develop from the beginning of his life as a Roman Catholic. As in other phases, there was continuity. Firstly, the Rule was influenced by the Ignatian spirituality which he had begun to practise whilst an Anglican. Secondly, like his evangelical spirituality, Faber's Roman spirituality was essentially practical, as he believed that a spirituality that was contemplative or eremitical could foster delusions, selfishness and unreality. An important facet of the early part of this phase is that Faber doubted the rightness of his conversion, a position that is not mentioned by any of his biographers. We also discussed Faber's inability to make the Wilfridian venture a success, and doubts concerning his vocation. An important discovery of this part of our study is that Faber wished to bring the Oratory to England himself, and was disappointed when Wiseman gave the task to Newman, an idea that changes our historical perception of the founding of the English Oratory. We suggested that Faber did not achieve a true spiritual equilibrium as a Roman Catholic until his move to London. In Stage Six of Faber's spirituality, between 1847 and 1849, we discussed the details of the closing down of the Wilfridian Order, and the transfer of its members to the Oratory in Birmingham; and Faber's move to London in order to found the London Oratory. We also discussed Faber's personal spirituality.

Stage Seven, 1850 to 1863, is the period during which Faber achieved what is recognisable as the outward face of his mature spirituality. We highlighted the ecclesiastical climate of London, disagreements between the clergy, and the opprobrium to which Faber's community were subjected, partly as a result of the Ultramontane character of their spirituality. This was fuelled by the 'papal aggression' and the restoration of the Roman Catholic hierarchy of England and Wales, during 1850. In this chapter, we also put forward some observations regarding the relationship between Newman and Faber, although not in detail as this has been discussed at length in biographies of both individuals. As we have seen throughout this study, Faber's personality polarised individuals who encountered him during his lifetime, and those who wrote about him after his death, between antipathy and empathy. Although we did not dwell on Faber's leadership of the London Oratory, it becomes apparent that his skill as a leader was founded upon his charismatic and distinctive personality, which influenced younger friends who shared his spiritual worldview, such as J. B. Morris and J. E. Bowden, and female acquaintances such as Margaret Hallahan. Several individuals recognised the dangers inherent in being overly attracted by Faber's highly emotional personality, particularly Dominic Barberi and Elizabeth Thompson (who chose not to have eye contact with him during their first meeting, in order to ensure that she was influenced by his spirituality rather than by his personality).[3] Those who were influenced by him can be characterised as being intelligent, individual, eccentric, in the sense of being liminal by virtue of being Catholic converts, and independent. In this chapter we also highlighted biographical references in Faber's major books, particularly his reference in the *Spiritual Conferences* to the fact that he had been taught whilst a child to prefer his second best to his best work; and hypothesised that this teaching, which remained with Faber for the whole of his life, effectively ruined his early intellectual development and overshadowed his potential. We noted that, because of ill-health, Faber's life became less eventful during this period. In discussing Faber's spirituality, use of theology, and spiritual reading, we formed the important conclusion that the character of Faber's spirituality became increasingly contemplative during the final years of his life.

In Chapter 5, we considered the style and content of Faber's major books written between 1853 and 1863, in order to assess Faber's spiritual writing and to illustrate the similarities and differences between his public and private spirituality. *All for Jesus* is an example of Faber's popular style and, perhaps because of this, is his least satisfactory book. We highlighted notions that occur both within the book and throughout this study, such as Faber's innate silliness and sense of sarcasm and ridicule. We discussed the positive influence of Ignatian spirituality, and distrust of spirituality that is excessively intellectual; also his major fault, that of treating questionable, or lesser, ideas as being of equal merit with those of higher theological value. The book, although successful in terms of the number of copies sold, led to polarisation between those who admired it and those who thought it could lead to accusations of heresy, a trait that is applicable to all of Faber's books. *Growth in Holiness* highlights the austere side of Faber's spirituality, and we discussed his opinion that individuals are unable to be spiritual, and his use of notions such as the theology of the Fall, and the dangers of worldliness. We noted that the book is stylistically mature and well written; that it highlights the variety of Faber's reading of theology, and shows that he was able to elucidate academic theology for individuals who were not theologically educated. *The Blessed Sacrament*, which was written in order to popularise theology and demonstrate its superiority to other sciences, also exhibits the variety of Faber's reading. Our primary criticism of the work is that it is a hybrid, which is neither good theology nor convincing devotion, and does not fit into either category convincingly, whilst its second major flaw is that it does not distinguish between theology and pious anecdote. The book highlights the major preoccupations of Faber's spirituality, as well as his cynicism, criticism of worldliness, and moral serious-ness. Faber's impressionistic and sensitive use of words and creation of atmosphere are present, and we highlighted the influence of Ignatian methods of meditation on Faber's literary style. In discussing Faber's *Complete Poems*, we illustrated the major themes and preoccupations present, and presented the views of several contemporaries regarding the poems. *The Creator and the Creature*, which is concerned with predestination, nature and grace, is the most successful and academic of Faber's books. It is an atypical work within Faber's mature Catholic writing, because it is stylistically reminiscent of the works written at Oxford, and whilst an Anglican. *The Foot of the Cross* is also distinctive, as it is the most personal of Faber's books. We discussed the primary limitation of the book, its dense and impenetrable style, and suggested that it contains few of the facets that we have noted throughout this study as being characteristic of Faber's literary and spiritual world. The *Spiritual Conferences* is concerned with grace and nature and with inauthentic and authentic forms of spirituality. In our discussion, we examined ideas within the book that are central to Faber's thought and spirituality, such as the 'spirit of the age', and dissatisfaction with the spiritual milieu of the nineteenth century. Although *Ethel's Book* was not a major work, it was included in our survey, albeit briefly, as an illustration of a work that several critics found problematic because they believed that Faber was encouraging individuals to think themselves more spiritually qualified than they were. *The Precious Blood* highlights the Ignatian spirituality that Faber uses in order to create a dramatic, almost mythical, spiritual world. The main negative aspects of the book are its sugary emotionalism, which appeals to a folksy rather than to a sophisticated apprehension of religion, and Faber's trait of expressing a fundamentally orthodox idea in a way that is vulgar, banal and sometimes strange. The book succeeds in presenting difficult concepts to his readership, and the piety expressed is characteristically personal rather than remote. *Bethlehem* demonstrates Faber's use of French spirituality and Carmelite spirituality, and we noted that his works may have influenced the spirituality of St Thérèse of Lisieux, some twenty years after Faber's death. The book illustrates that, at one level, Faber must be approached by historians as a storyteller, rather than as an academic theologian. We discussed the piety present in Faber's *Complete Hymns,* and noted characteristic traits present within them; illustrating those which were successful and less successful. We completed this chapter by briefly discussing the inclusion of Faber's hymns in twentieth-century hymn books.

Faber's books continued to be published during the final decades of the nineteenth century and the first forty years of the twentieth century; and individual ideas from them were included within books containing selections from several spiritual writers or poets.[4] Several letters at the London Oratory demonstrate their influence on individuals, one of whom wrote from South Africa to inform them of his 'great and increasing love for the works of Father Faber'.[5] In 1924, the publishers Burns and Oates notified the Oratory that, 'The average sale is ... 250 copies per year'[6] in England, and '50 sets per annum'[7] in America. Several of Faber's books were reprinted during the 1990s. We can concur with Gilley, who observed that Faber's 'emotive combination of romanticism and evangelicalism is a little strong for modern sensibilities'.[8] Although these no longer possess wide appeal, their essential message is significant; however, they are representative of a certain type of nineteenth-century spirituality and their ideas are submerged within a language and literary style that does not transfer easily from its literary milieu. It is unlikely that Faber established a polemical slant within English Roman Catholicism. However, his fusion of theology, mysticism, and poetic imagination, which evolves from his use of Ignatian spirituality, and which occasionally borders on being allegorical, is original, and has its logical conclusion within the genre of early twentieth-century English spiritual writing.

In Chapter 6, we presented a detailed discussion of the sermons written by Faber, as an Anglican and as a Roman Catholic, between 1837 and 1863. Faber preached his Anglican sermons from a copy that was written out; and we noted that they are examples of the formal, unemotional style of sermon writing popular in Protestant denominations during the eighteenth and early- to mid-nineteenth centuries. We discussed the main themes and preoccupations of the sermons, such as the idealisation of childhood, the 'spirit of the age', and Faber's use of doctrine and the *Book of Common Prayer*. We also highlighted Faber's characteristic austerity and the presentation of ideas which stem from his personal spirituality. We noted that Faber's Roman Catholic sermons, lectures and novice conferences exist only as detailed notes, as he conformed to the Roman practice of extemporisation. We discussed Faber's presentation of ideas and use of theology, his Mariology and the Christocentricity of the sermons. We highlighted the controversy generated by the sermons and lectures, and the devotional world within them, and considered further Faber's preoccupations, such as the critique of Protestantism, worldliness, the British Empire, and the influence of history. The 'spirit of the age' was discussed in a separate section, in order to highlight its importance within Faber's thought, both in sermons and throughout his life. In conclusion, we highlighted the similarities and differences in the sermons of three other nineteenth-century Roman Catholic priests, two of them converts, in order to place Faber's sermons in their historical context.

Faber was associated with a significant number of denominational groups within Christianity in mid-nineteenth-century England, and his primary appeal to the historian lies in the complexity and discrepancies in his responses to them. Our interest in Faber is founded on his inability to be wholly part of the movements with which he associated, and his position within mid-nineteenth-century history is as one who lacked confidence in, and constantly questioned the validity of, the religious milieu in which he lived. Faber's volatile personality, which was composed of irreconcilable contradictions, defies neat categorisation; and therefore, study of Faber's life enlarges the broader historical understanding of the relationship between the doctrinal, theological, spiritual and personal aspects of the process of conversion.

Faber's contribution to the mid-nineteenth-century Roman Catholic Church was threefold: as founder of the London Oratory, as an influence during the formative years of the Diocese of Westminster, and as a Roman Catholic polemicist. Each of these facets underlines Faber's role as an apologist for Ultramontane Roman Catholicism, through books, hymns and preaching, and as an important instigator of popular devotion. Although we can concur with Gilley's comment that Faber 'defined the tone and temper of mid-Victorian Ultramontane Catholicism',[9] we note that Faber was essentially an apologist for his own individual reading of Roman Catholicism. Paradoxically, Faber was mistrusted in England by both liberal and Old Catholics, who viewed him as promulgating foreign religious practices, and mistrusted by those abroad because of his Englishness.

Faber has not been universally popular during the 142 years since his death. There is no cult associated with him, and, although they admire and preserve his memory as their founder, the London Oratorians have not kept Faber's room as a shrine in the same way that the Birmingham house has preserved the rooms of Newman. This is mainly due to practical concerns as, because of illness, Faber's clothing and bedding were burned after his death. His room is now used as a library. On the surface, it seems more difficult to separate Faber and mid-nineteenth-century Catholicism than it is to do the same for an individual such as Newman; however, this is because those who support Newman have successfully represented his works as being relevant to the late twentieth and early twenty-first centuries, whilst there are no individuals willing to do the same for Faber. Another major problem with Faber is one of reputation, as those who have approached him from within the twentieth century have too readily assumed that the syrupy emotionalism, which is occasionally surprisingly modern in its vulgarity, is the only side to Faber. In the course of this study we have demonstrated that this is not so, and that he is a more multi-faceted and complex individual than has hitherto been realised.

Notes

1 I. Ker (1990), *John Henry Newman*, Oxford, OUP, pp. 503–4.
2 M. Trevor (1962), *Newman: The Pillar of the Cloud*, London, Macmillan & Co., p. 455 and p. 460.
3 Addington, *Faber: Poet and Priest*, pp. 307–8.
4 M. Drury to C. Bowden, 26 September 1868, and Lord Aberdeen to C. Bowden, 16 September 1881. Unpublished MS, LO, packet, drawer 3.
5 C. Rolfe to C. Bowden, LO, Vol. 21, No. 131, n.d. 1905.
6 Burns, Oates & Washbourne Ltd. to R. Kerr, 21 November 1924. Unpublished MS, LO, packet, drawer 3.
7 Ibid.
8 S. Gilley, *F. W. Faber (1814–1863)*, in DNB (OUP, Oxford, 2004), Vol. 18, p. 873.
9 Ibid.

Bibliography

Primary Sources: F. W. Faber

London Oratory

Letters
Vol. 1. F. W. Faber to J. H. Newman: 1843–1849.
    2. F. W. Faber to J. H. Newman: 1849–1850.
    3. F. W. Faber to J. H. Newman: 1850–1861.
    8. J. H. Newman to F. W. Faber: 1838–1850.
        (Copies of letters in Birmingham Oratory Archives)
    9. J. H. Newman to F. W. Faber & Misc: 1850–1862.
        (Copies of letters in Birmingham Oratory Archives)
  16. F. W. Faber: Letters from abroad: 1846–1851.
  17. F. W. Faber to J. B. Morris: 1833–1863.
  20. F. W. Faber to J. Bowden: 1843–1863.
  21. F. W. Faber: Various documents and letters.
  22. F. W. Faber: Various letters.
  23. F. W. Faber to S. Keogh and various.
  24. To and from Fr Dalgairns.

Manuscript files
Packet No. 1. Notes on Doctrinal and Spiritual Subjects:
               Vol. 1: Mysteries and Festivals.
Packet No. 2. Notes on Community life in the Oratory.
Packet No. 3. Notes on Doctrinal and Spiritual Subjects:
               Vol. 2: The Faith and Spiritual Life.
Packet No. 4. 1. Sermons.
               2. Misc. essays, chiefly spiritual, before 1845.
               6. MSS F. W. Faber.

Miscellaneous documents (black box file).
F. W. Faber Sermons [Anglican]: 1837–1845 (light brown box).
Miscellaneous documents (maroon folder).
MSS of Sermons and on Spiritual Subjects: Fr Faber.
Notes from books (dark brown folder).

Miscellaneous manuscript documents
A Christian Ideal of Friendship (23 January 1836).
AMD Sitorum que Josephic et Wilfridi Gloriam (n.d.), black box file,
    No. 10.
An Essay on the beatification and canonisation of Saints (1848) in
    Miscellaneous Essays.
Devotion to the Church (1861), in LO Vol. *Miscellaneous Faber*.
Essay for the Chancellor's Prize, Oxford University (1837).
Faber's Baptism Certificate (copy), black box file, No. 19.
The Idea of Man (n.d.).
*Journal: Sights and Thoughts in Foreign Churches and Among
    Foreign Peoples*, University College, Oxford (1841).
Notes on the Spiritual Exercises of St Ignatius Loyola. Untitled
    (n.d.), black box file, No. 8.
Rule of Brothers of the Will of God, black box file, No. 18.
Seven Books of St Optatus Against the Donatists, trans. F. W. Faber
    (1838).
*Various memoranda relating to London Oratorian History by Frs P.
    Gordon, R. F. Kerr, etc.*

Printed books
All for Jesus: or the Easy Ways of Divine Love, 5th edn, London,
    Richardson & Sons, 1855.
Bethlehem, new edn, London, Burns & Oates, n.d.
The Blessed Sacrament: or the Works and Ways of God, 3rd edn,
    London, Burns & Oates, 1861.
The Cherwell Water-Lily and Other Poems, London, Rivington,
    1840.
The Creator and the Creature: or the Wonders of Divine Love, new
    edn, London, Burns & Oates, n.d.
Devotion to the Pope, London, Richardson & Sons, 1860.
Essay on Catholic Home Missions, London, Richardson & Sons,
    1851.
Essay on the Characteristics of the Lives of the Saints, in *Life of St*

Francis of Assisi, London, Thomas Richardson & Sons, 1853.

Ethel's Book or Tales of the Angels, London, Burns & Oates, 1858.

The Foot of the Cross, or the Sorrows of Mary, London, Richardson & Sons, 1858.

Grounds for Remaining in the Anglican Communion: A Letter to a High Church Friend, London, Toovey, 1846.

Growth in Holiness: or the Progress of the Spiritual Life, 3rd edn, London, Burns & Oates, n.d.

Hymns, London, Burns & Oates, n.d.

Life of St Ignatius Loyola, London, Thomas Richardson & Son, 1847.

Life of St Philip Neri – Apostle of Rome, London, Thomas Richardson & Son, 1847.

Saints and Servants of God: Rose of Lima, London, Thomas Richardson & Son, 1847.

Lives of the English Saints: St Wilfrid, Bishop of York, London, Toovey, 1844.

The London Oratory and the Union Newspaper, London, Richardson & Sons, 1857.

Maxims and Sayings of St Philip Neri, Leominster, Gracewing, 1994.

Notes on Community Life in the Oratory, London, Richardson & Sons, 1867.

Poems, 3rd edn, London, Richardson & Sons, 1857.

The Precious Blood: or The Price of Our Salvation, 3rd edn, USA, Peter Reilly, 1959.

The School of St Philip Neri, trans. F. W. Faber, London, Burns & Lambert, 1850.

Sights and Thoughts in Foreign Churches and Among Foreign Peoples, London, Rivington, 1842.

Spiritual Conferences, 9th edn, London, Burns & Oates, n.d.

The Styrian Lake and Other Poems, London, Rivington, 1840.

British Library

F. W. Faber: Poems and Letters: Add. MSS 58225.

Calverley Church Archive

Faber and the Dibon Families.
Five letters from the 1970s relating to the association of the
Faber family with Calverley.

Cambridge University Library

Letters: F. W. Faber to Lord Acton (1858–1860): Add.
8119/1/F1–2.
Letters: F. W. Faber to H. Bence Jones: Add. 8546/1/78–79.

Carmelite Monastery, St Charles' Square, London

Letters: F. W. Faber to M. Howard: 1861–1863.
Letters: F. W. Faber to E. Thompson.

Huntingdon County Record Office

Faber's Mandate of Induction – 27 March 1843. Archdeaconry
Records Ref. A238/66.

Keble College, Oxford

Letters: (2) F. W. Faber to J. Keble. No ref.

Pusey House, Oxford

Letter: F. W. Faber to E. B. Pusey – 9 June 1845. No ref.

Ripon and Leeds Diocesan Registry

Entry in the Bishop's Act Book: F. W. Faber, 6 August 1837.

University College, Oxford

Entry in the Admission Register: F. W. Faber: 6 December
1834.

Westminster Diocesan Archives

(Quotations from correspondence used with the permission of the Archbishop of Westminster.)

Letters: F. W. Faber to N. Wiseman, Misc. Oratorians, *Dublin Review*: AAW: W3/16.

Letters: F. W. Faber to N. Wiseman, A. W. N. Pugin, J. Acton: AAW: W3/52.

Other correspondence

Lambeth Palace Library

Correspondence of Charles Wordsworth, Bishop of St Andrews, 1830–1891: MS 1823.

Correspondence of Charles Wordsworth, Bishop of St Andrews, 1825–1891: MS 1824.

Correspondence of Christopher Wordsworth Jnr: MS 2141, 2142.

Correspondence of Christopher Wordsworth, Master of Trinity College, Cambridge, 1803–1845: MS 1822.

Secondary Sources

Addington, R. H. L. (ed.) (1974) *Faber, Poet and Priest: Selected Letters by Frederick William Faber 1833–1863*, Cowbridge, D. Brown & Sons.

Albion, G. (1975) '"Convert and Extrovert": *Faber, Poet and Priest*, Selected Letters by Frederick William Faber, from 1833–1863, by Raleigh Addington' *Clergy Review* 60, 267–8.

Altholz, J. L. (1960) *The Liberal Catholic Movement in England: The Rambler and its contributors, 1848-1864*, London, Burns & Oates.

____ (1995) 'The Warfare of Conscience with Theology', in G. Parsons (ed.), *Religion in Victorian Britain*, Vol. 4: *Interpretations*, Manchester, Manchester University Press.

Anon. (1834) 'Life in Oxford', *Oxford University Magazine*, Vol. 1, 95–106.

—— (1845) 'Recent Secessions, 1845–46: Mr Faber', *Oxford and Cambridge Review*, September, 60–67.

—— (1849) '*Jesus and Mary; or, Catholic Hymns*. By Frederick William Faber, Priest of the Oratory of St Philip Neri', *Dublin Review* Vol. XXVII, No. LIII, September, 163–81.

—— (1854) '*All for Jesus, or the Easy Ways of Divine Love*. By Frederick William Faber, Priest of the Oratory of St Philip Neri', *Dublin Review*, Vol. XXXVI, No. LXXI, March, 194–212.

—— (1854) 'Review of F. W. Faber, *All for Jesus*', *Dublin Review*, Vol. XXXVI, No. LXXI, March, 194–212.

—— (1855) '*The Spiritual direction of Fr. Louis Lallemant*, ed. F. W. Faber DD,' *Dublin Review*, No. XXXIX, Vol. XIX, December, 494.

—— (1857) '*The Creator and the Creature, or, the Wonders of Divine Love*. By Frederick William Faber, DD, Priest of the Oratory of St Philip Neri', *Dublin Review*, Vol. XLIII, No. LXXXV, September, 235–6.

—— (1857) 'Review of F. W. Faber, *Creator and Creature*', *Dublin Review*, Vol. XLIII, No. LXXXV, September, 235–56.

—— (1858) '*Ethel's Book or Tales of the Angels*, by the Very Rev. F. W. Faber', *Dublin Review*, Vol. XLV, December, 532–3.

—— (1858) '*Oratory Hymns*, by the Very Rev. F. W. Faber, set to Music by Wilhelm Schulthes', *The Rambler*, NS, Vol. IX, 421–2.

——(1860–61) 'Living English Poets', *Dublin Review*, Vol. XLIX, No. XCVIII, 503–42.

—— (1863) Death Notice, 'F. W. Faber', *The Times*, 29 September, 1.

—— (1863) 'F. W. Faber', *Athenaeum*, Vol. 2, 3 October, 436.

—— (1863) 'F. W. Faber', *Morning Post*, 28 September, 5.

—— (1863) 'Frederick William Faber', *The Saturday Review*, 10 October, 488–9.

—— (1863) 'Letter from the Parish Priest on Father Faber's Centenary', *[London] Oratory Parish Magazine, Faber Centenary Number*, Vol. 42, No. 513, September, 1–9.

—— (1864) 'Father Faber', *Dublin Review*, NS, Vol. 2, January, 159–63.

—— (1869) 'F. W. Faber's Life and Letters', *Blackwood's Magazine*, Vol. CVI, December, 693–700.

—— (1869) 'Father Faber as a Writer', *The Month*, Vol. XI, 154–8.

—— (1869) 'The Life of Father Faber', *Dublin Review,* NS, Vol. XIII, July, l09–43.

—— (1869) 'The Life of Father Faber', *The Catholic World*, Vol. X, No. 56, November, 145–61.

—— (1869) 'Review of J. Bowden's Life of F. W. Faber', *Dublin Review,* NS, Vol. XIII, July, 109–43.

—— (1870) 'Father Faber's work in the Church: *Devotion to the Church and Devotion to the Pope*', *Dublin Review,* Vol. XIV, January, 95–123.

—— (1872) 'Saints' Lives as Spiritual Reading', *Dublin Review,* NS, Vol. XVIII, 309–33.

—— (1885–1902) 'F. W. Faber', in *A Literary and Biographical History or Bibliographical Dictionary of the English Catholics, from the Breach with Rome in 1534 to the Present Time*, 5 Vols, London, Burns & Oates, Vol. 2, pp. 207–18.

—— (1885–1902) 'J. B. D. Dalgairns', in *A Literary and Biographical History or Bibliographical Dictionary of the English Catholics, from the Breach with Rome in 1534 to the Present Time*, 5 Vols, London, Burns & Oates, Vol. 2, pp. 3–5.

—— (1885–1902) 'R. Stanton', in *A Literary and Biographical History or Bibliographical Dictionary of the English Catholics, from the Breach with Rome in 1534 to the Present Time*, 5 Vols, London, Burns & Oates, Vol. 4, pp. 525–9.

—— (1885–1902) 'W. A. Hutchison', in *A Literary and Biographical History or Bibliographical Dictionary of the English Catholics, from the Breach with Rome in 1534 to the Present Time*, 5 Vols, London, Burns & Oates, Vol. 3, pp. 511–14.

—— (1888) [Reference to F. W. Faber], *Notes and Queries*, 7th Series, Vol. 5, January to June, 505.

—— (1889) 'F. W. Faber (1814–1863)', in *Dictionary of National Biography*, London, Smith, Elder & Co, Vol. 18, pp. l08–11.

—— (1927) *Brief Chronology of the Life of F. W. Faber*, Harrow School Archives, Easter.

—— (1956) 'F. W. Faber', *The Harrovian*, 17 May, 88–9.

—— (1964) *In the Silence of Mary*, London, Carmel, Notting Hill.

—— (1966) '*F. W. Faber*', in *New Catholic Encyclopedia*, Vol. 5, Catholic University of America, pp. 781–2.

Arand, L. A. (1961–62) 'Review of Father Faber by Ronald Chapman', *Catholic Historical Review*, Vol. 47, 384–7.

The Baptist Hymn Book (1964) 5th Printing, London, Novello and Co.

Battiscombe, G. (1963) *John Keble: A Study in Limitations*, London, Constable.

Bellenger, D. (1999) 'Religious Life for Men', in V. A. McClelland and M. Hodgetts (eds), *From Without the Flaminian Gate: 150 Years of Roman Catholicism in England and Wales 1850–2000*, London, DLT, pp. 142–66.

Best, K. D. (*c*.1880) *Faber's Grave*, London, n.p.

_____ (1913) *The memorial discourse at the solemn requiem for Fr Wilfrid Faber, on September 26 1913, the 50th anniversary of his death*, London, n.p.

Bevan, J. (1985) *Index and Finding List to Joseph Gillow's Bibliographical Dictionary of the English Catholics*, Ross on Wye, St Francis Press.

Bidstrup, P. L. (1964) *Toxicity of Mercury and its Compounds*, Amsterdam, Elsevier Publishing Company.

Book of Common Prayer (n.d.) London, Eyre and Spottiswoode Ltd.

Bossy, J. (1975) *The English Catholic Community 1570–1850*, London, DLT.

Bowden, J. E. (1869) *The Life and Letters of Frederick William Faber, DD: Priest of the Oratory of St Philip Neri*, 5th edn, London, Burns & Oates.

Bradley, I. (1976) *The Call to Seriousness: The Evangelical Impact on the Victorians*, London, Jonathan Cape.

Brendon, P. (1974) *Hurrell Froude and the Oxford Movement*, London, Paul Elek.

—— (1975) *Hawker of Morwenstow*, London, Cape.

—— (2004) 'R. S. Hawker (1803–1875)', in *Dictionary of National Biography*, Oxford, Oxford University Press, Vol. 25, pp. 898–900.

Bridgeman, R. O. (1956) '125 years ago', in *Harrow School Register*, 17 May, pp. 88–9.

Bridgett, T. E. (ed.) (1898) *Characteristics from the Writings of Nicholas Cardinal Wiseman, Archbishop of Westminster*, London, Burns & Oates.

Bright, R. (1937) *Original Papers of Richard Bright on Renal Disease*, Oxford, Oxford University Press.

Brilioth, Y. (1933) *The Anglican Revival: Studies in the Oxford*

Movement, London, Longmans, Green & Co.

Brock, M. G. and M. C. Curthoys (eds) (1997) *The History of the University of Oxford*, Vol. 6, Part I, *Nineteenth Century Oxford*, Oxford, Clarendon Press.

Burrow, J. W. (1981) *A Liberal Descent: Victorian Historians and the English Past*, Cambridge, Cambridge University Press.

Bushell, T. (1949) *The London Oratory 1849–1949*, London, CTS.

Butler, C. (1926) *Life and Times of Bishop Ullathorne 1806–1889*, 2 Vols, London, Burns, Oates & Washbourne.

Butler, J. (1849) *The Analogy of Religion*, 2 Vols, Oxford, Oxford University Press.

Butler, P. (ed.) (1983) *Pusey Discovered*, London, SPCK.

Cassidy, J. F. (1946) *The Life of Father Faber, Priest of the Oratory of St Philip Neri*, London, Sands & Co.

Celebration Hymnal (1986), Essex, Mayhew Macrimmon.

Chadwick, O. (1971) *The Victorian Church*, Part 2: 1860–1901, Oxford, Oxford University Press.

—— (1972) *The Victorian Church*, Part 1: 1829–1859, Oxford, Oxford University Press.

—— (1990) *The Spirit of the Oxford Movement: Tractarian Essays*, Cambridge, Cambridge University Press.

—— (ed.) (1960) *The Mind of the Oxford Movement*, London, Adam and Charles Black.

Chapman, R. (1959) 'English Spiritual Writers 8: Father Faber', *Clergy Review*, NS XLIV, 385–94.

—— (1961) *Father Faber*, London, Burns & Oates.

—— (1970) *Faith and Revolt: Studies in the Literary Influence of the Oxford Movement*, London, Weidenfeld & Nicolson.

Church, R. W. (1900) *The Oxford Movement: Twelve Years – 1833-45*, London, Macmillan & Co. Ltd.

Churchill's Illustrated Medical Dictionary (1991) London, Churchill, Livingstone.

The Collected Poems of William Wordsworth (1994) Hertfordshire, Wordsworth Editions Limited.

Cooper, T. (revised M. Clifton) (2004) 'R. W. Sibthorp (1792–1879)', in *Dictionary of National Biography* Oxford, Oxford University Press, Vol. 50, pp. 498–500.

Cranny, T. (1953) 'A Study in Contrasts: Newman and Faber', *American Ecclesiastical Review* 129, No. 5, November, 300–13.

Cunningham, F. A. (1901) 'Father Faber', *Donahoe's Magazine*, 540–56.

Davies, H. (1961) *Worship and Theology in England, Vol. 3: From Watts and Wesley to Maurice, 1690–1850*, London, Oxford University Press.

—— (1961) *Worship and Theology in England, Vol. 4: From Newman to Martineau, 1850–1900*, London, Oxford University Press.

Delaney, J. J. and J. E. Tobin (1961) *Dictionary of Catholic Biography*, London, Robert Hale.

Dessain, C. S. (1980) *John Henry Newman*, 3rd edn, Oxford, Oxford University Press.

Dictionary of National Biography (1889) London, Smith, Elder & Co.

Dictionary of National Biography (1921–2) Oxford, Oxford University Press.

Dictionary of National Biography (2004) Oxford, Oxford University Press.

Disraeli, B. (1986, 1998) *Sybil*, Oxford, Oxford University Press.

Dwyer, J. J. 'Review of *Apostle of Rome. St Philip Neri, 1515–1595*, by Meriol Trevor', *Clergy Review* LII (1967) 78–9.

The English Hymnal (1933) revised edn, Oxford, Oxford University Press.

Englander, D. (1998) 'The Word and the World: Evangelicalism in the Victorian City', in G. Parsons (ed.) *Religion in Victorian Britain, Vol. 2, Controversies*, Manchester, Manchester University Press, pp. 14–38.

Faber, F. A. (1869) *A Brief Sketch of the Early Life of the Late F. W. Faber*, London, Thomas Richardson & Son.

Faber, G. S. (1854) *The Many Mansions in the House of the Father, with a Prefatory Memoir of the Author by Francis A. Faber, BD*, 2nd edn, London, Royston & Brown.

Faber, R. (1987) *Young England*, London, Faber and Faber.

Faber, T. H. (1815) *Will of Thomas Henry Faber*, Public Record Office, Kew, PROB 11/1815.

Ffinch, M. (1991) *Cardinal Newman, the Second Spring*, London, Wiedenfeld & Nicholson.

Fitzpatrick, J. (1903) *Characteristics from the Writings of Fr Faber*, London, R & T Washbourne.

—— (1903) *May Readings*, London, R & T Washbourne.

—— (1907) *Our Lady and the Eucharist*, London, R & T Washbourne.

—— (1907) *Selected Poetry of Father Faber*, London, R & T Washbourne.

—— (1908) *The Holy Souls: November Leaves from Fr Faber*, London, R & T Washbourne.

—— (1909) *The Christmas Eucharist. Selections from F. W. Faber*, 3rd edn, London, R & T Washbourne.

Forrester, D. (1989) *Young Doctor Pusey: A Study in Development*, London, Mowbray.

Foster, J. (1888) *Alumni Oxoniensis*, Oxford, Parker.

Fothergill, B. (1963) *Nicholas Wiseman*, London, Faber.

Frost, A. (2004) 'Father Faber', *Catholic Life*, June, July, August, 2004.

Froude, R. H. (1838) *Remains of the Late Rev R. H. Froude, MA, Fellow of Oriel College, Oxford*, London, Rivington.

G, W. A. [*sic*] (1921–2) 'J. B. Morris (1812–1880)', in *Dictionary of National Biography*, Oxford, Oxford University Press, Vol. XIII, pp. 996–7.

Galloway, P. J. (1987) *Frederick Oakeley: The Career of a Tractarian*, Ph.D., King's College London.

—— (2000) *A Passionate Humility: Frederick Oakeley and the Oxford Movement*, Leominster, Gracewing.

—— (2004) 'F. Oakeley (1802–1880)', in *Dictionary of National Biography*, Oxford, Oxford University Press, Vol. 41, pp. 312–14.

Gardner, W. H. and N. H. MacKenzie (eds) (1988) *The Poems of Gerard Manley Hopkins*, 4th edn, Oxford, Oxford University Press.

Garrard, J. R. (2004) 'C. T. Longley (1794–1868)', in *Dictionary of National Biography*, Oxford, Oxford University Press, Vol. 34, pp. 398–400.

Gill, S. (1998) *Wordsworth and the Victorians*, Oxford, Clarendon Press.

Gilley, S. (1969) 'English Catholic Charity and the Irish Poor in London, II: 1840–1870', *Recusant History*, 10, 253–69.

—— (1969) 'Protestant London, No Popery and the Irish Poor, II: 1850–1860', *Recusant History*, 10, 21–46.

—— (1969) 'The Roman Catholic Mission to the Irish in

London, 1840–1860', *Recusant History*, 10, 123–45.

—— (1981–2) 'Vulgar Piety and the Brompton Oratory, 1850–1860', *Durham University Journal*, Vol. LXXIV, NS Vol. XLIII, 15–21.

—— (1990) *Newman and His Age*, London, DLT.

—— (1996) 'The Ecclesiology of the Oxford Movement: A Reconsideration', in P. Vaiss (ed.), *Newman: From Oxford to the People*, Leominster, Gracewing.

—— (2004) 'F. W. Faber (1814–1863)', in *Dictionary of National Biography*, Oxford, Oxford University Press, Vol. 18, pp. 871–3.

—— (2004) 'J. B. D. Dalgairns (1818–1876)', in *Dictionary of National Biography*, Oxford, Oxford University Press, Vol. 14, pp. 945–6.

—— (2004) 'T. F. Knox (1822–1882)', in *Dictionary of National Biography*, Oxford, Oxford University Press, Vol. 32, pp. 44–5.

—— (2004) 'W. G. Ward (1812–1882)', in *Dictionary of National Biography*, Oxford, Oxford University Press, Vol. 57, pp. 362–5.

Gillow, G. (1885–1902) *A Literary and Biographical History or Bibliographical Dictionary of the English Catholics, from the Breach with Rome in 1534 to the Present Time*, 5 Vols, London, Burns & Oates.

Gloag, D. (*c*.1864) *Memoir of the Very Rev. Fr F. W. Faber DD*, London, n.p.

Godwin, T. (1901), 'Personal Recollections of Fr Faber' in *Various Memoranda Relating to London Oratorian History*, LO, pp. 206–14.

Hall-Patch, W. (1914) *Father Faber*, London, Burns & Oates.

Hamer, Sr D. S. (2001) 'The Impact of the Irish on the Missionary Activities of Dominic Barberi, 1840–1849', *Recusant History*, Vol. 25, No. 4, October, 670–707.

Hanshell, D. (1961) Review, '*Father Faber* by Ronald Chapman', *Heythrop Journal*, Vol. 2, 277–9.

Hardelin, A. (1965) *The Tractarian Understanding of the Eucharist*, Uppsala.

Harvie Greenfield, R. (1983) 'Such a Friend to the Pope' in P. Butler, *Pusey Rediscovered*, London, SPCK, pp. 162–84.

Heimann, M. E. (1995) *Catholic Devotion in Victorian England*, Oxford, Clarendon Press.

—— (1996) 'Devotional Stereotypes in English Catholicism, 1850–1914', in F. Tallett and N. Atkin, *Catholicism in Britain and France since 1789*, London, Hambledon Press Ltd, pp. 13–25.

Heyer, F. (trans. D. W. D. Shaw) (1969) *The Catholic Church from 1648–1870*, London, A & C Black.

Hoblyn, R. D. (1892) *Hoblyn's Dictionary of Medical Terms*, London, n.p.

Hogan, D. C. (1984) 'The Four Westminster Provincial Synods', *Clergy Review* 69, 444–50.

Holmes, D. (1978) *More Roman than Rome*, Tunbridge Wells, Burns & Oates.

Holmes, J. D. (1968) 'How Newman Blunted the Edge of Ultramontanism', *Clergy Review* LIII, 353–62.

—— (1975) 'The Character of English Catholicism', *The Month*, 352–4.

Hooker, R. (1890) *The Works of Richard Hooker, with an account of his life and death by Isaac Walton*, Oxford, Clarendon Press.

—— (1907) *Of the Laws of Ecclesiastical Polity*, 2 Vols, London, Dent.

Hooper, R. (ed.) (1839) *Lexicon Medicum or Medical Dictionary*, London, n.p.

Houghton, W. E. (1957) *The Victorian Frame of Mind: 1830–70*, Newhaven, Yale University Press.

Hutton, A. W. (1892) *Cardinal Manning*, London, Methuen.

Hylson Smith, K. (1988) *Evangelicals in the Church of England 1734–1984*, Edinburgh, T&T Clark.

Hymns Ancient and Modern (1939) London, Wm Clowes and Sons.

Hymns Old and New (1991) Bury St Edmunds, Kevin Mayhew Ltd.

Kaiser, E. G. (1945) 'Father F. W. Faber: One Hundred Years ago', *Ave Maria* No. 19, 10 November, 293–5.

Keble, J. (1840) 'Tract 89: *On the Mysticism attributed to the early Fathers of the Church*', in *Tracts for the Times by Members of the University of Oxford*, 3 Vols, London, Rivington.

Kelly, B. (ed.) (1954) *Butler's Lives of the Fathers, Martyrs, and other Principal Saints*, London, Virtue & Co. Ltd.

Ker, I. (1990) *John Henry Newman: A Biography*, Oxford, Oxford University Press.

Ker, I. and A. G. Hill (eds) (1990) *Newman After a Hundred Years*, Oxford, Oxford University Press.

Kilburn, E. (1987) *A Walk Round the Church of the London Oratory*, 13th edn, London, Caldra House.

Kitson Clark, G. (1962) *The Making of Victorian England*, London, Methuen & Co. Ltd.

—— (1973) *Churchmen and the Condition of England 1832–1885: A Study in the Development of Social Ideas and Practice from the Old Regime to the Modern State*, London, Methuen & Co. Ltd.

Klaus, R. J. (1987) *The Pope, the Protestants and the Irish: Papal Aggression and Anti-Catholicism in Mid-Nineteenth Century England*, London, Garland Publishing Inc.

Knight, F. (1995) *The Nineteenth Century Church and English Society*, Cambridge, Cambridge University Press.

—— (1996) 'The influence of the Oxford Movement in the Parishes *c*.1833–63', in P. Vaiss (ed.), *Newman: From Oxford to the People*, Leominster, Gracewing.

Knox, R. (1945) 'Many Mansions: The Conversions of Newman and Faber', Sermon preached at the London Oratory on 26 June 1945, *The Tablet* No. 5486, 30 June, 310.

—— (ed.) (1958) *Autobiography of a Saint: Thérèse of Lisieux*, London, The Harvill Press.

Laudate (1999) Suffolk, Decani.

Lossky, N. (1996) 'The Oxford Movement and the Revival of Patristic Theology', in P. Vaiss (ed.), *Newman: From Oxford to the People*, Leominster, Gracewing.

Malins, M. S. B. (1913) *Father Faber 1814–1863*, London, CTS.

Manners, J. (1869) 'Father Faber's Life and Letters', *Blackwood's Magazine* CVI, December, 693–700.

MacGregor, A. J. (1999) 'There's a Wideness in Variety – F. W. Faber Reassessed', *Ushaw Library Bulletin*, 10, December, 32–8.

MacRaild, D. M. (1999) *Irish Migrants in Victorian Britain 1750–1922*, London, Macmillan.

Martin, B. W. (1975) 'Wordsworth, Faber and Keble: Commentary on a triangular relationship', *Review of English Studies*, NS 26, 436–42.

Martin, R. B. (1992) *Gerard Manley Hopkins: A Very Private Life*, London, Flamingo.

Martin Murphy, G. (2004) 'J. B. Morris (1812–1880)', in

Dictionary of National Biography, Oxford, Oxford University Press, Vol. 39, pp. 282–3.

Martindale, C. C. (1961) Review, '*Father Faber* by Ronald Chapman', *The Month*, NS Vol. 26, 305–6.

McClelland, V. A. (1973) *English Roman Catholics and Higher Education, 1830–1903*, Oxford, Clarendon Press.

—— (1999) 'The Formative Years', in V. A. McClelland and M. Hodgetts (eds), *From Without the Flaminian Gate: 150 Years of Roman Catholicism in England and Wales 1850–2000*, London, Darton, Longman & Todd, pp. 1–20.

McClelland, V. A. and M. Hodgetts (eds) (1999) *From Without the Flaminian Gate: 150 Years of Roman Catholicism in England and Wales 1850–2000*, London, Darton, Longman & Todd.

McPherson, G. (ed.) (2001) *Black's Medical Dictionary*, 39th edn, London, A & C Black.

Mercedes, M. (1959) Review, 'A Father Faber Heritage', *Clergy Review*, NS 44, 384.

Meynell, W. (1914) *The Spirit of Father Faber: Apostle of London*, London, Burns & Oates.

Milnes Gaskell, D. (1890) 'Frederick William Faber', in M. E. G. Duff, *Addresses*, Kingston-on-Thames, W. Drewett, pp. 3–23.

Möhler, J. A. (1997) *Symbolism*, New York, Crossroad Herder.

Moorman, M. (1968) *William Wordsworth: A Biography*, 2 Vols, Oxford, Oxford University Press.

Morris, K. L. (1984) 'The Cambridge Converts and the Oxford Movement', *Recusant History*, 17, 386–98.

—— (1994) 'Rescuing the Scarlet Woman: The Promotion of Catholicism in English Literature, 1829–1850', *Recusant History*, 22, 75–87.

Munden, A. F. (2004) 'J. W. Cunningham (1780–1861)', in *Dictionary of National Biography*, Oxford, Oxford University Press, Vol. 14, pp. 693–4.

Munitiz, J. A. and P. Endean (1996) *Saint Ignatius of Loyola: Personal Writings*, London, Penguin.

Murray, P. (1969) *Newman the Oratorian: His Unpublished Oratory Papers*, Dublin, Gill & Macmillan Ltd.

Napier, M. (1984) *The London Oratory Centenary: 1884–1984*, London, Trefoil.

Newman, J. H. (1837) *Lectures on the Prophetical Office of the Church, Viewed Relatively to Romanism and Popular*

Protestantism, London, Rivington.

—— (1840) *Parochial and Plain Sermons, Vol. 1*, 4th edn, London, J. G. & F. Rivington.

—— (1870) *An Essay in aid of a Grammar of Assent*, London, Burns Oates & Co.

—— (1876) *Discourses Addressed to Mixed Congregations*, 5th edn, London, Burns Oates & Co.

—— (1885) *Lectures on the Doctrine of Justification*, London, Rivingtons.

—— (1918) *Fifteen Sermons Preached Before the University of Oxford*, London, Longmans Green & Co.

—— (ed. C. S. Dessain) (1957) *Catholic Sermons of Cardinal Newman*, London, Burns & Oates.

—— (1968) *An Essay on the Development of Christian Doctrine*, Westminster MD, Christian Classics Inc.

—— *The Letters and Diaries of John Henry Newman* (ed. C. S. Dessain, V. F. Blehl SJ and T. Gornall SJ)

(1978–1984) Vols I–VI, Oxford, Oxford University Press.

(1961–1972) Vols XI–XXII, London, Nelson.

(1973–1977) Vols XXIII–XXXI, Oxford, Oxford University Press.

Newsome, D. (1966) *The Parting of Friends: A Study of the Wilberforces and Henry Manning*, London, John Murray.

—— (2004) 'H. E. Manning (1808–1892)', in *Dictionary of National Biography*, Oxford, Oxford University Press, Vol. 36, pp. 492–9.

Nicholls, D. (ed.) (1991) *John Henry Newman: Reason, Rhetoric and Romanticism*, London, The Bristol Press.

Nockles, P. B. (1983) 'Pusey and the Question of Church and State', in P. Butler, *Pusey Rediscovered*, London, SPCK, pp. 255–97.

—— (1994) *The Oxford Movement in Context: Anglican High Churchmanship, 1760–1857*, Cambridge, Cambridge University Press.

—— (1996) 'Church and King: Tractarian Politics Reappraised', in P. Vaiss (ed.), *Newman: From Oxford to the People*, Leominster, Gracewing.

—— (1997) '"Lost Causes and … impossible Loyalties": The Oxford Movement and the University', in M. G. Brock and M. C. Curthoys (eds) *The History of the University of Oxford, Vol.*

6, Part 1, Nineteenth Century Oxford, Oxford, Clarendon Press.
—— (2004) 'R. Bagot (1782–1854)', in *Dictionary of National Biography*, Oxford, Oxford University Press, Vol. 3, pp. 240–2.
Norman, E. R. (1968) *Anti-Catholicism in Victorian England*, London, Geo. Allen & Unwin.
—— (1976) *Church and Society in England 1770–1970: A Historical Study*, Oxford, Clarendon Press.
—— (1984) *The English Catholic Church in the Nineteenth Century*, Oxford, Clarendon Press.
Oakeley, F. (1839) *Christ Manifested to the Faithful through His Church*, Oxford, J. H. Parker.
—— (1842) *Homilies for Holy Days and Seasons Commemorative of Our Lord and Saviour Jesus Christ from Advent to Whitsuntide, Translated from Writings of the Saints*, London, James Burns.
—— (1848) *Practical Sermons Preached in 1847–8*, London, James Burns.
—— (1855) *Popular Lectures Addressed to the Islington Catholic Popular Club*, London, Henry Teulon.
Ollard, S. L. (1915) *A Short History of the Oxford Movement*, London, A. L. Mowbray & Co. Ltd.
The Oxford History of the Christian Church (1957), London, Oxford University Press.
Oxford University Magazine, Vol. 1 (1834).
Palmer, W. (1863) Obituary, 'Frederick William Faber', *The Saturday Review*, Vol. XVI, 10 October, 488–9.
The Parish Hymn Book (1968) London, L. Carey and Co.
Parsons, G. (1988) 'Reform, Revival and Realignment: The Experience of Victorian Anglicanism', in G. Parsons (ed.), *Religion in Victorian Britain, Vol. 1: Traditions*, Manchester, Manchester University Press, pp. 14–67.
—— (1988) *Religion in Victorian Britain. Vol. 1: Traditions*, Manchester, Manchester University Press.
—— (1988) 'Victorian Anti-Catholicism: Emancipation, Expansion and Achievement', in G. Parsons (ed.), *Religion in Victorian Britain, Vol. 1: Traditions*, Manchester, Manchester University Press, pp. 146–83.
Pawley, M. (1993) *Faith and Family: The Life and Circle of Ambrose Phillipps de Lisle*, Norwich, The Canterbury Press.
Peacock, E. (1888) 'Lines by Faber', *Notes and Queries*, 7th series, Vol. 5, 505.

Peek, K. M. (1969) *Wordsworth in England: Studies in the History of his fame*, New York, Octagon.

Philips, C. (1991) *Gerard Manley Hopkins: Selected Letters*, Oxford, Oxford University Press.

Pickering, W. S. F. (1989) *Anglo-Catholicism: A Study in Religious Ambiguity*, London, Routledge.

Poston, L. (1986) "'Words not Realised": Wordsworthian Poetry in the 1830s', *Texas Studies in Literature and Language*, 28, pp. 51–81.

Pratt, A. E. (1997) *A Study of Frederick William Faber's Hymns on the Four Last Things in the Context of his Hymnody as Presented in the Collection of 1861*, unpublished MA Thesis, University of Durham, Department of English Studies.

Prestige, L. (1933) *Pusey*, London, Philip Allan and Co. Ltd.

Prickett, S. (1976) *Romanticism and Religion: The Tradition of Coleridge and Wordsworth in the Victorian Church*, Cambridge, Cambridge University Press.

Purcell, E. S. (1896) *Life of Cardinal Manning: Archbishop of Westminster*, 2 Vols, London, Macmillan & Co.

Ralls, W. (1988) 'The Papal Aggression of 1850: A Study in Victorian Anti-Catholicism', in G. Parsons (ed.), *Religion in Victorian Britain, Vol. 4: Interpretations*, Manchester, Manchester University Press, pp. 115–34.

Reardon, B. M. G. (1971) *From Coleridge to Gore: A Century of Religious Thought in Britain*, London, Longman.

Roberts, M. (1983) 'Coleridge as Background to the Oxford Movement', in P. Butler, *Pusey Rediscovered*, London, SPCK, pp. 34–50.

Root, J. D. (1981) 'Catholicism and Science in Victorian England,' *Clergy Review*, 66, Part 1: 138–47; Part 2: 162–70.

Rowell, G. (1974) *Hell and the Victorians*, Oxford, Clarendon Press.

—— (1983) *The Vision Glorious: Themes and Personalities of the Catholic Revival in Anglicanism*, Oxford, Oxford University Press.

—— (1996) "'Church Principles" and "Protestant Kempism", some Theological Forerunners of the Tractarians', in P. Vaiss, *Newman: From Oxford to the People*, Leominster, Gracewing.

Smith, R. J. (1987) *The Gothic Bequest: Medieval Institutions in*

British Thought, Cambridge, Cambridge University Press.

Songs of Fellowship (1994) Eastbourne, Kingsway Music.

Songs of Praise (1931) London, Oxford University Press.

Sutton, C. W. (1921–2) 'P. C. Claughton (1814–1884)', in *Dictionary of National Biography*, Oxford, Oxford University Press, Vol. IV, pp. 458–9.

—— (2004) (revised K. Prior) 'P. C. Claughton (1814–1884)', in *Dictionary of National Biography*, Oxford, Oxford University Press, Vol. II, pp. 949–50.

Tallett, F. and N. Atkin (1996) *Catholicism in Britain and France since 1789*, London, The Hambledon Press.

Tennyson, G. B. (1981) *Victorian Devotional Poetry: The Tractarian Mode*, London, Harvard University Press.

Toon, P. (1979) *Evangelical Theology 1833–1856: A Response to Tractarianism*, London, Marshall, Morgan & Scott.

Tracts for the Times by Members of the University of Oxford (1835–40) 3 Vols, London, Rivington.

Trevor, M. (1962) *Newman: Light in Winter*, London, Macmillan & Co.

—— (1962) *Newman: The Pillar of the Cloud*, London, Macmillan & Co.

Türks, P. (1995) *Philip Neri: The Fire of Joy*, Edinburgh, T&T Clark.

Ullathorne, W. B. (1892) *Letters of Archbishop Ullathorne*, London, Burns & Oates.

—— (1941) *From Cabin-Boy to Archbishop*, London, Hollis & Carter.

Vaiss, P. (ed.) (1996) *From Oxford to the People*, Leominster, Gracewing.

Vidler, A. R. (1961) *The Pelican History of the Church, Vol. 5: The Church in an Age of Revolution: 1789 to the Present Day*, London, Hodder & Stoughton.

Walsh, W. (1897) *The Secret History of the Oxford Movement*, London, Swan Sonnenschein & Co. Ltd.

Whibley, C. (1925) *Lord John Manners and His Friends*, Edinburgh, William Blackwood and Sons.

Whistler, R. F. (1892) *The History of Ailington, Aylton or Elton*, London, Mitchell & Hughes.

Wilkinson, M. J. (2004) *An Exploration of the Roman Catholic Sermons, Lectures, and Novice Conferences of Frederick William*

Faber, 1846–1863, Paper for the Catholic Record Society Conference, 3 August.

—— (2005) *An Exploration of the Intellectual and Spiritual Development of Frederick William Faber (1814–1863)*, Ph.D., University of Wales, Lampeter.

—— (2005) *Evangelical Traits in the Roman Catholic Spirituality of Frederick William Faber (1814–1863)*, Paper for Seminar on the Theme of Evangelicalism, University of Wales, Lampeter, 4 April.

Williams, I. (1838) 'Tract 80: *On Reserve on Communicating Religious Knowledge*', in *Tracts for the Times by Members of the University of Oxford*, 3 Vols, London, Rivington.

Wiseman, N. (1862) 'Rome and the Catholic Episcopate', *Dublin Review*, Vol. LII, November, 44–70.

Wolffe, J. (ed.) (1991) *The Protestant Crusade in Great Britain, 1829–60*, Oxford, Clarendon Press.

—— (1995) *Evangelical Faith and Public Zeal: Evangelicals and Society in Britain, 1790–1980*, London, SPCK.

Woollen, W. (1929) *Father Faber*, London, CTS.

Yates, N. (1999) *Anglican Ritualism in Victorian Britain, 1830–1910*, Oxford, Oxford University Press.

Index of Subjects

Index of Names